ADOBE® ILLUSTRATOR® CS2

level two

Dean Bagley

Prentice Hall
Upper Saddle River, New Jersey 07458

Library of Congress Cataloging-in-Publication Data
Bagley, Dean.
 Adobe Illustrator CS2, level two/Dean Bagley. — 2nd ed.
   p. cm. — (Essentials for design)
 Includes bibliographical references and index.
 ISBN 0-13-187554-X (alk. paper)
 1. Computer graphics. 2. Adobe Illustrator (Computer file) I. Title. II. Series.

T385.B293 2005
006.6'86—dc22   2005025320

Vice President and Publisher: Natalie E. Anderson
Executive Acquisitions Editor, Print: Stephanie Wall
Executive Acquisitions Editor, Media: Richard Keaveny
Acquisitions Editor: Melissa Sabella
Product Development Manager: Eileen Bien Calabro
Editorial Project Manager: Anne Garcia
Editorial Supervisor: Brian Hoehl
Editorial Assistants: Alana Meyers, Kaitlin O'Shaughnessy
Executive Producer: Lisa Strite
Content Development Manager: Cathi Profitko
Senior Media Project Manager: Steve Gagliostro
Director of Marketing: Sarah Loomis
Senior Marketing Manager: Jason Sakos
Marketing Assistant: Ann Baranov
Sr. Sales Associate: Joseph Pascale
Managing Editor: Lynda J. Castillo
Production Project Manager/Buyer: Vanessa Nuttry
Production/Editorial Assistant: Sandra K. Bernales
Art Director/Interior Design: Blair Brown
Interior Design: Thistle Hill Publishing Services, LLC.
Cover Illustration/Photo: FoodPix®
Composition/Full-Service Project Management: Progressive Publishing Alternatives
Cover Printer: Coral Graphics
Printer/Binder: Von Hoffman Press

Credits and acknowledgments borrowed from other sources and reproduced, with permission, in this textbook appear on the appropriate page within the text.

A portion of the images supplied in this book are copyright © PhotoDisc, Inc., 201 Fourth Ave., Seattle, WA 98121, or copyright ©PhotoSpin, 4030 Palos Verdes Dr. N., Suite 200, Rollings Hills Estates, CA. These images are the sole property of PhotoDisc or PhotoSpin and are used by Prentice Hall with the permission of the owners. They may not be distributed, copied, transferred, or reproduced by any means whatsoever, other than for the completion of the exercises and projects contained in this book.

Photoshop, PageMaker, Acrobat, Adobe Type Manager, Illustrator, InDesign, Premiere, and PostScript are trademarks of Adobe Systems Incorporated. Macromedia Flash, Generator, FreeHand, Dreamweaver, Fireworks, and Director are registered trademarks of Macromedia, Inc. QuarkXPress is a registered trademark of Quark, Inc. Macintosh is a trademark of Apple Computer, Inc. CorelDRAW!, procreate Painter, and WordPerfect are trademarks of Corel Corporation. FrontPage, Publisher, PowerPoint, Word, Excel, Office, Microsoft, MS-DOS, and Windows are either registered trademarks or trademarks of Microsoft Corporation.

Other product and company names mentioned herein may be the trademarks of their respective owners.

Copyright © 2006 by Prentice Hall, Inc., Upper Saddle River, New Jersey, 07458. All rights reserved. Printed in the United States of America. This publication is protected by copyright and permission should be obtained from the publisher prior to any prohibited reproduction, storage in a retrieval system, or transmission in any form or by any means, electronic, mechanical, photocopying, recording, or likewise. For information regarding permission(s), write to: Rights and Permissions Department.

10 9 8 7 6 5 4 3 2 1

ISBN 0-13-187554-X

ABOUT THE AUTHOR

Dean Bagley has been writing instructional books about Adobe Illustrator for a number of years. He first began when he wrote about Illustrator's version 5.0. Dean received his degrees in Speech-English-Education from the University of South Florida in Tampa, Florida. Upon graduation he spent several years teaching English and Speech in secondary schools.

A multi-talented person, Dean has been in the arts most of his life as a graphic artist, designer, cartoonist, typographer, writer, editor, and publication designer. He spent ten years working as Head of Advertising for his father in his well-known business in the fishing industry, Bagley Bait Company. It was during these years that Dean won both an ADDY Award and a first place award from the Florida Print Industry for the package and catalog design of their monofilament fishing line, Silver Thread.

Also a computer programmer in such languages as BASIC, Pascal, and dBase, Dean found himself in the world of the Internet where he creates Web sites, animations and images for use on the Web, using Adobe Illustrator.

Dean also has his own line of children's books about his cartoon character, Baggy Gator. These stories can be found online at http://baggygator.no-ip.com.

ACKNOWLEDGMENTS

I must extend my heartfelt thanks and undying appreciation to the one person who made writing these books possible for me — Ellenn Behoriam — a woman who took me under her wing, gave me this opportunity to write her books, and introduced me to the world of publishing. She is the one person whom I produced all my previous Illustrator books for and her company, Against the Clock.

I would also like to thank Lynn Bowen, Dan Workman, and John Griffin for their hard work in tech editing this book.

And special thanks to Anne Garcia and Eileen Calabro, who were traffic-managers for this book, keeping me updated, informed and receiving all necessary files and information.

LEVEL 2 IV

CONTENTS AT A GLANCE

Introduction XV

CHAPTER 1 Page Geometry 1

CHAPTER 2 Effects, Styles, and Appearances 46

CHAPTER 3 Working with Symbols 100

CHAPTER 4 Working with Animations 146

CHAPTER 5 Creating Web Objects 189

CHAPTER 6 SVG Graphics and Interactivity 242

CHAPTER 7 Working with Dynamic Graphics 288

CHAPTER 8 Enhancing Your Workflow 336

Integrating Project 391

Task Guide 419

Glossary 425

Index 429

TABLE OF CONTENTS

INTRODUCTION . . . . **XV**

CHAPTER 1   PAGE GEOMETRY 1

Lesson 1	Using Guides and Layers	.5
Lesson 2	Laying Out Web Pages	.10
Lesson 3	Understanding the Crop Area	.13
Lesson 4	Manage the Startup Document	.18
Lesson 5	Using the Grid Tools	.21
Lesson 6	Perspective Layout	.27
	Checking Concepts and Terms	.33
	Skill Drill	.34
	Challenge	.40
	Portfolio Builder	.45

CHAPTER 2   EFFECTS, STYLES, AND APPEARANCES 46

Lesson 1	Applying Vector Effects	.49
Lesson 2	Applying Photoshop Effects	.53
Lesson 3	Using the Appearance Palette	.59
Lesson 4	Graphic Styles	.64
Lesson 5	Creating Gradient Meshes	.73
	Checking Concepts and Terms	.89
	Skill Drill	.90
	Challenge	.94
	Portfolio Builder	.99

CHAPTER 3   WORKING WITH SYMBOLS 100

Lesson 1	Using the Symbols Palette	.104
Lesson 2	Creating Symbols	.108
Lesson 3	Editing Symbols and Links	.115
Lesson 4	Using Symbol Libraries	.120
Lesson 5	Using the Symbolism Tools	.124
Lesson 6	Symbolism Tool Options	.132
	Careers in Design	.135
	Checking Concepts and Terms	.136
	Skill Drill	.137
	Challenge	.141
	Portfolio Builder	.145

LEVEL 2 VI

CHAPTER 4 WORKING WITH ANIMATIONS 146

Lesson 1	Creating an Animation	150
Lesson 2	The Build (Cumulative) Animation	155
Lesson 3	The Sequence (Noncumulative) Animation	158
Lesson 4	Raster Animations	162
Lesson 5	Animating Blends	164
Lesson 6	Using Symbols and Release to Layers	170
	Checking Concepts and Terms	176
	Skill Drill	177
	Challenge	183
	Portfolio Builder	188

CHAPTER 5 CREATING WEB OBJECTS 189

Lesson 1	Using Save for Web	193
Lesson 2	Banding and Color Modification	204
Lesson 3	Refining Images for the Web	209
Lesson 4	Creating Image Maps	214
Lesson 5	Saving for the Web—HTML	217
Lesson 6	Slicing Images	220
	Careers in Design	227
	Checking Concepts and Terms	228
	Skill Drill	229
	Challenge	235
	Portfolio Builder	241

CHAPTER 6 SVG GRAPHICS AND INTERACTIVITY 242

Lesson 1	Exploring Scaleable Vector Graphics	246
Lesson 2	Adding Interactivity with JavaScript	251
Lesson 3	JavaScript and XML Naming Conventions	256
Lesson 4	JavaScript Events	261
Lesson 5	Embedding the SVG File	266
Lesson 6	Using SVG Filters	269
	Checking Concepts and Terms	274
	Skill Drill	275
	Challenge	280
	Portfolio Builder	287

CHAPTER 7 WORKING WITH DYNAMIC GRAPHICS 288

Lesson 1	What Is Dynamic Data?	292
Lesson 2	Assigning Variables	295
Lesson 3	Understanding Data Sets	302
Lesson 4	Using the Extensible Markup Language	306

VII | **LEVEL 2**

Lesson 5	Using the Graph Tools	313
Lesson 6	Customizing Graphs	318
	Careers in Design	324
	Checking Concepts and Terms	325
	Skill Drill	326
	Challenge	329
	Portfolio Builder	335

CHAPTER 8 — ENHANCING YOUR WORKFLOW 336

Lesson 1	Modifying Objects for Use in Photoshop	341
Lesson 2	Using Photoshop Techniques in Illustrator	345
Lesson 3	Using the Actions Palette	352
Lesson 4	Creating Your Own Actions	360
Lesson 5	Naming Objects and Menu Selections	365
Lesson 6	Using Acrobat to Combine Illustrator Files	373
	Checking Concepts and Terms	378
	Skill Drill	380
	Challenge	384
	Portfolio Builder	390

INTEGRATING PROJECT	391
TASK GUIDE	419
GLOSSARY	425
INDEX	429

HOW TO USE THIS BOOK

Essentials for Design courseware from Prentice Hall is anchored in the practical and professional needs of all types of students. The *Essentials for Design* series presents a learning-by-doing approach that encourages you to grasp application-related concepts as you expand your skills through hands-on tutorials. As such, it consists of modular lessons that are built around a series of numbered step-by-step procedures that are clear, concise, and easy to review.

Essentials for Design books are divided into chapters. A chapter covers one area (or a few closely related areas) of application functionality. Each chapter consists of several lessons that are related to that topic. Each lesson presents a specific task or closely related set of tasks in a manageable portion that is easy to assimilate and retain.

Each element in the *Essentials for Design* book is designed to maximize your learning experience. A list of the *Essentials for Design* chapter elements, and a description of how each element can help you, begins on the next page. To find out more about the rationale behind each book element and how to use each to your maximum benefit, take the following walk-through.

WALK-THROUGH

Chapter Objectives. Starting with an objective gives you short-term, attainable goals. Each chapter begins with a list of objectives that closely match the titles of the step-by-step tutorials. ▶

> **OBJECTIVES**
>
> *In this chapter, you learn how to:*
>
> - Create layouts using guides and layers
> - Manage the content of a Web page
> - Isolate specific objects in a document
> - Use the startup document
> - Create grids for unique jobs
> - Make perspective grids

◀ **Why Would I Do This?** Introductory material at the beginning of each chapter provides an overview of why these tasks and procedures are important.

Visual Summary. A series of illustrations introduces the new tools, dialog boxes, and windows you will explore in each chapter. ▼

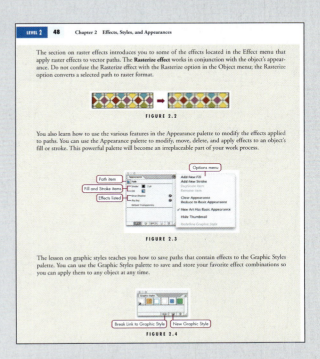

◀ **Step-by-Step Tutorials.** Hands-on tutorials let you learn by doing and include numbered, bold, step-by-step instructions.

LEVEL 2   x

? ◀ If You Have Problems. These short troubleshooting notes help you anticipate or solve common problems quickly and effectively.

◀ Careers in Design. These features offer advice, tips, and resources that will help you on your path to a successful career.

To Extend Your Knowledge. These provide extra tips, features alternative ways to complete a process, and special hints about using the software. ▶

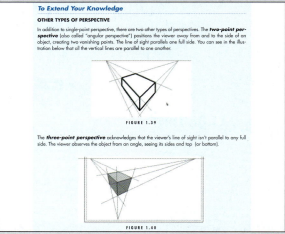

End-of-Chapter Exercises. Extensive end-of-chapter exercises emphasize hands-on skill development. You'll find three levels of reinforcement: Skill Drill, Challenge, and Portfolio Builder. ▼

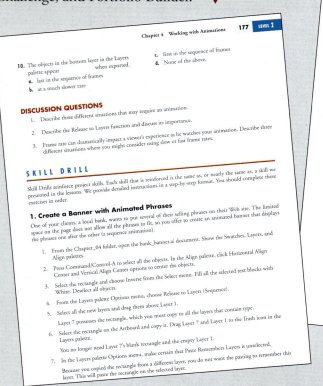

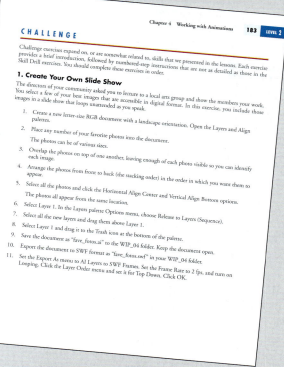

Portfolio Builder. At the end of every chapter, these exercises require creative solutions to problems that reinforce the topic of the project. ▶

◀ **Integrating Projects.** Integrating projects are designed to reflect real-world graphic-design jobs, drawing on the skills you have learned throughout this book.

Task Guides. These charts, found at the end of each book, list alternative ways to complete common procedures and provide a handy reference tool. ▶

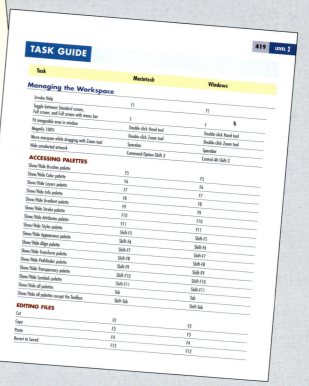

STUDENT INFORMATION AND RESOURCES

Companion Web Site (www.prenhall.com/essentials). This text-specific Web site provides students with additional information and exercises to reinforce their learning. Features include: additional end-of-chapter reinforcement material, online Study Guide, easy access to *all* resource files, and much, much more!

Before completing most chapters within this text, you will need to download the Resource files from the Student CD or from Prentice Hall's Companion Web site for the *Essentials for Design* Series. Check with your instructor for the best way to gain access to these files or simply follow these instructions:

If you are going to save these files to an external disk, make sure it is inserted into the appropriate drive before continuing.

1. Start your Web browser and go to http://www.prenhall.com/essentials

2. Select your textbook or series to access the Companion Web site. We suggest you bookmark this page, as it has links to additional Prentice Hall resources that you may use in class.

3. Click the Student Resources link.

4. Locate the files you need from the list of available resources and then click the link to download.

Moving forward the process will vary depending upon which operating system (OS) you are using. Please select your OS and follow the instructions below:

Windows OS:

5. Locate the files you need from the list of available resources and click the link to download.

6. When the File Download box displays, click the Save button.

7. In the Save As dialog box, select the location to which you wish to save the file. We recommend you saving the file to the Windows desktop or TEMP folder so it is easy to locate, but if you are working in a lab environment this may not be possible. To save to an external disk, simply type in or select your disk's corresponding drive. Example: a:\ where "a" designates an external disk drive.

8. Click the Save button to begin the downloading process.

9. Once the download is complete, navigate to the file using Windows Explorer.

10. Double click on the file to begin the self extraction process and follow the step-by-step prompts.

Mac OS with Stuffit Expander 8.0.2 or greater:

5. Locate the files you need from the list of available resources and click the link to download.

6. With default settings the file will be downloaded to your desktop.

7. Once Download Manager shows status as "complete", double-click on the file to expand file.

NOTE: Stuffit Expander can be downloaded free at http://www.stuffit.com/

Mac OS with Stuffit Expander 8:

5. Locate the files you need from the list of available resources and click the link to download.

6. With default settings the file will be downloaded to your desktop.

7. Once Download Manager shows status as "complete", double-click on the file and choose Stuffit Expander as the application to expand file.

NOTE: Stuffit Expander can be downloaded free at http://www.stuffit.com/

Need help? Contact Tech Support Online at http://247.prenhall.com

Resource CD.   If you are using a Resource CD, all the files you need are provided on the CD. Resource files are organized in chapter-specific folders (e.g., Chapter_01, Chapter_02, etc.), which are contained in the RF_Illustrator_L2 folder. You can either work directly from the CD, or copy the files onto your hard drive before beginning the exercises.

Before you begin working on the chapters or lessons in this book, you should copy the Work_In_Progress folder from the Resource CD onto your hard drive or a removable disk/drive.

Resource Files.   Resource files are organized in chapter-specific folders, and are named to facilitate cross-platform compatibility. Words are separated by an underscore, and all file names include a lowercase three-letter extension. For example, if you are directed to open the file "graphics.eps" in Chapter 2, the file can be found in the RF_Illustrator_L2> Chapter_02 folder. We repeat these directions frequently in the early chapters.

The Work In Progress Folder.   This folder contains individual folders for each chapter in the book (e.g., WIP_01, WIP_02, etc.). When an exercise directs you to save a file, you should save it to the appropriate folder for the chapter in which you are working.

The exercises in this book frequently build upon work that you have already completed. At the end of each exercise, you will be directed to save your work and either close the file or continue to the next exercise. If you are directed to continue but your time is limited, you can stop at a logical point, save the file, and later return to the point at which you stopped. In this case, you will need to open the file from the appropriate WIP folder and continue working on the same file.

Typeface Conventions.   Computer programming code appears in a monospace font that `looks like this`. In many cases, you only need to change or enter specific pieces of code; in these instances, the code you need to type or change appears in a second color and `looks like this`.

INSTRUCTOR'S RESOURCES

Instructor's Resource Center.   This CD-ROM includes the entire Instructor's Manual for each application in Microsoft Word format. Student data files and completed solutions files are also on this CD-ROM. The Instructor's Manual contains a reference guide of these files for the instructor's convenience. PowerPoint slides with more information about each project are also available for classroom use. All instructor resources are also available online via the Companion Web site at www.prenhall.com/essentials.

Companion Web site (www.prenhall.com/essentials).

TestGen Software.   TestGen is a test generator program that lets you view and easily edit test bank questions, transfer them to tests, and print the tests in a variety of formats suitable to your teaching situation. The program also offers many options for organizing and displaying test banks and tests. A built-in random number and text generator makes it ideal for creating multiple versions of tests. Powerful search and sort functions let you easily locate questions and arrange them in the order you prefer.

QuizMaster, also included in this package, enables students to take tests created with TestGen on a local area network. The QuizMaster utility built into TestGen lets instructors view student records and print a variety of reports. Building tests is easy with TestGen, and exams can be easily uploaded into WebCT, Blackboard, and CourseCompass.

Prentice Hall has formed close alliances with each of the leading online platform providers: WebCT, Blackboard, and our own Pearson CourseCompass.

INTRODUCTION

Adobe Illustrator CS2 is a remarkable application rich with features, and offering such a vast array of techniques, that mastering it becomes a process, not an event. No matter how long you use the program, there's always something new to learn.

In this book you will be able to use these Illustrator features to execute professional-looking illustrations, images, and documents. Designers who can create digital art dramatically expand their ability to communicate visually. Effectively controlling all the aspects of the digital design is a critical component in the creative process.

Illustrator CS2 provides a wide variety of tools and techniques for adding visual effects to illustrations. When you use Illustrator, you are on the threshold of its environment where you will have a world of tools, options and functions that allow you create artwork and designs of superlative nature.

Illustrator is a robust, design-oriented package and provides the tools you need to design and create effective pages. It allows you to integrate text and graphics — prepared in the program itself or imported from other sources — and produce files that may be printed to a local or networked printer, taken to a commercial printer or other graphic arts service provider, or published to the World Wide Web.

LEVEL 2

CHAPTER 1

Page Geometry

OBJECTIVES

In this chapter, you learn how to:

- Create layouts using guides and layers

- Manage the content of a Web page

- Isolate specific objects in a document

- Use the startup document

- Create grids for unique jobs

- Make perspective grids

Chapter 1 Page Geometry

Why Would I Do This?

Many of your illustrations will be used as stand-alone drawings, without being imported into a page-layout or Web-design application. For these types of jobs, many artists create their work solely in Illustrator. Other pieces of your artwork will become components in larger productions such as magazines, product packaging, brochures, instructional materials, Web pages and banners, posters, flyers, product and technical specification sheets, and more. These jobs involve either a page-layout or Web-design application to pull all of the components together to create one cohesive document.

Understanding the key concepts behind page layout and page geometry dramatically improves the appearance and effectiveness of your designs. In this chapter, you learn about *page geometry*, which is the division of a page into shapes and areas that hold (contain) the content you want to deliver to your audience.

VISUAL SUMMARY

"Page geometry" refers to the concept of creating containers that hold content on your documents' pages. As Illustrator becomes more appropriate for constructing Web pages and other interactive media, the term "container" can pertain to containers for Web banners, Web pages, and animations.

In this chapter, you explore various methods that allow you to maximize the Illustrator working environment and drawing surface. This makes it easier and more efficient to manage page geometry for different types of projects. In addition to working with standard page dimensions for print and distribution on the Web, you delve into the concept of *dimensionality* (adding the traditional methods of perspective drawing to Illustrator's powerful and accurate drawing and transformation tools).

You also discover that guides and layers allow you to store and access preset layout guides to expedite production of common jobs that require specific layouts.

FIGURE 1.1

Chapter 1   Page Geometry   **3**   LEVEL 2

You learn why you must design Web pages according to the average viewer's screen size. You also learn how to use the fold of a Web page to divide long pages into custom sizes that allow users with even the smallest screens to see the entire page.

FIGURE 1.2

Crop Area is a rarely used Illustrator feature that isolates a selected object from other objects in the document. You can use this tool to export or print only the cropped object.

FIGURE 1.3

As you learn how to manage the startup document, you discover how to save your most-used painting attributes, such as colors, gradients, and patterns. Once you save these attributes in the startup document, you can apply them to any of your Illustrator documents.

FIGURE 1.4

The Rectangular Grid and Polar Grid tools allow you to create customizable grids. Use the Rectangular Grid tool to produce grids with rows and columns, and use the Polar Grid tool to create circular and oval grids.

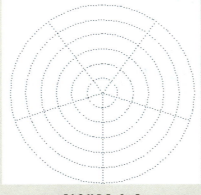

FIGURE 1.5

The lesson on perspective layout teaches you how to use measurements, guides, and angled paths to draw perspective grids. Illustrator does not offer a dedicated perspective grid tool, so you must use measurements, guides, and angled paths to produce a perspective layout.

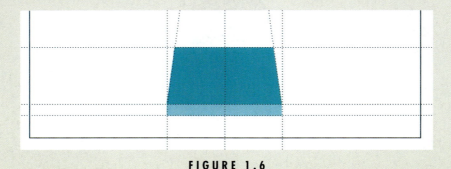

FIGURE 1.6

Chapter 1   Page Geometry   **5**   LEVEL **2**

LESSON 1   Using Guides and Layers

Many different types of companies — advertising, magazine publishers, and public relations, to name only a few — use standard page sizes and formats on a daily basis. If designers had to use guides and measurements to set up each page from scratch every day, creating the same layouts would quickly become a tedious task.

Designers can use templates, but if each layout had its own template, *managing* the layouts would become as tedious as *creating* them. A better idea is to place each layout, designated by guides, on its own layer in the document. Since a document can include multiple layers, you can keep several different layouts in a single document and show each layout individually by displaying its associated layer.

Create Layouts on Layers

To lay out common page sizes in advance, it is most productive to create the guides on layers and save the document as a template. In this exercise, you create a variety of tabloid magazine layouts using layers and guides.

1   **Create a new letter-size CMYK document with the units set for inches. Set the orientation to portrait (tall). Open the Layers palette and show the page rulers.**

2   **In the Layers palette, double-click Layer 1 and rename it "Margins" in the Layer Options dialog box. Click OK.**

3   **Drag guides to mark 1/2-inch margins at the top, bottom, and sides of the page.**

4   **Use the Type tool to draw an area text block that follows the margins from the upper-left corner to the lower-right corner.**

5   **Click the Create New Layer button at the bottom of the Layers palette four times.**

Every new layer appears above the currently selected layer. You now have five layers, with Layer 5 at the top of the layer list.

6   **Double-click Layer 5 and rename it "2-row, 3-col". Rename Layer 4 as "1/2-page ads", Layer 3 as "1/4-page ads", and Layer 2 as "1/16-page ads".**

7   **Use the Selection tool to select the text block. From the Type menu, choose Area Type Options.**

The *Area Type Options* dialog box opens.

8. In the Rows section of the dialog box, set the Number to 2. In the Columns section, set the Number to 3. Click OK. Keep the text block selected.

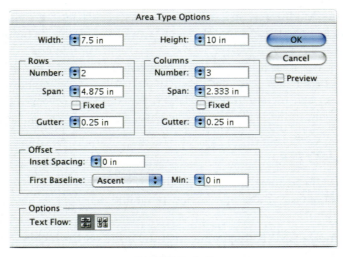

FIGURE 1.7

9. In the Layers palette, click the 2-row, 3-col layer to make it active.

10. Drag vertical guides to mark the two gutters between the three columns. Drag two horizontal guides to mark the single gutter between the two rows.

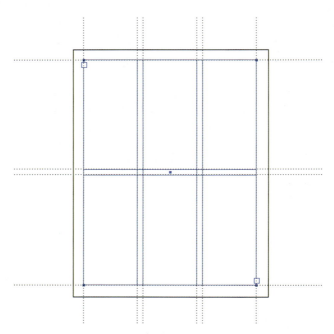

FIGURE 1.8

Chapter 1   Page Geometry   **7**   **LEVEL 2**

? If you have problems

If you do not set a guide correctly on the first attempt, choose Edit>Undo and try again.

11 **Click the Visibility icon of the 2-row, 3-col layer.**

Clicking the Visibility icon hides the guides on the layer. The margins on the visible margins layer remain in view because they are the same on each page of the tabloid.

12 **Save the document as a template with the name "tabloid_layouts.ait" to the Work_In_Progress>WIP_01 folder. Keep the document open for the next exercise.**

From now on, we refer to the Work_In_Progress>WIP_01 folder simply as the WIP_01 folder.

Add to the Layout

1 **In the open document use the Selection tool to select the text block. Choose Type>Area Type Options.**

The Area Type Options dialog opens.

2 **In the dialog box, keep the Rows Number set to 2, and change the Columns Number to 1. Click OK.**

You can use the Area Type Options attributes to modify an area text block at any time. The settings you apply to a text block are not permanent.

3 **Click the 1/2-page ads layer in the Layers palette to make it active. Drag two horizontal guides to mark the top and bottom lines of the gutter between the rows.**

The spaces above and below the gutter are custom-made, so you can insert two half-page ads.

4 **Click the Visibility icon of the 1/2-page ads layer to hide the guides.**

5 **Use the Selection tool to select the text block, and then choose Type>Area Type Options.**

6 **Leave the Rows Number set to 2, and change the Columns Number to 2. Click OK.**

7 **Click the 1/4-page ads layer to make it active. Drag vertical and horizontal guides to mark the gutters between the rows and columns.**

This sets up four quarter-page ad spaces on the page.

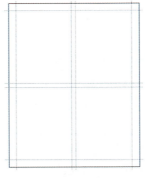

FIGURE 1.9

8   **Click the Visibility icon of the 1/4-page ads layer to hide the guides.**

9   **Select the text block on the Artboard. Return to the Type>Area Type Options dialog box.**

10   **Change the Rows Number to 8 and leave the Columns Number set to 2. Set the Rows and Columns Gutter to 0 (zero). Click OK.**

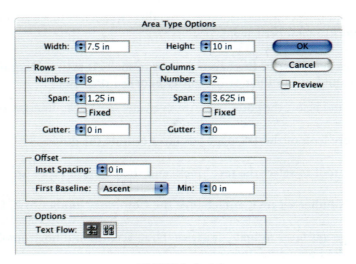

FIGURE 1.10

Chapter 1 Page Geometry   **9**   LEVEL 2

The small 1/16-page ads layout provides as much space as possible, with narrow gutters separating the individual sections.

11 **Click the 1/16-page ads layer to make it active. Drag vertical and horizontal guides to mark the single-line gutters between the rows and columns.**

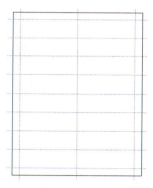

FIGURE 1.11

12 **Click the Visibility icon of each layer to hide or show the layer. Experiment with showing and hiding layer guides to see how they aid in laying out the page.**

You created a simple matrix of page layouts that a tabloid or magazine company could use. The 2-row, 3-column page provides three columns for text. The 1/2-page, 1/4-page, and 1/16-page ads provide various spaces and dimensions that meet the requirements for a wide variety of advertising projects.

13 **Save your changes and close the template document.**

To Extend Your Knowledge

ADDING OTHER ELEMENTS

You can use layers to retain other page elements besides guides. If your client has a logo or another type of page decoration, you can place these elements on layers and hide them along with the guides. If a logo or piece of art must always remain in view, place each element on its own layer and lock it to prevent changes.

LESSON 2 Laying Out Web Pages

As a Web designer, you cannot choose your audience, nor can you predict the size of your viewer's monitors. Computer monitors range from the most common 14-inch screens to 17-, 21-, and 24-inch screens. To accommodate the largest number of users, developers often size their sites at 640 × 480 pixels, which allows a little room for adjustment on the sides, top, and bottom of the screen. Some designers call this the *safe area* — the area of the screen where content displays unobstructed.

In the Illustrator New Document dialog box, you are given several Web-oriented sizes for the Artboard: 640 × 480 (for small monitors), 800 × 600 (for larger monitors), 468 × 60 (the standard size of a Web banner). We find that users with average-size monitors (14-inch screens) can see all the content of a Web page that is set for 640 × 480 pixels in size.

In the following illustration, the transparent frame shows the "fold" of a Web page. The *fold* is the location at the bottom of a viewer's monitor below which the user must scroll to see additional content. All viewers, including those using 14-inch monitors, can see objects positioned above the fold, if the page is designed at 640 × 480 pixels. To see objects below the fold, the user must scroll down through the window or click a link that moves the user down the page.

FIGURE 1.12

Chapter 1 Page Geometry   **11** LEVEL 2

If you know that your viewing audience has larger monitors and is therefore capable of seeing more material on each page, you can enlarge the Artboard and divide the rectangles to a more accessible size.

Modify a Web Page

In this exercise, you modify a Web page to fit within the fold of a common 640 × 480 pixel format.

1   **Open fold.ai from the RF_Illustrator_L2>Chapter_01 folder. Open the Layers palette and show the page rulers.**

From now on, we refer to the RF_Illustrator_L2>Chapter_01 folder simply as the Chapter_01 folder. In subsequent chapters, we refer to the RF folders as Chapter_02, Chapter_03, and so on.

2   **In the Preferences>Units & Display Preferences dialog box, set the General menu to Pixels.**

3   **Click the Default Fill and Stroke icon in the Toolbox. Change the Fill to None.**

4   **Activate the Rectangle tool and click its cursor on the top-left corner of the Artboard. In the dialog box, set the Width to 640 px and the Height to 480 px. Click OK.**

5   **Hold down Shift and drag the rectangle down until the duplicate rectangle's top segment rests on the original rectangle's bottom segment. Then press Option/Alt and release the mouse button to duplicate the rectangle.**

FIGURE 1.13

6   **Press Command/Control-D to make another duplicate.**

7. **Select the three rectangles and press Command/Control-5 to turn them into guides.**

    You divided the page into three Web pages; each page fits within a 640 × 480 pixel screen. Next, you must relocate the page materials so they appear balanced within each Web page.

8. **At the bottom of the Layers palette, click the Create New Layer button twice. Drag the new layers to below Layer 1, so the new order is Layer 1, Layer 2, and Layer 3.**

9. **Double-click Layer 1 and rename it "Home Page". Rename Layer 2 as "Page 2", and Layer 3 as "Page 3".**

10. **Save the document, keeping the same name, to your WIP_01 folder. Keep the document open for the next exercise.**

Divide the Web Page Components

1. **In the open document, select all the objects except the Growing Bananas text block and the images to its left. Press Command/Control-3 to hide the selected elements.**

2. **Select the Growing Bananas text block and its images. Center the objects within the borders of the second rectangular guide. Keep the objects selected.**

3. **In the Layers palette, drag the Selected Object icon from the Home Page layer to the Page 2 layer.**

    If you saved this document as HTML to create the separate Web pages, you must place each page on its own layer so you can hide all unsaved layers and keep them in Illustrator format.

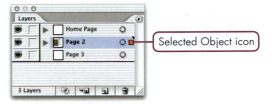

FIGURE 1.14

4. **Click the Visibility icon of the Page 2 layer to hide its components.**

5. **Choose Object>Show All to view the hidden objects.**

6. **Select the Banana Info text block and the image above it. Center the elements in the third rectangle. Keep the objects selected.**

    Your goal is to create a balanced appearance within each of the rectangles.

Chapter 1   Page Geometry   **13**   **LEVEL 2**

7 In the Layers palette, drag the Selected Object icon from the Home Page layer to the Page 3 layer.

You divided a lengthy Web page into convenient smaller-sized pages suitable for viewing on an average 14-inch monitor.

8 Save your changes and close the document.

To Extend Your Knowledge

DESIGN CONSIDERATIONS

The nation's leading Web designers consider the following as important rules for creating new Web pages/sites:

Always consider the size of your viewers' monitors when determining the size of your Web pages. Not every viewer has the luxury of a 17- or 21-inch monitor. Designing pages that perfectly fit large monitors results in pages that are too large to view on 14- or 15-inch monitors—by far the most common monitors in use today.

It is perfectly acceptable to require the viewer to scroll down to view the complete content of your page, but never force a viewer to scroll horizontally.

The first page of your site should require no scrolling at all. For the sake of those viewers with 14-inch monitors, keep the entire content of your first page within a single 640 × 480 pixel layout.

LESSON 3 Understanding the Crop Area

Adobe previously referred to the crop area as "crop marks." Some users confused crop marks with trim marks, which are also included in the document. Where *trim marks* show the printer where to crop (cut) an image from the printed page, the ***Crop Area*** feature isolates a specific object(s) from the other objects in the document.

You can also use the Crop Area feature for several other purposes. When you isolate an object from other objects, you can:

- Position the object anywhere on the printed page.
- Export the object as a TIFF image (or other formats) for commercial printing.
- Export the object as a JPG image for the Web.

Unfortunately, you cannot save an object in the crop area as an Illustrator EPS image. Even when exported in a legacy EPS format, the crop area does not isolate the object correctly.

Isolate Objects for Printing

In this exercise, you use the Crop Area feature to isolate an object and relocate it on the page for output.

1   **Open crop_area.ai from the Chapter_01 folder.**

2   **In the Preferences>Units & Display Preferences dialog box, set the General menu to Inches.**

3   **Click the Default Fill and Stroke icon in the Toolbox. Change the Fill to None.**

No fill allows you to see through objects so you can position them properly.

4   **Use the Rectangle tool to draw a 3.5-inch square. Position the square so it surrounds the Hourglass Productions logo in the bottom-right of the Artboard.**

Visually center the logo inside the square to leave ample distance between the two objects. Any part of the cropped object that extends past the square's borders will be cut off.

5   **Keep the rectangle selected. From the Object menu, choose Crop Area>Make.**

The square converts to crop marks. You cannot select crop marks, nor do they print. Only objects within the crop mark boundaries are acknowledged for output purposes.

FIGURE 1.15

? If you have problems

Do not confuse the crop area with the Crop Marks option found in the Filter>Create menu. Formerly called "trim marks" in previous versions of Illustrator, **crop marks** are necessary for the commercial printer to know where to trim the printed piece. Unlike crop area marks, you can select, modify, and paint crop marks.

6   **Press Command/Control-P to access the Print dialog box. Choose Setup in the options list located in the upper left side of the dialog box.**

Chapter 1   Page Geometry   **15**   LEVEL 2

7 In the Setup section of the dialog box, click the Crop Artwork To menu and choose Crop Area from the list.

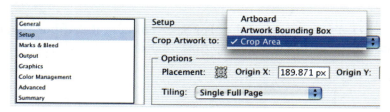

FIGURE 1.16

8 In the preview box in the bottom left of the dialog box, drag the Hourglass Productions logo to the upper-left corner.

The logo is the only object acknowledged because all the other objects were cropped off. You can place the cropped logo anywhere on the page.

FIGURE 1.17

9 Click the Print button at the bottom of the Print dialog box.

10 Inspect the printed page.

You isolated the logo and repositioned it on the page without actually altering any other objects in the document. The Crop Area feature is particularly useful when you want to isolate various logos and/or art pieces without deleting or hiding the other objects in the document.

11 Save the document with the same name to your WIP_01 folder. Keep the document open for the next exercise.

Export Objects for the Web

1 In the open document, choose Object>Crop Area>Release.

You've selected the released square object, but it possesses no paint attributes, which were stripped in the Crop Area>Make process.

2   **Click the Default Fill and Stroke icon in the Toolbox. Change the Fill to None.**

When unpainted objects are not in use, you should paint them. This square is painted, so you can select it and position it quickly.

3   **Position the selected square around the "For Sale" object in the Artboard's upper left. Keep the rectangle selected and go to Object>Crop Area>Make.**

FIGURE 1.18

4   **From the File menu, choose Export. In the Export dialog box, save the file as "for_sale.jpg" to your WIP_01 folder.**

5   **Set the Format to JPEG (jpg), and then click Export/Save.**

To retain the isolated crop area, you must export the file in a raster format. EPS formats do not export the cropped objects correctly.

6   **In the JPEG Options dialog box, set the Quality to Medium, the Color Model to RGB, the Format to Baseline (Standard), and the Resolution to Medium. Make certain the Anti-Alias option is checked, and then click OK.**

These settings save a 150-ppi JPEG image.

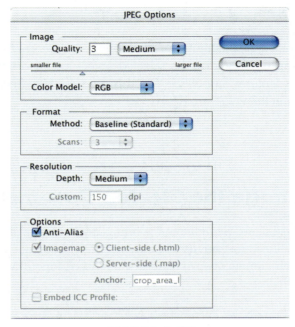

FIGURE 1.19

7. **From the Object menu, choose Crop Area>Release.**

    Once you release the square, it loses all paint attributes but remains selected and its edges visible.

8. **Reposition the square so it surrounds the compact discs in the top right of the Artboard. Apply the Crop Area>Make option to the square.**

9. **Export the file using the same JPEG settings you used in Step 5. Save the file as "compact_discs.jpg" to your WIP_01 folder.**

    Most of the settings reflect the last settings used except for the Color Model. This is a CMYK document, and the Color Model defaults to CMYK.

10. **Release the crop area and reposition the square so it surrounds the checkered flag object in the bottom left of the Artboard. Apply the Crop Area>Make option to the square.**

11. **Export the file using the same JPEG settings you used in Steps 5 and 6 . Save the file as "checkered_flag.jpg" to your WIP_01 folder.**

12. **Close the document without saving. From the WIP_01 folder, drag each of the JPEG images to its own browser window so you can see the exported objects.**

    You exported three images without deleting or hiding any of the other objects in the document.

LEVEL 2 · **18** · Chapter 1 Page Geometry

To Extend Your Knowledge

OTHER RASTER FORMATS

The File>Export dialog box contains many raster file formats, including BMP. Regardless of the raster format you choose, the crop area isolates the selected object for exporting in any of the available raster formats. Other raster features that utilize the crop area are File>Save For Web and File>Save For Microsoft, which results in the PNG format.

LESSON 4 · Manage the Startup Document

To make your favorite colors, gradients, patterns, and painting attributes available in all your new documents, you must save the items in the Illustrator *startup documents*. Inside the Adobe Illustrator CS2 folder is a sub-folder named "Plug-ins", which contains two startup documents: Adobe Illustrator Startup_CMYK.ai and Adobe Illustrator Startup_RGB.ai.

Illustrator refers to the appropriate startup document (CMYK or RGB) when you create a new document. The new document possesses all the paint attributes in the startup document. Illustrator loads the appropriate paint settings to the palettes. If you save new settings in the startup document, you must relaunch the program before the new settings become available.

Modify the Startup Document

In this exercise, you create and save various paint attributes to the startup document. The Brushes, Graphic Styles, Symbols, and Swatches palettes accept these settings.

1 **Make certain that the Illustrator program is not active. On your computer desktop, go to the Adobe Illustrator CS2 folder and open the Plug-ins folder.**

2 **Select the Adobe Illustrator_Startup_CMYK.ai document; then make a duplicate of this file.**

You revert to this copy of the original startup document at the end of the exercise.

3 **Launch the Adobe Illustrator CS2 program.**

Chapter 1   Page Geometry   **19**   LEVEL 2

4 Choose File>Open and navigate to the Adobe Illustrator CS2>Plug-ins folder. Open the Adobe Illustrator_Startup_CMYK.ai document.

FIGURE 1.20

5 Open the Color, Brushes, and Swatches palettes. Set the Swatches palette to Show Color Swatches and set the View to List.

6 In the Color palette, click the Fill box and create a CMYK color you like.

You can also pick a color from the color spectrum sampler at the bottom of the Color palette.

7 Drag the Color palette's Fill box color swatch to the Swatches palette to create a new color. Double-click the new swatch and rename it "My Color".

The Color palette's Fill box shows more of the color than the Stroke box. You can drag either box to the Swatches palette to create a new color.

8 Choose File>Open. Navigate to the Chapter_01 folder and open gradient_pattern.ai.

9 Select the two objects and copy them. Close this document without saving.

The left object is painted with a gradient; the other is painted with a pattern.

10 Back in the working document, click the Show Gradient Swatches icon at the bottom of the Swatches palette. Set the palette view to Large Thumbnail View.

11 Paste the two objects on the Artboard. Double-click the pasted gradient swatch and rename it "My Gradient".

The pasted gradient appears in the Swatches palette's gradient section. You did not have to drag the gradient swatch to the Swatches palette.

12 Click the Show Pattern Swatches icon in the Swatches palette. Set the view to Large Thumbnail View. Rename the pasted pattern "My Pattern".

The pasted pattern appears in the Swatches palette's pattern section without you having to drag its pattern swatch to the Swatches palette.

13 Save your changes. Close the document and quit Illustrator CS2.

Use the New Startup Document

1. Launch Illustrator CS2.

2. Create a new CMYK document.

3. Click the Show Color Swatches icon at the bottom of the Swatches palette. In the palette Options menu, set the view to List View and choose Sort by Name.

4. Scroll through the color swatches until you find your new swatch.

FIGURE 1.21

5. Click the Show Gradient Swatches icon at the bottom of the palette. Set the view to List View and choose Sort by Name.

6. Scroll through the gradients until you find your new gradient swatch.

FIGURE 1.22

7. Click the Show Pattern Swatches icon at the bottom of the palette. Set the view for List View and choose Sort by Name.

Chapter 1 Page Geometry **21** LEVEL 2

8 Scroll through the patterns until you find your new pattern swatch.

FIGURE 1.23

9 Close the document without saving. Quit Illustrator CS2.

10 At the desktop, return to the Adobe Illustrator CS2>Plug-ins folder and delete the Adobe Illustrator Startup_CMYK.ai file.

11 Rename the duplicate file you made in the previous exercise to "Adobe Illustrator Startup_CMYK.ai".

This step returns your startup document to its original state.

To Extend Your Knowledge

SAVING DOCUMENT SETTINGS

Even though you can use the startup document to save paint attributes to the various palettes, you cannot use the startup document to save document-related settings, such as showing rulers or guides. To save the physical document settings, use a template.

LESSON 5 Using the Grid Tools

Grids are quite useful for creating a layout. Creating grids, though, can be quite tedious with drawing lines and intricate measuring techniques. Illustrator has two grid tools that draw grids to your specifications: Rectangular Grid and Polar Grid. Use the **Rectangular Grid tool** to create rectangular-shaped grids, and use the **Polar Grid tool** to create oval/round grids.

When you need to place a graphic element in a specific area of the page, you can use these tools to quickly and easily create the necessary page divisions. Before the existence of these grid tools, designers created grids from scratch.

Use the Rectangular Grid Tool

1 **Open rectangular_grid.ai from the Chapter_01 folder.**

The page contains two half-pages that fold to a finished size of 5.5 × 8.5 inches.

2 **In the Toolbox, access the Line Segment tool's optional tools, and then choose the Rectangular Grid tool. Double-click this tool's icon in the Toolbox.**

The Rectangular Grid tool's Options dialog box opens.

3 **In the dialog box, set the Horizontal Dividers to 1, and set the Vertical Dividers to 1. Click OK.**

The divider lines separate the columns and the rows: The vertical dividers separate the columns; the horizontal dividers separate the rows.

4 **Starting at the upper-left corner of the left-side margin guide, drag the Rectangular Grid tool to match the rectangular margins exactly.**

5 **Press Command/Control-5 to convert the grid paths to guides.**

The single dividers separate the page into four sections, which you can use for four quarter-page ads.

FIGURE 1.24

6 **Click the Rectangular Grid tool's cursor on the upper-left corner of the right-side margin guide.**

7 **In the dialog box, set the Width for 4.5 in. and the Height for 7.5 in.; set the Horizontal Dividers to 6, and leave the Vertical Dividers set to 1. Click OK.**

By clicking the tool on the Artboard and assigning increments, the tool automatically draws the grid after you click OK. Before you assigned new increments, the dialog box reflected the increments of the hand-drawn grid you drew earlier.

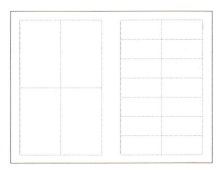

FIGURE 1.25

8   **Press Command/Control-5 to convert the selected grid paths to guides.**

You can use the multiple rectangles in this grid for small advertisements.

9   **Press Command/Control-Shift and double-click the first grid guide with the Selection tool. Deselect this released guide's path.**

At first, only the single guide that you clicked appears to be released and selected. This is not the case.

10   **Deselect the path. Press Command/Control-A to select all paths.**

Further selection shows that double-clicking the one guide releases the entire grid guide.

11   **Delete the selected grid. Release the other grid guide, and then delete it.**

12   **Use the two methods of the Rectangular Grid tool (manual drawing and its dialog box) to create other grids for the two page margins.**

Experiment with the number of dividers you include.

13   **When finished, save the document with the same name to your WIP_01 folder. Close the document.**

Use the Polar Grid Tool

In this exercise, you use the Polar Grid tool to create the art for an adhesive sticker for a vehicle's back window. Working with circular layouts can be difficult unless you use a grid to keep the elements positioned correctly.

1   **Open polar_grid.ai from the Chapter_01 folder. Show the Swatches and Align palettes.**

2   **Choose the Polar Grid tool from the Toolbox in the Line Segment tool's optional tools.**

| 3 | **Press Option/Alt and click the cursor in the approximate center of the Artboard.**

Wherever you click the cursor on the Artboard becomes the polar grid's center point.

| 4 | **In the Polar Grid tool's Options dialog box, set the Width and Height to 4 inches. Click OK.**

The Width and Height fields allow you to create circular or oval grids.

| 5 | **Press Command/Control-5 to convert the grid paths to guides.**

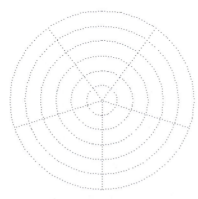

FIGURE 1.26

| 6 | **Activate the Ellipse tool. Press Option/Alt and click the cursor on the grid's center.**

| 7 | **In the dialog box, set the Width and Height to 4 inches. Click OK. Fill the circle with Sea Green and apply a Stroke of None.**

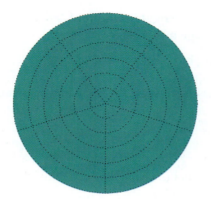

FIGURE 1.27

|8| While you press Option/Alt-Shift, drag the Ellipse tool on the grid's center to draw a circle that matches the fourth circle from the grid's center.

|9| Fill this circle with Pure Cyan and apply a Stroke of None.

|10| Draw another circle from the center that matches the third circle from the grid's center.

|11| Fill the circle with Pure Yellow and apply a Stroke of None.

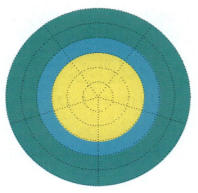

FIGURE 1.28

|12| Save the document with the same name to your WIP_01 folder. Keep the document open for the next exercise.

Add Type to the Sticker

|1| Select the two objects above the Artboard (the type and the fish). Press Command/Control-Shift-] (right bracket) to bring the objects to the front.

|2| Select the circular type object and move it onto the sticker.

|3| Select all the circles and the type object.

4 In the Align palette, click the Horizontal Align Center and the Vertical Align Center options.

FIGURE 1.29

5 Select the fish object above the Artboard and move it onto the sticker.

6 Visually center the object in the grid's middle.

If you use the Align palette to center the fish, the contours and width of the object make the design appear too heavy on the left. Visual placement is best for this type of object.

FIGURE 1.30

7 The fish sticker is finished.

8 Save your changes and close the document.

To Extend Your Knowledge

MODIFYING GRIDS

Rectangular and polar grids are simple vector paths grouped together. You can paint and otherwise modify these grids as you would any other path you create in Illustrator.

You can paint the fills and strokes of rectangular and polar grids, but if you ungroup a grid, its paths lose their paint attributes, and you must repaint them.

LESSON 6 Perspective Layout

If you want to add depth to a design, consider using a perspective viewpoint that gives two-dimensional artwork a three-dimensional appearance. A perspective drawing must include a horizon and a vanishing point. The ***horizon line*** is an imaginary horizontal (in most cases) line. All horizontal lines drawn in the design must run parallel to the horizon. The ***vanishing point*** is the exact location in a scene where objects disappear into the distance.

The simplest form of perspective uses a single vanishing point; the viewer directly faces the object as it recedes into the distance. A ***single-point perspective*** is also called a ***parallel view***. The two sets of blocks shown below illustrate how you can tip the horizon line from true horizontal without affecting the vanishing point.

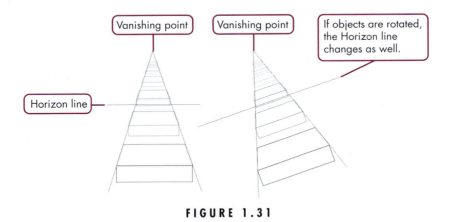

FIGURE 1.31

The vanishing point for these rectangles is at the top of the image. The horizon line on the left is horizontal; on the right, it's tipped. As you can see, the relationship of horizontal and vertical lines corresponds to the angle of the horizon line.

Create a Perspective

In this exercise, you create a perspective with a single vanishing point.

1 Create a new letter-size CMYK document with the units set for inches and a portrait orientation. Show the page rulers.

2 Drag horizontal guides to the 10-in, 2-in, 1.25-in, and 1-in marks on the vertical ruler.

At the top of the page, the guide on the 10-inch mark becomes the horizon of this perspective.

3 Drag vertical guides to the 3-in, 4.25-in, and 5.5-in marks on the horizontal ruler.

The intersection of the 4.25-inch vertical guide and the 10-inch horizontal guide becomes the vanishing point.

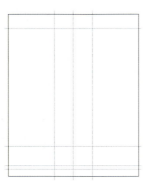

FIGURE 1.32

4 Click the Default Fill and Stroke icon in the Toolbox. Change the Fill to None.

5 Select the Pen tool. Click on the following locations: First, click where the 1.25-in horizontal guide intersects the 3-in vertical guide; then click the vanishing point (where the 4.25-in vertical guide intersects the 10-in horizontal guide); and finally, click where the 5.5-in vertical guide intersects the 1.25-in horizontal guide.

This triangular design defines the perspective as it descends toward the vanishing point.

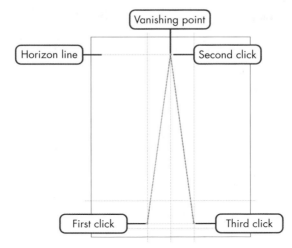

FIGURE 1.33

6 Press Command/Control-5 to convert the path to a guide.

7 Use the Rectangle tool to draw a rectangle that fits within the area where the 3-in and 5.5-in vertical guides meet the 1-in and 1.25-in horizontal guides.

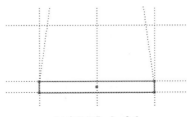

FIGURE 1.34

8 Fill the rectangle with C = 45, M = 0, Y = 0, K = 0 and change the Stroke to None. Deselect the path.

9 Click the Default Fill and Stroke icon in the Toolbox and change the Fill to None.

10 Use the Pen tool to draw a polygon closed path that fits the angled area above the rectangle you drew in Step 7 (see Figure 1.35).

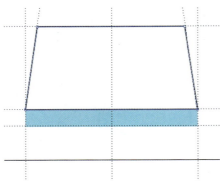

FIGURE 1.35

11 Fill the rectangle with Pure Cyan and change the Stroke to None. Select the two paths and group them.

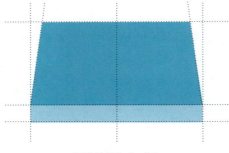

FIGURE 1.36

12 Save the document as "perspective.ai" to your WIP_01 folder. Keep the document open for the next exercise.

Create Additional Perspective

1 Select the grouped object and click the Scale tool in the Toolbox.

2 Press Option/Alt and click the Scale tool cursor on the vanishing point at the page's top.

3 In the Scale dialog box, set the Uniform Scale to 80, and then click Copy.

The object reduces in size as it moves toward the vanishing point.

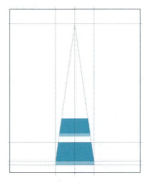

FIGURE 1.37

4 **Press Command/Control-D to create another reduced copy that heads toward the vanishing point.**

5 **Continue to press Command/Control-D until the reduced objects reach the vanishing point.**

You used a grid to draw objects that fit within the perspective lines and that reduce proportionally in size as they descend toward the vanishing point on the horizon.

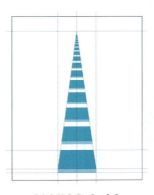

FIGURE 1.38

6 **Save your changes and close the document.**

To Extend Your Knowledge

OTHER TYPES OF PERSPECTIVE

In addition to single-point perspective, there are two other types of perspectives. The **two-point perspective** (also called "angular perspective") positions the viewer away from and to the side of an object, creating two vanishing points. The line of sight parallels one full side. You can see in the illustration below that all the vertical lines are parallel to one another.

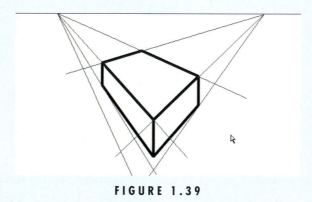

FIGURE 1.39

The **three-point perspective** acknowledges that the viewer's line of sight isn't parallel to any full side. The viewer observes the object from an angle, seeing its sides and top (or bottom).

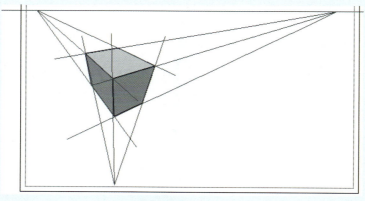

FIGURE 1.40

Entire books have been written about perspective drawing. We only touch the surface of the subject in this chapter, but now you know a few techniques that add realistic dimensionality to objects.

Chapter 1 Page Geometry **33** **LEVEL 2**

SUMMARY

In Chapter 1, you learned that Illustrator is much more than a digital drawing program and that you can use it to create complex page layouts and designs and to publish pages. You discovered how to create page layouts with guides that you can save to layers and use again in the future. We introduced you to the fold of a Web page and taught you how the fold aids in developing Web pages that accommodate viewers with smaller monitor sizes.

You also learned how to use the Crop Area function to isolate specific objects in a document from the other objects in the same document. You discovered how to save paint attributes to the Adobe Illustrator startup files, making the attributes available in any new documents you create. You learned how to use the Rectangular Grid and Polar Grid tools to customize grids, and you discovered how to create perspective grids using ruler guides and guides made from paths.

KEY TERMS

Area Type Options	Page geometry	Startup documents
Crop area	Parallel view	Three-point perspective
Crop marks	Polar Grid tool	Trim marks
Dimensionality	Rectangular Grid tool	Two-point perspective
Fold	Safe area	Vanishing point
Horizon Line	Single-point perspective	

CHECKING CONCEPTS AND TERMS

MULTIPLE CHOICE

Circle the letter that matches the correct answer for each of the following questions.

1. Other than the Guides option in the View menu, you can use _____ to hide guides.
   a. Outline viewing mode
   b. Layers
   c. Preferences
   d. Document setup

2. The fold of a Web page is _____.
   a. the line of division between two frames on the page
   b. the bottom scroll bar of a frame on the page
   c. the bottom of the browser window
   d. None of the above.

3. The Crop Area feature _____.
   a. shows the commercial printer where to trim off the designated area
   b. isolates the cropped object from the other objects in the document
   c. masks the selected object
   d. applies crop marks

4. When you apply the Crop Area feature to an object, you cannot export the image as a(n) _____.
   a. TIFF image
   b. JPEG image
   c. Encapsulated PostScript (EPS)
   d. BMP image

5. The Adobe Illustrator startup document can retain _____.

   a. any document settings

   b. only paint attributes

   c. increments in palettes

   d. positions of palettes

6. Once you save settings in the Adobe Illustrator startup document, _____.

   a. they take effect immediately

   b. you must restart the Illustrator program before they take effect

   c. they are only available in new documents

   d. they become available in all documents

7. The Rectangular Grid tool _____.

   a. alters the document grid, toggled in the View menu

   b. draws guides on the page

   c. creates a grid of paths divided into rows and columns

   d. None of the above.

8. The Polar Grid tool _____.

   a. can only draw when you drag the tool on the page

   b. creates grids in two shapes: circle and oval

   c. has vertical and horizontal divider lines

   d. is an optional tool of the Ellipse tool

9. A perspective grid includes _____.

   a. vertical and horizontal lines

   b. vanishing point and horizon

   c. portrait and landscape orientation

   d. angles and viewpoint

10. You must use the _____ to create a perspective grid.

   a. Rectangular Grid tool

   b. Polar Grid tool

   c. Pen tool

   d. None of the above.

DISCUSSION QUESTIONS

1. Name three different types of projects you could complete within Illustrator without using a page-layout program for final output.

2. What is the reason for keeping Web pages at a smaller size in relation to browsers and how they appear on various monitors?

3. Describe three different assignments that might require a round design framework.

4. Name three situations where using perspective grids would aid in the development of your design.

SKILL DRILL

Skill Drills reinforce project skills. Each skill that is reinforced is the same as, or nearly the same as, a skill we presented in the lessons. We provide detailed instructions in a step-by-step format. You can work through one or more exercises in any order.

1. Lay Out a Custom Page

You are a layout artist in the art department of a printing company. A new client publishes coupon booklets that they mail to the public. The client has standard pages that hold stories, articles, and various coupons and ads. Create a document template that lays out each page with the correct columns and rows to accommodate the various pages.

1. Create a new CMYK document. Set the dimensions of the Artboard to 8.5 × 5.5 inches. Set the units to inches. Open the Layers palette and show the page rulers in the document.

2. In the Layers palette, double-click Layer 1 and rename it "Margins".

3. Drag guides to mark 1/4-inch margins at the top, bottom, and sides of the page.

4. Use the Type tool to draw an area text block that matches the margins from its upper-left corner to its lower-right corner.

5. In the Layers palette, click the Create New Layer icon at the bottom of the palette five times.

6. Starting at the top of the layer list in the palette, rename the layers as follows: "2-row, 4-col", "1/2-page ads", "1/4-page ads", "1/8-page coupons", and "1/16-page coupons".

   Double-clicking a layer in the Layers palette brings up the Layer Options dialog box, allowing you to rename the layer.

7. One at a time, click a named layer, such as 4-row, 4-col, and use the Type menu's Area Type Options to set the text block for the appropriate number of rows and columns. Draw guides to match the text block's layout (see Figure 1.41).

   Each layer should have a different set of guides that apply to the layer's name.

   In a booklet of this small size, the gutters should be set to 0 (zero) to give the clients extra space for their ads and coupons.

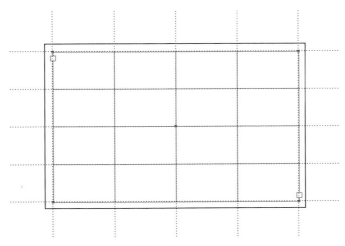

FIGURE 1.41

LEVEL 2   **36**   Chapter 1   Page Geometry

8. Click the Visibility icon for all the layers except one to see how you can choose grid layouts from the Layers palette. To see the guides, continue clicking the Visibility icons to show other single layers.

9. When you are finished, save the file as a document template with the name "coupons.ait" to your WIP_01 folder.

2. Inspect the Internet for Sites Needing Folds

Sites on the Internet fall into two categories: those professionally designed and laid out, and those slapped together simply to create a presence on the Web. Quickly surf the Web to see numerous examples of both types.

1. Launch your Internet browser.

2. Use your favorite search engine to find various Web sites.

3. Inspect the content of each site's home page.

    The home page should only contain pertinent photos, text, and links to other related pages or sites.

4. Determine how far you must scroll down (if at all) to reach the site's personal information and info link, such as About Us or Contact Us.

    The experienced Web designer places all this personal information across the bottom of the home page but well within the user's view.

5. Find a long Web page that you have to tediously scroll down through. As you scroll, take screen shots of the browser window until you have shots of the entire page.

    If you do not have a screen-shot program, use these built-in methods:

    For Macintosh users, to get a screen shot, press Command-Shift-3. A PDF file of the screen shot appears on your desktop. Move this to your Chapter_01 folder for placing.

    For Windows users, press the Print Screen key at the top of your keyboard (to the right of the "F" keys). The TIFF image is captured into your memory clipboard. Return to the Illustrator document and paste the image from your clipboard.

6. Go to the active Illustrator program and create a new RGB document of any size. Hide the Artboard. Place the screen shots you made of the Web page.

7. Use a clipping mask to mask out the unnecessary sections until you have pieced together the entire Web page in your document.

8. Create a 640 × 480 pixel rectangle. Fill the rectangle with None and apply a Stroke of Black. Position the rectangle at the top of the Web page you pieced together.

9. Duplicate the rectangle downward to divide the Web page into increments, showing where the folds should appear.

Analyzing other people's work gives you a good idea of what to do (and what not to do) when designing Web pages.

FIGURE 1.42

10. When you are finished, close the document without saving.

3. Draw an Angled Perspective Grid

You are a commercial artist. A client hired you to design a billboard that he will eventually install on a desert highway that heads toward some distant mountains. He wants to see a rough layout of how the billboard will look in this setting. Your first task is to create a perspective grid that you will use to draft the design.

1. Create a new letter-size CMYK document with Units set for Inches. Set the Orientation for Landscape (wide). Show the page rulers.

2. Drag vertical guides to the 1-inch, 5-inch, and 9-inch marks on the horizontal ruler.

3. Drag horizontal guides to the 8-inch, 4-inch, and 1-inch marks on the vertical ruler.

4. Click the Default Fill and Stroke icon in the Toolbox and change the Fill to None.

5. Select the Pen tool. Click where the 1-inch vertical guide intersects the 4-inch horizontal guide (see Figure 1.43).

6. Click again where the 9-inch vertical guide intersects the 8-inch horizontal guide near the top of the Artboard (see Figure 1.43).

This is your vanishing point.

7. Click a third time where the 5-inch vertical guide intersects the 1-inch horizontal guide at the lower part of the Artboard (see Figure 1.43).

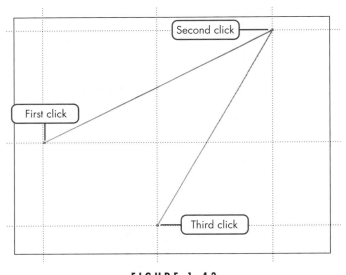

FIGURE 1.43

8. Select the path, and then press Command/Control-5 to convert the path to a guide.

9. Experiment with drawing rectangular objects that represent parts of the billboard. Place the objects along the angled lines of the perspective grid you created.

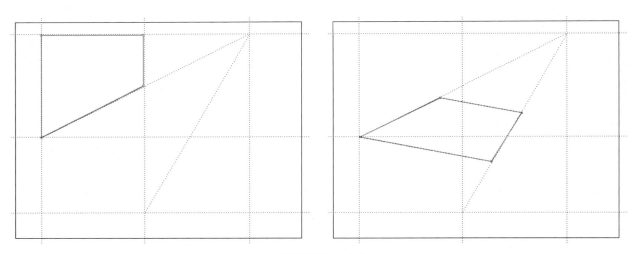

FIGURE 1.44

10. Save the document as "my_grid.ai" to your WIP_01 folder. Close the document.

Chapter 1   Page Geometry   **39**   **LEVEL 2**

4. Draw a Polar Grid for a Round Logo

A client hired you to design a round logo for a new product package. He asked you to use the words "Digital Flowers for You!" in the logo. The package will be printed in 4-color process, so your choice of colors is limitless. Your task is to produce a comprehensive layout to show the client.

1. Create a new letter-size CMYK document set for portrait orientation. Show the page rulers.

2. Drag vertical and horizontal guides to mark the center of the Artboard.

3. Select the Polar Grid tool. Press Option/Alt and click the cursor in the center of the Artboard. In the dialog box, set the Width and Height for 3 inches and click OK.

    The polar grid appears where you clicked on the Artboard.

4. Press Command/Control-5 to convert the grid paths into guides.

5. Use the Ellipse tool to draw a circle from the grid's center that matches the size of the second circle from the grid's center. Fill the circle with Jade and stroke with None.

6. Draw a thin oval that fits above the circle and extends up to the last circle in the grid. Fill the oval with Pure Yellow. Center the oval on the vertical center guide.

    The oval will be the flower's top petal. You now need to duplicate more petals around the circle.

7. Select the Rotate tool in the Toolbox. Press Option/Alt, and click the center of the circle guide. In the Rotate dialog box, set the angle for 22.5 and click Copy.

    A copy of the oval (flower petal) appears, rotated to the left.

8. Press Command/Control and press the "D" key 14 times. Select all the ovals and the circle and group them. Copy the group.

9. Press Command/Control-B to paste in back. Press the Right Arrow and Down Arrow keys one time each. Fill the pasted objects with Black.

10. Click the Swap Fill and Stroke icon in the Toolbox.

11. Select the Ellipse tool. Press Option/Alt and Shift, and drag a circle from the marked center to match the outer circle in the grid.

12. Select the Type on Path tool and click its cursor on the top anchor point of this circle. Type the words "Digital Flowers".

13. Apply the font of your choice (we used Textile in the example). Make the size approximately 60 pt, maintaining a tight tracking. Kern any letters you think should have their spacing adjusted.

14. Select the circular text block with the Selection tool and use its middle I-beam to center the type above the flower.

The logo is finished.

FIGURE 1.45

15. Save the document with the name "digital_flowers.ai" to you WIP_01 folder. Close the document.

CHALLENGE

Challenge exercises expand on, or are somewhat related to, skills that we presented in the lessons. Each exercise provides a brief introduction, followed by numbered-step instructions that are not as detailed as those in the Skill Drill exercises. You can work through one or more exercises in any order.

1. Create Raster Images for the Web

You are working on a site that promotes your skills as a Web designer. You already placed a significant amount of artwork on the site, but you need to choose the best examples to show a prospective client. Your images must be saved in the JPEG format.

1. Create a letter-size RGB document set to portrait orientation. Show the page rulers.
2. Use the Type tool to draw an area text block that matches the size of the Artboard. From the Type menu, choose Area Type Options.
3. Set the Rows Number to 5 and the Columns Number to 3. Change the Gutters to 0. Click OK.
4. Use guides to mark the lines that separate the columns and rows.

You created a grid to hold your artwork.

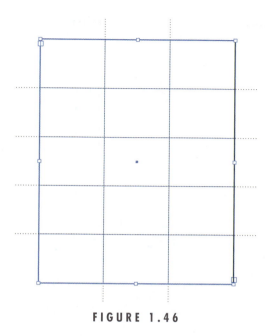

FIGURE 1.46

5. Collect about 15 of your favorite images (vector and/or raster) and place them into the document.
6. Scale each image and position it within its own section on the grid.
7. Once you place all the images, draw a rectangle (filled with None, stroked with Black) in the size of the first (top-left) section.
8. From the Object menu, choose the Crop Area>Make option.
9. Export the image to your WIP_01 folder in the JPEG format, using an appropriate file name.
10. Release the crop area, and then relocate the rectangle to the next image to the right.
11. Apply the Crop Area>Make option to the rectangle and export the image as a JPEG to the WIP_01 folder.
12. Continue to apply the Crop Area>Make option to each of the artwork pieces on the page and export them as JPEGs.
13. When you are finished, close the file without saving. On your desktop, view the exported images in your browser window.

2. Use a Rectangular Grid for a Bottle Label

One of your clients wants you to produce a label for a new line of women's shampoo. Your task is to create a grid for the label you will create. The client asked you to use pink as the background color.

1. Create a new CMYK document with the Units set for Inches and the Artboard size set for 2.5 × 4 inches.
2. Double-click the Rectangular Grid tool in the Toolbox.

3. In the dialog box, set the Horizontal Dividers to 6 and the Vertical Dividers to 4. Click OK.
4. Draw a grid that matches the Artboard.

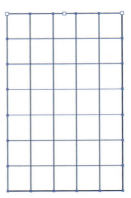

FIGURE 1.47

5. Press Command/Control-5 to convert the grid paths to guides.
6. Use the Rounded Rectangle tool to draw a rectangle that matches the size of the Artboard.
7. Fill the rectangle with 25% Magenta and stroke with None.
8. Lock the rectangle. From the View menu, select Hide Artboard.

   The layout is complete and ready to build the label with type and graphics.

FIGURE 1.48

9. Save the document as "shampoo_label.ai" to your WIP_01 folder. Close the document.

Chapter 1 Page Geometry 43 LEVEL 2

3. Save the Startup Document

Saving your most frequently used colors, gradients, and patterns in a single document speeds up the painting process, because you don't have to search through multiple documents to find the attributes you need. In this exercise, you locate a number of your favorite paint attributes and save them to the startup document.

1. Choose File>Open, and navigate to the Adobe Illustrator CS2>Plug-ins folder. Open the Adobe Illustrator Startup_CMYK.ai document. Open the Swatches palette.

2. Open your own Illustrator documents that contain custom colors, gradients, or patterns that you have used or created.

3. Paint objects, such as squares, with these paint attributes.

4. Cut and paste the various paint-filled objects into the Adobe Illustrator Startup_CMYK.ai document.

5. Once you finish pasting the objects, close all the documents except the Adobe Illustrator Startup_CMYK file.

   All the gradients and patterns you pasted into the document appear automatically in the Swatches palette. The color swatches, however, are the only paint attributes that don't appear automatically.

6. If you pasted any objects based on their color swatch, select each object (one at a time) and drag its Fill or Stroke box from the Color palette to the Swatches palette to create a new swatch.

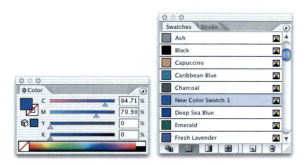

FIGURE 1.49

7. Double-click the new swatch in the Swatches palette and name it.

8. Continue to select the pasted objects, drag their fills to the Swatches palette, and rename the new swatches. Do this for all of the objects.

9. Save your changes and close the document. Quit Illustrator CS2.

10. Launch Illustrator CS2. Go to the Swatches palette to see your own colors, gradients, and patterns.

4. Create a Perspective Grid from a Rectangular Grid

You are an artist at a billboard company. Your team is preparing to present a new design to a client. The more realistic the design appears, the better your chances of selling it to the client — who is due to arrive at your office in an hour. It will be difficult to draw a perspective grid from scratch, one path at a time, in one hour, but do your best to complete the task before the client arrives.

1. Create a new letter-size CMYK document with Units set for Inches. Set the Orientation for Landscape.

2. Select the Rectangular Grid tool. Click the upper-left corner of the Artboard.

3. In the dialog box, set the Width to 7 inches and the Height to 5 inches.

4. Set the Horizontal Dividers to 4 and the Vertical Dividers to 8. Click OK.

   The grid appears on the Artboard.

5. Activate the Free Transform tool.

6. Position the tool's cursor over the grid's bottom-right control handle. Click and hold the mouse button on this handle.

7. Press Command/Control to change the tool into Shear mode.

8. Continue to hold Command/Control and move the anchor point upward while pressing the Shift key to constrain the move.

9. Move the anchor point up so the height of the right side is about half the size of the grid's left side.

   You quickly created a perspective grid without having to measure, make guides, or draw paths.

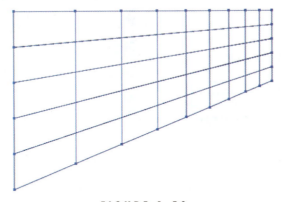

FIGURE 1.50

10. Use your own artistic judgment to draw a design that follows this perspective grid. A fence that descends into the horizon is one suggestion.

11. Save the document as "shear_perspective.ai" to your WIP_01 folder. Close the document.

Chapter 1 Page Geometry 45 LEVEL 2

PORTFOLIO BUILDER

Build an Image Library

Webmasters need quick access to JPEG images for the Web sites they create for clients. In this Portfolio Builder, you create a folder of images. You can use this folder as a library so you can quickly find an image when you need one.

1. Create a new letter-size RGB document.

2. Draw twelve 1.5-inch squares, three per row, evenly aligned and distributed to fill the Artboard.

3. Turn the squares into guides.

4. You can use this matrix to place 12 art objects.

5. Open Illustrator documents that contain your favorite designs, and copy/paste the designs into the new matrix. Fit one of the pasted art pieces inside each square guide on the page.

6. Starting with the top-left image, return its guide to a path. Use the Crop Area>Make option to isolate the image inside the square.

7. Export the object as an RGB image in JPEG format with a Quality and Resolution of Medium. Save the image to your WIP_01 folder and name it.

8. Release the crop area and delete the square. Use the same procedure to isolate and export all the other objects on the page, one by one. When finished, close the document without saving.

9. Drag each JPEG file to a browser window so you can observe your work.

LEVEL 2

CHAPTER 2

Effects, Styles, and Appearances

OBJECTIVES

In this chapter, you learn how to:

- Apply vector effects

- Add raster effects

- Manage attributes with the Appearance palette

- Create graphic styles

- Modify effects and graphic styles

- Create and modify a gradient mesh

- Design with a gradient mesh

Chapter 2　Effects, Styles, and Appearances　　**47**　　LEVEL 2

Why Would I Do This?

Adobe Illustrator is a remarkable application that is rich with features and offers such a vast array of techniques that mastering the program becomes a process, not an event. No matter how long you use the program, there's always something new to learn — such as the efficient use of effects, appearances, and styles. Each of these functions, particularly when combined with gradients, can reduce development time, increase productivity, and allow you to achieve dramatic results that are impossible to accomplish using basic drawing techniques.

In this chapter, you learn how to apply effects, styles, and appearances to objects. You discover how to expand your creative possibilities while preserving original drawing elements. You work with styles, which allow you to apply an appearance or other attributes to a drawing element with a single click. You also learn how to use the gradient mesh — one of Illustrator's must powerful coloring and shape-creation tools. After you complete this chapter, you can use these advanced Illustrator features to execute professional-looking illustrations, images, and documents.

VISUAL SUMMARY

A designer who can create digital art dramatically expands his or her ability to communicate visually. Effectively controlling the appearance of the digital design is a critical component in the creative process. Illustrator CS2 provides a wide variety of tools and techniques for adding visual effects to illustrations. You can access the most commonly used colors, gradients, and patterns in the Swatches palette, but the options in the Effect menu take the appearance of painted paths to an all-new level.

The lesson on vector effects introduces you to some of the many effects located in the Effect menu that utilize only vector paths. As you explore these effects, you learn about a new Illustrator concept called *appearance*, which describes how the object *appears* to be modified according to the settings you apply. In truth, the selected path is not altered in any way. You can add effects sequentially to achieve unusual and unique appearances.

FIGURE 2.1

The section on raster effects introduces you to some of the effects located in the Effect menu that apply raster effects to vector paths. The **Rasterize effect** works in conjunction with the object's appearance. Do not confuse the Rasterize effect with the Rasterize option in the Object menu; the Rasterize option converts a selected path to raster format.

FIGURE 2.2

You also learn how to use the various features in the Appearance palette to modify the effects applied to paths. You can use the Appearance palette to modify, move, delete, and apply effects to an object's fill or stroke. This powerful palette will become an irreplaceable part of your work process.

FIGURE 2.3

The lesson on graphic styles teaches you how to save paths that contain effects to the Graphic Styles palette. You can use the Graphic Styles palette to save and store your favorite effect combinations so you can apply them to any object at any time.

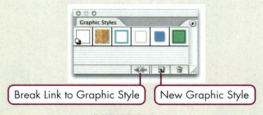

FIGURE 2.4

Chapter 2 Effects, Styles, and Appearances   49   LEVEL 2

You also learn how to create and modify a gradient mesh to achieve free-form-style gradients. Before the advent of the gradient mesh, you could only apply linear or radial gradients that cut off sharply at the path's edge. With the gradient mesh, however, you can create gradients that extend their gradations, similar to blends.

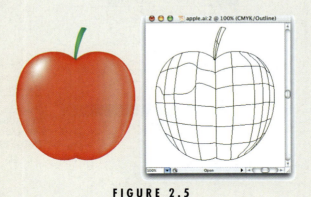

FIGURE 2.5

LESSON 1 Applying Vector Effects

When you apply effects from the Effect menu, you are modifying only the object's "appearance," not the actual path itself. Under the Effect menu are two sets of options.

The first set of options, called Illustrator Effects, contains effects you can apply to vector paths only. Most of these effects are like those found in the Filters menu (but the Filters menu items physically shape, cut, and distort the object's actual path).

The Illustrator Effects only apply these changes to the path's "appearance." You can use the Appearance palette to remove these effects from the object.

The second set of options, called Photoshop Effects, contains effects you can apply to both vector and raster objects. When you apply one of these effects to a vector path, its appearance is automatically rasterized so as to receive one of the Photoshop Effects.

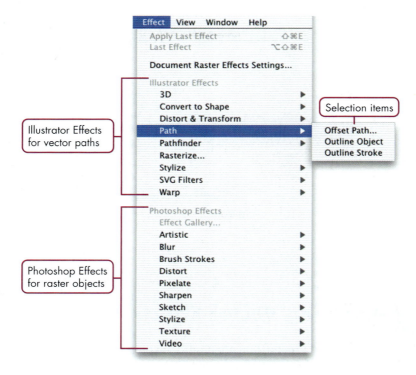

FIGURE 2.6

- The Illustrator Effects section of the menu contains the effects you can apply to vector paths in the document.
- The Selection items pop-out menu for each option contains an assortment of related effects.
- The items under Photoshop Effects apply Photoshop filters to the object's appearance. You do not need to rasterize images prior to applying these effects; the rasterizing is included in the process.

Apply Vector Effects

In this exercise, you apply some of the more prominent effects that alter and/or enhance the appearances of vector paths.

1. Open vector_effects.ai from the Chapter_02 folder.

2. Select all three objects on the Artboard. From the Effect menu, choose Distort & Transform>Twist.

    The Twist dialog box opens.

Chapter 2 Effects, Styles, and Appearances 51 LEVEL 2

3 **In the dialog box, set the Angle to 35 and click OK.**

Once you click OK, all three objects twist. The twisted circle shows little change, but the other objects are obviously affected.

FIGURE 2.7

4 **Press Command/Control-Y to switch to Outline view.**

In Outline view, the twisting effects are no longer visible. Effects are based on the new image function known as "appearance." Despite the shape of the path, which remains unaltered, you can see only the appearance of the painted effects in Preview mode.

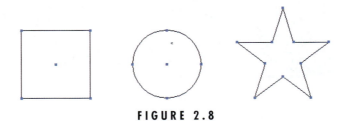

FIGURE 2.8

5 **Return to Preview mode.**

? If you have problems

If you apply the wrong effect settings or if you want to remove an effect completely, you must use Edit>Undo for now. The best way to remove or modify an effect is in the Appearance palette, which you learn about later in this chapter.

6 **From the Effect menu, choose Stylize>Scribble. Make no changes in the dialog box and click OK.**

The objects now appear as though a child scribbled with a crayon on a piece of paper.

FIGURE 2.9

7. **Choose the Effect menu, choose Warp>Arc Upper. Make no changes in the dialog box and click OK.**

The twisted objects now have rounded tops — the arc effect. At any time during these effect applications, you may toggle back and forth between Preview and Outline viewing modes to see how the original paths remain unchanged.

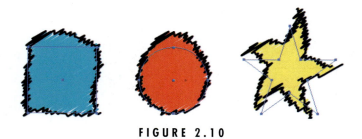

FIGURE 2.10

8. **From the Effect menu, choose Stylize>Drop Shadow. Make no changes in the dialog box and click OK.**

A drop shadow appears on each object. This effect is similar to the Drop Shadow filter in the Filter menu, but the filter creates an actual raster image that becomes the shadow. Here, the effect's drop shadow appears only in Preview mode.

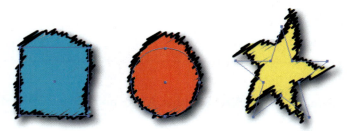

FIGURE 2.11

9. **From the Effect menu, choose Stylize>Outer Glow. In the dialog box, click the swatch to the right of the Mode menu. In the Color Picker, click the upper-right corner of the large spectrum window to set a yellow color. Click OK.**

The yellow glow appears around the extremities of each object — in this case, outside the drop shadow.

FIGURE 2.12

10 Save the document with the same name to your WIP_02 folder. Close the document.

In this exercise, you applied effects to vector paths and observed how they only affected the appearance of the paths, visible only in Preview mode.

To Extend Your Knowledge . . .

EFFECTS VS. FILTERS

Effects are similar to filters, but where a filter physically changes the selected path's anchor points and segments, effects alter only the appearance of the object's preview seen in Preview mode.

LESSON 2 Applying Photoshop Effects

The Effect menu has its own raster section called Photoshop Effects, which are the appearances that the Photoshop Filters (possessing the same name as the Photoshop Effects) apply. These Photoshop Effects work on three kinds of objects in the document: vector paths, paths that have been rasterized in Illustrator, and photographs (or raster artwork) that have been placed.

The biggest difference between using these raster effects and the raster filters of the Filter menu is that you don't need to rasterize the selected object prior to applying the Photoshop Effects. A vector path that has a Photoshop Effect applied to it remains a path and is not actually rasterized as if the Rasterize option in the Object menu were used.

The Photoshop Effects, when applied to a vector path, do their own rasterizing of the "appearance" in preparation for the effect. The Photoshop Effect dialog box then appears and allows customizing of the settings, if needed.

Once you apply an effect to an object, you can modify it by double-clicking the effect name in the Appearance palette, which brings up a dialog box where you can make changes.

These uses and applications of raster effects fall into the following categories:

- The effect adds a separate raster element to the vector path. A good example is the blurred shadow in the Effects>Stylize>Drop Shadow option.

FIGURE 2.13

- The effect applies a raster appearance to the path's preview, shown here in the Effects>Stylize>Feather effect.

FIGURE 2.14

- The Photoshop Effects options Blur, Pixelate, and Sharpen rasterize a path's whole appearance, as shown in this example of the Effects>Blur>Gaussian Blur.

FIGURE 2.15

In this exercise, you utilize the raster-related options located in the Effect menu to create a banner for the Internet.

Create a Banner with Raster Effects

1 **From the Chapter_02 folder, open the document spider_banner.ai.**

Make certain that the Preferences>Units & Display Performance dialog box has its General menu set for Pixels.

2 **Click the Default Fill and Stroke icon in the Toolbox.**

Chapter 2 Effects, Styles, and Appearances   55   LEVEL 2

3 Select the Round Cornered Rectangle tool and draw a rectangle that fits the Artboard.

4 Change the Stroke of the rectangle to None.

5 From the Effect menu, choose Stylize>Inner Glow.

Position the dialog box so you can see the rectangle clearly.

6 In the dialog box, set the Mode to Normal, and click the color swatch to the menu's right.

The Color Picker opens.

7 In the Color Picker, set the RGB values to R = 30, G = 101, and B = 163. Click OK.

8 Set the Blur for 14.4 px. Click the Preview button in the dialog box.

The edges of the rectangle take on the inner glow, which resembles the Photoshop Feather effect. The Edge button, which you selected, applies the effect to the edge of the object.

FIGURE 2.16

9 Click the Center button, and click OK. Lock the rectangle. Press Command/Control-H to hide the edges of the selected rectangle.

Without a stroke or visible edge, the white rectangle remains invisible until you apply the effects. The hidden edge does not interfere with the effect's appearance.

The glow changes; it now fills the center of the rectangle.

FIGURE 2.17

10 Send the rectangle to the back.

11 Save the document as "spider_banner.ai" to your WIP_02 folder. Keep the document open for the next exercise.

Add More Effects

1 Above the Artboard, select the "Spider's Web Design" text outlines and position them on the banner's left side.

2 Apply a 1-point Yellow Stroke to the text and vertically center it on the banner.

FIGURE 2.18

3 From the Effect menu, choose Stylize>Drop Shadow. Change the Y Offset to 3.6 px, and set the Blur to 2.88 px. Leave all other settings the same. Click OK.

For the size of the type, the default Y Offset of 7 pixels positions the shadow too low. The 3.6-pixel setting lifts the shadow closer to the letters. The 2.88-pixel Blue darkens the shadow so it contrasts well with the background color.

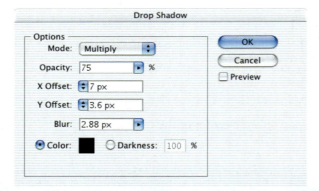

FIGURE 2.19

If you have problems

When you apply effects, we recommend that you click the Preview button in the effect's dialog box. This allows you to adjust the settings as necessary before you commit the change.

Chapter 2   Effects, Styles, and Appearances   **57**

4 To the right of the shadowed type, draw a 108 × 36 pixel round-cornered rectangle and fill it with the Spiral pattern in the Swatches palette. Stroke the rectangle with 1-pt Mediterranean Blue.

FIGURE 2.20

5 Keep the rectangle selected. From the Effect menu, choose the Rasterize option. Set the Resolution for Medium and the Background for Transparent. Click OK.

This effect does not rasterize the actual path. Only the path's appearance receives the raster effect.

It is not necessary to rasterize any object before applying a Photoshop Effect, but if you have specific settings that you require for the clarity of the effect, it is best to use the Effect>Rasterize option to make these settings.

6 With the rectangle selected, return to the Effect menu. Choose the Brush Strokes>Ink Outlines option. Make no changes in the dialog box and click OK.

7 From above the Artboard, select the "We spin to please!" text object and position it onto the rasterized rectangle.

8 Paint this text White and move it to the left side of the rasterized rectangle.

The white type is difficult to read over the white-flecked image.

FIGURE 2.21

9 Hide the selected text outlines and select the rasterized rectangle. From the Effect menu, choose Blur>Gaussian Blur. Set the Radius to 1.5 pixels and click OK.

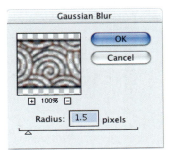

FIGURE 2.22

10 Show the hidden type.

The slight blur subdued the rectangle image so the type reads better, but some contrast would help even more.

11 **From the Effect menu, choose Stylize>Outer Glow. In the dialog box, click the swatch to the right of the Mode menu. In the Color Picker, click the upper-right corner of the large spectrum window to set a yellow color. Click OK.**

A subtle yellow glow gives the type some contrast against the raster design behind it.

FIGURE 2.23

The banner design is finished. Using only two rectangles and some type, you created an entire banner with the help of the Effect menu and its options.

FIGURE 2.24

12 Save your changes and close the file.

To Extend Your Knowledge . . .

PREVIEWING OPTIONS

Raster effects are not totally dependent upon the Preview mode to exist. To extract these otherwise invisible effects from your design and convert them to actual objects, choose Expand Appearance from the Object menu, and then choose Object>Expand. The raster effect becomes a raster image suitable for further modification.

Chapter 2   Effects, Styles, and Appearances   **59**   LEVEL 2

? If you have problems

It is important to note that CMYK documents will have only three of the Photoshop Effects items available: Blur, Pixelate, and Sharpen. If your document must be CMYK in the final form, you can use the File>Document Color Mode option to switch to RGB Color. Then apply the Photoshop Effects and switch back to CMYK Color using the same menu item.

LESSON 3   Using the Appearance Palette

The ***Appearance palette*** offers several ways to view and modify the appearance of a path that is painted with basic fills and strokes or that is altered with any of the effects from the Effect menu. When you select an object in the document, its paint attributes display in the Appearance palette. From here, you see the details of the fill and stroke and a list of the effects you used to create its appearance. Double-clicking the effects listed in the Appearance palette displays the corresponding dialog box, from which you can edit the object's appearance.

The Appearance palette does not show other path operations, such as those located in the Filter menu. Nevertheless, the features in the Appearance palette are powerful and varied and offer some controlling functions not available in the other Illustrator palettes or menus. You can use the Appearance palette to apply effects to an object's fill and stroke, or you can apply effects to each attribute individually. You can remove paint attributes with one click of the Clear Appearance button. The Appearance palette allows the discerning designer to carefully manage the paint attributes and effects assigned to his or her images and illustrations.

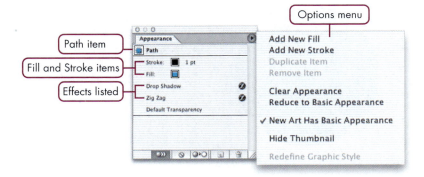

FIGURE 2.25

- The Path item is the default selection, which applies all effects to both the fill and stroke of the object.

- The Fill and Stroke items section shows the fill and stroke items of the painted object. You can apply an effect to either the fill or stroke once you select the specific item.

- The Effects listed identifies the effects applied to the object. Double-clicking an effect's name shows its dialog box, where you can make changes.

- The Options menu shows additional options related to the settings. Some of these options also have corresponding icons at the bottom of the Appearance palette.

Manage Effects with the Appearance Palette

1 Open appearance.ai from the Chapter_02 folder. Open the Appearance and Swatches palettes.

2 Select the object on the Artboard.

3 Click the Reduce to Basic Appearance button at the bottom of the Appearance palette.

This removes the effects applied to the vector path but leaves the original fill and stroke attributes intact.

4 Click the Clear Appearance button at the bottom of the Appearance palette.

This removes all paint attributes, including the fill and stroke.

5 Fill the square with Pure Cyan, and apply a Stroke of 4-point Caribbean Blue.

6 From the Effect menu, choose Distort & Transform>Pucker & Bloat.

The Pucker & Bloat dialog box opens.

7 In the dialog box, set the Percentage to 45, and click OK.

The square changes appearance. The Pucker & Bloat effect appears in the Item list on the Appearance palette. You can move the items in the list, the same as you would layers in the Layer list.

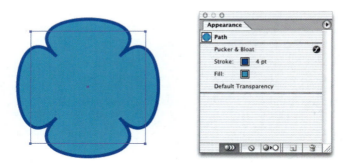

FIGURE 2.26

8 From the Effect menu, choose Distort & Transform>Twist. In the dialog box, set the Angle to 80, and click OK.

Chapter 2   Effects, Styles, and Appearances   **61**   LEVEL 2

The bloated object twists. The Item list in the Appearance palette now includes the Twist effect.

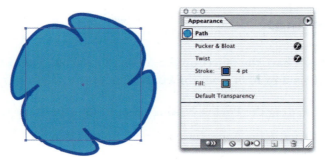

FIGURE 2.27

9   **Drag the Twist item down to the Trash icon at the bottom of the Appearance palette.**

This removes the Twist effect from the selected path.

10   **Drag the Pucker & Bloat item down to the Stroke item.**

This applies the effect to the stroke of the path. The fill remains the same.

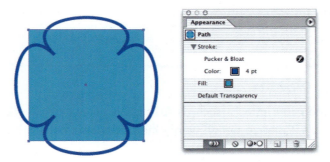

FIGURE 2.28

11   **Click the Fill item in the Appearance palette. Choose Effect>Stylize>Drop Shadow, and click OK without making any changes in the dialog box.**

This applies a drop shadow to the fill of the path. If you wish to deselect either the Stroke or Fill items, click the Path item at the top of the palette.

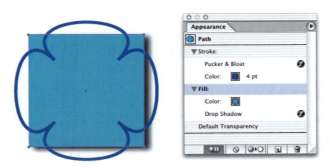

FIGURE 2.29

LEVEL 2   **62**   Chapter 2   Effects, Styles, and Appearances

12   Save your changes. Keep the document open for the next exercise.

Use Appearance Settings

1   Make certain that you have the object on the Artboard selected. Go to the Appearance palette and drag the Drop Shadow item from the Fill section to the palette's Trash icon.

2   In the Stroke section, drag the Pucker & Bloat item to the Path item at the top of the palette.

You can control the items in the Appearance palette simply by dragging them to different locations.

3   Click the Fill item in the palette. In the Swatches palette, click the Blended Rainbow gradient.

This method selects the Fill attribute without having to click the Fill boxes in either the Toolbox or the Color palette.

4   Click the Path item in the Appearance palette.

5   Choose Rasterize from the Effect menu. Set the Color Model to CMYK, the Resolution to Medium, and the Background to White. Click OK.

The appearance, not the actual path, becomes rasterized and is capable of receiving the raster effects in the Effect menu.

? If you have problems

If you cannot get the raster effects (such as Artistic>Watercolor) to work on a path you rasterized with the Effect menu's Rasterize option, verify the document's color mode. Most raster effects only work with RGB color mode.

---

6   Click the Fill item in the Appearance palette. From the Effect menu, choose Pixelate>Color Halftone. Make no changes in the dialog box and click OK.

Note that the raster effect was applied only to the fill of the object. When you use the Object menu to rasterize an object, the whole path — including the fill and stroke — is rasterized as one unit. In this case, even though both fill and stroke were rasterized through the Path item, you could isolate the fill and apply the effect to that element only.

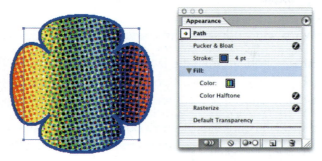

FIGURE 2.30

7 **Close the Fill item by clicking the triangle icon next to the fill's name. Click the Path item at the top of the palette.**

Clicking the Path item at the top of the Appearance palette deselects the Fill item. When the Path item is selected, all attributes are applied to both the fill and the stroke.

8 **Double-click the Pucker & Bloat item in the Appearance palette.**

The effect names in the Appearance palette identify what effects were applied; double-click any of the names to show their dialog box.

9 **In the dialog box, change the Percentage to 25, and click OK.**

The shape of the appearance adjusts to the new setting, even though you rasterized the object's appearance.

10 **Click the Fill item's triangle icon to show its settings. Drag the Color Halftone item to the Trash icon in the Appearance palette.**

The fill returns to its rasterized Rainbow Gradient setting.

11 **Drag both the Rasterize and Pucker & Bloat items to the Trash icon.**

The path returns to its basic appearance, with only a fill and stroke applied.

12 **Close the document without saving.**

To Extend Your Knowledge . . .

APPEARANCES POINTERS

Keep these pointers in mind as you work with appearances:

Objects with basic fill or stroke attributes from the Swatches palette appear in the Appearance palette. However, objects with special appearances must possess effects applied from the Effect menu. Filters and other operations outside the Effect menu do not show up in the Appearance palette.

The Appearance palette reflects the attributes of single paths only. If you select more than one path (for example, objects in a group), the Appearance palette merely states "Object: Mixed Appearances." You must use the Direct Selection tool to isolate a single path for it to appear in the Appearances palette.

If you press Option/Alt while you drag an effect from one item to another in the Appearance palette, the effect duplicates and is immediately applied to the selected path.

If an object has no applied effects, only the object's fill and stroke attributes appear in the Appearance palette.

When you click the Fill or Stroke item in the Appearance palette, the corresponding boxes in the Toolbox and the Color palette are also activated.

You can move the Stroke and Fill items in the Appearance palette. For instance, if the Stroke item resides at the bottom of the Appearance palette, you can drag it to the top of the Appearance list. The corresponding attribute in the selected object's appearance moves in front of the other attributes.

LESSON 4 Graphic Styles

Graphic styles are not single operations or effects you apply to a path to achieve appearance. Rather, graphic styles are composite effects already applied to an object (must be a single path) and saved to the ***Graphic Styles palette***.

For example, if you applied the Drop Shadow, Outer Glow, and Twist effects to an object, you could drag the painted object to the Graphic Styles palette to save the appearance and its settings in the palette. When you want to apply those particular effects and settings to another selected object, simply click that graphic style in the palette to apply all three effects and their settings to the object.

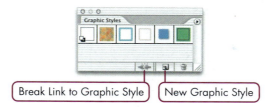

FIGURE 2.31

- The ***Break Link to Graphic Style*** option breaks the connection between an object and a graphic style. After you break the link between an object and its style, you can edit the style without affecting the object; its painting attributes remain unchanged.

- When you click the ***New Graphic Style*** button, you turn the attributes of a selected object into a graphic style and add it to the Graphic Styles palette.

If you have problems

You cannot apply any filters from the Filter menu and save them as a graphic style — you must use effects from the Effect menu. You cannot use several paths painted with effects to create a design that you can save as a graphic style. All the effects you use must be applied to a single path, which can then become a graphic style.

Create and Apply Styles

1   **Open vector_effects.ai from your WIP_02 folder. Open the Swatches, Appearance, and Graphic Styles palettes.**

2   **Select the far left object on the page and drag it into the Graphic Styles palette. Deselect the square object.**

When you drag a painted path into the Graphic Styles palette, you automatically create a new style. Styles can include any paint attribute, such as colors, gradients, patterns, and effects.

Remember, only single paths can be dragged to the Graphic Styles palette to create a new style. If you drag two or more paths to the palette, nothing will happen or an empty white box will appear.

FIGURE 2.32

3 **Double-click the new graphic style and name it "Scribble Style".**

4 **Click the Default Fill and Stroke icon in the Toolbox. Use the Polygon tool to draw a 1.5-inch 6-sided polygon underneath the other objects.**

5 **Click the new Scribble Style in the Graphic Styles palette.**

The polygon displays the new style.

6 **Click several of the other graphic styles in the palette to see how they look when applied to the polygon.**

The styles include specific effects and settings, but the actual shape of the path to which you apply the style alters the appearance of the style, as seen with the original square, circle, and star of the document.

7 **Use the Ellipse tool to draw a 1.5-inch circle to the polygon's right. Fill the circle with the Vega Blue radial gradient from the Swatches palette.**

8 **Select the Gradient tool and drag its cursor from the circle's upper-left part to the path's lower-right edge.**

FIGURE 2.33

Chapter 2 Effects, Styles, and Appearances 67 LEVEL 2

9. **From the Effect menu, choose Stylize>Drop Shadow. Make no changes in the dialog box and click OK.**

FIGURE 2.34

10. **Drag the circle to the Graphic Styles palette to create a new style. Rename the style "Gradient Shadow".**

    The shape of the path you drag to the Graphic Styles palette does not determine any specific qualities of the appearance. The graphic style holds only the paint attributes and appearance of the object. You can apply graphic styles to single vector paths of any shape, either open or closed.

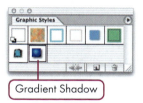

FIGURE 2.35

11. **Press Command/Control-A to select all the objects on the page. Click the new Gradient Shadow style in the palette.**

    Note how different the graphic style looks on the various paths. A graphic style is only a paint attribute, independent of the shape of a path.

FIGURE 2.36

LEVEL 2   **68**   Chapter 2   Effects, Styles, and Appearances

12   Save your changes. Keep the document open for the next exercise.

To Extend Your Knowledge . . .

MODIFY GRAPHIC STYLES

To modify one of the default styles that appears in the Graphic Styles palette, click the style and use the Appearance palette to make your changes. This will not alter the actual default style in the Adobe Illustrator startup document; if you want to change this default style, you must make your changes in the startup document. Otherwise, the modified style remains only in the document in which you made the alterations.

Duplicate Graphic Styles

1   In the open document, select any object on the page and copy it. Close the document without saving.

The shape of the path does not matter. You are copying the object in order to paste it in another document which will transfer the graphic style.

2   Open styles_gradient.ai from the Chapter_02 folder.

3   Paste the copied object into the document.

The graphic style of the object immediately appears in the Graphic Styles palette. Also note that the Vega Blue gradient appears in the Fill box of the Toolbox. Fills and strokes of graphic styles appear in the Fill and Stroke boxes.

4   Delete the pasted object. Press Command/Control-A to select all the objects on the Artboard.

5   Click the Gradient Shadow style in the Graphic Styles palette.

Chapter 2   Effects, Styles, and Appearances   **69**   LEVEL 2

All the selected objects become painted with the pasted graphic style.

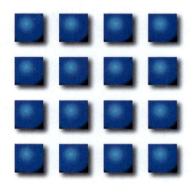

FIGURE 2.37

6   **Deselect all the objects on the page.**

Despite being unselected, all the objects are linked to the Gradient Shadow graphic style. Any alterations you make to this style will be reflected in the linked objects.

7   **The Gradient Shadow style should still be selected in the Graphic Styles palette. Use the palette's Options menu to choose Duplicate Graphic Style.**

The duplicate appears next to the original style. You can duplicate and modify graphic styles. In the next exercise, you modify the original style, which is linked to the squares. The duplicate allows you to have a copy of the original style in case you need it again.

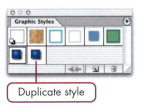

FIGURE 2.38

8   **Save the document with the same name to your WIP_02 folder. Keep the document open for the next exercise.**

Modify Graphic Styles

1   **In the open document, show the Color and Gradient palettes. Click the White, Black Radial gradient in the Swatches palette.**

2   **In the Gradient palette, click the Ending color slider to select it. In the Color palette, change the sliders to CMYK and set them for C = 0, M = 100, Y = 100, K = 0.**

If you cannot see the gradient color sliders, click the gradient swatch in the Gradient palette.

3. **Select the Ellipse tool and draw a 1.5-inch circle above the squares. Deselect the circle.**

    The circle fills with the new red gradient in the Fill box. Note that the gradient in the circle still retains the alteration you made earlier to the Vega Blue radial gradient with the Gradient tool. Modified gradients that remain unchanged in the Fill box will apply their alteration to other gradients of the same type (linear or radial) when applied to objects. To remove this alteration from the gradient in the Fill box, you must change the gradient to another type (linear or radial).

4. **Select the upper-left square on the Artboard. Select the Eyedropper tool and click the red-gradient circle. Keep the square selected.**

    The selected square takes on the new red gradient.

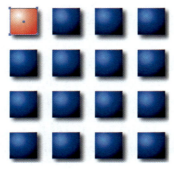

FIGURE 2.39

5. **In the Appearance palette's Options menu, choose the Redefine Graphic Style "Gradient Shadow" option. Keep the upper-left square selected.**

    In the Graphic Styles palette, the selected Gradient Shadow style takes on the new red gradient that appears in the Fill item of the Appearance palette. The redefined Graphic Shadow style changes all objects that are painted with it — even unselected objects such as the squares.

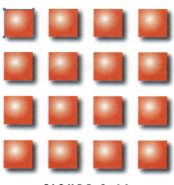

FIGURE 2.40

Chapter 2 Effects, Styles, and Appearances   **71**   LEVEL 2

6   **Use the Gradient tool to drag the cursor from the square's lower-right area to the upper left. Keep the square selected.**

The white highlight on the circle is relocated.

7   **From the Options menu of the Appearance palette, choose the Redefine Graphic Style "Gradient Shadow" option.**

The selected circle acts as a model from which the Gradient Shadow style is redefined. Note that the squares, painted with the Gradient Shadow, now take on the new alterations.

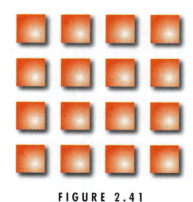

FIGURE 2.41

8   **Save your changes and close the document.**

To Extend Your Knowledge . . .

READY-MADE STYLES

The Window>Graphic Style Libraries option is a good place to find ready-made styles and to get ideas for creating your own graphic styles. Libraries are available in CMYK and RGB color modes. You can use features from the Effect menu and the Appearance palette to alter any of the styles in these libraries, but you must drag a style to the Graphic Styles palette of an active document before you can edit the style.

TIPS ON GRAPHIC STYLES

Keep these suggestions in mind as you explore Illustrator's Graphic Styles features:

Graphic styles can be as simple or as elaborate as you need. We often have you click the Default Fill and Stroke icon in the Toolbox and change the Fill to None. However, you can create a style that possesses a black 1-point stroke with a fill of None.

A single graphic style can take on different appearances, depending on the shape of the path to which you apply the style.

To apply changes to every object of the same graphic style, you must use the Appearance palette's Redefine Graphic Style option to replace the original style. If you change any of the default styles that appear in the Graphic Styles palette and want these changes to remain, you must save these changes in the Illustrator startup document.

The Break Link to Graphic Style option breaks the global connection between an object and its assigned graphic style. If you then edit the applied style, the object remains painted with the original graphic style.

You can drag only one object at a time to the Graphic Styles palette to convert the object to a style. If you drag more than one object at a time to the palette, Illustrator rejects all of the objects.

? If you have problems

Before you modify a graphic style's fill or stroke, make sure you select either the Fill item or the Stroke item in the Appearance palette. Remember to choose Redefine Graphic Style in the Appearance palette's Options menu after you make your changes.

Chapter 2   Effects, Styles, and Appearances   **73**   LEVEL 2

LESSON 5 Creating Gradient Meshes

You are used to only two types of gradient: linear and radial. The hard edge of the path to which you apply these gradients sharply cuts off the gradient. What if you wanted a gradient to look as if it was airbrushed with fine extending sprays? You can now achieve this by using the newly developed "gradient mesh."

The *gradient mesh* provides a new way to create realistic blends that follow the contours of a specific shape. The feature provides an outstanding method of fine-tuning the way colors blend into one another, allowing you to create superior textures, contours, and designs.

You must apply gradient meshes to existing objects; you cannot draw a gradient mesh from scratch. Once an object becomes a gradient mesh, you cannot convert it back into a regular path without extensive techniques.

The gradient mesh is an advanced feature; the more you understand it, the more effectively you will apply it to your own designs. Let's explore the components of a gradient mesh.

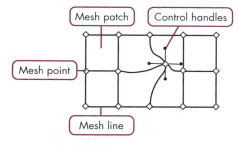

FIGURE 2.42

- The *mesh patch* is the inner space of the mesh cells that displays the gradient's colors.
- Each mesh patch has four connecting *mesh points* that are much the same as anchor points but are actually smooth points that allow for adjustments.
- The *mesh line* is the connecting segment between mesh points.
- Each mesh point is a curving smooth point with its own *control handle* for adjusting the curve of the mesh lines.

Create a Gradient Mesh

1 **Create a new letter-size CMYK document.**

2 **Use the Rectangle tool to draw a 2-inch square. Fill the object with Black and stroke with None.**

Make certain the square has a black fill before proceeding. If you forget to fill objects that are to become a gradient mesh, it is difficult to paint the object after the conversion. The black fill gives you the foundation from which to start painting the mesh's elements.

3 From the Object menu, choose Create Gradient Mesh. In the dialog box, change the Rows to 3, and set the Columns to 4. Set the Appearance to Flat. Click OK.

The mesh appears on the selected square.

FIGURE 2.43

4 Deselect the square. In the middle row, use the Direct Selection tool to click the second mesh patch. Use the Swatches palette to fill this patch with Sunshine.

The mesh patch and its connecting corner mesh points receive the new paint attribute. Notice that the gradient radiates from these points in an airbrush fashion. Gradient meshes can only be painted with the Fill attributes and with colors.

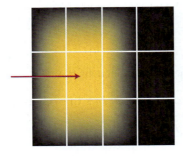

FIGURE 2.44

5 Deselect the gradient mesh object. Use the Direct Selection tool to click anywhere inside the gradient mesh or on the object's border.

The Direct Selection tool shows all the mesh points for easy selection.

6 Click the center mesh point on the second mesh line (see Figure 2.45) to select it. Fill the patch with Red.

The most difficult part of working with a gradient mesh is selecting its mesh points. In Preview mode, you can hardly see the mesh points you need to select. In Outline mode, the mesh and points are obvious.

Chapter 2   Effects, Styles, and Appearances   **75**   LEVEL 2

7   **Keep the mesh point selected.**

The red color emanates from the painted mesh point and extends into the color of the other gradient. Selected mesh points are more distinguishable in Preview mode.

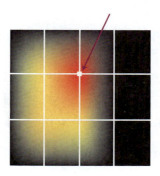

FIGURE 2.45

8   **Use the Direct Selection tool to drag the selected mesh point down to the left.**

The mesh lines are curved and are connected to the smooth mesh point. The red gradient is longer, extending its mesh point into the patch from which it was dragged.

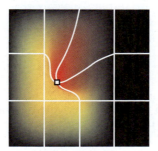

FIGURE 2.46

9   **With this mesh point still selected, press the Delete key.**

The mesh lines connected to this point are also deleted.

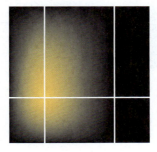

FIGURE 2.47

10 Save the document with the name "gradient_mesh.ai" to your WIP_02 folder. Keep the document open for the next exercise.

Continue Painting the Gradient Mesh

1 **If the object is selected, deselect it. Click the Fill box in the Toolbox. Click the Pure Cyan swatch in the Swatches palette to set the Fill color.**

Remember, the Fill box must be active in the Toolbox if you are applying paint attributes to a gradient mesh. Stroking a gradient mesh will not work.

2 **Activate the Mesh tool in the Toolbox and click the approximate center of the square.**

New mesh lines appear, along with the mesh point. The Pure Cyan color radiates upward into the taller mesh patches.

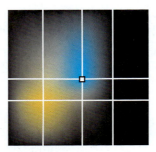

FIGURE 2.48

3 **Use the Direct Selection tool to marquee-select the two mesh points on the square's right edge. Fill these points with Squash. Deselect the points.**

The color extends into the square, coloring only the patches that touch the mesh points.

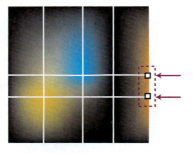

FIGURE 2.49

Chapter 2   Effects, Styles, and Appearances   **77**   LEVEL 2

4   **Show the Color palette and set its CMYK sliders for C = 0, M = 25, Y = 0, K = 0. Drag the Fill swatch from the Color palette to touch the second patch on the square's left side.**

The four mesh points that define the patch are now pink, extending the color into adjoining patches. Deselect the patch.

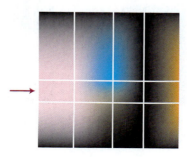

FIGURE 2.50

5   **Set the Fill box in the Toolbox to Black. Activate the Mesh tool and click directly above the top horizontal mesh line (see Figure 2.51).**

The black gradient radiates from only this point.

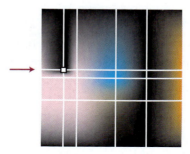

FIGURE 2.51

6   **Use the Direct Selection tool to marquee all the horizontal mesh points (see Figure 2.52) on this new mesh line to select them. Click the Black swatch in the Swatches palette.**

The black extends upward into patches above the points, and the narrow patches below these points are half-filled with the black gradient.

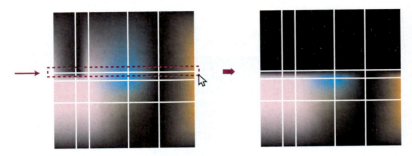

FIGURE 2.52

15 Save your changes and close the document.

Use Gradient Meshes in Design Work

1 Open apple.ai from the Chapter_02 folder.

2 Click the apple-shaped path and fill it with Ruby from the Swatches palette. Set the Stroke to None.

3 From the Object menu, choose Create Gradient Mesh. In its dialog box, set both the Rows and Columns to 6, and set the Appearance to Flat. Click the Preview option. Click OK.

The apple shape takes on this gradient mesh.

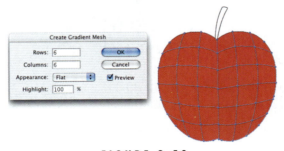

FIGURE 2.53

4 From the Window menu, choose New Window. Resize Window 2 and position it to the right of the apple in Window 1.

Chapter 2 Effects, Styles, and Appearances   **79** LEVEL 2

Opening one window for Outline mode and one for Preview mode allows you to easily select mesh points while you see your changes in Window 1.

5 **Click into Window 1 and choose Hide Edges from the View menu.**

You see the gradient mesh appearance without the distraction of the blue edges.

6 **From the Window menu, select Window 2 to show it.**

7 **Click inside Window 2 and change its view to Outline mode. Deselect the gradient mesh object.**

Work in Window 2 as you apply meshes and colors. The results appear instantly in Window 1 as you do the work.

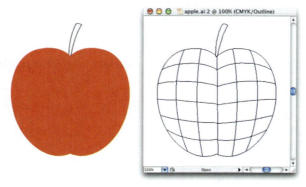

FIGURE 2.54

8 **Save the document with the same name to your WIP_02 folder. Keep the document open for the next exercise.**

Continue Painting the Apple

1 **Show the Color palette. The Ruby color should be showing its four CMYK colors. Press Shift and drag the Magenta slider to approximately 45%.**

This lightens the Ruby color proportionally in the CMYK sliders.

2 **Activate the Mesh tool in the Toolbox. In Window 2, click a mesh point halfway between the apple's left border and the first vertical mesh line.**

A new mesh line appears with the lighter color.

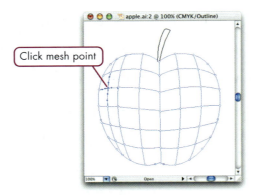

FIGURE 2.55

3. **Select the Direct Selection tool and press Shift to select the other mesh points on this new mesh line; ignore the points on the outer border.**

When we tell you to select mesh points, do not select any that are on the surrounding apple border.

FIGURE 2.56

If you have problems

When you select a single mesh point, it does not always show its curve handles, especially in Preview mode. To fully see the curve handles, choose Outline mode and marquee the desired mesh point with the Direct Selection tool.

When you click a mesh patch with the Direct Selection tool, the four mesh points defining the path become selected. You can deselect a single point by clicking it while you hold down the Shift key.

Chapter 2   Effects, Styles, and Appearances   **81**   LEVEL 2

4 **Select the Eyedropper tool and click the mesh point that appeared where you clicked the Mesh tool in step 2.**

The Eyedropper tool is useful for painting mesh points by sampling other existing colors. The apple's left side takes on a lighter tone to act as a light source.

FIGURE 2.57

5 **Move to the next vertical mesh line to the right and select all the interior mesh points.**

6 **In the Color palette, press Shift and drag the Magenta slider to approximately 70%. Deselect the mesh points.**

When the Magenta slider (or any slider with the most color percentage) is dragged, all the other sliders change proportionally.

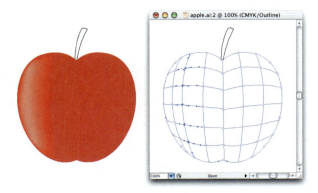

FIGURE 2.58

7 Select the interior mesh points on the next three mesh lines. Use the Color palette to apply the color, with C = 16, M = 66, Y = 65, K = 0.

The apple takes on a lighter tone on its facing surface.

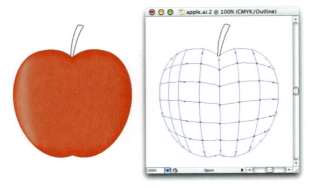

FIGURE 2.59

8 Save your changes. Keep the document open for the next exercise.

Finish the Apple Gradient Mesh

1 Move to the last vertical mesh line before the apple's right edge. Use the Direct Selection tool to select and move the mesh points farther to the right. Deselect the mesh points.

When repainted, this mesh line adds contour along the right side of the apple. Moving it also makes room for another mesh line.

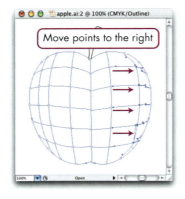

FIGURE 2.60

Chapter 2   Effects, Styles, and Appearances   **83**   LEVEL 2

2 Use the Color palette to set the CMYK sliders to C = 10, M = 41, Y = 41, K = 0. Select the Mesh tool to click a mesh line to the left of the line you just moved.

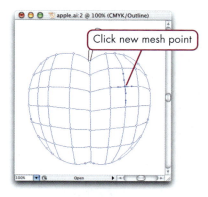

FIGURE 2.61

3 Select the mesh points along this vertical mesh line. Select the Eyedropper tool and click the first mesh point that you clicked to create this new mesh line.

Additional highlights appear, creating curvature on the apple.

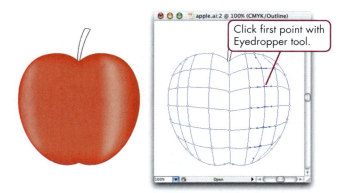

FIGURE 2.62

4 **Move the selected mesh points to the right, closer to the next mesh line. Deselect the mesh points.**

The moved mesh point creates more of a curvature on the surface of the apple.

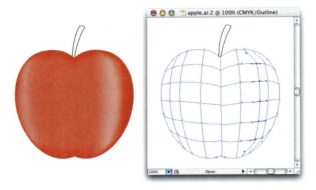

FIGURE 2.63

5 **Select the mesh points on the next vertical mesh line to the right. Use the Color palette to set the CMYK sliders for C = 14, M = 60, Y = 60, K = 0. Deselect the mesh points.**

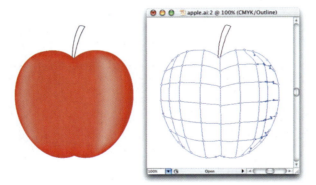

FIGURE 2.64

6 **Select the Mesh tool and click one of the mesh lines to the right of the previously selected mesh line.**

A new mesh line appears next to the edge of the apple.

Chapter 2 Effects, Styles, and Appearances

7 Select the interior mesh points along this vertical mesh line. Use the Eyedropper tool to click one of the mesh points on the first vertical mesh line from the apple's left border. Deselect the mesh points.

This adds a light highlight along the edge of the apple. The color tones are complete, but you still need to add a highlight to the apple.

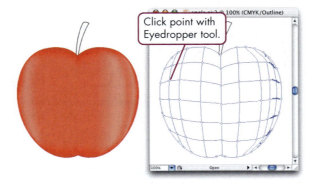

FIGURE 2.65

8 Save your changes and keep the document open for the next exercise.

Create the Apple's Highlight

1 Select the single mesh point at the top of the second vertical mesh line on the left. Click the White color box in the Color palette.

Spread this highlight up and down the apple contour, rather than leave it in one small place.

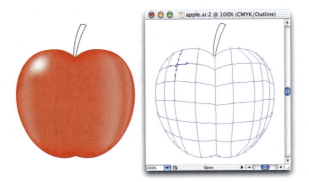

FIGURE 2.66

2 Select the mesh point under the selected point. Press Shift and select the mesh point to its left. Drag both mesh points downward.

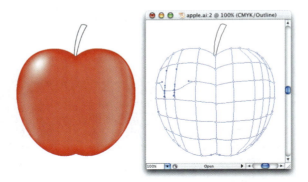

FIGURE 2.67

3 Select the top and second mesh points on the third mesh line from the left. Use their control handles to increase the rounded effect of the highlight.

The apple is finished, but you still need to apply a gradient mesh to the stem to finalize the design.

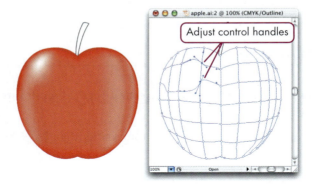

FIGURE 2.68

4 Select the apple stem path and use the Color palette to fill it with C = 95, M = 5, Y = 100, K = 0. Apply a Stroke of None.

5 Choose Create Gradient Mesh from the Object menu, and apply 2 Rows and 1 Column. Click OK. Deselect the path.

You see the mesh line in the middle of the stem.

6 Use the Color palette to set the CMYK sliders for C = 60, M = 0, Y = 80, K = 0. Use the Mesh tool to click the stem's mesh line to create a mesh point.

Chapter 2   Effects, Styles, and Appearances   **87**   LEVEL 2

The entire apple design is finished and painted with an appearance you could not create with only linear or radial gradients.

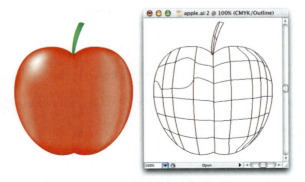

FIGURE 2.69

7 Close Window 2.

8 Save your changes and close the document.

To Extend Your Knowledge . . .

GRADIENT MESH FACTS AND FIGURES

Here are some facts and reminders about working with the gradient mesh:

You cannot select or paint mesh lines; you select mesh points and mesh patches for painting purposes. Remember, the mesh patch refers to the fill regions that lie between the mesh lines.

You can't simply click a mesh line to select the whole mesh object for painting. You must individually select the mesh points and mesh patch.

Always fill the original object with black or the desired original color before applying a gradient mesh. If you fill the object with white or None, you must apply considerable paint attributes to make the object visible.

You can delete mesh points by clicking them with the Gradient Mesh tool while holding the Option key (Macintosh) or the Minus key (Windows).

The default style of the Gradient Mesh tool is Flat. To use To Center or To Edge, you must use the Object>Create Gradient Mesh menu to make the mesh.

All internal mesh points (not on the enclosing path) are smooth points.

It is easier to select individual mesh points by marquee-selecting them in Outline mode, without the interference of the fill.

You can fill mesh points, but you cannot stroke them. If the Fill box in the Toolbox is not active when you paint mesh points, the applied color goes to the stroke. Even though the Stroke box in the

Toolbox assumes the color, a gradient mesh cannot accept stroke color, so nothing happens to the selected point.

If you select and delete a single mesh point, its connecting mesh lines are also deleted, as are the mesh points that were present when these lines touched other mesh lines.

When you paint a mesh patch, you actually apply paint attributes to the mesh points that define the patch.

If an object is not a closed path, it becomes closed when converted into a gradient mesh.

BEWARE OF THE ANCHOR POINT TOOLS

You can use the Add Anchor Point and Delete Anchor Point tools to add points to and delete points from a mesh — but be careful! The Add Anchor Point tool adds regular anchor points, not mesh points. You cannot paint regular points when you add them to a mesh. Use regular anchor points only to fine-tune the shapes of the mesh lines.

FINDING MESH POINTS

In Preview mode, it can be difficult to locate the mesh points of a gradient mesh. To see the points clearly, click the gradient mesh with the Direct Selection tool; the mesh points appear, and then you can select them.

SUMMARY

In Chapter 2, you learned about Adobe's concept of "appearance." You found that you must use Preview mode to see the changes you apply to an object. You learned that when you alter an object's appearance, the original path remains intact and completely unaltered. You also learned how to use the Effect menu to apply effects to a path, changing the path's appearance according to the particular settings you assign. You discovered two types of effects — vector and raster — and found that you can use the vector options to affect any path, but the raster effects only affect paths that you rasterize with the Rasterize option in the Effect menu.

You explored the features of the Appearance palette and discovered that it shows the fill, stroke, and applied effects of a path. You learned how to use the Appearance palette to modify a path's attributes. You also learned about graphic styles and used the Graphic Styles palette to create styles from paths that contain paint attributes and effects. Finally, you painted a gradient mesh and observed how this feature generates free-form gradients that create realistic 3-D effects.

KEY TERMS

Appearance	Graphic Styles palette	Rasterize effect
Appearance palette	Mesh line	Raster paths
Control handles	Mesh patch	Sampling
Gradient mesh	Mesh point	Vector paths

Chapter 2   Effects, Styles, and Appearances   **89**   **LEVEL 2**

CHECKING CONCEPTS AND TERMS

MULTIPLE CHOICE

Circle the letter that matches the correct answer for each of the following questions.

1. You can view an effect you applied to an object from the Effect menu _____.
   a. at any time
   b. only in Outline mode
   c. only in Preview mode
   d. only when the object is selected

2. An effect applied to a path _____.
   a. alters the anchor points and segments of the path
   b. makes no changes to the anchor points and segments of the path
   c. locks the path
   d. cannot be removed once applied

3. When you select a path, the Appearance palette shows _____.
   a. the fill and stroke of the path, as well as applied effects
   b. only the effects applied to the path
   c. the applied filters from the Filter menu
   d. None of the above.

4. You can make a graphic style from a path possessing _____.
   a. effects only
   b. effects and filters
   c. any paint attribute
   d. fill, stroke, and effects

5. You can adjust the radiating colors in a gradient mesh by dragging _____.
   a. a mesh line
   b. a mesh point or its control handles
   c. a mesh patch
   d. the Mesh tool

6. The gradient mesh's gradients _____.
   a. are unique and cannot be created by any other tool
   b. can be imitated by a radial gradient
   c. can be imitated by a linear gradient
   d. can be created with the Gradient tool

7. After you apply a graphic style to multiple objects in a document, modifying the style _____.
   a. means you must reapply the style to the objects
   b. automatically updates all of the objects linked to the style
   c. does not affect the objects that possess that style
   d. automatically unlinks the style from the applied objects

8. The raster effects in the Effect menu only work on _____.
   a. objects rasterized by the Rasterize effect in the Effect menu
   b. all raster objects, whether placed or rasterized through the Object menu
   c. TIFF images
   d. JPEG images

9. To extract the paths and raster images from an appearance, you must _____.
   a. access Clipping Mask>Release from the Object menu
   b. drag a graphic style out of the Graphic Styles palette and onto the Artboard
   c. choose Expand Appearance>Expand options from the Object menu
   d. rasterize the object with the Rasterize option from the Effect menu

LEVEL 2 · **90** · Chapter 2 Effects, Styles, and Appearances

10. You can use the Eyedropper tool to sample colors from a raster image if _____.

a. the document is in RGB color mode

b. the image was rasterized by the Effect menu's Rasterize option

c. you press the Shift key while clicking the image

d. None of the above.

DISCUSSION QUESTIONS

1. Explain how Adobe's concept of "appearance" works and how it utilizes the Preview mode.

2. List some circumstances where you would use the powerful features of the Appearance palette.

3. The Graphic Styles palette includes a Break Link with Graphic Style option. Why would you want to break an object's link with its graphic style? What benefits does this feature offer?

4. The gradient mesh is a unique feature you can use to create free-form gradients that appear three-dimensional. List specific items that would require you to use a gradient mesh to create a realistic-looking illustration.

SKILL DRILL

Skill Drills reinforce learned skills. Each reinforced skill is the same as, or nearly the same as, a skill we presented in the lessons. We provide detailed instructions in a step-by-step format. You can work through one or more exercises in any order.

1. Create 3-D Contours

You are a graphic artist in a printing company. A client supplied you with a black-and-white flower she drew and asked you to add colors and three-dimensional surfaces to the various parts of the flower.

1. Open mesh_flower.ai from the Chapter_02 folder.

   The object on the page contains several paths that represent a flower's petals, leaves, and stem.

2. Select the main flower object and fill it with any color you prefer.

3. Convert the path to a gradient mesh and use your artistic judgment to determine what colors to apply to the mesh points.

   You can also paint the points on the border, with mesh points, surrounding the gradient mesh object. Do not ignore these.

4. Move the mesh points as necessary to achieve the appearance of a rounded surface for the flower.

Chapter 2   Effects, Styles, and Appearances   **91**   LEVEL 2

5. Paint the other components of the flower and convert them to gradient meshes so they can receive appropriate colors. Use your artistic judgment to select the colors and tones.

FIGURE 2.70

6. Save your changes and close the document.

2. Add Effects to a Painter's Palette

You are a freelance commercial artist. You submitted a color drawing of a painter's palette to your client, who owns an art supplies store. To finish the job, you must add realistic shadows and highlights to the various objects in the drawing.

1. Open painter_palette.ai from the Chapter_02 folder.

    The design is a painter's palette with color swatches on it.

2. Select the red circle on the painter's palette. Drag the object while pressing Option/Alt to make seven duplicates that wrap around the palette's contour (see Figure 2.71).

3. Select all the circles. From the Effect menu, choose Distort & Transform>Roughen.

4. Set the Size to 12 and the Detail to 20. Select the Relative and Smooth boxes if they are not selected. Click OK.

    The round objects take on rough edges, representing swatches of paint on the palette.

5. Show the Swatches and Appearance palettes.

6. Select the paint swatch to the right of the original red swatch.

7. In the Appearance palette, click the Fill item. Select another color from the Swatches palette.

    The Fill swatch in the Appearance palette changes to the color you choose, as does the selected object on the painter's palette.

8. Select, one at a time, the other duplicate swatches on the palette and use the Appearance palette to change each swatch to a color of your choice.

9. Select all the objects on the Artboard.

10. From the Effect menu, choose Stylize>Drop Shadow. In the Drop Shadow dialog box, make no changes and click OK.

    All the objects take on the drop shadow effect.

11. Save the document with the same name to your WIP_02 folder and close the document.

FIGURE 2.71

3. Create a Road Sign

You are an artist at a sign company. Your client hired you to design a sign that he will place on the roadside outside his city. Your task is to create a comprehensive layout of the proposed sign.

1. Open caribbean_sign.ai from the Chapter_02 folder.

2. Use the Line Segment tool to draw a horizontal line between "UTA" and "Caribbean Island."

   The width of the line should be as wide as the Caribbean Island text.

3. Paint the line with a Fill of None and a 6-pt Starry Night Blue Stroke with Round Caps.

4. From the Effect menu, choose Distort & Transform>Zig Zag. Set the Size to 0.06 in and the Ridges to 9. Select the Smooth option, and click OK.

   The appearance of the line becomes wavy.

5. Select the background rectangle. In the Graphic Styles palette, click the Tissue Paper Collage style.

6. Select both sets of letters on the rectangle. Choose Effect>Stylize>Outer Glow.

7. Set the Mode to Normal and click the color swatch to the right of Normal.

8. In the Color Picker, set the color to C = 0, M = 0, Y = 100, K = 0. Click OK.

9. Back in the Outer Glow dialog box, set the Opacity for 100 and the Blur for 0.1 inch. Click OK.

   The Outer Glow effect adds contrast between the letters and the multicolored background.

10. Select "UTA" and the background rectangle. From the Effect menu, choose Warp>Arc Upper. Make no changes in the dialog box and click OK.

    The upper portions of "UTA" and the rectangle take on a rounded appearance.

11. Save the document with the same name to your WIP_02 folder and close the document.

FIGURE 2.72

4. Create a Web Banner

You are a Webmaster. A client who owns a fish market in town has hired you to create a Web site for him. The site needs an identifying banner at the top of the home page. Your task is to create this banner using some eye-catching effects.

1. Open fish_house.ai from the Chapter_02 folder.

   In the Preferences>Units & Display Performance dialog box, set the General menu for Pixels.

2. Draw a 468 × 60 pixel rectangle that matches the Artboard. Fill this with the Ocean pattern from the Swatches palette.

3. From the Effect menu, select the Document Raster Effects Settings option. Make certain that Color Model is set for RGB, the Resolution is set for Medium (150 ppi), and the Background is set for Transparent. Leave all other settings. Click OK and lock the rectangle.

   Unlike the Photoshop filters in the Filter menu, the Photoshop Effects in the Effect menu do not need prior rasterizing to function. When the Photoshop Effects are selected, Illustrator automatically rasterizes the object and then applies the effect. The Document Raster Effects Settings dialog box makes the necessary settings that control the automatic rasterizing process. Be aware that making changes in this dialog box changes all other existing objects that possess raster effects from the Effect menu.

4. From the Effect menu, select the Photoshop Effect Distort>Ocean Ripple. In the upper-right of the Ocean Ripple dialog box, set both the Ripple Size and Ripple Magnitude to 3. Click OK.

   The Ocean Ripple gives the waves in the pattern a rippling texture, and the rectangle's edges take on an uneven appearance, adding to the carefree style of the beach environment.

5. From above the Artboard, select the Seaside Fish House text object and bring it to the front. Position the text object onto the banner and visually center it.

6. Fill the text outlines with Latte and copy the object.
7. Set the stroke with 4-pt Aloha Blue.
8. From the Effect menu, select Stylize>Drop Shadow. Set the X and Y Offsets, and set the Blur for 3 px. Click OK.
9. Press Command/Control-F to paste the copied text into place.
10. From the Effect menu, choose Texture>Craquelure. Make no changes in the dialog box and click OK.

    The Craquelure effect gives the beige type an old, wooden appearance.

11. Select both text outline objects and choose Effect>Warp>Fish. Make no changes in the dialog box and click OK.

    This is the Effect version of Envelope Distort's function, Make with Warp>Fish, which gives the objects a fish shape.

FIGURE 2.73

12. The banner is finished. Save the Illustrator document with the same name to your WIP_02 folder.
13. Use the File>Save for Web option to save the images as a JPEG to the WIP_02 folder. Use your browser to view the new banner. When finished, close the document.

CHALLENGE

Challenge exercises expand on, or are somewhat related to, skills that we presented in the lessons. Each exercise provides a brief introduction, followed by numbered-step instructions that are not as detailed as those in the Skill Drill exercises. You should complete these exercises in order.

1. Create an Art Department Logo

A local elementary school asked you to create a design for a sign they will place on the door of their school's art department.

1. Open art_dept.ai from the Chapter_02 folder. Show the page rulers.
2. Select the smaller square of the pencil design.
3. Show the Graphic Styles palette and click the Scratchboard style.
4. Click the Break Link to Graphic Style icon at the bottom of the Graphic Styles palette.

    This allows you to modify the attributes of the style in the object, rather than alter the original graphic style in the palette.

5. Show the Appearance palette. Lengthen the palette so you can see all the items.
6. Click the Fill item that shows a black swatch.
7. Open the Color palette. Use the Options menu to choose Grayscale. Change the percentage to 50.

   The background becomes lighter.
8. Select the larger background square.
9. In the Graphic Styles palette, click the Hair Ball style.

   Though the squares had black strokes, they were removed when the Graphic Style was applied. Graphic styles remove the original paint attributes of objects.

FIGURE 2.74

10. Save the document with the same file name to your WIP_02 folder. Keep the document open for the next exercise.

2. Add Type to the Art Department Logo

You have altered the appearance of the Style's color. Now you must add further effects to the type that will finish the logo.

1. From the open document, select the Art Department text outlines.
2. Choose Stylize>Scribble from the Effect menu.
3. In the dialog box, click the Preview button to see the effect on the text block.

   You may have to relocate the large dialog box on the screen to see your artwork.
4. Select the Settings menu at the top of the dialog box. Choose each of the options to see how each looks on the text.
5. When finished browsing, choose the Swash option in the Settings menu and click OK.
6. Use the Line Segment tool to draw a 2-pt horizontal line below the text outlines. The line should be the same width as the word "Department."
7. From the Effect menu, choose Distort & Transform>Zig Zag.
8. Set the Size for 0.1 in and the Ridges for 10. Click the Absolute and Smooth boxes (if they are not already selected). Click OK.

The straight line becomes wavy.

FIGURE 2.75

9. Save your changes and close the document.

3. Enhance the Ace of Hearts Logo

A new client owns an establishment in town called "Ace's." A member of his staff created a basic logo design on his computer. The club president asked you to add some special effects to enhance the logo to make it more interesting.

1. Open ace_logo.ai from the Chapter_02 folder. Open the Swatches, Graphic Styles, and Appearance palettes.

2. Select the letter "A" outline in the upper left of the card. Fill the letter with the White and stroke with None. Copy the letter.

3. Fill the selected letter with Red and stroke it with 1-pt Black.

4. In the Appearance palette, click the Stroke item.

   By selecting this section in the Appearance palette, you apply the next effect to only the stroke of the object.

5. From the Effect menu, choose Path>Offset Path. Set the Offset for 2.88 points, and click OK.

   Only the stroke becomes offset.

6. From the Effect menu, choose Stylize>Drop Shadow.

7. Set the Mode to Multiply and Opacity to 100%. Set the X and Y Offsets, and set the Blur to 2 pt.

8. Click the Color swatch at the bottom of the dialog box. In the Color Picker, click on the upper-right corner of the large red spectrum square. Click OK.

9. Drag the "A" object to the Graphic Styles palette. Rename the new style "Red Offset".

10. Press Command/Control-F to paste the white letter in front of the letter with the effects.

FIGURE 2.76

11. Save the document with the same name to your WIP_02 folder. Keep the document open for the next exercise.

4. Add More Effects to the Ace of Hearts

You have created customized styles to the top letter "A". Now you must apply them to the bottom "A" in the card. Also, you must apply effects to the large heart and the hearts that surround it.

1. In the open file, select the "A" in the card's bottom right. Fill the object with White and a stroke of None. Copy the white object.

2. Keep the "A" selected and click the Red Offset style in the Graphic Styles palette.

    The object takes on the paint attributes and effects that were saved as a graphic style.

3. Press Command/Control-F to paste the copied "A" in front of the copied white letter.

4. Select the large heart in the middle of the card. From the Effect menu, choose Stylize>Inner Glow.

5. Set the Mode to Screen, the Opacity to 75, and the Blur to 20 pt. Click the Center box, and click OK.

    The heart takes on a glowing effect that emanates from its center. The glow's color is taken from the heart's red color.

6. From the Effect menu, choose Stylize>Outer Glow. Set the Mode to Multiply, the Opacity to 76, and the Blur to 15 pt.

7. Click the swatch to the Mode menu's right. Set the color for Red and click OK. Click OK in the Outer Glow dialog box.

    The heart takes on a glow around its path.

8. Select the grouped small hearts that surround the large heart.

9. From the Effect menu, choose Stylize>Drop Shadow. Set the Mode to Multiply and the Opacity to 50. Set the X and Y Offsets, as well as the Blur to 3 pt.

10. Click the Darkness option at the bottom of the Drop Shadow dialog box. Set the percentage for 100. Click OK.

    The hearts take on the drop shadow you applied.

FIGURE 2.77

11. Save your changes and keep the document open for the next exercise.

5. Add Drop Shadow to the Card

You are finished adding the effects to the Ace of Hearts logo. The card border looks dull since all the objects on the card have drop shadows. You must add a drop shadow to the card.

1. Select the card rectangle.
2. From the Effect menu, choose Stylize>Drop Shadow.
3. Set the X and Y Offsets, plus the Blur, to 0.07 in. Set the Opacity to 75%.
4. Click the Darkness button. Set the percentage for 50. Click OK.

   The Darkness option defaults to black. The percentage field allows you to customize the amount of black in the shadow.

FIGURE 2.78

5. Save your changes and close the document.

PORTFOLIO BUILDER

Create a Personal Library of Graphic Styles

You are a commercial artist working with a client whose company products and corporate image require that the graphics you create possess special effects. Your task is to prepare a library of Graphic Styles that may be repeatedly applied to path objects whenever you work on this client's jobs.

1. Create a new letter-size CMYK document. Open the Align, Graphic Styles, and Appearance palettes.

2. On the Artboard, create twelve 1.5-inch squares that are evenly aligned and distributed to fill the page.

3. Select the first square and apply a Rounded Rectangle effect.

4. Apply the Drop Shadow and then the Outer Glow effects to the selected path.

5. Use the Appearance palette to apply the Zig Zag effect to the Stroke item.

6. Turn the painted object into a graphic style that is named "Corporate 1".

7. Continue to select each object and paint it with any colors, gradients, patterns, and effects you desire.

8. Turn the painted objects into graphic styles and name them "Corporate 2", "Corporate 3", and so on.

9. Delete all styles but your corporate ones and save them as a graphic style library with the name "corporate_styles.ai" to your WIP_02 folder.

10. You have created a customized library of Graphic Styles that can be used for future jobs. Close the document without saving.

LEVEL 2

CHAPTER 3

Working with Symbols

OBJECTIVES

In this chapter, you learn how to:

- Work with the Symbols palette
- Create symbols
- Edit symbols
- Manage links to symbols

- Create and access symbol libraries
- Apply the Symbolism tools
- Utilize the Symbolism tools' options

Chapter 3   Working with Symbols   **101**   **LEVEL 2**

Why Would I Do This?

Knowing how and when to incorporate symbols in your illustrations offers a number of measurable benefits. *Symbols* are virtual copies of existing elements that you can use repeatedly without adding to the complexity or size of your drawings. In addition to the obvious benefit of reduced file size (particularly important when you develop artwork for the Web), there are other benefits. For example:

- Once you create a symbol, you can drag it into any of your drawings wherever you need to use it.

- You can quickly spray numerous symbols onto the page.

- You can replace symbols one at a time or all at once.

- You can apply changes to one symbol, and every other occurrence of that symbol changes automatically, saving significant time and effort.

- You can share symbols with other artists working with you or on other projects.

Symbols are key components in creating animations — a form of rich content that is becoming increasingly important on the Web and as part of interactive projects. In this chapter, you learn how to apply symbols to a wide variety of assignments, including content for the Web and other real-life situations.

VISUAL SUMMARY

Symbols were originally developed as a method to control the size of Web graphics. As you know, file size is a critical factor when creating graphics for the Internet. If a page containing multiple graphics takes too long to download — which can occur when a user has a standard dial-up modem — the visitor may abandon the site and move on to another.

While the ability to minimize file sizes is an important asset, symbols also provide time-saving advantages to graphic designers who must use multiple objects in a design; symbols provide an excellent alternative to traditional patterns. Another time-saving feature is the ability to edit one symbol and apply those edits to every other instance of that symbol — with one click of your mouse. This feature is of monumental importance in the graphic arts field, as it saves considerable amounts of time and effort.

You discover that to place a symbol on your page, you can simply drag the symbol from the Symbols palette and place it in the desired location. Once you drag a symbol from the palette to the Artboard, the symbol becomes an *instance*, which you can unlink from the original symbol. Once unlinked, the instance returns to its vector path format, and you can edit it however you prefer. You can replace instances on the Artboard with other symbols from the Symbols palette.

FIGURE 3.1

You also learn methods for creating symbols. You can turn both vector and raster images into symbols, but you must unlink placed images so they have no connection to the external image. You can apply any Illustrator painting attribute to a path and turn it into a symbol.

FIGURE 3.2

You also learn techniques for modifying existing symbols to meet your specific requirements. Once you edit a symbol, you can use the linking feature in the Symbols palette to update all of the symbol's instances — saving time and effort.

FIGURE 3.3

The Symbols palette has only a few symbols in it. This is because Adobe has so many symbols in their repertoire that they cannot show them all in one palette. These symbols are divided into categories and included in 25 external symbol libraries (see Figure 3.4), which you learn how to quickly access. You also discover how to gather symbols into a collection and save them to a customized symbol library.

FIGURE 3.4

In this chapter, you discover the various symbolism tools available in the Toolbox and use many of their features. When you apply the symbolism tools to instances, you create impressive results that are impossible to generate with any other Illustrator tool. For example, the Symbol Sprayer sprays symbols on the Artboard, as if you were using a can of spray paint. Other tools allow you to move, size, spin, stain, style, and screen your symbols.

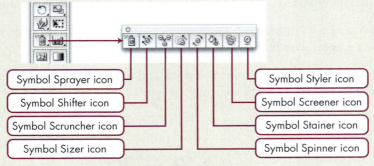

FIGURE 3.5

You also learn about the symbolism tool options, which provide a wide range of additional settings that allow you to manipulate the tools' effects. These options go far beyond simply clicking and dragging the symbolism tools to customize a symbol or instance; with these options, you can create incredibly innovative designs.

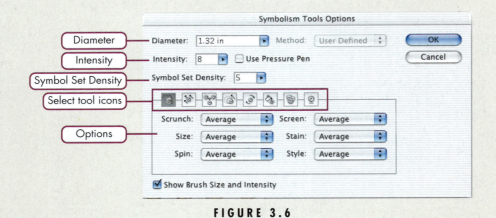

FIGURE 3.6

LESSON 1 Using the Symbols Palette

Symbols are art pieces stored in the Symbols palette. When you drag a symbol from the palette onto the Artboard, the art piece is not a duplicate of the symbol; rather, the art piece is a graphic icon that represents (and is linked to) the original symbol in the Symbols palette. The theory behind symbols and instances is best illustrated by an "alias" (Macintosh) or "shortcut" (Window), which is an icon that links to an original file.

To better understand symbols and instances, you must understand the terminology we use. Become familiar with the following terms:

- Symbol. The actual symbol exists only in the Symbols palette, where you store and manage symbols.
- Instance. When you drag a symbol from the Symbols palette into the document, the symbol becomes an "instance," or a graphic icon that represents the symbol it is linked to.
- From the **Symbols palette**, you create, control, store, and manage your symbols. You use the four buttons at the bottom of the palette to control your symbols and the links between symbols and their instances.

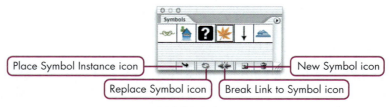

FIGURE 3.7

- **Place Symbol Instance.** When you click the Place Symbol Instance button, the selected symbol in the Symbols palette appears as an instance on the Artboard. This method's shortcut is simply to drag the symbol onto the Artboard.

- **Replace Symbol.** You can change the link between an instance and its original symbol to any symbol in the Symbols palette. To do so, select an instance, click the new symbol in the Symbols palette, and click the Replace Symbol button. The selected instance takes on the appearance of the new symbol.

- **Break Link to Symbol.** With an instance selected, click this button to remove the link between the instance and its original symbol. The unlinked instance becomes an individual path object. If you modify the original symbol, the unlinked instance remains unchanged.

- **New Symbol.** If you select a vector path or group of paths, and click the New Symbol button, the selected object becomes a new symbol in the Symbols palette. To use a quicker method to create a new symbol, drag the object into the Symbols palette, which converts the object into a symbol.

In this exercise, you create symbols and instances and use the Symbols palette to manage the objects.

Create Symbols and Instances

1 Create a new letter-size CMYK document with the units set for points. Open the Swatches and Symbols palettes.

Make certain that the Preferences>Units & Display Performance dialog box has its General menu set for Points.

2 From the Symbols palette, drag the Arabesque-Symmetrical, House, Leaf, and Storm Clouds symbols onto the Artboard.

Symbols, when dragged out of the Symbols palette, are known as "instances" when they reside on the Artboard or surrounding pasteboard. You now have four instances on your Artboard.

FIGURE 3.8

3 Change to Outline mode. Use the Direct Selection tool to try selecting the paths you see.

You find that you cannot select the paths. What you see is only an "appearance" of the paths making up the design. To extract the paths so you can select them, break the instance's link to the symbol in the Symbols palette.

FIGURE 3.9

4   **Return to Preview mode. Drag the Storm Clouds instance downward and press Option/Alt to make a duplicate. Keep the copied instance selected.**

You don't have to keep dragging the same symbol from the Symbols palette to make multiple copies of the symbol. Symbol instances are like any other object and may be copied, transformed, and rasterized. You can easily recognize an instance by its rectangular bounding box when selected (see Figure 3.10).

FIGURE 3.10

5   **At the bottom of the Symbols palette, click the Break Link to Symbol button. Return to Outline mode to see the paths better.**

Clicking this button removes the selected instance's bounding box and automatically selects all the object's paths.

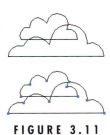

FIGURE 3.11

6 In the Symbols palette, select the Info symbol. Click the Place Symbol Instance button at the bottom of the palette.

This is another way to place symbols onto the Artboard, but it is easier to drag the symbols.

FIGURE 3.12

7 Select all the objects on the Artboard. Click the House symbol in the Symbols palette.

8 Click the Replace Symbol button at the bottom of the Symbols palette.

The House symbol replaces all of the instances on the Artboard. The one Cloud instance that you unlinked from the Symbols palette remains unchanged.

FIGURE 3.13

9 Deselect all objects on the Artboard. In the Symbols palette Options menu, choose Select All Unused.

This command selects all the symbols in the palette except the House, because it is linked to the instances on the Artboard. If necessary, you could drag the selected symbols to the Trash icon to delete them.

FIGURE 3.14

10 Click the House symbol in the Symbols palette. From the palette Options menu, choose Select All Instances.

This option selects all instances linked to the selected symbol in the palette. This is a fast way to select multiple instances on the Artboard, rather than clicking each instance individually.

11 In the Symbols palette, drag the House symbol to the Trash icon at the bottom of the palette. Click Cancel in the warning dialog box that appears.

You cannot delete a symbol that is linked to instances in the document until you either expand or delete the instances.

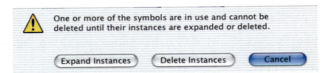

FIGURE 3.15

12 Save the document as "using_symbols.ai" to your WIP_03 folder. Keep the document open for the next exercise.

To Extend Your Knowledge . . .

BROKEN LINKS

When you break the link between an instance and a symbol, the instance loses its bounding box and becomes an object with editable paths. You cannot relink these paths to an existing symbol. Instead, you must drag the symbol from the Symbols palette to the Artboard to create a new instance.

LESSON 2 Creating Symbols

When you create a symbol, you don't need to follow any special procedures or processes — you simply drag a painted object or raster image into the Symbols palette. Unlike the Graphic Styles palette, which restricts you to dragging only one object at a time, the object you use for a symbol can contain multiple paths.

If an object exists in an Illustrator document, you can use it to create a symbol. Vector paths painted with colors, gradients, or patterns, and objects that include effects, can all become symbols. You can convert raster objects to symbols, regardless of the raster's source. You can place raster objects from outside the document, or you can use rasterized paths from inside the document. In addition, you can easily turn masked objects into symbols by dragging the object and its clipping mask into the Symbols palette.

In the following exercises, you convert a variety of objects to symbols.

Create Symbols

1   **In the open document, show the Graphic Styles palette.**

2   **On the Artboard, select the Storm Clouds paths that you broke the link with in the previous exercise, step 5. Choose Show Bounding Box from the View menu. On the bounding box, drag the bottom handle down slightly to lengthen the clouds.**

FIGURE 3.16

3   **Hide the bounding box. Drag the selected object to the Symbols palette. Double-click the new symbol and rename it "Clouds".**

Dragging paths or raster objects to the Symbols palette creates a new symbol. Unlike Graphic Styles, which can accept only a single path, symbols can be made from multiple paths that have been painted with any paint attribute, including Effects.

FIGURE 3.17

4   **Delete the selected Clouds object on the Artboard.**

Once you convert an object to a Symbol, you no longer need the original.

5   **Click the House symbol in the Symbols palette. From the palette Options menu, choose Select All Instances.**

This again selects all the House instances on the Artboard.

6   **Click the Clouds symbol in the Symbols palette. Click the Replace Symbol button at the bottom of the palette.**

The new Clouds symbol replaces all of the selected instances.

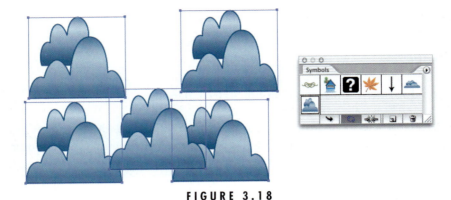

FIGURE 3.18

7 Click the Break Link to Symbol button in the Symbols palette.

Breaking the link between the instances and their symbol returns all the paths in the instances back to their original vector path format. They are now like any other path that you may select and modify.

8 Use the Direct Selection tool to select any of the paths. When finished, select all the objects on the Artboard and delete them.

9 Save your changes. Keep the document open for the next exercise.

Add Symbols

1 Use the Rectangle tool to draw a 36 pt square above the Artboard. Fill the square with Red and stroke with None.

2 Use the Ellipse tool to draw a 21 pt circle on top of the square. Fill the circle with Black and stroke with None.

3 Show the Align palette. Select the two objects and use the Align palette to center them.

4 Drag the two selected objects to the Symbols palette to create a new symbol. Rename the new symbol "Black Dot".

FIGURE 3.19

Chapter 3 Working with Symbols   **111**   LEVEL 2

5 **Select the Black Dot symbol in the palette. Click the Place Symbol Instance button five times.**

Only one symbol seems to appear, but all five of the instances are stacked on top of one another.

6 **Drag the instances so they line up horizontally in a row (see Figure 3.20).**

As an instance, the two objects move as one unit, even though they were not grouped. Your placement of the moved instances does not need to be perfect.

7 **Select the five instances. In the Align palette, click the Vertical Align Top and Horizontal Distribute Center buttons.**

These commands align and distribute the symbols.

FIGURE 3.20

8 **From the Object menu, choose Transform>Transform Each. In the dialog box, set the Rotate to 45 degrees and click OK.**

The instances all rotate. You can transform instances as you would any other object in a document.

FIGURE 3.21

9 **Keep the instances selected. Click the Leaf symbol in the Symbols palette.**

10 **Click the Replace Symbol button in the Symbols palette.**

The Leaf symbol replaces the selected instances. The new instances take on the 45-degree rotation assigned to the former instances.

FIGURE 3.22

11 **Save your changes and keep the document open for the next exercise.**

Use a Graphic Style to Create a Symbol

1 In the open document, show the Graphic Styles palette.

2 Select the black circle on the original red square you created and delete it.

3 Select the red square. In the Graphic Styles palette, click the Chiseled style.

The graphic style paints the square.

FIGURE 3.23

4 Drag the square to the Symbols palette. Rename the new symbol "Chiseled Symbol".

You can convert to symbols paths that are painted with graphic styles.

5 Select the five Leaf instances on the Artboard.

6 Click the Chiseled Symbol and press the Replace Symbol button on the Symbols palette.

This command links the selected instances to the Chiseled Symbol. The instances retain their 45-degree rotation.

FIGURE 3.24

7 From the Effect menu, choose Stylize>Drop Shadow. Make no changes in the dialog box and click OK.

Similar to applying effects to paths, you can also apply effects to instances.

FIGURE 3.25

8 Drag the five selected instances into the Symbols palette to create a new symbol. Drag this new symbol onto the Artboard.

You can combine several instances into a symbol.

FIGURE 3.26

9 Select all the objects in the document and delete them.

10 Save your changes. Keep the document open for the next exercise.

Use Raster Images and Symbols

1 From the Chapter_03 folder, place (without linking) greeting_duck.jpg into the open document.

Even though you can convert all raster image formats to symbols, the images must be unlinked when you do. You receive error messages if you try.

2 Drag the placed image to the Symbols palette and rename it "Greeting Duck".

The raster image becomes a symbol.

FIGURE 3.27

3 Delete the placed image on the Artboard.

4 Drag the Greeting Duck symbol to the Artboard.

5 Click the Default Fill and Stroke icon in the Toolbox and change the Fill to None. Draw a circle that surrounds the duck in the instance.

6 Select the instance and the circle. Press Command/Control-7 to mask the two objects.

Similar to raster images and paths, you can use the Clipping Mask feature to mask instances, too.

Chapter 3 Working with Symbols

7   **Drag the masked instance to the Symbols palette and rename it "Masked Duck". Delete the masked objects on the Artboard.**

You can convert masked objects to symbols.

FIGURE 3.28

8   **Drag the Masked Duck symbol from the Symbols palette to the Artboard. Keep it selected.**

9   **Click the Chiseled Symbol in the Symbols palette and click Replace Symbol.**

Despite its larger size, the Masked Duck instance becomes as small as the Chiseled Symbol.

10   **Click the Greeting Duck symbol in the Symbols palette and click Replace Symbol.**

11   **Click the Break Link to Symbol button in the Symbols palette.**

The duck image returns to its original raster image state.

12   **Save your changes and close the document.**

To Extend Your Knowledge . . .

REPLACING SYMBOLS

Clicking the Replace Symbol button replaces all the selected instances on the Artboard with the symbol you select in the Symbols palette. This feature is an excellent time-saver when you need to replace multiple objects, such as the objects used to create a border.

LESSON 3 Editing Symbols and Links

Symbols are objects, either vector or raster, that you dragged to the Symbols palette. You can no longer select or modify a symbol's paths once you convert it to a symbol format. If you need to alter a symbol, you must drag it to the Artboard as an instance and break the link between the instance and its symbol. Once unlinked, the instance returns to its original vector or raster state, and you can edit it as necessary. To return the edited object to a symbol state, you must drag it back to the Symbols palette to create a brand-new symbol.

Access Symbol Libraries

In this exercise, you use the Symbols palette to unlink and edit symbols.

1 **Open iceblue_earth.ai from the Chapter_03 folder. Open the Symbols and Graphic Styles palettes.**

This file contains the initial layout for a Web site. Many of these graphics need editing and updating. This document is RGB, which has a few different symbols in the Symbols palette (see Figure 3.29) than the CMYK document.

FIGURE 3.29

2 **In the Symbols palette, use the Options menu to select Open Symbol Library. In the pop-out menu, scroll to the bottom and select Other Library.**

3 **Navigate to the Chapter_03 folder and open Essentials.ai.**

This imported palette of symbols appears on the screen's right side. You can use the Other Library option to access any Illustrator document that contains symbols.

4 **In the imported Essentials palette, click the River Foliage, Blue Circle, and Earth symbols. Close the Essentials palette.**

Clicking symbols from imported libraries places a copy into the Symbols palette. You no longer need the imported palette.

5 **From the Symbols palette, drag the River Foliage symbol to the Artboard. Position it on top of the Earth type. Click the Break Link to Symbol icon in the palette.**

The instance reverts back to its original path format.

6 **Send the River Foliage to the back. In the View menu, show the bounding box.**

7 Use the bounding box to scale the foliage object proportionally so its width extends past the edges of the Earth type and the lower ends of the foliage extend slightly beneath the type.

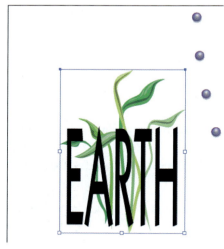

FIGURE 3.30

8 Use the View menu to hide the bounding box.

9 Save the document with the same name to your WIP_03 folder and keep it open for the next exercise.

Modify Symbols

1 In the Graphic Styles palette, use the Options menu to select Open Graphic Style Library>Other Library. Navigate to the Chapter_03 folder and access the Essentials.ai file.

Though the Symbols palette previously opened the Essentials.ai document, the Graphic styles palette now opens it. The document now shows only the graphic styles.

2 In the Essentials graphic styles palette, click the Ice Type style to make a copy in the Graphic Styles palette. Close the Essentials palette.

This places the Ice Type style in the Graphic Styles palette.

3 From the Symbols palette, drag the Blue Circle and the Earth symbols to the open area on the Artboard's right side.

4 Select the Blue Circle instance and click the Break Link to Symbol icon at the bottom of the Symbols palette.

The selected instance reverts to its original vector path format.

5 With the Blue Circle paths now selected, click the Ice Type style in the Graphic Styles palette.

The circle takes on this style, comprised of various shades of blue, which resemble the Earth's oceans.

6 Select the Earth instance. Click Break Link to Symbol to convert the instance to paths.

7 Use the Direct Selection tool to select the earth object's outer circle path and change the Fill to None. Apply a stroke of 1 pt Aloha Blue.

8 Use the Selection tool to select the modified earth object and bring it to the front. Position it on top of the Ice Type object.

FIGURE 3.31

9 Select the Earth and Ice Type objects. Drag them to the Symbols palette. Rename the new symbol "Blue Earth".

10 In the Symbols palette, click the Button 1 Mouse Down symbol. In the palette Options menu, choose Select All Instances.

This selects all the Button 1 Mouse Down instances on the Artboard. This convenient shortcut eliminates the need to individually select multiple objects on the Artboard.

11 Select the new Blue Earth symbol in the Symbols palette. Click the Replace Symbol icon at the bottom of the palette.

All the selected instances, which were scaled to create this pattern, take on the Blue Earth symbol. The Blue Earth symbol reduces in size, the same as the symbols it replaces.

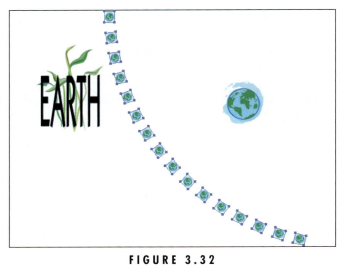

FIGURE 3.32

12 Save your changes and keep the document open for the next exercise.

Replace Symbols

1 Return to the Earth object that you painted with a stroke of Aloha Blue.

2 Use the Direct Selection tool to select the Aloha Blue circle path and change its Stroke to None.

FIGURE 3.33

3 Use the Selection tool to select the Earth and Ice Type objects. Drag them to the Symbols palette.

4 Rename this new symbol "Earth Iced".

5 Select the Earth and Iced Type objects that you used to create the symbols and delete them.

6 Drag the new Earth Iced symbol from the Symbols palette to the Artboard's upper-right area. Use the View menu to show the bounding box.

7 Use the bounding box to proportionally scale the instance to a larger size.

8 Position the scaled instance in the Artboard's upper-right corner.

Use your artist's eye to create a balanced and aesthetic design.

FIGURE 3.34

9 Save your changes. Close the document.

To Extend Your Knowledge . . .

SCALE SETTINGS

If you scale an instance on the Artboard and replace that instance with another symbol instance from the Symbols palette, the new instance assumes the same scale settings applied to the original instance.

LEVEL 2 **120** Chapter 3 Working with Symbols

LESSON 4 Using Symbol Libraries

Collections of graphics, such as clip-art books and graphics saved to CDs, are extremely convenient and excellent time-savers when deadlines arise and you need ready-made artwork to complete a job. The same rule applies to symbols — keeping symbols in *symbol libraries* (collections) can cut production time in half. Illustrator offers two types of symbol libraries:

■ Illustrator Symbol Libraries. You can access the Illustrator symbol libraries from either the Window menu (Window>Symbol Libraries) or the Symbols palette Options menu (Open Symbol Library). When you choose the Options menu's Save Symbol Library command, you save the new symbol library to the Illustrator Symbols folder, and the new library appears in the Window and Options menus after you quit and relaunch Illustrator.

```
3D Symbols
Arrows
Artistic Textures
Buildings
Charts
Communication
Decorative Elements
Default_CMYK
Default_RGB
Document Icons
Food
Hair and Fur
International Currency
Logos
Maps
Nature
Networking
Occasions
Office
People
Science
Weather
Web Buttons and Bars
Web Icons

Other Library...
```

FIGURE 3.35

■ Other Library. The Other Library option is located at the bottom of the Open Symbol Library menu in the Symbol palette's Options menu. Alternately, you can also use Window>Symbol Libraries>Other Library. When you choose the Other Library option, a dialog box appears. From here, you can navigate to any folder and open an Illustrator document that contains the symbols you need. The actual document does not open; the symbols appear in a separate palette.

Access Symbol Libraries

In this exercise, you use various methods to access symbol libraries.

1   **Create a new letter-size CMYK document with portrait orientation. Open the Symbols palette.**

2   **In the Symbols palette Options menu, choose Open Symbol Library.**

The pop-out menu displays a long list of symbol collection categories (libraries) that come with the Illustrator program. Each of these categories appears in the Illustrator document as a single palette containing many symbols.

3   **Select the Arrows library.**

The Arrows symbols appear in a separate palette. Note the pencil with the red line in the lower left of the Arrows palette. This icon means that you may not edit the symbols in the palette, nor may you add new symbols to the palette. To edit symbols you find in a library, you must first transfer the symbols to the main Symbols palette.

4   **Click several of the symbols in the Arrows palette.**

When you click a symbol in the imported library, it appears in the main Symbols palette.

FIGURE 3.36

5   **Use the Symbols palette's Options menu to choose Open Symbol Library. Choose the Logo Elements library.**

6   **If necessary, separate the Logo Elements palette from any palette it is grouped with and position it under the Arrows palette.**

7   **From the Logo Elements palette, drag the Airplane, Car, Coffee, and Figure symbols to the Artboard.**

The selected symbols also appear in the Symbols palette.

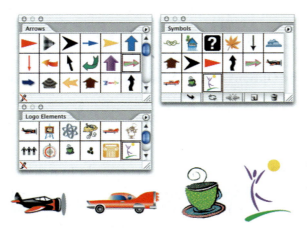

FIGURE 3.37

8 Return to the Symbols palette Options menu and choose Open Symbol Library>Celebration. Position the Celebration palette under the Logo Elements palette.

9 Click several of the symbols in the Celebration palette to transfer them to the Symbols palette.

10 Close the Arrows, Logo Elements, and Celebration palettes.

11 From the Symbols palette, select the six default symbols in the top row. Drag them to the Trash icon in the bottom of the palette.

All that should remain in the Symbols palette are the symbols that you clicked from the imported libraries. Even if you have not yet placed any instances of a new symbol in a document, you can save the symbol in the Symbols palette in a separate document. You can access this document through the Open Symbol Library>Other Library menu.

12 Name the document "favorite_symbols.ai" and save it to your WIP_03 folder. Close the document.

Save Symbol Libraries

1 Create a new letter-size CMYK document with portrait orientation.

2 Use the Symbols palette Options menu to choose Open Symbol Library. From the list in the pop-out menu, choose the Web Buttons and Bars library.

All symbol libraries that appear in this menu reside in the Presets>Symbols folder that is in the Adobe Illustrator CS2 folder.

Chapter 3   Working with Symbols   **123**   LEVEL 2

3   **From the Web Buttons and Bars palette, drag four symbols of your choice to the Artboard.**

Observe the main Symbols palette. Clicking the symbols in the imported palettes to drag them to the Artboard simultaneously places them in the Symbols palette.

4   **Return to the Open Symbol Library menu and choose Web Icons.**

5   **From the Web Icons palette, drag five icons of your choice to the Artboard.**

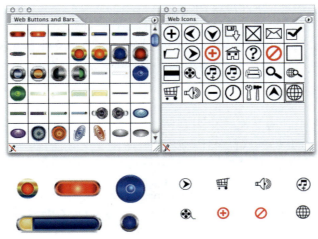

FIGURE 3.38

6   **Close the two imported library palettes.**

7   **In the Symbols palette Options menu, choose Select All Unused. Drag these selected symbols to the Trash icon to delete them.**

8   **In the palette Options menu, choose Save Symbol Library. Save the library as "my_web_icons.ai" to the Adobe Illustrator CS2>Presets>Symbols folder. Close the document.**

Any document located in the Presets>Symbols folder appears in the Open Symbol Library menu after you restart Illustrator.

9   **Quit Illustrator and relaunch it.**

10 **Create a new CMYK document and open the Symbols palette. Use the palette Options menu to choose Open Symbol Library.**

Your new my_web_icons library is available in the list of names. If you do not want this menu item to show, take the my_web_icons.ai document out of the Symbols folder and restart Illustrator.

11 **Use the Window menu to choose Symbol Libraries>Other Library. Go to the WIP_03 folder to open the favorite_symbols.ai document you saved earlier.**

The Window menu is another method you can use to access Symbol libraries. The symbols you saved in the favorite_symbols.ai document appear in their own palette, available for use.

12 Close the document without saving.

To Extend Your Knowledge . . .

IMPORTING SYMBOL LIBRARIES

When you import symbol libraries, several library palettes may appear grouped. If this happens, you can drag a palette's name tab out of the group so the palette appears separately.

LESSON 5 Using the Symbolism Tools

In addition to the Symbols palette, which you use to manage symbols, you can use the symbolism tools to either apply symbols directly to the page or set controls for how the symbols appear. These tools are in the *Tearoff menu* accessed through the Symbol Sprayer tool in the Toolbox.

The Symbol Sprayer is the default symbolism tool that displays in the Toolbox — this tool's icon resembles a spray paint can. Once you select another symbolism tool in the Tearoff menu, the new tool's icon replaces the Symbol Sprayer in the Toolbox. When the Symbol Sprayer tool is used, it creates a *symbol set*, which is a collection of the same symbol residing in a rectangular container.

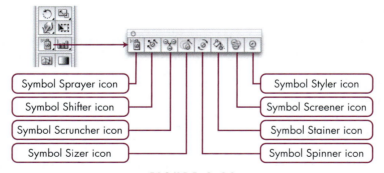

FIGURE 3.39

Use the Symbolism Tools

1 Create a new letter-size CMYK document with landscape orientation. Open the Symbols palette.

2 From the palette Options menu, choose Open Symbol Library. From the pop-out menu, choose the Nature library.

Chapter 3 Working with Symbols **125** LEVEL 2

3 Use the Nature palette Options menu to set the view to Small List View. Click the Bee symbol.

4 Access the Symbol Sprayer tool's optional tools in the Toolbox. Drag the Tearoff menu onto the screen to see all the symbolism tools.

5 Drag the Symbol Sprayer tool quickly across the page to spray Bee symbols.

The faster you drag the cursor, the farther apart the instances appear. If you drag the cursor slowly, the instances mound up on top of one another — they spray rapidly onto the page.

The Symbol Sprayer's cursor is a large circle. You need to use the tool a few times to get accustomed to how it applies symbols to the page. Drag the tool several times, and choose Edit>Undo to remove unsuccessful attempts.

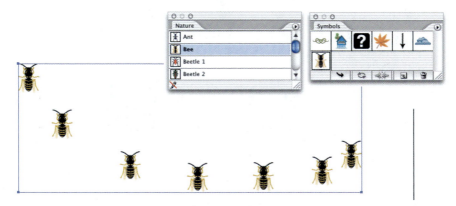

FIGURE 3.40

6 Press Option/Alt and click a couple of the Bee instances with the Symbol Sprayer tool cursor.

Pressing Option/Alt allows you to delete an instance from a symbol set.

7 Drag the Symbol Sprayer tool cursor on the existing Bee symbol set.

You added more Bee instances to the active symbol set.

FIGURE 3.41

8 **Choose the Butterfly symbol in the Nature palette. Drag the Symbol Sprayer tool under the rectangle that is holding the Bee instances.**

Even though you didn't touch the Bee set with the tool cursor, you added Butterfly instances to the Bee symbol set. As long as you select a set, all the symbols you spray become part of the active set.

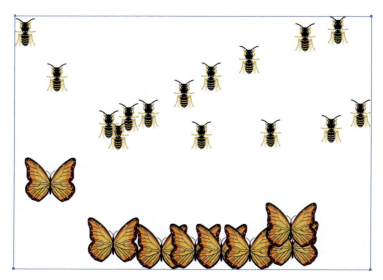

FIGURE 3.42

9 **Choose Edit>Undo to remove the Butterfly instances. Use the Selection tool to deselect the active symbol set.**

10 **Click the Butterfly symbol in the Symbols palette.**

11 **Activate the Symbol Sprayer tool. Press the "[" (left bracket) key eight times.**

This reduces the size of the large circle on the Symbol Sprayer tool cursor. Press the Right Bracket key to make the cursor/circle larger.

12 **Drag the tool below the Bee instances on the page.**

The Butterfly instances appear in their own set. You can use the Selection tool to select sets and move them around.

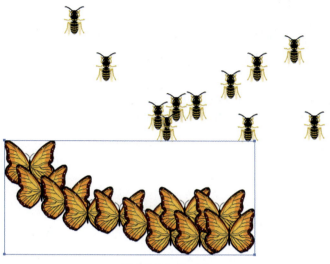

FIGURE 3.43

13 Save the document as "symbolism_tools.ai" to your WIP_03 folder. Keep the document open for the next exercise.

Explore Other Symbolism Tools

1 In the open file, select all the symbol sets on the page and delete them. Close the Nature symbol palette.

2 From the Window menu, choose Symbol Libraries>Other Library. Navigate to the Chapter_03 folder and select the Weather.ai library.

The Weather palette appears with its own symbols.

3 Select the Cloudy symbol in the Weather palette. Activate the Symbol Sprayer tool and drag it briskly across the page to create a cloud-filled sky.

If you don't like the way your sprayed symbols look, simply choose Edit>Undo and try again.

FIGURE 3.44

4 | **Select the Sunny symbol and make a quick, single click to create one Sun instance in the symbol set.**

The sun is in front of the clouds, but it should be behind them.

FIGURE 3.45

5 | **Activate the Symbol Shifter tool (the tool to the right of the Symbol Sprayer). Double-click this tool's icon in the Tearoff menu to show its Options dialog box.**

The Options dialog box for each symbolism tool contains some brief instructions about how to use the tool, such as keys you must press to achieve a specific result. For example, when you Shift-Option/Alt-click an instance, you send it backward.

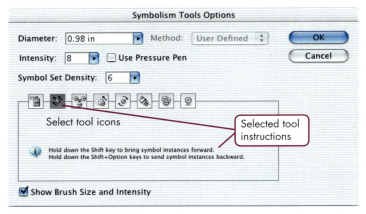

FIGURE 3.46

6 | **Click OK in the dialog box. Hold down the Shift-Option/Alt keys and click the Sun instance.**

The sun moves behind the clouds.

FIGURE 3.47

7 | **Double-click the Symbol Scruncher tool icon in the Tearoff menu.**

The dialog box states that pressing Option/Alt causes instances to move away from the cursor when clicked.

8 | **Close the dialog box. Press Option/Alt and quickly click the Sun instance.**

The Cloud instances move away from the cursor, revealing the sun. This behavior supports the name "Scruncher," because the instances scrunch together as they move away from the cursor.

Chapter 3   Working with Symbols   **129**   LEVEL 2

It takes time and practice to know how long to hold down the mouse button when you click the symbolism tools' cursors. Remember, if you don't produce the result you need, simply choose Edit>Undo and try again.

FIGURE 3.48

9 **Double-click the Symbol Sizer tool, the next tool in the Tearoff menu.**

The Symbol Sizer dialog box states that if you press the Option/Alt key when you click an instance, the instance decreases in size.

10 **Press Option/Alt and quickly click the cursor on the sun.**

The sun reduces slightly in size.

FIGURE 3.49

11 Save your changes. Keep the document open for the next exercise.

Explore More Symbolism Tools

1 **In the open document, select the Hurricane symbol in the Weather palette. Use the Symbol Sprayer tool to place the Hurricane instance above the sun.**

FIGURE 3.50

2 **Activate the Symbol Spinner tool in the Tearoff menu, but do not double-click it.**

This tool has no modifier keys.

3   **Click the tool cursor on the center of the Hurricane instance and continue to hold down the mouse button.**

4   **Move the cursor slightly to the right to see the arrow underneath the cursor.**

    The arrow shows you the angle that the instance will spin.

5   **Move the arrow a little more to the right and release the mouse button.**

    The Hurricane instance rotates the specified angle in the symbol set.

FIGURE 3.51

6   **Activate the Symbol Sprayer tool, and click the Raindrop symbol in the Weather palette. Single-click seven or eight times to create random raindrops below the Hurricane instance.**

FIGURE 3.52

7   **Keep the raindrop set selected. In the Color palette, set the Fill box for Cyan of 50% and zero for M, Y, and K.**

    You use the Symbol Stainer tool next, and it requires that the Fill box have a color set in it. The 50% Cyan subdues the raindrops' color.

8   **Select the Symbol Stainer tool from the optional tools and click its cross-hair cursor on each raindrop.**

Chapter 3 Working with Symbols 131 LEVEL 2

This tool reduces the colorization (amount of color) when you click an instance. The tool's Options dialog box provides more information on the tool's modifier keys.

FIGURE 3.53

9 **Open the Graphic Styles palette and click the Harmony Collage style. Select the Hurricane symbol in the Symbols palette.**

You must select the Hurricane instance in the Symbols palette for the Symbol Styler tool to know which instance on the page to affect.

10 **Activate the Symbol Styler tool in the Tearoff menu. Click the tool cursor on the Hurricane instance.**

The Symbol Styler tool paints the Hurricane symbol's path with the selected graphic style.

FIGURE 3.54

11 **Activate the Symbol Screener tool in the Tearoff menu, and click its cursor on the Hurricane instance.**

The Symbol Screener tool fades the appearance of the painted style, the same way you screen colors to subdue them.

FIGURE 3.55

12 **Save your changes. Close the document.**

LESSON 6   Symbolism Tool Options

In the previous lesson, you probably noticed that the same Options dialog box pertains to all eight of the symbolism tools. Open the Options dialog on your screen to choose which of the symbolism tools you want to customize. From the Options dialog box, you can modify the tools' behavior, including changing the brush size and several other tool-specific attributes.

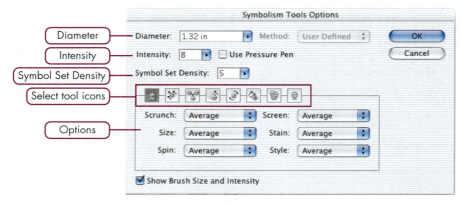

FIGURE 3.56

Double-click any symbolism tool in either the Toolbox or the Tearoff menu to access the Symbolism Tools Options dialog box. Let's review the features on this dialog box:

- The Diameter setting controls the tool cursor's size. Rather than use the dialog box to change the cursor's size, however, it's faster to use the Left or Right Bracket key shortcuts.

- The *Intensity* control determines how heavily a tool affects an instance or a symbol set. A low setting produces a sparse amount of instances; a higher setting applies a dense amount. If you check Show Brush Size and Intensity at the bottom of the dialog box, the brush outline becomes lighter at lower settings and darker at higher settings.

- *Symbol Set Density* controls the spacing between instances in a symbol set. A lower setting adds more space between instances. A high setting (the maximum is 10) reduces the space.

- In the Select Tool section, you choose the specific symbolism tool you want to modify.

- The Options section includes Scrunch, Size, Spin, Screen, Stain, and Style, which control how tightly the symbols scrunch together and their size and style.

Chapter 3   Working with Symbols   **133**   LEVEL 2

Use Symbolism Tool Options

1   **Create a new letter-size CMYK document with a landscape orientation. Open the Symbols palette.**

2   **From the Symbols palette Options menu, choose Open Symbol Library. Select the Nature library.**

3   **Double-click the Symbol Sprayer tool in the Tearoff menu. Set the Intensity to 2 and click OK.**

Double-clicking the Symbol Sprayer tool shows its Options dialog box.

4   **In the Nature palette, scroll down and select the Trees 1 symbol.**

5   **Slowly drag the Symbol Sprayer cursor across the page.**

Only a few trees appear because of the low Intensity setting.

6   **Show the Symbolism Tools Options dialog box again, and change the Intensity to 10. Click OK.**

7   **Drag the Symbol Sprayer tool across the page at a quicker rate.**

At one point in the spraying process, stop the tool cursor and watch as the symbols stack on top of one another. Many more trees spray on the page because of the higher Intensity setting.

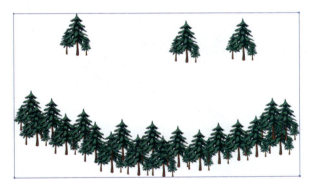

FIGURE 3.57

8   **Use the Selection tool to select the symbol set. Delete it.**

9   **Show the Symbolism Tools Options dialog box again. Change the Intensity to 8 and the Symbol Set Density to 2. Click OK.**

10 **Drag the Symbol Sprayer tool in a slight curving motion on the page. Keep the symbol set selected.**

At this low Density setting, the trees are quite far apart.

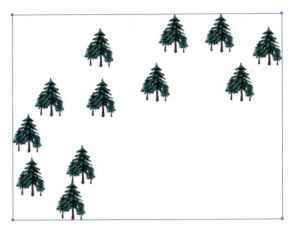

FIGURE 3.58

11 **Show the Symbolism Tools Options dialog box again, and change the Symbol Set Density to 6. Click OK.**

Making changes in the Symbolism Tools Options dialog box automatically rearranges/changes selected symbol set instances.

FIGURE 3.59

12 **Return to the Symbolism Tools Options dialog box and change the Symbol Set Density to 5. Click OK.**

You have observed how the Symbol Set Density controls the amount of symbols sprayed when you drag the tool cursor.

13 **Close the document without saving.**

Chapter 3 Working with Symbols   135   LEVEL 2

To Extend Your Knowledge . . .

SYMBOL SET DOS AND DON'TS

You can see the paths of individual instances when you drag the instances or use Outline mode, but you cannot see the paths of instances after you place them within a symbol set.

You can position symbol sets on top of one another to create interesting designs, which is not possible when you place additional symbols inside a symbol set.

You cannot isolate instances within a symbol set for selection, no matter what tool you use. You can, however, delete instances in a symbol set when you click the instance with a symbolism tool while holding down Option/Alt.

CAREERS IN DESIGN

BUILDING A FUNCTIONAL PORTFOLIO

Unless you work for a family member who is willing to ensure you'll have a job for the rest of your life, you must prepare yourself for the unlucky (and uncomfortable) position of needing to find a new job. Even if you currently have a wonderful position and feel happier than ever before, we highly recommend that you keep your portfolio up-to-date — just in case.

Prepare your portfolio by keeping samples of not only your best work, but of all your work. You may feel a particular project is of average quality, but a client may find that your "average" project precisely meets her needs.

In most cases, you will not own the rights to the work you create for your clients or employer; as you know, if you don't own the copyright, you don't own the work. Copyright law clearly states that you can't use anyone else's work for professional purposes, but it says nothing about including the work in your portfolio. Before you publish samples of your professional jobs on a Web site or some other public forum, you must get permission from the person or organization that holds the work's copyrights. For hard copies of your work, however, printed solely to demonstrate your skills to potential employers, copyright law is vague and should pose no legal issue.

LEVEL 2 **136** **Chapter 3 Working with Symbols**

SUMMARY

In Chapter 3, you discovered the many uses of symbols. You found that symbols save development time and file size — allowing you to create smaller files that download quickly from the Web. You learned how to use the Symbols palette to manage symbols and their instances. You created and saved symbols and symbol sets, and you learned that you can modify instances and save them as brand-new symbols in the Symbols palette. You discovered how to break the link between an instance and its symbol, so you can edit the instance as necessary. You also learned that you can replace one symbol with another simply by updating a link.

You discovered symbol libraries and found various methods to access them. You also used the symbolism tools to create a number of interesting effects. Finally, you used the Symbolism Tools Options dialog box to customize symbols before and after you apply the symbols to the page.

KEY TERMS

Instance

Intensity

Symbol

Symbol library

Symbol set

Symbol Set Density

Symbols palette

Tearoff menu

CHECKING CONCEPTS AND TERMS

MULTIPLE CHOICE

Circle the letter that matches the correct answer for each of the following questions.

1. When you drag a symbol to the Artboard from the Symbols palette, it becomes _____.

   a. a variable

   b. an instance

   c. a set

   d. an appearance

2. You cannot create symbols from _____.

   a. paths

   b. raster images

   c. masked objects

   d. effects-filled objects

   e. None of the above.

3. To return a symbol to its original path format, you must choose _____ from the Symbols palette.

   a. Expand

   b. Expand Appearance

   c. Break Link to Symbol

   d. Rasterize

4. Once you edit a symbol, you must _____ before you can use it.

   a. return it to the Symbols palette

   b. link it to its original symbol

   c. ungroup it

   d. replace it with another symbol

5. You can _____.

   a. mask a symbol with a clipping mask

   b. transform a symbol with any transformation tool

   c. enhance a symbol by applying an effect to its appearance

   d. All of the above.

6. You can only access symbol libraries through the _____.

   a. Window menu

   b. File>Open option

c. Symbols palette Options menu

d. None of the above.

7. From the Symbols palette Options menu, the Open Symbol Library>Other Library command _____.

a. opens symbol libraries from the Symbols folder

b. imports symbols from other Illustrator documents

c. converts graphic files from other programs into a symbol library

d. None of the above.

8. You can find the symbolism tools in the _____.

a. Window menu

b. Symbols palette

c. Toolbox

d. Symbols palette Options menu

9. You access the Symbolism Tools Options dialog box _____.

a. by clicking a symbolism tool cursor on the page

b. through the Window menu

c. by double-clicking a symbolism tool icon in the Toolbox or Tearoff menu

d. by clicking a symbolism tool icon while pressing the Command/Control key

10. You can delete a single instance in a symbol set by _____.

a. selecting it with the Direct Selection tool and pressing the Delete key

b. clicking the instance with a symbolism tool while pressing the Option/Alt key

c. unlinking the symbol set, selecting an instance, and pressing the Delete key

d. None of the above.

DISCUSSION QUESTIONS

1. What was the original reason for creating symbols, and how do they meet that requirement?

2. Breaking the link to a symbol allows you to modify an instance as a stand-alone graphic. What's the major disadvantage to doing so, and how can you work around it?

3. Site a situation where using symbols would improve your workflow, and why.

4. Site a design situation for using symbol sets.

SKILL DRILL

Skill Drills reinforce learned skills. Each skill that is reinforced is the same as, or nearly the same as, a skill we presented in the lessons. We provide detailed instructions in a step-by-step format. You should complete these exercises in order.

1. Create Symbols Painted with Styles

Your art director asked you to create several symbols based on geometric shapes for a new brochure.

1. Create a new letter-size CMYK document with units set for inches and portrait orientation. Show the page rulers.

2. In the middle of the page, use the Rectangle tool to draw a 0.75-inch square.

3. Copy the square and press Command/Control-5 to turn it into a guide.

4. Paste the copied square onto the Artboard and drag the copy to the page's upper-left corner.

5. Use the other geometric drawing tools to draw a circle, a polygon, and a star that fit within the square guide. Place the objects in a row beside the square in the upper-left corner.

6. Apply any colors, gradients, patterns, or effects that you prefer.

7. After you paint the objects, drag each one to the Symbols palette. Name the new symbols appropriately.

FIGURE 3.60

8. Save the document as "my_symbols.ai" to your WIP_03 folder.

9. Close the document.

2. Save Symbols to Other Library

You are a graphic designer creating a Web site for a client who owns a restaurant. He has asked you to develop some food-related icons for the site you design.

1. Create a new letter-size RGB document with portrait orientation.

2. From Window>Symbol Libraries, choose Other Library. Navigate to the Chapter_03 folder and select the Food.ai library.

3. Drag the Beef, Chicken, Fish, Chef, Escargot, and Grapes symbols onto the Artboard.

4. Select all the instances and click the Break Link to Symbol icon in the Symbols palette.

   You do not have to select a single symbol before clicking the Break Link to Symbol icon. Multiple symbol instances may be selected on the Artboard and the Break Link to Symbol icon clicked once.

5. Use the Direct Selection tool to select the various paths of the unlinked instances. Paint the objects however you prefer.

FIGURE 3.61

Chapter 3 Working with Symbols 139 LEVEL 2

6. Save the document as "food_symbols.ai" to your WIP_03 folder. Keep the document open for the next exercise.

3. Save a Symbols Library

Save the newly painted symbols in a library so you access them from the Symbol Libraries menu.

1. In the open food_symbols.ai document, drag the painted objects to the Symbols palette.

2. Rename each new symbol appropriately: "Beef", "Chicken", "Fish", "Chef", and "Grapes". Rename the Escargot Shell symbol as "Seafood".

3. Drag each of these new symbols to the Artboard so you can use them.

4. From the Symbols palette Options menu, choose Select All Unused.

5. Delete all the selected symbols in the palette.

   If you get the error message that suggests expanding or deleting instances, choose Delete Instances. This does no harm and appears because the first symbols you dragged were later unlinked, but the palette still thinks the dragged symbols are active.

FIGURE 3.62

6. From the Symbols palette Options menu, choose Save Symbol Library.

7. Save the library with the name "Painted Food.ai" to the Adobe Illustrator CS2>Presets>Symbols folder.

   Under normal circumstances, Illustrator automatically saves the library to its Symbol folder. If you have navigated to other folders using this saving feature, you may have to navigate back to the Illustrator Symbols folder.

8. Close the document. Go to the next exercise.

4. Replace Web Symbols from a Library

In creating the rough layout of a Web page, you used generic instances for position only. Now you are ready to replace preset placeholder instances with the final symbols you saved earlier as a library.

1. Quit the Illustrator program and relaunch it.

   This adds the Painted Food library to the Symbol Libraries menu.

2. Open online_market.ai from the Chapter_03 folder.

   This Web page layout includes some generic placeholder instances that you need to replace. You also need to apply some new symbols to the page.

3. From the Window>Symbol Libraries menu, choose the Painted Food library.

4. Return to the Window>Symbol Libraries menu and choose Other Library. Navigate to the Chapter_03 folder and access the Essentials.ai library.

5. Drag the Green Apple symbol from the Essentials palette to the empty area in the page's upper left.

6. Choose Show Bounding Box from the View menu, and use the box to proportionally scale the apple to a larger size to fit the space.

7. On the left side of the Web page, under the apple, select each generic instance and replace it with the symbol of the same name from the Painted Food palette.

8. Scale the replaced symbols to fit, if necessary.

FIGURE 3.63

9. Save the document with the same name to your WIP_03 folder. Keep the document open for the next exercise.

5. Continue Replacing Web Symbols

Easily identified symbols have replaced the generic instances on the Artboard's left side. You now must replace the other generic instances in the document.

1. From the Painted Foods palette, drag the Chef symbol near the Online Market type area. Manually scale the chef until it is slightly larger than the generic instances under the Online Market headline.

2. Click the Break Link to Symbol icon in the Symbols palette.

3. Drag the scaled chef to the Symbols palette and rename the symbol "Little Chef". Select and delete the unlinked, scaled chef object on the Artboard.

4. Select all the generic instances under the Online Market type and replace them with the Little Chef symbol.

5. Select the generic symbol for the Fruit Market type at the bottom of the Artboard. Replace it with the Grapes symbol from the Painted Food palette.

6. Use the symbols in the Essentials palette to replace the generic instances as follows: Honey Market receives the Bumble Bee symbol, Email receives the Web Mail symbol, and Shop receives the Web Shopping symbol.

7. Scale any of these instances to fit, as necessary.

FIGURE 3.64

8. Save your changes. Close the document.

CHALLENGE

Challenge exercises expand on, or are somewhat related to, skills that we presented in the lessons. Each exercise provides a brief introduction, followed by numbered-step instructions that are not as detailed as those in the Skill Drill exercises. You should complete these exercises in order.

1. Create Raster Objects from Symbols

You are the artist who created the geometric symbols used in the Skill Drill section. The client wants to use the symbols as spot-art decorations in his fall catalog. Your task is to convert the symbols to raster objects.

1. Create a new letter-size RGB document set for portrait orientation. Show the page rulers.

2. From the Window menu, choose Symbol Libraries>Other Library.

3. Navigate to the WIP_03 folder and open my_symbols.ai.

4. One at a time, drag the four symbols from the my_symbols palette onto the Artboard.

5. One at a time, select each instance and use Object>Rasterize to rasterize each instance with a Medium Resolution and White Background.

6. From the Filter menu, apply a raster Photoshop Filter of your choice to each instance.

   You should have four rasterized, filtered objects on the page.

7. Drag each of the rasterized objects to the Symbols palette.

8. In the order you dragged the instances to the palette, rename the new symbols "Raster 1", "Raster 2", "Raster 3", and "Raster 4".

FIGURE 3.65

9. Save the document as "raster_objects.ai" to your WIP_03 folder. Close the document.

2. Create Notepad Designs

A client asked you to develop four notepad designs. The designs must include a border of decorations across the top of the notepad.

1. Open notepads.ai from the Chapter_03 folder.

    The page is divided into four quarter-page notepads with generic instances across the top of each pad.

2. From the Window menu, select Symbol Libraries>Other Library. Navigate to the Chapter_03 folder and choose the Occasions.ai library.

3. In the Artboard's upper-left, select the six generic instances.

4. Click the Heart symbol in the Occasions palette. Click the Replace Symbol icon in the Symbols palette.

5. Use the Object>Transform>Transform Each dialog box to scale the selected instances to a uniform 40%.

6. View the other libraries in the Symbol Libraries menu and experiment with replacing the other generic instances on the three remaining notepads.

    Scale the instances, if necessary.

7. After experimenting, choose three symbols to decorate the remaining three notepads.

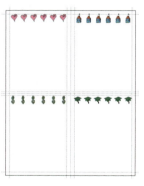

FIGURE 3.66

8. Save the document with the same name to your WIP_03 folder. Close the document.

3. Create a Scene of Nature

You were hired to create a rustic nature scene to support an article in a local magazine. Your task is to use the symbolism tools to create the scene.

1. Create a new letter-size CMYK document with a landscape orientation.

2. From the Window menu, select Symbol Libraries. From the pop-out menu, choose the Nature library.

3. Set the Nature palette view to Small List View, and lengthen the palette to see all the available symbols.

4. From the Toolbox, select the Symbol Sprayer tool to show its optional tools in the Tearoff menu. Drag the Tearoff menu and its symbolism tools into the document. Activate the Symbol Sprayer tool.

5. Use any of the various symbols from the Nature palette to spray a rustic scene with grass, trees, ants, bees, and other objects.

   Try to keep all the instances in one symbol set.

6. Utilize the various symbolism tools to adjust the instances to fit your design.

7. Use the Symbolism Tools Options dialog to further customize the distribution of the instances in the symbol set.

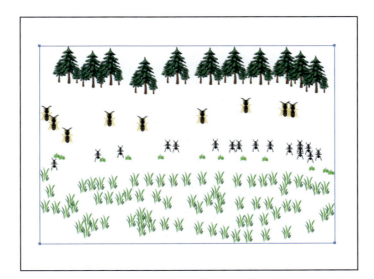

FIGURE 3.67

8. Save the document as "my_rustic_scene.ai" in the WIP_03 folder and close the document.

4. Create an Office Supply Design

A local office supply store hired you to create a design that displays a variety of office supplies.

1. Create a new letter-size CMYK document with a portrait orientation. Set the units for inches and show the page rulers.

2. Drag vertical and horizontal guides to mark the center of the Artboard.

3. Activate the Ellipse tool, hold down Option/Alt, and click the cursor on the center of the Artboard, which is marked by the guides.

4. Set the width and height for 4 in, and click OK to draw a circle.

5. Press Command/Control-5 to convert the circle to a guide.

    The circle represents a clock with the guides marking the 12:00, 3:00, 6:00, and 9:00 hours.

6. From the Window menu, select Symbol Libraries>Other Library. Navigate to the Chapter_03 folder and choose the Office.ai library.

7. Drag each symbol from the Office palette to the Artboard, and use your artist's judgment to scale, rotate, or reflect the instance (if necessary) to serve as a number on the clock guide.

    Start with the CD symbol, and drag it to the center of the circle guide.

8. Scale and fit the instances into the number areas of the clock guide from the 1:00 to the 12:00 hours.

    Twelve objects should follow around the circle guide.

9. Save the document as "office_clock.ai" to your WIP_03 folder. Close the document.

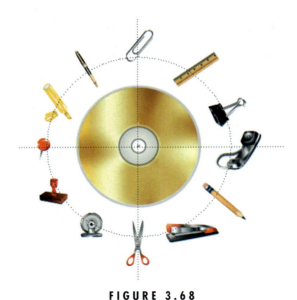

FIGURE 3.68

Chapter 3 Working with Symbols   145   LEVEL 2

PORTFOLIO BUILDER

Create Patterns with Symbols

You are a graphic designer working in an advertising agency. A new client owns a fashion clothing company and likes repetitive designs and objects to decorate the pages of their catalog you are working on. Your task is to create symbols of various styles that you can use repeatedly as spot art in the catalog.

1. Create a new letter-size CMYK document, with portrait orientation. Set the units for inches.
2. Draw a 2-inch square in the middle of the page and make the path a guide.
3. From the Window>Symbol Libraries menu, choose the Fashion option. Drag its symbols from the palette onto the Artboard.
4. Unlink the instances and modify them with transformations or painting techniques.
5. Either use the single instances by themselves or combine several in the square guide to make your design.

    The idea is to create spot-art pieces that reflect the floral look of typical wallpaper types.

6. Create four different spot-art objects using pieces of, or whole, instances.
7. Convert each spot-art piece to a new symbol, naming it however you want.
8. Save the document to your WIP_03 folder with the name "fashion_spot_art.ai" and close the document.

LEVEL 2

CHAPTER 4

Working with Animations

OBJECTIVES

In this chapter, you learn how to:

- Export objects to animations

- Create an animation using the Layers palette

- Generate an animation using the build process

- Use the sequence process to build an animation

- Apply the Blend feature to create frames

- Use symbols to create animations

- Apply the Release to Layers command

Why Would I Do This?

Using drawing programs such as Illustrator to create animations is a relatively new phenomenon — one that's increasing in popularity and acceptance throughout the graphic arts industry. While Illustrator is not by definition an animation program, its powerful features and functions make it a strong contender for the next generation of animation artwork. Learning to use Illustrator to generate motion graphics will expand your creative horizons as you develop complex and compelling animations for use on the Web or in other interactive media.

In this chapter, you expand on the Illustrator techniques you already know as you learn the core concepts of animation, which include time and motion. You also learn to output your drawings in formats that are compatible for direct delivery to the Web and for further development within dedicated animation and video applications.

VISUAL SUMMARY

Because Illustrator isn't an animation program per se, it lacks certain critical tools — specifically control over time and motion, which form the foundation of animation technology. As one of the most powerful commercial illustration and design applications, however, you can certainly use Illustrator to generate objects from which you can build *animations*. With a small amount of planning and effort, you can use familiar tools and techniques to build illustrations that appear to move. You can also use Illustrator to output files that are compatible with several animation players, most notably **Flash Player** from Macromedia.

The lesson on creating an animation in Illustrator shows you everything you need to know — from assigning *layers* to exporting the document to an animated format. To ensure your animation works as expected, you must perform these steps in the proper sequence. You discover that when you use layers to create an animation in Illustrator, you must use the Macromedia SWF format to export the file. This process provides you with the Macromedia Flash (SWF) Format Options dialog box, where you customize the animation's settings.

FIGURE 4.1

You learn how the objects in a cumulative type of animation remain in view; the frames continue to build on top of one other until all of the objects display in the animation's final frame. This popular type of animation keeps Internet viewers interested while they watch the banner build to its final frame.

FIGURE 4.2

In noncumulative animations, the objects appear only once, and then disappear as another frame comes into view. Web designers frequently use this type of animation to produce special effects that grasp the viewer's attention and that advertise a particular product or site.

FIGURE 4.3

You also discover that you are no longer restricted to using only vector paths to create animations in Illustrator. You learn how to assign raster images to layers so you can export the images to animation frames and use the frames in slide shows.

FIGURE 4.4

You also learn how to use the **Blend option** to add objects in-between two originals. These in-between objects are called *tweens*, which you can easily create using blending techniques. You can use the new tweened objects in their own frames of an animation. Using tweens, you can morph one object into another as the animation advances through its frames.

FIGURE 4.5

You also learn the advantages of using symbols in animations that include multiple objects — objects you may need to change or repurpose later. You discover the time-saving options of the Layers palette, specifically the Release to Layers command. This powerful operation relocates objects in the document to individual layers so you can export the layers to an animation.

FIGURE 4.6

Chapter Setup: All the animations you make with Illustrator are exported to the Macromedia Flash Player format. There are two methods to see this type of animation: (1) you must have Macromedia Flash Player installed on your computer (can be versions 4.0 to the current 7.0). To install this, go to http://www.macromedia.com/software/flashplayer/ and click Get Macromedia Flash Player on the right of the page. (2) You can view the exported animation file in your Internet browser. Create a new browser window and, from the desktop, drag the exported animation to the window.

LESSON 1 Creating an Animation

Illustrator is not a dedicated animation program capable of producing awe-inspiring special effects and sounds. Even so, Illustrator allows you to organize objects, whether vector or raster, into *frames* (individual scenes) that, when viewed in rapid succession, result in an animation. The animation process is quite simple. It involves only two basic steps:

- First, you place each object in the animation on its own layer in the Layers palette. Every object/frame in the animation must have its own layer (i.e., 10 objects/frames require 10 layers).

- You then export the document as a Macromedia Flash (SWF) file. It is important that you install the Macromedia Flash Player on your computer so you can test the SWF file and ensure that it works correctly.

As you export the document to the SWF format, you must make certain changes in its Macromedia Flash (SWF) Format Options dialog box. Figure 4.7 shows a basic overview of this dialog box's important aspects (keep in mind that Adobe's default settings present the animation at its best, and fastest, uploading quality).

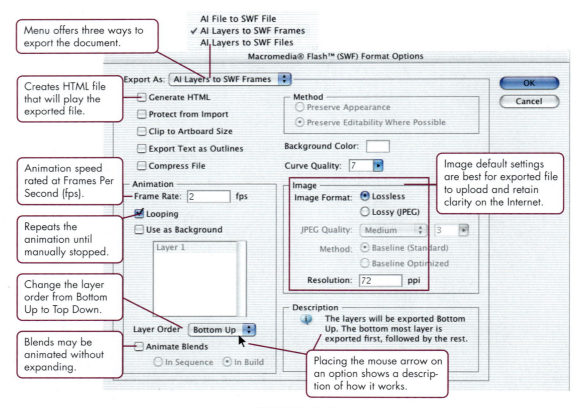

FIGURE 4.7

In the following exercise, you perform the basic procedures necessary to create an animation in Illustrator: create the objects, assign the objects to layers, and export the document.

Chapter 4 Working with Animations **151** LEVEL 2

Create and Export an Animation

1 From the Chapter_04 folder, open the neon_sign.ai document. Open the Layers palette.

2 Use the Ellipse tool to draw a 2-inch circle in the middle of the page. Paint the circle with a Fill of Pure Cyan and a Stroke of None.

3 From above the Artboard, select the "Eat At Joe's" text outlines. Bring the outlines to the front.

4 Paint the text White and position it on the circle.

5 Select the circle and text objects. In the Align palette, click the Horizontal Align Center and the Vertical Align Center buttons.

The type centers on the circle.

FIGURE 4.8

6 In the Layers palette, rename Layer 1 "Frame 1".

Each single moving segment of an animation is called a "frame" in technical jargon. A complete animation is made up of these frames.

7 Drag Frame 1 down to touch the Create New Layer icon at the bottom of the Layers palette.

When you drag a layer to this icon, the layer duplicates, along with any objects residing on the dragged layer.

8 Rename the new layer "Frame 2".

Illustrator defaults the first frame of the animation to the bottom layer of the *layer list*. Each consecutive frame appears above it. The last frame you build should appear at the top of the layer list.

This sequence can be changed, if necessary, in the Macromedia Flash (SWF) Format Options dialog box that appears when exporting the file. We will explore this later.

FIGURE 4.9

9 Click the Visibility icon of Frame 1 to hide it. Keep Frame 2 selected.

The object on Frame 2 looks the same as the object on Frame 1. We hid Frame 1 so that you can do the needed work on Frame 2. It can become confusing when you work with multiple layers and objects.

10 Select the circle and text block. From the Effect menu, choose the Stylize>Outer Glow option.

11 Set the Mode menu to Normal. Click the color swatch to the right of the Mode menu.

12 In the Color Picker set the CMYK Yellow color to 100%. Click OK, which brings you back in the Outer Glow dialog box. Change the Opacity to 100% and set the Blur to 0.1 in Click OK.

When this image is exported as an animation, it will blink back and forth from one frame to the other. The first frame shows only the object without a glow. The second frame shows a yellow glow, similar to a neon sign.

FIGURE 4.10

13 Save the document with the same name to your WIP_04 folder. Keep the document open for the next exercise.

Chapter 4   Working with Animations   **153**   **LEVEL 2**

Export the Animation

1   **In the open document, click the Visibility icon of Frame 1 to show its objects.**

This shows the objects on Frame 1, but the layer is under Frame 2, so you cannot see it.

2   **Click the Visibility icon of Frame 2 to hide it. Continue to click it several times to show and hide it to get a rough idea of how the animation looks.**

Showing and hiding the layer frames is a fast way to see an animation at work.

3   **Leave the Visibility icon of Frame 2 active to show the objects on that layer.**

To export correctly, all layers must be visible to be included in the animation. A hidden layer will not export to the animation.

4   **From the File menu, choose Export. Save the file to your WIP_04 folder and name it "neon_sign.swf".**

5   **In the dialog box, set the Format menu (Macintosh) or File Type (Windows) for Macromedia Flash (SWF). Click Export (Macintosh) or Save (Windows).**

The Macromedia Flash Player requires the SWF file format to play the animation.

6   **In the Macromedia Flash Format Options dialog box, set the Export As menu to AI Layers to SWF Frames.**

This setting converts each layer in the document to an individual frame.

7   **Set the Frame Rate for 2 frames per second (fps).**

The *frame rate* controls how fast your animation advances through its sequence of frames. *Frames per second (fps)* determines how many frames of your movie will play per second. A higher number speeds up the animation; a lower number slows it down. Depending on your specific animation and its frames, you will have to use your own judgment to determine what is the correct fps setting.

8   **Make certain the Looping option is selected.**

When you *loop* an animation, it plays through in sequence and starts over again (loops) at Frame 1. A looped animation continues to play until you stop it manually.

9 **Leave the Image Format set to Lossless (default) and the Resolution set to 72 ppi (default). Click OK.**

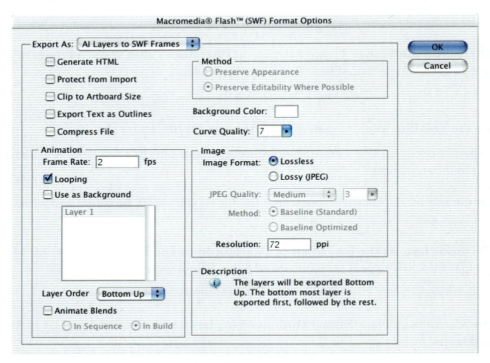

FIGURE 4.11

10 **From the desktop, go to your WIP_04 folder and double-click the neon_sign_swf file to launch Macromedia Flash Player and see your animation.**

The exported SWF file can be viewed two ways: by using the Macromedia Flash Player or by dragging the exported file into a new window of your Internet browser program.

If Flash Player is installed on your computer, the player should launch and play the animation. Since Illustrator exported the file, it may try to open it and will give you an error message. If this happens, open the SWF file through the Flash Player program's File>Open option.

If you want to see the animation as it will appear on the Internet, open a new browser window. From the desktop, drag the exported SWF file to the browser. The size of the browser window controls the size of the animation. Reduce the size of the window, if necessary, to see a smaller animation.

11 **Close the animation after you view it. Return to the Illustrator document. Save your changes and close the document.**

Chapter 4   Working with Animations   **155**   LEVEL 2

To Extend Your Knowledge . . .

ADDING SWF TO HTML

To find out how to incorporate SWF animations into HTML code, check the Generate HTML box in the Macromedia Flash Format Options dialog box. The HTML file appears separately, along with the SWF file. If you open the HTML file in a word processor, you will see how the code uses the <embed> tag to access this type of file.

LESSON 2   The Build (Cumulative) Animation

In a ***build (cumulative)*** animation, the first object appears, then the second, third, and so on, until all the objects in the animation are visible on your screen. This type of animation is applied to some banners on the Internet, where one element of the banner appears, and another, until the final frame of the animation includes all of the elements, images, and logos.

Even though this may sound complicated, it's really quite simple — you just continue to add frames/objects to each successive frame of the animation until you reach the final frame, which contains all the elements. Once all the elements are in place, you can work in reverse — deleting the elements in sequence until you reach the first frame and only the original object displays on the screen.

In this exercise, you use the build method to create an animated Web banner.

Create a Build Animation

1. Open tips_trix.ai from the Chapter_04 folder. Open the Layers palette.

2. Use the Rectangle tool to draw a rectangle that fits the banner-sized Artboard. Fill the object with Sea Green from the Swatches palette, and stroke with None.

3. Send the rectangle to the back. From above the banner, select all the type outlines and drag them on top of the rectangle.

   The type outlines are already in position for you to select and move.

4. Select the ampersand (&) and Adobe Photoshop text and change the Fill to White.

FIGURE 4.12

5. Double-click Layer 1 in the Layers palette and rename it "Frame 1".

6. Drag Frame 1 to the Create New Layer icon at the bottom of the Layers palette four times to create four new layers.

   You have a total of five layers, including Frame 1.

7. Moving up the layer list from Frame 1, rename all consecutive layers "Frame 2", "Frame 3", "Frame 4" and "Frame 5".

   Frame 5 should be at the top of the layer list.

8. Click Frame 1 to make it active. Press Option/Alt and click the Visibility icon of Frame 1.

   This hides all the other layers in the palette, with only Frame 1 remaining visible.

9. Select all the type outline objects and delete them, leaving only the rectangle.

   This starts the animation with a blank green screen.

10. Click Frame 2 to make it active. Click its Visibility icon to show the objects on the layer.

    The objects on Frame 2 obscure those on Frame 1, which is underneath.

11. Delete all the type outline objects except "Tips".

    The second frame in the animation contains only the word "Tips".

FIGURE 4.13

12. Save the document with the same name to your WIP_04 folder. Keep the document open for the next exercise.

Add "Trix" to the Banner

1. Click Frame 3 to make it active.

2. Click its Visibility icon so you can see the objects on the layer.

3. Delete all the type objects except "Tips" and the ampersand (&).

Chapter 4 Working with Animations 157 LEVEL 2

The ampersand is added to the banner. "Tips" did not disappear as it would have in a sequence-type animation. The objects begin building on the green banner.

FIGURE 4.14

4 Click Frame 4 to make it active.

5 Click Frame 4's Visibility icon to see the objects. Select the Adobe Photoshop outlines and delete them.

"Trix" is added to the animation, continuing the build.

FIGURE 4.15

6 Click Frame 5 to make it active.

7 Click the Visibility icon of Frame 5. Make no changes to the objects.

The objects on Frame 5 are all in place, showing final frame and the complete banner.

FIGURE 4.16

8 Save your changes. Keep the document open for the next exercise.

Export the Trix Banner

1 In the open document, make certain that all the layers' Visibility icons are showing. Choose Export from the File menu.

2 Choose the SWF format and save the exported file to your WIP_04 folder.

Since the document is already named, the Export dialog box should use the assigned name and add the "swf" extension automatically. If this does not happen, save the file as "tips_trix.swf".

LEVEL 2   **158**   Chapter 4   Working with Animations

3   In the Macromedia Flash Export Options dialog box, make certain the Export As menu is set for AI Layers to SWF Frames. Set the Frame Rate to 3 fps.

4   Make certain that Looping is selected. The Layer Order menu should be set for the default setting Bottom Up.

By default, all exported animations work in sequence from the bottom layer in the *Layers palette* up to the top layer in the layer list.

5   Leave all the other options at their default settings. Click OK.

6   From the desktop, go to your WIP_04 folder and double-click the tips_trix.swf file.

Watch your animation play in the Flash Player.

7   As the animation is playing, enlarge or reduce the window size of the Flash Player.

The animated objects scale along with the size of the playing window.

8   When finished viewing, close the Flash Player window.

9   Return to the tips_trix.ai document. Save your changes and close the document.

To Extend Your Knowledge . . .

RELEASE TO LAYERS

The easiest way to create a build (cumulative) animation is to use the Release to Layers (Build) option in the Layers palette. When you use this method, however, you need to prepare the objects and ensure proper stacking order. You learn more about this method in Lesson 6.

LESSON 3   The Sequence (Noncumulative) Animation

In a *sequence (noncumulative)* animation, one frame disappears as the next frame appears on the screen. Unlike a build animation, the objects in a sequence animation do not all appear in the final frame. You can use a sequence animation to:

- Create a single banner in which an advertising phrase appears, then disappears as another phrase appears.

- Develop a fireworks animation in which various bursts of colored sparkles appear and disappear in the sky.

- Generate a slide show of photographs — one photo appears for a few seconds, and another photo replaces it, until the final photo appears on the screen.

Chapter 4   Working with Animations   **159**   LEVEL 2

In this exercise, you create a sequence animation that shows how objects appear to move out of the picture.

Create a Sequence Animation

1 Open zoom.ai from the Chapter_04 folder. Open the Layers palette.

2 In the Layers palette, double-click Layer 1 and rename it "Frame 1".

3 Drag Frame 1 four times to the Create New Layer icon at the bottom of the Layers palette.

You should have five layers.

4 Rename each layer so you have Frame 1 at the bottom, then, above this, Frame 2, Frame 3, and Frame 4 until Frame 5 is at the top of the list.

5 Click Frame 1 to make it the working layer. Press Option/Alt and click the Frame 1 Visibility icon to hide the other layers.

6 Zoom in closer to the small banner object.

7 Use the Direct Selection tool to select the zooming lines to the left of the word "Zoom" and delete them.

The "Zoom" type is stationary in the first frame.

FIGURE 4.17

8 Click Frame 2 to make it active. Press Option/Alt and click the Visibility icon of Frame 2 twice to make it the visible layer.

9 Use the Selection tool to select "Zoom" (it's grouped with the lines). Move it to the right until the second "O" hangs halfway off the edge of the yellow rectangle.

Remember to hold down the Shift key to constrain the move.

FIGURE 4.18

10 Select the yellow rectangle and copy it. Deselect the rectangle.

11 Select all the objects on the Artboard and press Command/Control-F.

This command pastes a copy of the rectangle in front of the selected objects.

12 Press Command/Control-A to select all the objects, including the pasted rectangle; press Command/Control-7 to mask the banner.

You can use masked objects in animations. The hidden, masked-off part of the object does not affect the bounding box of the exported animation.

FIGURE 4.19

13 Save the document with the same name to your WIP_04 folder. Keep the document open for the next exercise.

Modify the Objects

1 In the open document, click Frame 3 to make it active. Press Option/Alt and click the Visibility icon of Frame 3 twice.

2 Select the "Zoom" type and move it to the right until the first "O" is halfway off the rectangle.

Remember to press the Shift key to constrain the move.

FIGURE 4.20

3 Select and copy the yellow rectangle. Select all the objects and press Command/Control-F to paste the copy in front.

4 Again, select all the objects. Press Command/Control-7 to mask the objects.

The right-hand portion of the word "Zoom" is masked off.

FIGURE 4.21

5 Click Frame 4 to make it active. Press Option/Alt and click the Visibility icon of Frame 4 twice.

6 Select the Zoom type and move it (pressing the Shift key) to the right until the right side of the bottom speed line touches the yellow triangle's right edge.

FIGURE 4.22

7 Select all the objects and press Command/Control-F to paste the rectangle copy in front.

8 Again, select all the objects. Press Command/Control-7 to mask the objects.

FIGURE 4.23

9 Save your changes. Keep the document open for the next exercise.

Build the Zoom Banner

1 In the open document, click Frame 5 to make it active. Press Option/Alt and click the Visibility icon of Frame 5 twice.

2 Select the "Zoom" type and speed line objects. Delete them.

The empty rectangle shows the viewer that the "Zoom" type has zoomed off the banner.

3 Press Option/Alt and click Frame 1 twice.

Only Frame 1 and its object should be showing on the Artboard.

4 Starting at Frame 1, move up the layer list, clicking the Visibility icon of each frame to see how the animation looks at each stage.

Do not press the Option/Alt key at this time, so you do not hide any layers.

5 When you're finished viewing the above simulation, make certain that the Visibility icon is showing on all layers.

Only visible layers will export to an animation.

6 Export the file as an SWF file. Save the file to your WIP_04 folder as "zoom.swf".

7 From the Macromedia Flash Export Options dialog box, choose AI Layers to SWF Frames in the Export As menu. Make certain that Looping is selected. Set the Frame Rate to 5 fps. Click OK.

The 5-fps rate gives the zooming object some speed.

8 From the desktop, go to the WIP_04 folder and double-click the zoom.swf file. Watch the animation as it plays.

You can also see the animation by opening a new browser window and dragging the SWF file to the window. Resize the window to see the animation at a smaller size.

9 When you've finished viewing the animation, return to the Illustrator document. Save your changes and close the document.

To Extend Your Knowledge . . .

CREATE A STORYBOARD

When designing an animation, we suggest that you map out a rough draft that describes what each frame will show. These sketches are known as a storyboard. Many artists prefer to draw their storyboards by hand, rather than on the computer. They feel it aids in the creative process.

LESSON 4 Raster Animations

In addition to using vector paths when you create animations, you can place raster images and rasterized vector objects within your documents. When you use raster images, you can create photographic slide shows, which display a sequence of pictures, one after another.

When you develop a slide show, you may find that a 1-fps speed is too fast. Luckily, you can enter frame-rate values between 0.01 and 120 into the Frame Rate field. You experiment with various frame-rate values in the following exercises.

In this exercise, you create a slide show by assigning raster images to layers and exporting the layers to an animation.

Create a Photo Animation

1. Open photo_show.ai from the Chapter_04 folder. Show the Layers palette.

2. Select the various photos and position them on the Artboard so that they overlap one another.

   Use your artistic judgment as you position the photos. Don't worry if the photos overlap one another; the photos appear one at a time.

FIGURE 4.24

Chapter 4   Working with Animations   **163**   LEVEL 2

3   In the Layers palette, click the Create New Layer icon five times. Rename Layer 1 "Photo 1".

4   Move up the layer list and rename the other layers "Photo 2", "Photo 3", and so on, until "Photo 6" is at the top of the list.

5   Select each photo on the Artboard and relocate it from the Layers palette to its own individual layer.

Each photo should reside on its own layer.

6   Save the document with the same name to your WIP_04 folder. Keep the document open.

7   Export the file in SWF format. Save the file to your WIP_04 folder as "photo_show.swf".

8   In the Macromedia Flash Export Options dialog box, set the Export As menu to AI Layers to SWF Frames.

9   Make certain that the Looping option is selected. Make certain that the Layer Order menu is set for Bottom Up.

10   In the Frame Rate field, type "0.50". Click OK.

This setting adds a brief pause between photos.

11   From the desktop, go to the WIP_04 folder and double-click the photo_show.swf file.

Watch as the Flash Player plays the animation for you.

12   When you're finished viewing the animation, return to the Illustrator document and close it.

In this next exercise, you create a slide show with photos and their descriptive comments.

Create a Digital Slide Show with Comments

1   Open slides_comments.ai from the Chapter_04 folder. Show the Layers and Align palettes.

We supply the same pictures you used in the previous exercise, but we added descriptive comments to the photos.

2   Select all the photos on the page. In the Align palette, click the Horizontal Align Center and Vertical Align Top options.

This centers the photos so each one appears in the same place on your screen.

3   In the Layers palette, rename Layer 1 "Photo 1". Click the Create New Layer icon five times at the bottom of the Layers palette.

You now have six layers.

4   Rename the other layers "Photo 2", "Photo 3", and so on, until "Photo 6" is at the top of the list.

LEVEL 2   **164**   Chapter 4   Working with Animations

5   **Select each photo on the Artboard and relocate it from the Layers palette to its own individual layer.**

Each photo should reside on its own layer.

6   **Make certain the Visibility icon of all layers is showing.**

7   **Save the document with the same name to your WIP_04 folder. Keep the document open.**

8   **Export the file to the SWF format. Save the file to your WIP_04 folder as "slides_comments.swf".**

9   **In the Macromedia Flash Export Options dialog box, set the Export As menu for AI Layers to SWF Frames.**

10   **Select the Looping option.**

11   **In the Frame Rate field, type "0.10". Click OK.**

This frame rate adds a long pause so the viewer can read the comments on the photos.

12   **From your WIP_04 folder, double-click the slides_comments.swf file.**

Watch as the Flash Player plays the animation for you. If you widen the Flash Player window while it's playing, the objects increase in size in relation to the size of the window.

13   **Return to the Illustrator document. Save your changes and close the document.**

To Extend Your Knowledge . . .

USE RASTER IMAGES

A raster image is basically the same as any other object in a document. As long as you place a raster image on its own layer, it can appear in any animation you export from Illustrator.

LESSON 5   Animating Blends

The Illustrator blending operation is a powerful feature that allows you to create multiple objects between two original objects. Depending on the type of blend you choose, the intermediate objects change shape or color as they transform from one object to the other. The professional animation term for the in-between objects is "tweens."

The appearance and color of tweens is based upon the two original objects and their shape and color. In the examples here, the original objects are selected and the blend applied, showing the tweens, which exist only in Preview mode. Outline view shows only the original objects and the spine, which holds the tweens. If you select and move the spine (with the Direct Selection tool) in Preview mode, the tweens move with it.

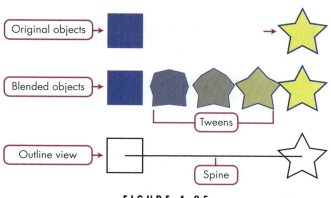

FIGURE 4.25

There are two ways to use blends in an animation:

Modified. Once you apply the blend, the objects may need further changes of position or alterations. To separate the tweens, you must expand the blend object from the Object menu. The expanded tweens become actual paths that you must ungroup from the blend. You may now move or modify these individual paths to suit the animation.

Unmodified. Even though the unexpanded blend objects are nonexistent in Outline mode, you can export the document to Macromedia Flash format and click the Animate Blends options to retain these appearance-based objects. The only alteration you can make to an unmodified blend (other than repainting the original objects) is relocating the spine endpoints so the tweens change position. If you relocate the two endpoints so that they are on top of each other, all the objects will appear in one location.

Create an Animation from Blends

In this exercise, you use blends to create an animation that enlarges type on a banner while it changes colors.

1 **From the Chapter_04 folder, open the theater_blend.ai document. Show the page rulers.**

This document is in RGB color mode. We have been using CMYK documents for our past animations. In most cases, CMYK color models will not appear on the Internet. However, when exported into SWF format, the color model does not matter. In this Flash format, both CMYK and RGB images will show animations on the Internet.

2 **Select the Rectangle tool and click its cursor on the Artboard's upper-left corner.**

3 **In the dialog box, set the Width to 468 px and the Height to 60 px to match the Artboard. Click OK. Fill the rectangle with Pure Red and apply a Stroke of None.**

4. **Send the rectangle to the back. Drag vertical and horizontal guides to mark the center of the selected rectangle.**

   This is to make certain that all the objects you use are centered on the banner.

   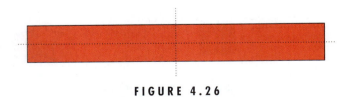

   FIGURE 4.26

5. **From above the Artboard, select the "Now Coming to a Theater Near You" text block.**

6. **Fill the text with Yellow. Show the bounding box from the View menu.**

7. **Position the text block near the top of the rectangle. The center handles of the bounding box should rest on the vertical center guide.**

   FIGURE 4.27

8. **Drag the text block to the bottom of the rectangle while pressing Option/Alt to duplicate the block. Hold the Shift key as you drag to constrain the move.**

   This creates a duplicate text block.

9. **With the duplicate text block selected, double-click the Scale tool in the Toolbox and set the Uniform Scale to 50%. Click OK.**

10. **Fill the selected text with White. Hide the guides to see the banner more. Hide the bounding box.**

    FIGURE 4.28

11. **Save the document with the same name to your WIP_04 folder. Keep the document open for the next exercise.**

Set the Blend Options

1 From the Object menu, choose Blend>Blend Options. In the dialog box, set the Spacing menu to Specified Steps and type "3" in the input field. Click OK.

The Specified Steps option tells the blend operation to create copies of the selected paths in between the originals. The number you type in the text field represents the number of copies you want Illustrator to make.

FIGURE 4.29

2 Select the two text blocks. Choose Object>Blend>Make to apply the blending operation.

The keyboard shortcut for Blend>Make is Option/Alt-Command/Control-B. The blend creates three "tweens" in between the two originals. The tweens' color ranges from the white type at the bottom to the yellow type at the top.

FIGURE 4.30

3 Choose Object>Expand to extract the objects from the blend. Select Object>Ungroup to ungroup the five lines of text objects.

Each line of text is now a separate object with grouped letters.

If you want the text blocks to appear in the exact blended positions (see Figure 4.30), you would not expand the blend. Instead, the blend would remain unchanged and you would export the animation with the Animate Blends option selected in the Macromedia Flash Options dialog box. However, you will rearrange these blended objects, so you must expand and ungroup them to select them.

4 In the Layers palette, double-click Layer 1 and rename it "Frame 1".

5 Drag the Frame 1 layer down to the Create New Layer icon in the Layers palette four times.

You should have five layers in the Layers palette.

6 Moving up from Frame 1, rename the other layers "Frame 2", "Frame 3", and so on, until you have "Frame 5" at the top of the list.

LEVEL 2   168   Chapter 4   Working with Animations

7 **Click the Frame 1 layer to make it active. Press Option/Alt and click Frame 1's Visibility icon.**

This hides all the other layers except the active Frame 1 layer.

8 **Select and delete all individual text groups except the group at the bottom.**

The animation starts with the smaller text group. As the animation runs, the text becomes larger and larger while it changes colors, until it reaches the final yellow type at the top of the banner.

FIGURE 4.31

9 **Click Frame 2 to make it active. Press Option/Alt and click Frame 2's Visibility icon twice.**

The first click shows all layers; the second click hides all layers except Frame 2.

10 **Select and delete all text groups except the second group from the bottom.**

FIGURE 4.32

11 **Save your changes. Keep the document open for the next exercise.**

Customize the Objects on the Layers

1 **Click Frame 3 to make it active. Press Option/Alt and click the Visibility icon of Frame 3 twice.**

2 **Select and delete all text groups except the third group from the bottom.**

FIGURE 4.33

3 **Click Frame 4 to make it active. Press Option/Alt and click the Visibility icon of Frame 4 twice.**

4 **Select and delete all text groups except the second group from the top.**

FIGURE 4.34

Chapter 4   Working with Animations   **169**   LEVEL 2

5   Click Frame 5 to make it active. Press Option/Alt and click the Visibility icon of Frame 5 twice.

6   Select and delete all text groups except the group at the top.

NOW COMING TO A THEATER NEAR YOU!

FIGURE 4.35

7   Press Option/Alt and click the Visibility icon of Frame 5 once.

This shows all layers, bringing all the objects back into view. All objects to be included in an animation must have the Visibility icon of their layer showing.

8   Press Command/Control-A to select all the objects on the Artboard, including the red rectangles. In the Align palette, click the Horizontal Align Center and the Vertical Align Center options.

This moves all the text groups onto one line. In the animation, they appear to originate from the same location. Do not be concerned if the aligned objects move slightly away from the Artboard, which does not affect animations. The Artboard was used only to position the elements.

9   Save your changes. Keep the document open for the next exercise.

Export the Blends Into an Animation

1   From the open document, choose File>Export.

2   Save the exported file in Macromedia Flash (swf) format.

3   Save the file to your WIP_04 folder as "theater_blend.swf". Click Export (Macintosh) or Save (Windows).

4   In the Macromedia Flash Export Options dialog box, set the Export As menu to AI Layers to SWF Frames.

5   Set the Frame Rate for 2 fps.

6   Select the Looping option. Click OK.

7   From the desktop, go to your WIP_04 folder and double-click the theater_blend.swf file.

Watch as the Flash Player plays the animation for you. If the Flash Player animation window is too small, enlarge it to see the objects more clearly.

8   When you've finished viewing the animation, close the Flash Player animation window.

9   Return to the Illustrator document, save your changes, and close the file.

LEVEL 2   **170**   Chapter 4   **Working with Animations**

To Extend Your Knowledge . . .

METAMORPHOSIS AND TWEENS

You can use the powerful Blend operation to create animation tweens. Once you understand how blending affects different objects, you can enter a whole new world of creative possibilities as you morph objects from one form into another.

To Extend Your Knowledge . . .

ANCHOR POINTS AND THE SPINE

If you are very creative, the Add Anchor Point tool can add anchor points to the spine. You can use the Convert Anchor Point tool to convert the new points into smooth points and adjust the spine on a curving basis.

LESSON 6 Using Symbols and Release to Layers

As you learned in Chapter 3, symbols are reusable graphical elements that maintain relationships with their instances (copies), which you place within Illustrator documents. Similar to blends, symbols were not specifically created for animations, but their ability to alter and control objects makes symbols another excellent source of objects to use in animations.

In addition to using symbols, you can use two additional time-saving options located in the Layers palette Options menu: *Release to Layers (Sequence)* and *Release to Layers (Build)*.

- The Release to Layers (Sequence) command relocates all the objects on a single layer to individual layers, which completes the setup for exporting to an animation. Once exported, this animation behaves as do all sequence-type animations, where one layer displays and then disappears as the next layer comes into view.

- The Release to Layers (Build) command relocates all the objects on a single layer to individual layers. As "build"-type animations, the objects continue to accumulate as each new layer displays, until all the objects display in the animation's final frame. As you know from manually creating a build animation earlier, you must decide which objects to delete on specific layers. When you use the Release to Layers (Build) command, Illustrator makes these decisions for you and immediately performs the necessary deletions.

In the following exercise, you use symbols to create the objects for the animation, and you assign the symbols to layers using the Release to Layers (Build) menu option. Your goal is to create an animation that looks like leaves wafting down from a tree.

Use Symbols and Release to Layers (Build)

1 From the Chapter_04 folder, open the falling_leaves.ai document. Show the Layers palettes.

FIGURE 4.36

2 In the Layers palette, click the triangular icon to show the sublayers.

3 Click the top leaf object on the Artboard. Note its level in the sequence of sublayers. Click several of the other leaf objects and note their sublayer positions.

The objects on the page are not in consecutive order in the sublayers. In the animation, we want the top leaf to show first, then the second down, and so on as the leaves go down the Artboard. This means that they have to be in a proper stacking order, from top to bottom.

4 Select the top leaf and use the Object>Arrange menu to select Bring to Front. Select the second leaf and bring it to the front. Continue down the page (in order), bringing each leaf to the front.

The top leaf is now in back of all the others that were brought to the front.

5 Click the top leaf on the Artboard again and note its sublayer position at the bottom of the sublayer list. Click each leaf down the Artboard to see its sublayer position.

As we have stated, Illustrator wants the first frame (layer) of the animation at the bottom of the layer list. The leaf at the top of the Artboard is now listed at the bottom of the sublayers. When you click each leaf as you move down the Artboard, the next sublayer in the layer list is highlighted.

FIGURE 4.37

6 **Click Layer 1 to select it. Use the Layers palette's Options menu to choose Release to Layers (Build).**

This command needs some explaining. A build animation means that each appearing object stays in view as other objects appear. At the end of the sequence, all the objects appear in the last frame.

To do this, Illustrator copies the objects and relocates them to their own layers. This process creates a total of 28 instances that you would normally have to keep track of, relocate on individual layers, and delete as necessary. Think of how tedious and mistake-ridden this process could be.

The Release to Layers (Build) command did all of the work for you in seconds.

7 **Click Layer 2's triangular sublayer icon to see its sublayers. View the sublayers and close the sublayer icon.**

Chapter 4 Working with Animations   173   LEVEL 2

Layer 2 is at the top of the layer list inside Layer 1 and is the last frame of the build animation. This means that all the objects in Layer 2 have appeared and are in view. So there are seven sublayers to match the seven objects on the Artboard.

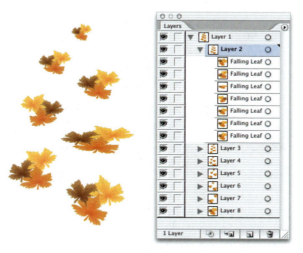

FIGURE 4.38

8 **Show the sublayer of Layer 8 and view the single object there. Close this sublayer.**

This is the first frame of the animation, which means that it is showing only the top leaf object.

9 **Press the Shift key as you select Layers 2 through 8. Drag the selected layers to be above Layer 1 in the layer list.**

10 **Select Layer 1 and drag it to be above Layer 2 in the layer list to keep the numbers in sequence. Keep Layer 1 selected.**

We will have Layer 1 be an empty frame between the ending frame and the starting frame as the animation loops.

11 **Use the Rectangle tool to draw a small square under the top instance on the Artboard (see Figure 4.39). Paint the square with a Fill of White and a Stroke of None.**

The white square creates a blank frame (layer), so the animation pauses slightly at its end before starting over. The animation process does not include empty layers, so you must place an object on the layer. This object, however, cannot be painted with None. The background is white, so the square was painted white. For an animation that takes place on a colored background, paint the empty frame object the same color as the background.

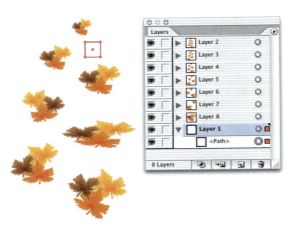

FIGURE 4.39

12 Save the document with the same name to your WIP_04 folder. Keep the document open for the next exercise.

All the objects and their layers are in sequence. The only step left is to export the document to an animation.

Export the Build Animation

1 In the open document, choose File>Export. Save the file to your WIP_04 folder in SWF format; name it "falling_leaves.swf".

2 In the Macromedia Flash Export Options dialog box, set the Export As menu to AI Layers to SWF Frames.

3 Set the Frame Rate to 3 fps. Select the Looping option.

4 This time select Generate HTML. Click OK.

When the Generate HTML option is selected another file named falling_leaves.html will be saved to the same folder as the animation. If you open this HTML file in your browser, you will see the animation at work.

5 From the desktop, go to the WIP _04 folder and double-click the falling_leaves.swf file.

Watch as the Flash Player displays your animation, which shows the top leaf first and remains in view as the second leaf appears. All the appearing leaves remain in view until the last leaf appears, ending the animation sequence. This is what a "build" animation does — builds the final frame.

6 Close the animation in the Flash Player.

Chapter 4   Working with Animations   **175**   **LEVEL 2**

7   Use your browser to open the falling_leaves.html document from your WIP_04 folder.

The browser will play the animation. The HTML code in the falling_leaves.html text file is the code you should include in your own HTML documents to play animations on your Web sites. Resize the browser window to see how the animation reduces or enlarges in size.

8   Close the browser window that is playing the animation.

9   Return to the Illustrator document. Save your changes and close the file.

To Extend Your Knowledge . . .

STACKING ORDER

When you use the Release to Layers options, pay close attention to the stacking order of the objects on the Artboard. The Release to Layers operations do exactly what you tell them to do. If you do not place the objects in the proper stacking order, the animation will not work correctly.

S U M M A R Y

In Chapter 4, you learned how to use Illustrator to export animated files created and developed in the Layers palette. You learned about two types of animations: build (cumulative) and sequence (noncumulative). You used the Export option of the File menu and applied settings in the Export dialog boxes to customize the animations according to the build and sequence types.

You learned that you can include raster objects in animations, either by themselves or with vector objects. You discovered how to use blends in animations and how the blend operation creates multiple objects in an animation. You learned additional features of the Layers palette and discovered how objects on layers become frames when exported as SWF files.

You found that you can incorporate symbols in an animation, which allows you to replace multiple instances with a single click, maintaining all of the transformations applied to the original instances. Finally, you became familiar with two of the Layers palette's options — Release to Layers (Build) and Release to Layers (Sequence). These features automatically assign objects to layers and delete layers as necessary, saving significant amounts of development time.

K E Y   T E R M S

Animations	Build (cumulative)	Frame
Blend options	Flash Player	Frames per second (fps)

Frame rate	Layers palette	Release to Layers (Sequence)
Layers	Loop	Sequence (noncumulative)
Layer list	Release to Layers (Build)	Tween

CHECKING CONCEPTS AND TERMS

MULTIPLE CHOICE

Circle the letter that matches the correct answer for each of the following questions.

1. When exporting a document as an animation, use the _____ file format.
   a. BMP (bmp)
   b. Macromedia Flash (SWF)
   c. Windows Metafile (wmf)
   d. Photoshop (psd)
   e. None of the above.

2. The _____ palette is crucial when you construct an animation.
   a. Links
   b. Layers
   c. Appearance
   d. Swatches

3. The two types of animations are _____.
   a. flip book and cinematic
   b. SVG and GIF
   c. build (cumulative) and sequence (noncumulative)
   d. build (noncumulative) and sequence (cumulative)

4. The Illustrator feature that produces copies of objects between two originals is _____.
   a. the Effects option
   b. Graphic Styles
   c. Envelope Distort
   d. the Blend option

5. The professional term for the objects in between originals is _____.
   a. tween

   b. frame
   c. loop
   d. mask

6. Which of the following cannot be used to create an animation in Illustrator?
   a. Raster images
   b. Vector paths
   c. Masked objects
   d. Gradients and patterns
   e. None of the above.

7. During a _____ animation, all the objects display in the final frame.
   a. sequence
   b. JavaScript
   c. build
   d. dynamic

8. The _____ value sets the speed of the exported animation.
   a. Looping
   b. Generate HTML
   c. Export As
   d. Frame Rate

9. When you use either of the Release to Layers options, the stacking order of the objects _____.
   a. is irrelevant
   b. has no bearing on these options
   c. is extremely important
   d. is changed by the Layers palette

Chapter 4   Working with Animations   **177**   **LEVEL 2**

10. The objects in the bottom layer in the Layers palette appear _____ when exported.

a. last in the sequence of frames

b. at a much slower rate

c. first in the sequence of frames

d. None of the above.

DISCUSSION QUESTIONS

1. Describe three different situations that may require an animation.

2. Describe the Release to Layers function and discuss its importance.

3. Frame rate can dramatically impact a viewer's experience as he watches your animation. Describe three different situations where you might consider using slow or fast frame rates.

SKILL DRILL

Skill Drills reinforce project skills. Each skill that is reinforced is the same as, or nearly the same as, a skill we presented in the lessons. We provide detailed instructions in a step-by-step format. You should complete these exercises in order.

1. Create a Banner with Animated Phrases

One of your clients, a local bank, wants to put several of their selling phrases on their Web site. The limited space on the page does not allow all the phrases to fit, so you offer to create an animated banner that displays the phrases one after the other (a sequence animation).

1. From the Chapter_04 folder, open the bank_banner.ai document. Show the Swatches, Layers, and Align palettes.

2. Press Command/Control-A to select all the objects. In the Align palette, click Horizontal Align Center and Vertical Align Center options to center the objects.

3. Select the rectangle and choose Inverse from the Select menu. Fill all the selected text blocks with White. Deselect all objects.

4. From the Layers palette Options menu, choose Release to Layers (Sequence).

5. Select all the new layers and drag them above Layer 1.

   Layer 7 possesses the rectangle, which you must copy to all the layers that contain type.

6. Select the rectangle on the Artboard and copy it. Drag Layer 7 and Layer 1 to the Trash icon in the Layers palette.

   You no longer need Layer 7's blank rectangle and the empty Layer 1.

7. In the Layers palette Options menu, make certain that Paste Remembers Layers is unselected.

   Because you copied the rectangle from a different layer, you do not want the pasting to remember this layer. This will paste the rectangle on the selected layer.

8. Click Layer 6's Target button to select its text block. Press Command/Control-B to paste the rectangle behind the text block on that layer.

9. Move up the layer list. Target each layer text block and paste the rectangle behind it. Do this for all other layers.

   Check that each layer's sublayers have a pasted rectangle.

10. Save the document with the same name to your WIP_04 folder. Keep the document open.

11. Export the document in SWF format as "bank_banner.swf" to your WIP_04 folder. Set the Export As for AI Layers to SWF Frames. Select the Looping option. In the Frame Rate input field, type "0.50". Deselect Generate HTML (if selected). Click OK.

    This frame rate briefly pauses so the viewer has time to read the phrase.

12. From the desktop, go to the WIP_04 folder and double-click the exported file.

    Watch your animation as Flash Player plays it.

FIGURE 4.40

13. Return to the Illustrator document and close it.

2. Create Animated Arrows

A client asked you to build a banner with a moving arrow for his Web site. Your task is to create an animation with the arrow path we supplied for you.

1. Open arrows.ai from the Chapter_04 folder. Open the Swatches and Layers palettes.

2. Select the arrow object and drag it to the right edge of the rectangular guide. Press the Option/Alt-Shift key to make a duplicate and constrain the move (see Figure 4.41).

FIGURE 4.41

3. Select the two arrows. In the Object>Blend menu, select Blend Options and set the Spacing menu for Specified Steps. Type "2" in the input box and click OK.

   You have specified that there will be two duplicates in between the two originals.

4. Press Command/Control-Option/Alt-B to blend the objects.

   You now have four objects that move from left to right in sequence. You do not have to modify the blend. In Preview mode, you see that the blend contains four arrows. If you go to Outline view, you see the "spine" (single line path) that connects the two original arrow paths.

5. Use the Direct Selection tool to select the far-right duplicate. Choose Effect>Stylize>Inner Glow.

   Using the Direct Selection tool, you can still individually select blended original objects for modifications.

6. Set the Mode to Screen. Click the color swatch to the right of the Mode menu. In the Color Picker, set a yellow color and click OK. Back in the Inner Glow dialog box, select the Center option. Click OK.

   Blends have in-between steps that show the two original objects' graduation of paint attributes. The duplicate on the right was given an Inner Glow; the blend tweens now reflect this, showing an increase in color intensity as they move right.

FIGURE 4.42

7. From the File menu, choose Export.

8. In the Export dialog box, choose Macromedia Flash (swf). Save the file to your WIP_04 folder as "arrows.swf". Click Export (Macintosh) or Save (Windows).

9. In the Macromedia Flash Export Options dialog box, set the Export As menu to AI Layers to SWF Frames. Set the Frame Rate for 2 fps.

   You have not expanded and ungrouped the blended objects from the blend, so you may select the Animate Blends option in the Macromedia Flash Options dialog box.

10. Turn on Looping. Make sure the Generate HTML is unselected. Select the Animate Blends in the bottom-left of the dialog box. Click OK.

    With the Animate Blends option selected, the entire blend and its components are automatically assigned to the animation. This option eliminates all the work we did before in layers — expanding, ungrouping, and deleting objects.

11. From the desktop, go to the WIP_04 folder and double-click the arrows.swf file to see your animation.

12. Return to the Illustrator document and save it with the same name to your WIP_04 folder. Close the document.

3. Create a Flaming Apple Animation

The owner of The Flaming Apple restaurant hired you to create a special animation for her Web site. She wants the animation to show an apple suddenly bursting into flames.

1. From the Chapter_04 folder, open the flaming_apple.ai document. Open the Layers, Symbols, and Align palettes.

2. Drag the Green Apple and Prometheus symbols from the Symbols palette to the Artboard. Select the two instances and scale them a uniform 50%.

3. Position the Green Apple instance on the Artboard's left side and the Prometheus instance to the right side.

4. From the Object menu, choose Blend>Blend Options. Set the Spacing menu for Specified Steps with a Number of 3. Click OK.

5. Select the two instances. Press Command/Control-Option/Alt-B to apply the blend. Keep the blend selected.

    The blend creates a sequence of tweens to give the impression that the normal apple is gradually bursting into flames.

FIGURE 4.43

6. From the Object menu, choose Expand. Ungroup the expanded objects. Click the Horizontal Align Center and Vertical Align Bottom options in the Align palette.

7. In the Layers palette, click the triangular icon of Layer 1 to see its sublayers.

    The original apple, which you dragged to the Artboard first, should reside on the bottom sublayer.

8. Choose Release to Layers (Sequence) from the Layers palette Options menu.

    Layer 1 is selected as you do this, so all of its sublayers are converted to normal layers. They reside, however, inside Layer 1; you must relocate them.

9. Save the document with the same name to your WIP_04 folder. Keep the document open for the next exercise.

4. Continue the Flaming Apple Animation

1. Press the Shift key as you select all the new layers inside Layer 1. From the Layers palette's Options menu, choose Reverse Order.

    The original apple (the first in the animation sequence) is now at the top of the new layers list. We have been using Illustrator's default setting, which makes the bottom layer the first animation frame. You can change this as you export the animation.

Chapter 4   Working with Animations   **181**   LEVEL 2

2. Drag the selected layers to above Layer 1 in the layer list.

3. Click Layer 1 to make it active.

   The layers' numbers are out of sequence, but this does not affect the sequence of frames in an animation. The physical order of the layers (or frames) in the Layers palette controls the animation.

4. Use the Rectangle tool to draw a small rectangle on Layer 1 that is within the bounding box of the other objects. Paint the rectangle with a Fill of White and Stroke of None.

   This unpainted object makes Layer 1 an empty frame that appears by itself at the end of the animation.

5. Export the document to SWF format as "flaming_apple.swf" in your WIP_04 folder.

6. The Export As should be AI Layers to SWF Frames. Select Looping and set the Frame Rate for 3 fps. The Generate HTML and Animate Blends options should not be selected.

7. At the bottom of the Macromedia Flash (SWF) Format Options dialog box, select the Layer Order menu and choose Top Down. Click OK.

   This changes the sequence of the layers to be exported, from the top layer down to the bottom layer.

8. From the desktop, go to your WIP_04 folder and double-click the flaming_apple.swf file to see your animation play.

   Enlarge the Flash Player window, if necessary, so you see the animation more clearly. The animation remains in proportion to the size of the window.

FIGURE 4.44

9. Return to the Illustrator document and close it.

5. Create an Animation from Raster Objects

A new client brought you GIF images created by another artist. She hopes that you can use the images to make an animation. Your task is to apply the images to layers and export the layers as an animation.

1. Open bouncing_heart.ai from the Chapter_04 folder. Open the Layers and Align palettes.

   In this exercise, you create a sequence animation with the Release to Layers option. The objects must be in proper sequence in the stacking order to appear correctly. The images are in the order they should appear, but the stacking order needs adjustment.

2. In the Layers palette, click the triangular sublayer icon to the left of Layer 1's name.

   This expands the sublayers view.

3. Select the top object on the Artboard.

   Note that the corresponding sublayer is at the bottom of the layer list. To keep the top-to-bottom arrangement more synchronized, we need to put the top Artboard object at the top of the layer list.

4. Press the Shift key and click all the other sublayers to select them. In the Layers palette Options menu, choose Reverse Order.

   The Reverse Order option reverses the layer order of all selected layers (or sublayers). The top object on the Artboard is now at the top of the sublayer list.

5. Select Layer 1. From the Layer's palette's Options menu, choose Release to Layers (Sequence).

   This converts the sublayers to actual layers, though they still reside inside Layer 1.

6. Select all the new layers and drag them above Layer 1. Select Layer 1 and drag it above Layer 2.

7. Click Layer 1 to make it active. Draw a small square within the Artboard's boundaries. Fill the square with White and apply a Stroke of None.

   This adds a blank transitional frame between the ending and beginning frames when the animation loops.

8. Select all the images on the Artboard. In the Align palette, click the Horizontal Align Center and Vertical Align Center options.

   The objects are aligned to appear from one location.

9. Export the document to SWF format as "bouncing_heart.swf" in your WIP_04 folder.

10. In the Macromedia Flash (SWF) Format Options dialog box, set the Export As menu to AI Layers to SWF Frames. Select Looping and set the Frame Rate to 3. Click the Layer Order menu and set it for Top Down. Click OK.

    The Top Down layer order starts the animation with the top layer (frame).

11. From the desktop, go to your WIP_04 folder and double-click the bouncing_heart.swf file.

    Watch your animation play in Flash Player. Enlarge the Flash Player window if necessary.

FIGURE 4.45

12. Return to the Illustrator document. Save your changes and close the document.

Chapter 4   **Working with Animations**   **183**   **LEVEL 2**

CHALLENGE

Challenge exercises expand on, or are somewhat related to, skills that we presented in the lessons. Each exercise provides a brief introduction, followed by numbered-step instructions that are not as detailed as those in the Skill Drill exercises. You should complete these exercises in order.

1. Create Your Own Slide Show

The directors of your community asked you to lecture to a local arts group and show the members your work. You select a few of your best images that are accessible in digital format. In this exercise, you include those images in a slide show that loops unattended as you speak.

1. Create a new letter-size RGB document with a landscape orientation. Open the Layers and Align palettes.

2. Place any number of your favorite photos into the document.

   The photos can be of various sizes.

3. Overlap the photos on top of one another, leaving enough of each photo visible so you can identify each image.

4. Arrange the photos from front to back (the stacking order) in the order in which you want them to appear.

5. Select all the photos and click the Horizontal Align Center and Vertical Align Bottom options.

   The photos all appear from the same location.

6. Select Layer 1. In the Layers palette Options menu, choose Release to Layers (Sequence).

7. Select all the new layers and drag them above Layer 1.

8. Select Layer 1 and drag it to the Trash icon at the bottom of the palette.

9. Save the document as "fave_fotos.ai" to the WIP_04 folder. Keep the document open.

10. Export the document to SWF format as "fave_fotos.swf" in your WIP_04 folder.

11. Set the Export As menu to AI Layers to SWF Frames. Set the Frame Rate to 2 fps, and turn on Looping. Click the Layer Order menu and set it for Top Down. Click OK.

12. From the desktop, go to your WIP_04 folder and double-click the fave_fotos.swf animation to see your animation play.

13. Return to the Illustrator document and close it.

2. Create a Raster Animation

One of your clients is a manager at an airline company. He hired you to create an animated sign for the projector screen that warns people to fasten their seat belts before taking off.

1. Open the document airliner.ai from the Chapter_04 folder. Open the Layers palette.

2. Select the airline photo that is grouped with the yellow type.

3. From the Object menu, rasterize the objects with an RGB Color Model, High Resolution (300 ppi), and the Background set to White.

FIGURE 4.46

4. Copy the rasterized object and press Command/Control-F four times to paste duplicates in the same position as the original.

5. In the Layers palette, click the triangular sublayer icon on Layer 1 to see the photos on their sublayers.

6. In the Layers palette Options menu, choose Release to Layers (Sequence).

   This converts all the sublayers to actual layers. They are no longer sublayers despite being inside Layer 1. To be accessible to animation, you must relocate them from the Layers palette to become individual layers.

7. Press the Shift key and select all the new layers inside Layer 1. Drag them above Layer 1 in the layer list.

8. Select Layer 1 and drag it to the Trash icon in the Layers palette.

9. Save the document with the same name to your WIP_04 folder. Keep the document open for the next exercise.

3. Finish the Seat Belts Animation

The layer frames are set up for your Fasten Your Seat Belts animation. The next step is to change the opaque qualities of each photo frame so that the photo in the animation fades in and out.

1. In the open document, click Layer 3's Target button to select the photo on this layer.

   We have ignored working on Layer 2, which is the first to appear in the animation. The Layer 2 photo will be 100% opacity, so we have moved on to Layer 3.

2. Show the Transparency palette. In the Opacity input field, type 85. Press Return/Enter to apply this.

   This sets the Layer 3 photo opacity to 85%. The idea of the animation is to have the photo become lighter and lighter as the frames progress.

3. Click the Target button of Layer 4 to select its photo on the Artboard.

4. Use the Transparency palette to apply an opacity of 65. Press Return/Enter to apply.

5. Click the Target button of Layer 5 to select its photo on the Artboard. Set the opacity to 50 and apply.

6. Click the Target button of Layer 6 to select its photo on the Artboard. Set the opacity to 35 and apply.

7. Make certain that all layers have their Visibility icon showing.

   Remember, hidden layers do not export to animations.

8. Export the document to SWF format as "airliner.swf" in your WIP_04 folder.

9. In the Macromedia Flash (SWF) Format Options dialog box, set the Export As menu to AI Layers to SWF Frames. Set the Frame Rate to 3 and select Looping. Set the Layer Order menu for Top Down. Click OK.

10. From the desktop, go to your WIP_04 folder and double-click the airliner.swf file to see the animation play.

FIGURE 4.47

11. Return to the Illustrator document. Save your changes and close the document.

4. Create an Animation with Blends

One of your clients owns a lightbulb company. He developed a new line of colored lightbulbs. The client hired you to design an animation for his corporate Web site.

1. Open lightbulb.ai from the Chapter_04 folder. Open the Swatches and Layers palettes.

2. Use the Direct Selection tool to click the bulb's top section. Fill the path with Starry Night Blue and apply a Stroke of None.

3. Use the Selection tool to select the entire bulb. Drag the bulb to the Artboard's right side (pressing the Shift key to constrain). Press Option/Alt and release the mouse to duplicate.

4. Use the Direct Selection tool to select the top section of the duplicate lightbulb. Fill the path with Pure Yellow and apply a Stroke of None.

5. From the Object menu, choose Blend>Blend Options. Change the Spacing menu to Specified Steps and set the Steps to 4. Click OK.

6. Select the two lightbulbs and press Command/Control-Option/Alt-B to apply the blend.

   Four duplicate bulbs appear in between the blue and yellow originals. With the blend selected, you can see the spine running through the various objects.

FIGURE 4.48

7. Change to Outline mode. In the View menu, make certain that Snap to Point has a checkmark next to its name.

   This gives you a much clearer view of the spine connecting the two lightbulbs.

8. Use the Direct Selection tool to click the spine's far-right anchor point and select it. Drag this point to the left (pressing the Shift key to constrain) so that the dragged point snaps on top of the far-left point.

   This moves all the objects to one place and is equivalent to using the Align palette to align all objects into one location.

9. Return to Preview mode. Save the document with the same name to your WIP_04 folder. Keep the document open for the next exercise.

5. Complete the Lightbulb Animation

You have created the lightbulb animation. You need only to export the blend to an animation.

1. In the open document, choose File>Export and set the file format to SWF.

2. Save the file to your WIP_04 folder as "lightbulb.swf".

3. Set the Export As menu to AI Layers to SWF Frames.

4. Select the Looping option. Set the Frame Rate to 2 fps. Click the Layer Order menu and set it for Bottom Up.

5. At the bottom of the Macromedia Flash (SWF) Format Options dialog box, click the Animate Blends option.

   This exports all the bulbs in the blend to the animation.

6. From the desktop, go to your WIP_04 folder and double-click the lightbulb.swf file.

   Watch your animation being played by Flash Player.

7. When finished viewing, return to the Illustrator document and close the document.

FIGURE 4.49

PORTFOLIO BUILDER

Create a Web Banner with Blinking Neon Edges

There is nothing more eye-catching (or irritating) than something blinking on an Internet Web page. It does do its job, however, and gets the viewer's attention. In this exercise, you create a blinking banner that could later be combined with text to show on a Web page.

1. Create a new RGB document with the Artboard set to 150 × 200 pixels. Open the Layers palette.

2. Draw a rounded-corner rectangle to match the Artboard. Fill the rectangle with Black Light Blue from the Swatches palette, and apply a Stroke of None.

3. From the Layers palette, drag Layer 1 to the Create New Layer icon.

4. Rename the new layer "Layer 2". Click its Target button to select its rectangle.

5. Apply an Inner Glow effect with default settings to the selected rectangle.

6. Save the Illustrator document to your WIP_04 folder as "blinking_banner.ai".

7. From the File menu, choose Export. Save the file in SWF format to your WIP_04 folder. Name the file "blinking_banner.swf".

8. Set the Export As menu to AI Layers to SWF Frames with a Frame Rate of 3 fps. Select Looping and make certain that Animate Blends is not selected.

9. From the desktop, go to your WIP_04 folder and double-click the blinking_banner.swf file to see your animation play.

10. Close the document.

LEVEL 2

CHAPTER 5

Creating Web Objects

OBJECTIVES

In this chapter, you learn how to:

- Save Internet images

- Correct banding

- Adjust color ranges

- Eliminate artifacts

- Create image maps

- Slice images

- Save documents as HTML Web pages

Why Would I Do This?

Ten short years ago, few designers placed much value in developing skills for creating and publishing Web objects. At that time, the technology was just starting to emerge, and only a relatively small group of forward-thinking designers realized its extensive possibilities. Today, a graphic designer who cannot develop objects for the Internet is at a severe disadvantage as a creative professional. Most clients and employers boast some sort of presence on the Web; if you want to work with those individuals or organizations, you must know how to prepare images for use on the Internet.

Fully half of the artwork and illustrations developed by today's professional graphic artists are destined for publishing on the World Wide Web. Illustrator is the perfect companion for the artist who needs to create buttons, navigation strategies, technical illustrations, banner ads, and entire Web pages. In this chapter, you learn how to develop all of these graphical elements, and you explore the issues surrounding color predictability and file size. You also discover which file formats work best for various applications on the Web.

VISUAL SUMMARY

Considered to be one of the preeminent illustration and graphics applications, Illustrator continues to provide the cutting-edge features and functions that meet the needs of today's graphic artists and designers. As the Web becomes increasingly prevalent in our everyday lives, the design community continues to demand that illustration and graphic applications effectively generate Web-compliant visuals. In response to that demand, the Illustrator program extends far beyond the tools and techniques required to produce printed images; the powerful new Illustrator CS2 features and functions allow users to create effective, highly complex graphic objects for delivery on the Web.

If you need to effectively build, manage, update, and maintain a Web site, Illustrator is not the right choice for the job. It is certainly an excellent tool for creating graphics for the Web, and it provides the necessary tools to develop simple individual Web pages — but it's not meant to replace dedicated applications such as Dreamweaver, FrontPage, GoLive, or similar programs. As you become more familiar with Illustrator and the features it offers for creating Web objects, you will better understand the program's strengths (and weaknesses) in creating Web objects.

We begin the chapter with an introduction to the Save for Web dialog. This feature provides a wide range of control over such things as colors, file formats, transparency, and other attributes.

Most importantly, you can compare as many as four different options at once, using various preview settings.

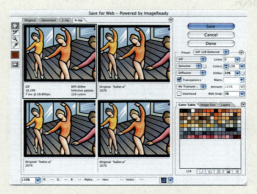

FIGURE 5.1

You learn the pitfalls of using gradients and how to avoid unsightly *banding*— visible lines and stripes that often appear in artwork incorrectly formatted for use on the Web.

FIGURE 5.2

You examine anti-aliased images and observe the obvious blemishes that appear when you place an image on a Web page with a colored background. Lesson 3 shows you several effective methods for rectifying this problem.

FIGURE 5.3

You learn how to use the Attributes palette to assign links to images. When you apply a URL to a vector path, you create an image map, known to Webmasters in Internet jargon as a "hotspot" link. For example, many Web graphics do not contain text links; instead, they show a pointing finger to indicate a link (hotspot) on an image map (the graphic).

FIGURE 5.4

In addition, you explore various options that allow you to save your artwork as a combination of HTML and images, images alone, or just the code required to accurately render your pages in today's most popular browsers.

FIGURE 5.5

You discover how to divide images and Web pages into slices, a specialized type of Web object that allows for faster uploading of larger images. Slices are commonly used by professionals to accommodate for slower connections while taking advantage of large illustrations.

FIGURE 5.6

Chapter 5   Creating Web Objects   **193**   LEVEL 2

LESSON 1   Using Save for Web

Illustrator offers two methods to save objects as external raster files. You are already familiar with the first method — the File>Export option. This method is a good choice in many situations but offers limited choices for saving files for use on the Web. File>Export does not include GIF or PNG formats, and you cannot use the Export dialog box to adjust image colors, matting, dithering, or a host of other specifications geared toward the Web.

The second method, File>Save for Web, offers a feature-rich dialog box that includes a preview of how the image will look when exported, as well as several settings that allow you to make critical adjustments before you save the image. Perhaps the most important choice in the Save for Web dialog box is the file format. Illustrator supports a wide variety of file formats, including several that are specifically engineered for use on the Internet, including JPEG, GIF, and PNG.

- Choose the JPEG (Joint Photographic Experts Group) format when the artwork includes continuous-tone images, such as photographs. You can also use the JPEG format when artwork contains many smooth blends, which would result in unattractive banding when saved as a GIF file.

- GIF (Graphic Interchange Format) is considered the standard for creating small images that contain mostly flat colors. When saving Illustrator files as GIF images, make sure to include *dithering*, which converts colors outside of the Web palette into Web-safe colors.

- *PNG* (Portable Network Graphic) is another bitmap format that's gaining popularity among Web designers. It supports a greater range of colors than GIF, and it supports transparency — often a critically important concern when developing complex, overlapping page elements for the Web.

Exercise Setup

Before you begin doing chapter exercises, go to the desktop and drag the following folders from the Chapter_05 folder to the WIP_05 folder: Feathered Friends, HTML Only, Shell, Sliced Bananas, Star Zoom, and Valentine Web. These folders must be in the proper location to ensure that the exercises work correctly with files and images.

In the following exercise, you use the Save for Web dialog box to save Illustrator objects to a variety of popular Web-compliant formats.

Explore Save for Web

1 Open ballet.ai from the Chapter_05 folder.

2 From the File menu, choose Save for Web. In the dialog box, click the Original tab in the upper-left corner.

Make sure the appropriate monitor setting is selected for Macintosh or Windows.

The Original preview image represents the artwork as you see it on the Artboard, without any settings applied to it. The Original preview can be used for comparison when you use the other tabs to apply the settings located on the dialog box's right side.

FIGURE 5.7

Chapter 5   Creating Web Objects   **195**   LEVEL 2

3   **Click the Optimized tab to the right of the Original tab.**

The Optimized view applies the GIF file format to the preview. This format's settings are set by Adobe to give the image the best attributes so that it uploads to and appears on the Internet with optimal quality. You can make changes with the setting menus located on the dialog box's right.

"GIF" appears in the bottom-left corner of the preview window. The number underneath this is the image's file size if saved with the current settings. Underneath the file size is the number of seconds it takes to upload the image to a viewer's browser; this speed is determined by "kbps" (kilobytes per second), which is the speed of the modem. In Figure 5.8, you are told that the image will take eight seconds to upload to a 28.8 kbps modem.

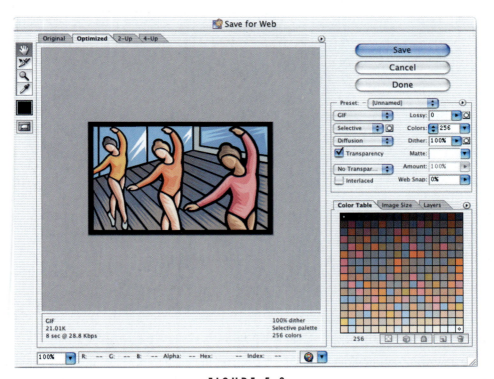

FIGURE 5.8

4 **Click the 2-Up tab to the right of the Optimized tab. Observe the numbers and information at the bottom of each preview type.**

This preview window compares the GIF image to the Original image. Viewing multiple versions at the same time allows you to compare the critical balance between quality and file size.

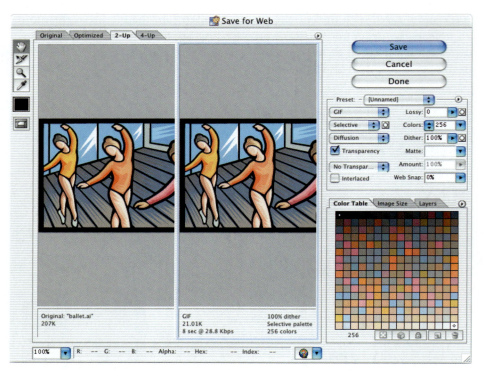

FIGURE 5.9

5 **Click the 4-Up tab to the right of the 2-Up tab.**

This preview window provides four samples of the image. The top-left image is the original, shown in its actual document preview. The other three images show how the file would look if you saved it in GIF format with various dithering settings and numbers of colors. Keep in mind that any preview window, including the Original, may be selected and new settings applied from the right of the dialog box.

Note that the entire image does not completely show in each preview window.

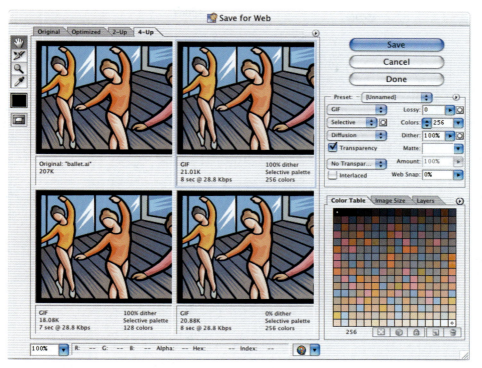

FIGURE 5.10

6 **Click the Zoom tool icon in the upper-left corner of the dialog box. Press Option/Alt and click the Zoom tool on the top-left preview image to reduce its size to 66.7%.**

The Zoom tool works only when clicked on a selected preview image, although all the images reduce in size to show the entire image in each window. The field in the dialog box's bottom-left corner shows the actual size percentage. You can also use the menu to the right of the percentage box to manually change the size of the preview images.

FIGURE 5.11

7   **Use the View Percentage menu in the dialog box's bottom-left to change the view to 200%.**

8   **Select the Hand tool in the dialog box's upper-left and drag the cursor on the top-left image.**

The Hand tool allows you to move the images. The images are synchronized, so moving one moves all of them simultaneously.

9   **Continue to the next exercise.**

Set File Formats

1 Click the top-right preview image. From the dialog box's right side, use the Preset menu to choose GIF 64 Dithered.

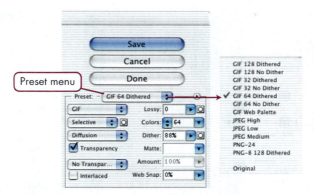

FIGURE 5.12

Full-color images may contain millions of colors with a wide range of color values. This is not acceptable in the limited Internet palette. Dithering reduces the color range of images to the 256 (or fewer) colors seen in 8-bit GIF images. Observe the image after choosing GIF 64 Dithered to see how the limited color range affects the clarity of the image elements.

2 Select the bottom-left preview image and use the Preset menu to choose GIF 32 No Dither.

3 Select the bottom-right image and use the Preset menu to set it for GIF Web Palette.

Each setting impacts the image's visual quality: GIF 64 has 64 colors, GIF 32 has 32, and the GIF Web Palette has 61 colors (based on the Web-safe color palette).

4 Use the dialog box Zoom tool to click the selected bottom-right image three times. Use the dialog box's Hand tool to drag the selected preview image to show more of the far-right dancer.

The Zoom tool takes you to 300% viewing. The details in the images' appearances become more apparent at this size. The **Color Table** in the dialog box reflects the colors applied to the selected preview image.

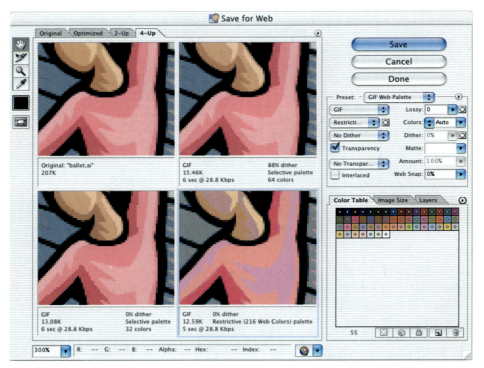

FIGURE 5.13

5   **Click the bottom-left image to select it.**

The settings change on the right side of the dialog box. The Color Table now shows 32 colors. The fewer colors an image contains, the smaller it is and the faster it loads into the viewer's browser.

6   **Use the View Percentage menu in the dialog box to return to 100% view. Click the top-right image to select it.**

7   **Use the Preset menu of the dialog box to set the format to JPEG Low.**

We highly recommend that you apply JPEG file formats to Web images that contain fine details. The JPEG format retains clarity and definition in the work. This is especially true of photographs.

8   **Click the bottom-left preview image. Change its format setting to JPEG Medium.**

You can change each of the preview images (including the Original) to different file formats and settings. You can simultaneously preview GIF, JPEG, and PNG formats, compare the results, and choose the best image for the job. When you hit Save, the settings of your selected preview image are applied to the exported file.

Chapter 5   Creating Web Objects   **201**   LEVEL 2

9 Click the bottom-right preview image. Change the format setting to JPEG High.

The information under each image shows the file size and number of seconds required to upload the file to a browser.

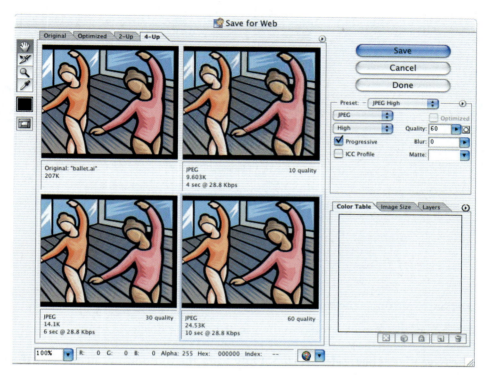

FIGURE 5.14

10 Continue to the next exercise.

In the next exercise, you use the Save for Web dialog box to create external images suitable for the Web.

Save File Formats

1 From the open document, choose JPEG Medium from the Preset menu in the dialog box.

2 In the dialog box's lower-right section, click the Image Size tab.

3 Change the Percent to 50 and click Apply.

The Percent value allows you to specify the file's finished size. The Width and Height values reflect the size of the image in pixels.

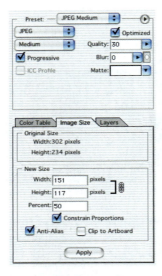

FIGURE 5.15

4. **Click the Save button at the top-right of the dialog box.**

   This step applies the current settings to the selected preview image.

5. **From the Save dialog box, select Images Only from the top pop-up menu. Save the image to your WIP_05 folder.**

   You do not need to name the saved file. Illustrator automatically appends the "jpg" extension to the file name and closes the dialog box. Saving images from the Save for Web feature also closes its dialog box.

   The Images Only saves only the raster image. The HTML and Images option saves the raster image and a separate HTML file that possesses the name of the saved image in its code. The HTML Only option saves just the HTML file, but does not save a raster image.

FIGURE 5.16

6. **From the File menu, choose Save for Web. Click the 4-Up tab.**

7. **Select the top-right preview image. Use the Preset menu on the right to choose GIF 128 Dithered. Leave all other settings the same.**

8. **Save the file to your WIP_05 folder, with the pop-up menu set to Images Only.**

   The file name automatically receives the "gif" extension.

Chapter 5   Creating Web Objects   **203**

9 Return to the Save for Web feature. Click the 4-Up tab. Select the bottom-left image and use the Preset menu to choose PNG-8 128 Dithered.

This 8-bit image has a dithering value of 88%.

10 Select the bottom-right image and choose PNG-24 from the Preset menu. Leave this preview image selected.

Note the file size and upload time of this 24-bit image, as compared to the PNG-8 128 image.

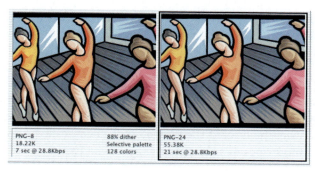

FIGURE 5.17

11 Click the Save button in the dialog box. Save the file to your WIP_05 folder, with the top pop-up menu set to Images Only.

12 Go to the desktop and launch your browser. Open your WIP_05 folder and, one at a time, drag each of the saved files to the browser window to inspect the results.

Observe how fast the images appear and note the quality of their appearance.

13 Return to the Illustrator document and close it without saving.

To Extend Your Knowledge . . .

MAINTAINING THE LOOK AND FEEL

Because various file formats support different attributes (such as transparency or continuous tones), you must ensure that converting your artwork to a Web-compliant file format doesn't substantially change the illustration's look and feel. You must find a balance between the file size and the quality of the Web-compliant file format.

You can rely on this basic rule of thumb: Any image with 256 or fewer colors can safely be saved as a GIF file, while images with more colors (generally photographic images or illustrations containing a wide range of subtle gradations) are better saved as JPEGs.

LESSON 2 Banding and Color Modification

When designing a site for viewers with 24-bit displays, you can use as many colors as you prefer. The majority of users, however, do not have the luxury of seeing millions of colors on 24-bit monitors. To reach the widest possible audience, you must design sites that accommodate the millions of people around the world who use 14-inch, 8-bit screens.

Due to the differences in the way operating systems define colors, only 216 colors (214 colors, plus white and black) share common definitions between Macintosh, Windows, and UNIX computers. These limited colors are known as **Web-safe colors**. As you observed in the previous Save for Web dialog box lesson, images with fewer colors appear less refined and "choppy." To retain the quality of your artwork, take special care in choosing the file format and number of colors to include.

The gradient is the graphic element most commonly affected by the limited Web-safe color palette. Figure 5.18 illustrates the palette's effect on a gradient. On the left, you see an object containing a colored gradient. The image on the right shows how the gradient looks when converted to Web-safe colors — which is certainly not what the artist intended when he created the design. This effect, called *banding*, is a series of unsightly *artifacts* (defects) that resemble stripes of color on your artwork. To retain the gradient's continuous tone, we recommend that you save the art to a JPEG format. Use the GIF format with caution, as it often results in banding.

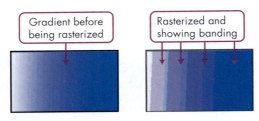

FIGURE 5.18

In this exercise, you use various methods to create high-quality Web images with small file sizes so they load quickly in a browser.

Fix Banding Problems

1. Open globe.ai from the Chapter_05 folder.

2. Zoom in on the circle painted with a radial gradient. We used the Gradient tool to alter the gradient so that the object looks like a 3-dimensional sphere.

Chapter 5 Creating Web Objects 205 LEVEL 2

Observe the excellent tonal quality of the gradient, which might suffer from banding if converted to the wrong format.

FIGURE 5.19

3 **From the File menu, choose Save for Web. Click the 4-Up tab at the top of the dialog box.**

The original image preview appears in the upper-left. The others default to GIF format.

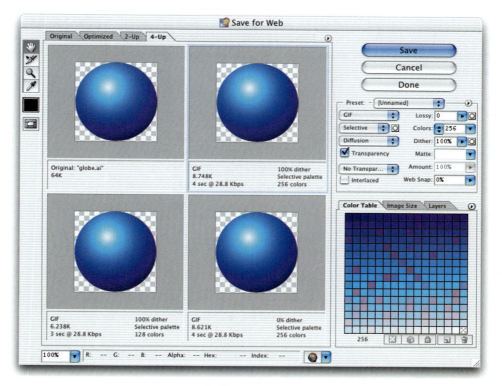

FIGURE 5.20

4 **Select the top-right preview image. Use the Preset menu to change the format to GIF 64 Dithered.**

5. **Open the pop-up options menu to the right of the Color Table; choose Select All Non-Web Safe Colors.**

   This command selects almost all the colors in the palette. Illustrator automatically shifts all non-Web-safe colors to the closest Web-safe hue or tint.

   FIGURE 5.21

6. **At the bottom of the Color Table dialog box, click the Shifts/Unshifts Selected Colors to Web Palette button.**

   This converts the unsafe colors to the 216 colors recognized in the Web-safe palette.

   FIGURE 5.22

Chapter 5   Creating Web Objects   **207**   LEVEL 2

7   **Enlarge the view to 300%. Compare this image to the Original image.**

The banding rings that result from shifting to Web-safe colors greatly affect the artwork's appearance. The fine gradations that exist in the original artwork make use of colors outside the 216-color limit imposed by the Web-safe color palette.

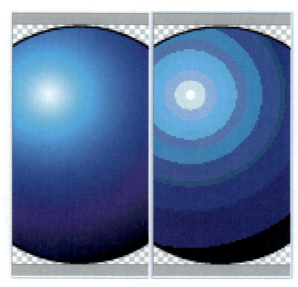

FIGURE 5.23

8   **Set the View Percentage back to 100%. Select the bottom-left image. Use the Preset menu to change the file format to JPEG Medium.**

The image still shows gradations, but the quality isn't as good as the original, and the texture appears somewhat mottled. The Preset menu does not have a JPEG Maximum option, but another menu offers this setting.

9   **Select the bottom-right image. Use the Preset menu to choose JPEG Medium. This reveals other menus. Beneath the Preset name is another menu; select JPEG. Underneath this menu is yet another menu; select Maximum.**

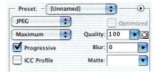

FIGURE 5.24

10 **Compare the different images to the Original image.**

The JPEG Maximum image looks as good as the Original. The JPEG Maximum takes 3 seconds to load, whereas the JPEG Medium and GIF images take 2 seconds to load. The increased quality of the JPEG Maximum image is well worth the additional 1 second it takes to upload to the browser.

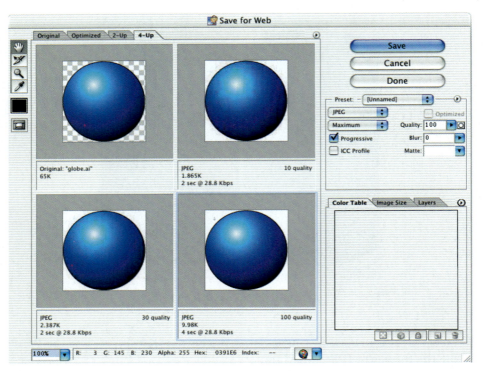

FIGURE 5.25

11 **Save the file in Images Only format to your WIP_05 folder.**

The "jpg" extension will automatically be added to the "globe" name.

12 **Go to the desktop and drag the saved file to your browser so you can see the quality of the image.**

13 **Return to the Illustrator document and close it without saving.**

To Extend Your Knowledge . . .

LOSSY COMPRESSION

JPEG is considered a ***lossy compression*** method because it throws away data in an effort to reduce file sizes. At lower quality levels, the file sizes become progressively smaller, but artifacts begin to creep into the image. At the highest (maximum) quality settings, the technique doesn't throw away any data and is therefore called ***lossless compression***.

UPLOAD TIMES

Upload times are the single most critical factor when designing for the Web. Sometimes you must sacrifice a little quality or redesign the object so its design characteristics fall within the limits imposed by Internet technology.

LESSON 3 Refining Images for the Web

Most of the images you see on the Web today have been ***anti-aliased***, which means the borders, especially on the curving contours (see Figure 5.26), were intentionally blurred to create a smoother appearance. Use anti-aliasing to create a soft transition between a sharp-edged image and its background.

FIGURE 5.26

If you position anti-aliased artwork onto a colored background, unsightly white or very light blemishes, called ***artifacts***, surround the image elements (see Figure 5.27). If the page background color is white, the problem does not occur; the soft-edged pixels blend into the white background. Artifacts only become a concern if the image contains irregular, curving, or angular shapes. Square-edged objects do not display this problem.

FIGURE 5.27

In the following exercises, you clean up the unsightly anti-aliased edges of a Web graphic.

Resolve Anti-Alias Artifacts

1. Open star_zoom.ai from the WIP_05>Star Zoom folder.

2. From the File>Menu, choose Save for Web. Click the Optimized tab in the dialog box.

3. From the Preset menu, choose GIF 64 Dithered. Under the Preset section, make certain that Transparency is selected.

   The GIF file format is the best choice when the white areas of the background need to be transparent. This allows only the colored elements of the art to show against the Web pages with colored backgrounds. Transparent areas display as a checkerboard pattern in the image preview.

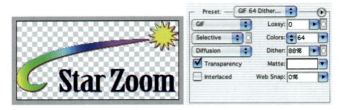

FIGURE 5.28

4. From the dialog box, save the illustration as "star_zoom.gif" in Images Only format. Save this to the WIP_05>Star Zoom folder.

5 From the desktop, go to the WIP_05>Star Zoom folder. Use your browser to open the star_zoom_white.html file that we supply.

Notice how seamlessly the artwork blends into the white background.

6 Close star_zoom_white.html and open star_zoom_blue.html in your browser.

The transparent background of the image allows the Web page's blue color (#0000CC) to show through. However, you can clearly see artifacts around the edges of the artwork.

FIGURE 5.29

7 Keep star_zoom_blue.html open in your browser. Return to the Illustrator document.

8 Draw a rectangle that matches the guide around the artwork and send it to the back.

9 In the Color palette, click the Fill box. In the palette's Options menu, choose Web Safe RGB. Set Red to 00 (zeroes), Green to 00 (zeroes), and the Blue (B) value to CC. Set the stroke to None.

The rectangle fills with the matching color of the blue Web page background.

10 Return to Save for Web and save the image with the same settings you used earlier. When asked if you want to replace the existing image, click Replace.

In this case, the Transparency option is unnecessary because the white background no longer touches the edges of the original art. The rectangle's 90-degree sides eliminate any chance of anti-aliased artifacts.

11 **Return to star_zoom_blue.html in your browser and refresh the page.**

This updates the image. As you can see, filling the rectangle with the background color eliminates the artifacts that were so obvious before the change.

FIGURE 5.30

12 **Keep star_zoom_blue.html open in your browser. In the Illustrator document, save your changes and keep it open for the next exercise.**

Another way to make objects float seamlessly on colored backgrounds is to use a technique called *matting*. Matting minimizes the artifacts that may appear on the edges of anti-aliased graphics. The Matting option is located in the Save for Web dialog box.

You soften anti-aliased edges by gradually transitioning pixels of the object's primary color values to white — since most Web pages have white backgrounds. You create the shades of the anti-aliased edges by mixing the primary color with increasing amounts of white. As long as the background of the page is white, this method works well. If the anti-aliased image rests on a colored background, however, you can see the white edges, which negatively impact the appearance of the graphic.

Instead of transitioning the edge colors to white, you can change the edge pixels to another color, called the *matte color*. The matte color is usually the color of the Web page background. With this method, the primary color blends with the matte color, resulting in a soft edge that fades to the matte color — not to white.

Once you set the matte color, the pixels that were progressively lighter shades of the object color change to the matte color. Matting is often a superior method for floating graphics over backgrounds, especially photographic backgrounds.

In this exercise, you use matting to repair the artifacts caused by anti-aliasing.

Use Matting to Eliminate Artifacts

1 **In the open Illustrator document, select the blue rectangle you drew earlier and delete it.**

We will show you how matting can alleviate the need to draw an extra object in the design.

2 **From the File menu, choose Save for Web. Click the Optimized tab in the dialog box.**

3 **Use the Viewing Percentage menu in the bottom-left to change the view of the preview image to 200%.**

Chapter 5   Creating Web Objects   **213**   LEVEL 2

4   **From the Matte menu (located on the dialog box's right), choose Other.**

The Matte menu allows you to choose another color to replace the white pixels in the anti-aliased edges. The Other selection allows you to choose a hexadecimal color from the Color Picker, which appears when Other is chosen.

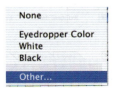

FIGURE 5.31

5   **At the bottom of the Color Picker, type "0000CC" (four zeros) in the "#" field. Click OK.**

The edges of the image in the Save for Web preview change to the assigned blue color. The white pixels that caused the artifacts are now the same color as the Web page background.

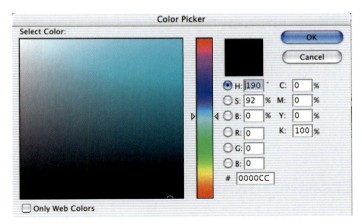

FIGURE 5.32

6   Click the Save button in the dialog box. Save the file with the same name to your WIP_05 folder. When asked if you want to replace the existing image, click Replace.

7   Return to star_zoom_blue.html in your browser and refresh the page.

The blue matte edges blend seamlessly with the background color of the Web page. The blue matte effectively removed the artifacts from the image.

FIGURE 5.33

8. Close the star_zoom_blue.html browser window.

9. Return to the Illustrator document and save your changes. Close the document.

To Extend Your Knowledge . . .

TRANSPARENCY AND ANTI-ALIASING

Images with 90-degree rectangular edges do not produce anti-alias artifacts. The alternative to a transparent background is white, which lays on top of the Web page background color and allows the image to display as intended.

LESSON 4 Creating Image Maps

An *image map* is a commonly seen navigation strategy that includes buttons as part of an underlying graphic. For example, think of a map of the United States. Clicking a state might link you to a page that offers that state's demographic information. To create such a navigation object, you would first create the map, and then add buttons that allow the user to click a state and view the actual data.

Image maps make use of objects called "hotspots." A *hotspot* is a "live" area directly connected to an external or internal URL. A *URL* (Universal Resource Locator) points the user to another page, either within the same site (internal) or on another site altogether (external). Think of a URL as a Web address. (These terms aren't Illustrator specific; they are common HTML terms.)

The advantage to using image maps is that you can turn any part of a raster image into a hotspot by drawing a path to designate the hot (clickable) area. You use the **Attributes palette** to assign a URL to a path and to determine the hotspot's shape. You can choose from rectangular or polygonal hotspots. Polygons are commonly used as hotspots because they can accommodate irregular shapes.

In this exercise, you draw objects and apply image maps by assigning URLs to the paths.

Chapter 5   Creating Web Objects   **215**   LEVEL 2

Create an Image Map

1 From the WIP_05 folder, go to the Feathered Friends folder and open the feathered_friends.ai document.

2 Use the Rectangle tool to draw a square that matches the size of the Swans photo. Change the Fill and Stroke of the rectangle to None.

The square designates the hotspot. When the cursor in the browser touches this area, it becomes the pointing finger icon, which indicates a link that can be clicked

FIGURE 5.34

3 Keep the path selected. From the Attributes palette, choose Rectangle from the Image Map menu.

Use the Rectangle option to create rectangular and square hotspots.

4 In the URL field, type "swans.html", and press Return/Enter to apply.

? If you have problems

Make sure you press Return/Enter after typing in the URL in the Attributes palette. This ensures you connect the link to the selected path. If the document contains an incorrect link when you choose the Save for Web command, you must return to the document, apply the correct link, and resave the document. This can quickly become a nuisance.

5 Drag the square to match the White Egret photo. Once it's in place, press Option/Alt and release the mouse button to make a duplicate. Keep the duplicate selected.

The copy possesses the same URL attributes as the original.

6 In the Attributes palette, change the URL to "egrets.html", and press Return/Enter to apply.

| 7 | Use the Ellipse tool to draw a circle to fit the Ducklings photo. Keep the object selected. |

FIGURE 5.35

| 8 | In the Attributes palette, use the Image Map menu to choose Polygon. |

Any object shapes other than rectangle or square are classified here as polygon.

| 9 | Set the URL to "ducklings.html" and apply. |

| 10 | Save your changes to the document and keep it open for the next exercise. |

Add More Hotspots to the Map

| 1 | Press Option/Alt and drag the Ducklings circle to make duplicates for the Coots and White Ibis objects. |

| 2 | Select the Coots circle. Change the URL to "coots.html" and apply. |

| 3 | Select the White Ibis circle. Change the URL to "ibis.html" and apply. |

| 4 | Draw a rectangle around the word "Information" in the image's bottom right. Keep the rectangle selected. |

| 5 | In the Attributes palette, use the Image Map menu to select Rectangle. |

| 6 | Set the URL to "info.html" and apply. |

| 7 | Press Option/Alt and drag the rectangle to the right to surround the words "Join The Club" with a duplicate. |

Press the Shift key as you drag to constrain the move.

FIGURE 5.36

8 Change the URL of this duplicate to "join.html" and apply. Deselect the rectangle.

9 Change the Stroke box to Pure Cyan. Use the Pen tool to draw a closed path around the larger duck's head in the image. After you draw the path, change the stroke to None.

FIGURE 5.37

10 Keep the path selected. Set the Image Map attribute to Polygon. Change the URL to "duck.html".

All the images that require links now have hotspots. In the next exercise, you save this document for the Web and see how the URLs/links work in a browser.

11 Save your changes and keep the document open for the next exercise.

To Extend Your Knowledge . . .

HOTSPOTS

Drawing the hotspot paths and applying the URLs is only half the job. You cannot see how the links work until you save the document for the Web, which creates an HTML file. (You learn more about HTML files later in this chapter.)

Image maps may contain other objects besides vector paths. You can also assign URLs to text blocks. Point text blocks are good choices, since they usually contain a limited number of words.

LESSON 5 Saving for the Web — HTML

As the popularity of the Internet rises, Adobe continues to provide increasingly effective tools for creating images for the Web. The File menu's Save for Web option includes many features for saving documents as external images and/or HTML files. The Save for Web dialog box displays the objects in the document and allows you to choose from a wide variety of settings to properly configure raster images, including GIF, JPEG, and PNG file formats. You can also modify the colors in an image to ensure it downloads as quickly as possible.

Once you use Save for Web to apply Web-safe colors, dithering, matting, and transparency to an image, you can save the image for the Web. If you prefer, you can use Save for Web to take the process one step further — to create an HTML file that describes all of the elements on the Artboard, making them accessible to your browser. The Save for Web feature offers three options for saving a document:

- **HTML and Images** saves the visible document elements into a single image (unless you sliced the image). This option also creates a separate HTML file that references the image and any image map information in the document.

- The **Images Only** selection saves all the visible elements into a single raster image (unless you used slices, which you learn about in the next lesson).

- The **HTML Only** option saves the positions of the Web page elements to HTML code but provides no images. You must supply the images manually.

✓ HTML and Images
Images Only
HTML Only

FIGURE 5.38

In the next exercise, you use the Save for Web feature to save an Illustrator document's images and text to a Web page.

Save a Document as a Web Page

1 From the open document, select Save for Web from the File menu.

2 Click the Optimized tab in the dialog box's upper left.

3 Set the View Percentage menu to 50%.

Chapter 5 Creating Web Objects 219 LEVEL 2

This shows you how the complete image looks when saved at these settings.

FIGURE 5.39

4 Click the Save button.

5 Save the document to your WIP_05>Feathered Friends folder. Set the top pop-up menu to HTML and Images. Click Save.

This option saves a separate HTML text file along with the raster image.

6 From the desktop, go to your WIP_05>Feathered Friends folder. Open the feathered_friends.html file in your browser.

The hotspot links are not obvious, because they are not underlined text links.

7 Move the cursor over the areas where you drew paths and turned them into hotspots.

The cursor turns into the pointing finger icon, which indicates a link.

8 Click one of the links.

You see the Web page associated with the link.

9 In your browser, close the Web page to return to the Feathered Friends home page. Click the hotspot on the duck's head.

You see the photo of the duck guarding a park.

LEVEL 2   **220**   Chapter 5   Creating Web Objects

10   **Close the browser windows. Return to the Illustrator document.**

11   **Save your changes and close the document.**

To Extend Your Knowledge . . .

USE THE PROPER FOLDER

When you save documents as HTML, the code must have access to the images to properly render the Web page. With the HTML and Images format, Illustrator saves the images in their own folder named "images." If you do not save your images in the location to which the HTML file refers, the dreaded "Page Cannot Be Found" error is sure to appear.

LESSON 6   Slicing Images

If you were to visit any average Web site that contains a large image, and you dragged on the image just to see what happens, you would probably find that only a small portion of the image moves. Even though the image appears to be one graphic element, it is actually made up of multiple smaller image sections. This method of dividing a graphical element into sections is known as *slicing*. Slicing allows you to cut a page into multiple sections, called "*slices*," and to save each slice to a different file.

Since the technique divides one file into several separate files, you can *optimize* (customize) each slice individually with the Save for Web feature. You can apply higher compression, greater dithering, and fewer colors to certain slices (such as backgrounds), while other slices require lower compression and a greater number of colors (such as photographic images). Optimizing each slice individually provides a quicker upload than when you optimize an entire page at the same (higher) settings.

Illustrator offers two methods for slicing a Web page: You can use the Slice tool to draw the area you want to slice, or you can select an object and apply the Object>Slice>Make command. For the most part, you convert sliced areas to the GIF format, which allows the image to paint quickly when the Web page loads. You can choose another file format if you prefer.

In this exercise, you use slicing techniques to isolate various parts of a Web page into separate sections that load quickly on the Internet.

Create Slices

1   **Open sliced_bananas.ai from the WIP_05>Sliced Bananas folder.**

2   **Click the photo at the top of the Web page.**

This single photo contains three separate scenes. An image of this size would take an unacceptably long time to upload to a browser. To shorten the upload time, slice it into separate sections.

Chapter 5   Creating Web Objects   **221**   LEVEL 2

3   **Activate the Slice tool in the Toolbox (under the Eyedropper tool). Place the blade's tip on the photo's upper-left corner. Drag the tool to enclose the left scene in the image.**

When you draw slices with the Slice tool, the tip of the blade is your starting point. Even though the edges of the slice snap to pixel edges and other slices, you may want to zoom in to ensure you make an accurate slice.

The two squares in the slice's upper left show the numbers of the slices, which display in the Save for Web dialog box.

FIGURE 5.40

4   **Click the Slice tool on the top-right corner of the first slice and drag another slice to enclose the middle scene.**

5   **To enclose the scene, drag the tool from the top-right corner of the middle scene to the bottom-right corner of the right scene.**

You now have three sections of the photo. When you access Save for Web, each slice will appear as a separate GIF file.

FIGURE 5.41

6   **Zoom in on the small photo of a banana bunch to the left of the text.**

7   **Select the Slice tool and trace the edges of the photo to enclose it.**

The Slice tool draws a rectangle around the area you want to include in the slice. The outlines of the rectangles are difficult to see because they are white. They sometimes disfigure the appearances of the items you slice, but they do no harm.

FIGURE 5.42

8 **Use the Selection tool to select the text block to this photo's right. From the Object menu, choose Slice>Make.**

The Slice tool is not the only method to slice objects. The Object>Slice menu options allow you to convert selected objects into slices.

9 **Select the next text block to the right, and use the same Slice>Make method to turn it into a slice.**

Obscuring the bold text headlines does not affect the text blocks. The upper-left corner of a slice contains the slice number, which names the slice when the Save for Web saves the HTML file. If the slice is number 39, the slice's exported file name would be 39.gif.

In Figure 5.43, you see a thin rectangular slice dimmed out between the two text block slices. All the artwork in the document is like a jigsaw puzzle, with the slices being the pieces. In between the slices you draw or create, Illustrator makes "filler" slices that fill in the empty spaces. This dimmed slice is a filler slice.

FIGURE 5.43

10 **From the View menu, choose Hide Slices. After viewing the result, return the slices to view with View>Show Slices.**

All of the slices you created so far have small squares in their upper-left corners and tinted rectangles that outline the sliced areas. Hiding the slices allows you to see the page without any distractions.

11 **Save your changes. Keep the document open for the next exercise.**

Add More Slices

1 Zoom in on the point text blocks under the small banana bunch photo.

2 Use the Rectangle tool to draw a rectangle around the top text block. Change the fill and stroke to None. Keep the path selected.

3 Use the Attributes palette to apply a rectangle image map. In the URL field, type "banana_care.html" and apply this.

4 Continue to create rectangular hotspots for the other blocks underneath.

5 The URLs for these additional hotspots should be (moving down): "banana_variety.html", "banana_splits.html", and "banana_recipes.html", respectively.

Be sure to press Return/Enter to apply the URLs.

6 Use the Selection tool to select all four of the point text blocks.

7 From the Object menu, choose Slice>Make.

Each individual text block becomes a separate slice with a dimmed slice (filler slice) in between. This is far too many slices to keep track of. All these text blocks can combine into one slice and remain linked with the image maps.

FIGURE 5.44

8 Select Edit>Undo to undo this slicing. Keep the text blocks selected. Return to the Object>Slice menu and choose Create from Selection.

The selected text blocks now combine into a single slice, which becomes a single GIF image with a hotspot over each link.

FIGURE 5.45

9. Save your changes to the document and keep it open for the next exercise.

View Slicing Concept

1. Zoom out to see the entire Artboard. Select all the objects on the page and press Command/Control-3 to hide them.

   Note that the entire bounding area made up of all the objects on the Artboard has been sliced. Whenever you create a slice, Illustrator automatically fills in between your slices. The combined art objects, when sliced, cannot contain empty spaces. The filler slices appear dimmed in view.

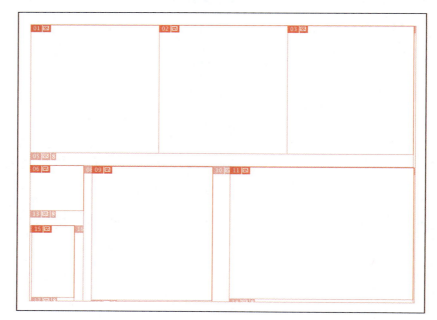

FIGURE 5.46

Chapter 5 Creating Web Objects **225** LEVEL 2

2 Show all the hidden objects.

3 From the File menu, choose Save for Web.

It may take a few moments for Illustrator to load the Web page and slices.

4 If the slices aren't visible (see Figure 5.47 to see visible slices), click the Toggle Slices Visibility icon on the dialog box's left side, below the tools.

All the slices appear with numbers in the squares in the upper-left corners.

5 Press Command/Control-A to select all the slices in the preview window. Set the Matte menu back to None.

6 Choose the Select Slice tool, the second tool in the dialog box tool list.

FIGURE 5.47

7 Click the slice that contains the photo of the small banana bunch. Use a JPEG Maximum setting to ensure the quality of the final image.

You can customize all of your slices to meet the requirements of the final Web page.

8 Click the Save button in the Save for Web dialog box.

9 Save the file in HTML and Images format to your WIP_05>Sliced Bananas folder. Click Save.

The bottom menu of the dialog box should read All Slices. You don't need to manually name the file. Illustrator automatically adds the "html" extension to the document's existing name. The Save for Web feature saves all the slices in a new folder it creates named "images" that is located in the folder you save to.

10 Save your changes to the Illustrator document. Keep the document open for the next exercise.

View the Web Page

1. **From your desktop, use your browser to go to the WIP_05>Sliced Bananas folder.**

   Note the new "images" folder Illustrator has created.

2. **Open sliced_bananas.html in your browser.**

3. **Drag the top-center photo downward. Release the mouse and it returns to its original position.**

   Depending on your computer platform (Macintosh or Windows) and your browser type (Internet Explorer, Netscape Navigator, or another brand), the selected image may or may not move. We used Internet Explorer on the Macintosh, and the image moved away from its original position so we could see the individual slice.

FIGURE 5.48

4. **Drag the sliced image of the four text links in the bottom-left corner. Release the mouse.**

   The single slice placed the four links into one image.

FIGURE 5.49

Chapter 5   Creating Web Objects   **227**   **LEVEL 2**

5   **Move the mouse cursor over any of the four links.**

The cursor changes to a pointing finger icon. Do not click the links, as we do not have actual Web pages they connect to. The URLs you typed were fictitious.

6   **Drag the white filler space between the two large text blocks.**

Illustrator added this white-spacing image to fill in between the designated slices.

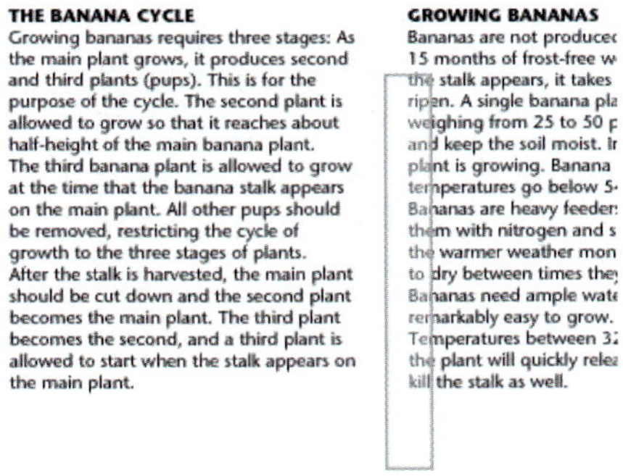

THE BANANA CYCLE
Growing bananas requires three stages: As the main plant grows, it produces second and third plants (pups). This is for the purpose of the cycle. The second plant is allowed to grow so that it reaches about half-height of the main banana plant. The third banana plant is allowed to grow at the time that the banana stalk appears on the main plant. All other pups should be removed, restricting the cycle of growth to the three stages of plants. After the stalk is harvested, the main plant should be cut down and the second plant becomes the main plant. The third plant becomes the second, and a third plant is allowed to start when the stalk appears on the main plant.

GROWING BANANAS
Bananas are not produce 15 months of frost-free w the stalk appears, it takes ripen. A single banana pla weighing from 25 to 50 p and keep the soil moist. Ir plant is growing. Banana temperatures go below 5- Bananas are heavy feeder them with nitrogen and s the warmer weather mon to dry between times they Bananas need ample wate remarkably easy to grow. Temperatures between 3: the plant will quickly relea kill the stalk as well.

FIGURE 5.50

7   **Close the browser window.**

8   **Return to the Illustrator document and save your changes. Close the document.**

CAREERS IN DESIGN

BUILDING AN ONLINE PORTFOLIO

As you continue to develop your skills, you should create samples of your work that potential clients may examine. The perfect vehicle for displaying your artwork is a personal Web site, where you can include information about yourself and provide access to your artwork. Most successful artists take advantage of the Web to showcase their work.

Building an effective Web presence is outside the scope of this book, but you've learned enough by now to build a few attractive pages to display thumbnails (small versions) of the images you created in this book and in *Essentials for Design: Illustrator CS2 Level 1*. Adding the artwork you completed on your own certainly enhances the interest and effectiveness of the Web page.

Build a single page that can show six, eight, or ten thumbnail images at a time. Make sure that each thumbnail contains a link that displays a larger version of the graphic, should a visitor want to inspect the artwork more carefully. Consider creating an SVG version of the page to accommodate those visitors who can view vector artwork with their browsers.

SUMMARY

In Chapter 5, you learned how to access the Save for Web dialog box and use its many features to modify and customize images for the Web. You learned about banding and found that Web-safe colors can contribute to this unsightly problem in some objects, most notably in gradients. You discovered that anti-alias artifacts can blemish an image, and you learned about the two most popular methods — matting and adding a colored rectangle to the art — that Webmasters use to rectify this problem. You used both methods to eliminate the unsightly borders that result from improper color selections.

You also learned about image maps and hotspots. You discovered that you can create a hotspot simply by assigning a URL to a vector path or text block. You learned how to create a Web page from an Illustrator document using the Save for Web feature. You used the Slice tool and the Object>Slice>Make option to cut images and text elements into smaller sections, each of which you can optimize individually in the Save for Web dialog box.

KEY TERMS

Anti-alias	Hotspot	Optimize
Artifacts	Image map	Slices
Attributes palette	Lossy compression	Slicing
Banding	Lossless compression	URL
Color Table	Matte color	Web-safe colors
Dithering	Matting	

CHECKING CONCEPTS AND TERMS

MULTIPLE CHOICE

Circle the letter that matches the correct answer for each of the following questions.

1. The Save for Web feature _____.
   a. saves images for the Web
   b. saves the document written in HTML code
   c. modifies color settings to refine Web images
   d. saves a document's content as a Web page
   e. All of the above.

2. The Save for Web features allows you to save files in the _____ raster formats.
   a. GIF, JPEG, TIF
   b. BMP, JPEG, PNG
   c. GIF, JPEG, PNG
   d. TIF, BMP, GIF

3. Banding occurs when a file _____.
   a. is saved in the wrong file format
   b. receives too few colors in its palette to retain the correct coloring in the image
   c. is dithered
   d. receives the wrong matte color

4. Artifacts occur on a Web image when you _____.
   a. make the image transparent
   b. apply too few colors in the palette
   c. use anti-aliasing to blur the edges to white
   d. use Web-safe colors

Chapter 5   Creating Web Objects   **229**   **LEVEL 2**

5. To create a hotspot on an image map, you can apply URL links to _____.

  a. vector paths only

  b. vector paths and text blocks

  c. raster images

  d. any object in a document.

6. Before you apply an image map, you must _____.

  a. save the document as an EPS image

  b. export the document as a raster image and use it in HTML code

  c. use Save for Web to export the HTML code and images

  d. None of the above.

7. Another term or nickname for an image map is _____.

  a. absolute link

  b. relative link

  c. hotspot

  d. link spot

8. The Slicing operation _____.

  a. places elements on various layers

  b. rearranges the elements on the Artboard

  c. divides the content into raster images

  d. isolates the vector, raster, and text objects

9. You can see the numbers of the slices _____.

  a. both on the Artboard and in the Save for Web dialog box

  b. only when you select a sliced image

  c. when you select Show Bounding Box

  d. in Outline view

10. To optimize a slice image, you _____.

  a. apply the same settings to every slice

  b. customize the settings for each slice

  c. create a file that will load quickly on the Internet

  d. None of the above.

DISCUSSION QUESTIONS

1. Besides preparing images for publishing on the Web, how else can you use the Save for Web feature?

2. Why do you need to control the colors that display in a Web image?

3. What is the reason for saving an image into a JPEG format?

4. What is the most important reason for slicing a large graphic that you use on a Web page?

SKILL DRILL

Skill Drills reinforce project skills. Each skill that is reinforced is the same as, or nearly the same as, a skill we presented in the lessons. We provide detailed instructions in a step-by-step format. You should complete these exercises in order.

1. Control Banding

One of your clients supplied you with three images he created on his computer. He asked you to incorporate the images into his Web site. The images contain gradients and other blending effects. Your task is to use the Save for Web features to make the image presentable on the Web.

1. Open save_images.ai from the Chapter_05 folder.

    The document contains four art pieces. You need to isolate each image so that it will be saved only to a raster image.

2. Click the Default Fill and Stroke icon in the Toolbox. Change the Fill box to None.

3. Use the Rectangle tool to draw a square around the circle object. In the Object menu, choose Crop Area>Make.

    You could assign each object to its own layer and hide and show the layers to see each object individually. The Crop Area option is a much easier and faster way to isolate images.

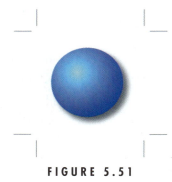

FIGURE 5.51

4. From the File menu, choose Save for Web.

5. Click the 4-Up tab in the dialog box.

6. Leave the top-left image as the Original image. One at a time, click the other three images, and use the Preset menu to assign your choice of GIF, JPEG, or PNG formats.

    Continue to experiment with the settings, and compare the results to the Original image in the top-left of the Save for Web dialog box. Your goal is to reduce the file size and number of seconds as much as possible, while retaining acceptable image quality.

7. When your settings are in place, save the file as "circle_gradient" with the correct file extension (such as .gif, .jpg, or .png) to match the final format. Save the file to your WIP_05 folder with the top pop-up menu set to Images Only.

8. Return to the Illustrator document, release the Crop Area, and relocate the square to surround the star-shaped object. From the Object menu, select Crop Area>Make.

9. Return to Save for Web, and customize the image as you did in Step 6. Save the file to your WIP_05 folder, using an appropriate name and extension.

10. To the remaining two images, apply the Crop Area and Save for Web techniques to save the raster images to the WIP_05 folder.

11. After you save all four images, close the document without saving.

12. From the desktop, go to the WIP_05 folder. One at a time, drag each of these saved raster images to a browser window to see them. Close the browser window when finished.

2. Create a Rough Layout

You are a Webmaster whose new client is a dating group called Valentine's Web. They have hired you to create a rough layout of their new Web site. You want to divide the site into four equal slices to reduce upload time. Your task is to slice the site as quickly and accurately as possible.

1. Open valentine_website.ai from the WIP_05>Valentine Web folder. Open the Layers palette. Show the page rulers.

2. Draw a vertical and horizontal guide to mark the center of the Artboard.

3. Select all the objects on the Artboard.

    This procedure works only if you select all the objects on the page.

4. From the Object menu, choose Slice>Create from Guides.

    The slices appear only around the bounding area of the selected objects. This procedure does not extend to the Artboard's edges (the dimensions of the Web page). If you want the slices to extend to the Artboard's edges, you must draw an object that matches the size of the Artboard, and it will be included in the slicing operation.

5. Choose Edit>Undo. Draw a rectangle that fits the Artboard. Fill and stroke the rectangle with None.

6. Select all the objects, including the rectangle. From the Object menu, choose Slice>Create from Guides.

    Even though the rectangle contains no paint attributes, it was included in the slicing procedure. The rectangle extended the boundaries of the object to the Artboard's edges.

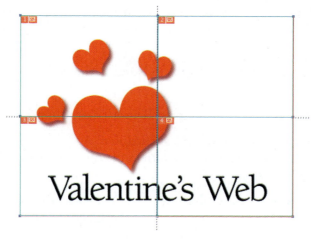

FIGURE 5.52

7. From the File menu, choose Save for Web.

    Examine the four slices. If you cannot see the slice numbers, click the Toggle Slices Visibility icon in the upper-left corner of the dialog box.

LEVEL 2   **232**   Chapter 5   Creating Web Objects

8. Click the Save button in the dialog box and save the document in HTML and Images format to the WIP_05>Valentine Web folder.

9. Go to the desktop. Use your browser to open valentine_website.html from the Valentine Web folder. On the Web page, drag the images to see how they were sliced into separate pieces.

10. Return to the Illustrator document and save your changes. Keep the document open for the next exercise.

3. Create an Image Map with Hotspots

The Valentine's Web client asked for a more comprehensive layout of their site. The home page contains several links that take viewers to the other pages on the site. Your task is to apply hotspots to the text blocks on the page.

1. In the open document, open the Layers and Attributes palettes. In the Layers palette, click the Visibility icon of the Links layer, which is hidden. Select the Links layer to make it active.

   Objects on hidden layers are not included in the Save for Web operations. Hiding/showing layers is a convenient way to exclude objects from being saved with Save for Web.

2. Deselect all objects. Click the Default Fill and Stroke icon in the Toolbox and change the Fill to None.

3. Use the Rectangle tool to draw a rectangle around the "Find a Friend" text block and the heart to its left.

4. Drag duplicates of the rectangle to surround each of the other links and their hearts. Remember to hold down the Shift key to constrain the move.

   You can apply an image map to only one object — a path, a text block, or a raster image. You cannot apply an image map to a grouped image; you have to apply the link to each object in the group. Another alternative is to surround a grouped object with a rectangle and apply the image map to the rectangle.

5. Select the top rectangle and change its Stroke to None. In the Attributes palette, apply a rectangle to the hotspot.

6. In the URL field, type "friends.html" and press Return/Enter to apply.

   Remember, the links you use in this exercise are fictitious. Always press Return/Enter to apply a URL to an image map. If you don't, you have to return to the Attributes palette, reapply the URLs, and complete the whole process again.

7. One at a time, select the rectangles of the other image maps, change the Strokes to None, and apply the links (moving down): "heart_throb.html", "members_photos.html", "wedding_agenda.html", and "contact_us.html".

8. Select all the hearts, text blocks, and rectangles in the links section. From the Object menu, choose Slice>Create from Selection.

All of the selected objects become part of a single slice, which Illustrator saves as a single raster image.

FIGURE 5.53

9. From the File menu, choose Save for Web. Click the Optimized tab at the top of the dialog box. Use the Preset menu to set the format to GIF 128 Dithered.

   The Optimized option shows one preview image, allowing you to see the entire Web page in one window. These link slices now become part of the slices you made in the previous exercise.

10. Save the file as HTML and Images to your WIP_05>Valentine Web folder. Use the same file name. When asked if you want to replace existing files, click Replace.

11. Use your browser to open valentine_website.html from the WIP_05>Valentine Web folder. Refresh the browser page. Move your cursor over the links to make sure they are active.

    Browsers usually cache the addresses of Web pages you visit, so you may not see the page you just saved. If this happens, refresh the page. If that doesn't work, restart your browser to clear its cache and reload this file.

12. Return to the Illustrator document and save your changes. Close the file.

4. Save for Web as HTML Only

You created a Web page that contains only text — no images. To expedite saving the Web page, you choose HTML Only as the format.

1. Open html_only.ai from the WIP_05>HTML Only folder.

   The page contains only text blocks, so you don't need to use HTML and Images as the Save for Web format . . . or do you?

2. Access the Save for Web dialog box and click the Optimized tab.

3. Click the Save button. In the next dialog box, set the Format menu to HTML Only.

4. Save the document to the WIP_05>HTML Only folder.

   Illustrator automatically adds the "html" extension to the file name.

5. From the desktop, go to the WIP_05 folder and use your browser to open the html_only.html document.

LEVEL 2   **234**   Chapter 5   Creating Web Objects

You see nothing on the page except the dreaded "missing image" icon and its bounding box, telling you that no image is available. Even though there are only text blocks on the Artboard, Illustrator saves all the objects in the document as a graphic image (unless sliced) and assigns the ".gif" extension. The HTML code refers to the image in its <IMG SRC> tag, though the image is missing.

6. Launch your word processor. Navigate to the WIP_05>HTML Only folder and open html_only.html as Text Only or Plain Text.

   The <IMG SRC> tag in the code references the image html_only.gif, which does not exist. Had you chosen the HTML and Images format, Illustrator would have saved the HTML file plus the image with the name html_only.gif. Note also that Illustrator created in the <IMG SRC> tag a folder called "images", which precedes the html_only,gif name. This is the folder that the HTML file looks to for its images.

7. Close the html_only.html text file in your word processor. In your browser, close the html_only.html window.

8. At the desktop, go to the WIP_05>HTML Only folder. Inside it, create a new folder called "images".

   This is the folder name Illustrator needs for the HTML file to access any images. When you choose Images Only, however, Illustrator does not create the "images" folder. Just the HTML and Images format creates an images folder. The HTML file exists now. All you need is the GIF graphic to show in the browser window.

9. Return to the Illustrator document.

10. In the Save for Web dialog box, click the Optimized tab. Set the Preset menu to GIF 128 Dithered. Name the document "html_only.gif" and save it as Images Only to the WIP_05>HTML Only>images folder you created.

    The file name must match the html_only.gif name referenced in the html_only.html text document.

11. Return to your browser. From the WIP_05>HTML Only folder, open html_only.html. Refresh the page if necessary.

The html_only.gif image now appears in the browser window. Although you are viewing nothing but text, the entire Web page was saved as a single GIF image.

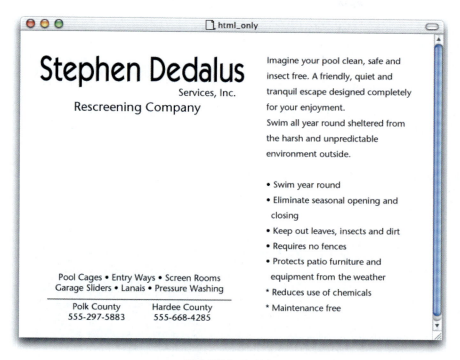

FIGURE 5.54

12. Close the browser window and return to the Illustrator document. Close the file without saving.

CHALLENGE

Challenge exercises expand on, or are somewhat related to, skills we presented in the lessons. Each exercise provides a brief introduction, followed by numbered-step instructions that are not as detailed as those in the Skill Drill exercises. You should complete these exercises in order.

1. Slice Photos and Text

You are the commercial artist who created the Stephen Dedalus Web site. The client asked you to add some photos to the site. To ensure the site uploads as quickly as possible, you must slice the photos.

1. Open html_only.ai from the WIP_05>HTML Only folder. Open the Layers palette.

2. Select the text block on the Artboard's right side and delete it.

3. In the Layers palette, click the Visibility icon of the Photos layer.

   The photos on the layer come into view.

4. Use the Slice tool to draw a slice around each photo and its shadow.

5. Use the Selection tool to select the "Stephen Dedalus", "Services, Inc.", and "Rescreening Company" text blocks. From the Object menu, choose Slice>Make.

   The individual text blocks become separate slices. Illustrator automatically makes other slices to fill in the gaps on the page. Each individual text block and slice becomes a GIF image when saved for the Web.

6. Select the large text block in the middle of the page and choose Object>Slice>Make.

7. Select the two lower text blocks and the black line between them. From the Object menu, choose Slice>Create from Selection.

   This command combines the three objects into a single slice. The Create from Selection combines all the selected objects into one GIF image when saved for the Web.

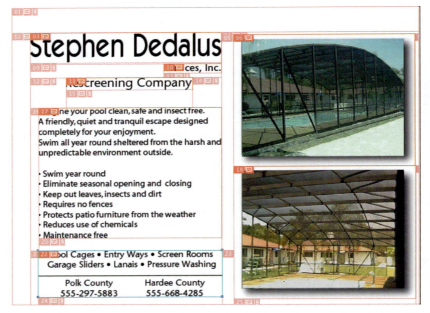

FIGURE 5.55

8. Go to the Save for Web dialog box. Click the Optimized tab to see the entire Web page in one image window. Click Save.

9. Save the file in HTML and Images format to the WIP_05>HTML Only folder. The menu at the dialog box's bottom should read All Slices. Click Save.

10. When you receive a message that says the files will replace existing files, click Replace.

11. Use your browser to go to the WIP_05>HTML Only folder and open html_only.html. Refresh the page if necessary. Drag any photo or text to see how the slices separated the elements into sections.

12. Return to the Illustrator document and save your changes. Close the document.

2. Eliminate Artifacts

You are a graphic designer who creates images for the Internet and sells them to various Web users. You create GIF images with transparency applied, which would create white artifacts if customers placed the images against colored backgrounds. You cannot guess what color backgrounds your customers will use, so you create self-contained images with their own artifact-removing matte color. Your task in this exercise is to produce such an image.

1. Open shell.ai from the WIP_05>Shell folder.

2. Open the Save for Web dialog box and click the Optimized tab.

3. Save the shell in Images Only format to the WIP_05>Shell folder.

   Illustrator automatically adds the .gif extension to the file name, which is shell.gif.

4. Use your browser to go to the WIP_05>Shell folder and open shell.gif.

   The rounded sections of the shell produce considerable white artifacts against the background.

5. Leave the browser window open. Return to the Illustrator document and open the Save for Web dialog box.

6. In the Matte menu, choose Eyedropper.

7. Zoom the image view to 200%.

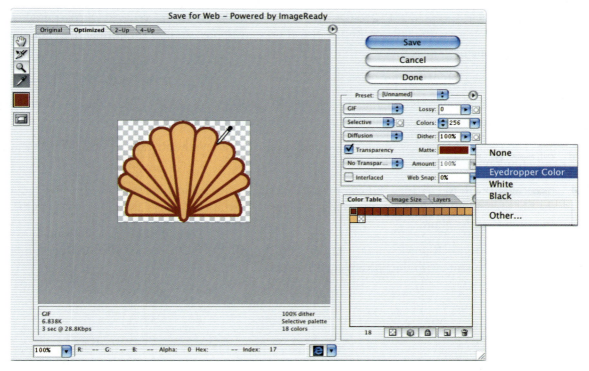

FIGURE 5.56

LEVEL 2   **238**   **Chapter 5**   **Creating Web Objects**

8. Click the Eyedropper Color tool on the darker outline of the shell to set this as the matte color.

   The anti-alias pixels will match the matte color. This technique allows the image to appear on any color background without having to customize the image to match the background color.

9. Save the image with the same settings as before to the WIP_05>Shell folder. When asked if you want to replace the existing file, click Replace.

10. Return to the active browser window and refresh the page.

    Matting the image edges eliminates the white artifacts. Regardless of the background color, the image remains artifact-free because of its own self-contained matte color.

11. Close the browser window and return to the Illustrator document. Save your changes and close the document.

3. Modify a Photograph

You offered to create a Web site for a friend who wants to put various pictures of his family members on the page. He supplied you with one photo, but the large file size requires too much time to load. Your task is to lower the upload time by applying a different file format or including fewer colors in the image.

1. Create a new letter-size RGB document.

2. From the Chapter_05 folder, place nicole_hat.tif.

3. Keep the image selected. Choose Filter>Colors>Convert to RGB.

   This is a CMYK image in TIFF format. You need to convert the colors to the RGB color mode. The Save for Web feature saves files as RGB GIFs, JPEGs, or PNGs, so the TIFF format does not matter. It becomes one of these formats.

4. In the Save for Web dialog box, click the 4-Up tab.

   Note the file information underneath each image in the viewing window. The high-resolution file would require 6–7 seconds to load, even in GIF format.

5. Select the top-right preview image. Apply various file formats with different numbers of colors and dithering options.

   Experiment with the settings and compare the results to the Original image. Your goal is to reduce the file size and number of seconds as much as possible, while retaining acceptable quality in the appearance of the photo.

6. Select the bottom-left preview image and experiment with the file formats, dithering, and numbers of colors. Do the same with the bottom-right image.

Give each image a different setting, lowering the upload seconds and file size.

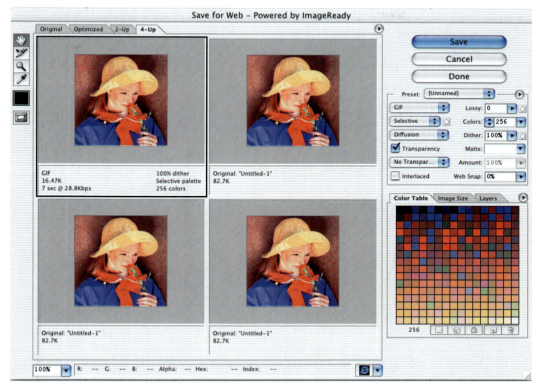

FIGURE 5.57

7. When your settings are in place, save the file as "nicole_hat" with the appropriate file extension (gif, jpg, or png) to match the final file format. Save the file to your WIP_05 folder in the Images Only format.

8. Return to the Illustrator document, and close it without saving.

4. Add a Photo to the Valentine Web Page

The Valentine's Web site wants to use a generic picture of a young woman to announce an article called "My Wedding Story." You have permission from your friend to use his daughter's photo for the job. You already modified the photo for the Web. Your task is to convert the photo to an image map so users can click the image and view the story.

1. Open valentine_website.ai from the WIP_05_Valentine Web folder. Open the Attributes palette. Choose Hide Slices from the View menu.

    The white lines and squares of the slices can be distracting.

2. From the File menu, use the Place option to import from the WIP_05 folder the nicole_hat.tif image you saved in the previous exercise.

    Note that the Images Only format in the previous exercise did not create an "images" folder.

3. Scale the photo at 50% Uniform. Position the photo below and flush left with the column of small hearts next to the links (see Figure 5.58).

4. Drag-duplicate the Contact Us text block below the photo. Change the text to "My Wedding Story", and manually center the text under the photo.

FIGURE 5.58

5. Use the Attributes palette to assign a rectangular image map to the selected photo. Apply the URL "wedding_story.html".

   Raster images and paths can receive URL link attributes.

6. Select the text block below the photo and assign a rectangular image map. To the right of the URL field, click the menu and choose wedding_story.html. Apply this.

   This menu stores all your URLs; it saves you from retyping.

7. Choose Show Slices from the View menu to see the slices.

   The photo and text have become part of the bottom-right slice, so there is no need to slice them.

8. In the Save for Web dialog box, click the Optimized tab. Make sure the format is set to GIF 128 Dithered, and click Save.

9. Save the file in HTML and Images format to the WIP_05>Valentine Web folder. When asked if you want to replace the existing files, click Replace.

10. Use your browser to go to the WIP_05>Valentine Web folder and open valentine_website.html. Refresh the page if necessary. Move the cursor over the photo and its text link to verify that they are now image map hotspots.

11. Return to the Illustrator document and save your changes. Close the document.

PORTFOLIO BUILDER

Slice a Background Image

You are a photographer creating a Web page to show your latest prize-winning shot. The large image, however, would load much faster on the page if it were sliced into sections. Your task is to divide the image into four pieces.

1. Create a new letter-size RGB document with the Artboard set for 640 × 480 points. Open the Layers palette. Show the page rulers.

2. Place one of your favorite photographs on the Artboard and scale the image so that it is slightly larger than the Artboard but in proper position.

3. Create a 640 × 480 pt rectangle that matches the Artboard border. Drag vertical and horizontal guides to mark the center point of the selected rectangle.

4. Select the rectangle and the photo and mask them, keeping the objects selected.

5. Use the Object>Slice menu to apply the Create from Guides option.

   The guides cut the objects into slices based on the guides' relationship with the outer extremities of the Web page, defined by the rectangle.

6. In the Save for Web dialog box, click the Optimized tab. Name the file "fave_foto.html" and save it as HTML and Images to the WIP_05 folder.

7. Use your browser program to go to the WIP_05 folder and open the fave_foto.html file.

8. Drag the slices slightly to see how the guides divided them. Close the browser window.

9. Return to the Illustrator document and close it without saving.

LEVEL 2

CHAPTER 6

SVG Graphics and Interactivity

OBJECTIVES

In this chapter, you learn how to:

- Create scaleable vector graphics (SVG)
- Generate static SVG files
- Add interactivity with JavaScript and SVG
- Create multiple events in a single file
- Embed SVG images in HTML files
- Apply SVG filters

Why Would I Do This?

Scaleable Vector Graphics (SVG) is rapidly becoming one of the most important underlying technologies in delivering interactive products. The SVG file format allows nonscaleable, nonbitmapped graphics to be distributed via the Internet. Until quite recently, the only graphic objects you could place on the Web were bitmapped (rasterized) objects. Adding vector graphics into the mix opens broad avenues for more effective information delivery.

With SVG, your site visitors can zoom in to see the details in a drawing; they can interact with the page and with a single page element — namely, your drawings. The creative possibilities are seemingly endless. The rapid acceptance of the technology and the ability to display SVG objects in today's browsers is proof that the technology's time has come. In this chapter, you learn how to develop SVG objects and publish them on the Web.

You must install the *SVG Viewer* plug-in on your computer so you can see the SVG files in your browser. You can download the SVG Viewer installation file at http://www.adobe.com/svg/viewer/install/main.html. (This file is available at no charge.) Scroll down the window and select the correct platform to download. Once installed on your computer, double-click the installation file and it installs in a matter of seconds. There are some browsers that may not be SVG-compliant. If you find you cannot view an SVG file in your browser, we suggest either Microsoft's Internet Explorer or Netscape's Navigator, which can be downloaded free from the Internet.

VISUAL SUMMARY

In this chapter, you delve deeper into the creation of advanced Web objects and begin to explore alternative methods to enhance and distribute the designs and graphics you develop with Illustrator. To accomplish this, you explore *Scalable Vector Graphics (SVG)*. SVG is a relatively new file format supported by the World Wide Web Consortium (W3C.org) and a number of software developers, including Adobe. Scalable Vector Graphics is a form of XML that allows you to use JavaScript to add *interactivity* to your graphics.

This chapter is about SVG and its relationship to *XML (eXtensible Markup Language)* and JavaScript. As you read the lessons in this chapter, you become acquainted with new technology — namely SVG — that produces small but very high quality line-art objects for Web designs. You also learn how to use JavaScript to add interactivity to SVG objects. These advanced techniques enable you to make your documents interactive, highly effective, and increasingly accessible to site visitors, which naturally increases hit rates and heightened success of your site.

You are introduced to static SVG images, which remain still and do not animate. You learn the benefits of using SVG images, such as scaling and moving the images around on a Web page, and you learn how these benefits offer significant advantages to Web designers. For example, designers can use this type of image to develop sites for realtors, where the viewer can take an online tour of a home. Users can zoom in to certain rooms and move the page around to better view specific areas, as shown in Figure 6.1, in which the browser window was zoomed in to enlarge the objects.

FIGURE 6.1

When you use JavaScript to add interactive elements to your sites, users become involved with the Web page; they can interact with the SVG images as they click and move around with the mouse. These user-oriented functions include the well-known onmouseover and onmouseout events, where a change takes place as the mouse moves over an image or text. Other events include *onclick*, *onload*, and onkeypress, all of which you explore in this chapter.

FIGURE 6.2

With the addition of XML functions to Illustrator, users must use appropriate names when the XML ID option in the Illustrator preferences is selected. You must follow the correct XML naming conventions, which we will show you, when naming layers, objects on layers, and sublayers to ensure the proper function of JavaScript events.

FIGURE 6.3

The use of events in a JavaScript file brings to light another way to use layers to control objects. With the objects named on sublayers, you can use events to show and hide objects. You use this technique to transform one image into another simply by moving the mouse over the original image.

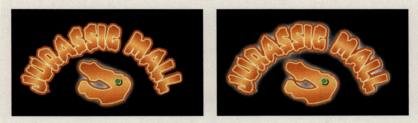

FIGURE 6.4

You also discover how to include an SVG file into an HTML text document. The key to adding SVG to HTML is the <EMBED> tag and its various settings, which allow you to access and view the SVG file on the Web. To illustrate this, you learn how to create a Web site on the Internet, upload the SVG and HTML files to your site, and observe how they operate.

```
<EMBED SRC="generic_image.svg" TYPE="image/svg-xml"
  PLUGINSPAGE="http://www.adobe.com/svg/viewer/install/" WIDTH="100" HEIGHT="200">
</EMBED>
```

FIGURE 6.5

You investigate Illustrator's collection of effects that alter objects, much the same as the other effects alter paths and raster objects. The SVG filters are reserved for images that will be saved in SVG format and placed on the Web.

FIGURE 6.6

LESSON 1   Exploring Scaleable Vector Graphics

Scalable Vector Graphics is a relatively new technology proposed by a group of software developers, including those at Adobe Systems, Corel, and Autocad. Their concept was to develop a standard method of describing and rendering vector images on the Web. It wasn't until 2001 that the World Wide Web Consortium (W3C.org) published the first draft for public release.

Similar to their EPS counterparts, SVG images retain clarity of appearance, regardless of the amount of scaling applied. This is not the case with high-resolution pixel-based images, which ***pixelate*** (break down) at some point during a scale. The easiest type of SVG image to create is the simple ***static*** (nonanimated) image. When you create static SVG images in an Illustrator document, you simply save the file in SVG format in the Save As dialog box. Static images contain no JavaScript, events, or XML, so there are no special naming requirements.

The SVG format allows the user to zoom in on an image, which is impossible with the GIF, JPEG, and PNG raster formats. Those who make architectural plans, maps, and technical illustrations would all benefit from publishing vector images on their Web sites, providing more useful and effective documents to their viewers. Let's take a moment to explore the modifier keys you can use to scale or move SVG on the Web page.

Chapter 6   SVG Graphics and Interactivity   **247**   **LEVEL 2**

- Command/Control changes the cursor to the Zoom In (+) tool so the image increases to 200%. The location where you click the tool on the image moves to the center of the browser window. It is best to click the tool on the approximate center of the image.

- Command/Control-Shift changes the cursor to the Zoom Out (−) tool to reduce the image to 50%.

- Option/Alt changes the cursor to the Hand tool so you can drag the image around the browser window; you can even drag the image to the window's edges so it's almost out of view.

If you did not already install the SVG Viewer plug-ins on your computer, do so now. You can download the free SVG Viewer plug-in file at http://www.adobe.com/svg/viewer/install/main.html.

In the following exercise, you create a static (nonanimated) SVG image and place it in a browser window to see how this type of image behaves with the addition of modifier key controls.

Explore Scaleable Vector Graphics

Exercise Setup:

Go to your desktop. Drag the SVG Interactivity folder from the Chapter_06 folder to the WIP_06 folder. This is necessary to keep all related files in the same folder for all the exercises in this chapter.

1   **From the WIP_06>SVG Interactivity folder, open the explore.ai document.**

2   **Choose File>Save As. Name the document as "explore.svg" and save the document in SVG Document format to the WIP_06>SVG Interactivity folder. In the SVG Options dialog box, click OK.**

       The default SVG settings are correct.

3   **Close the Illustrator SVG document.**

4   **Go to the desktop and open a new browser window. Open the WIP_06>SVG Interactivity folder on the desktop and drag the explore.svg file to the browser window.**

It takes a few seconds to load all the SVG information; then you will see the image in the browser window.

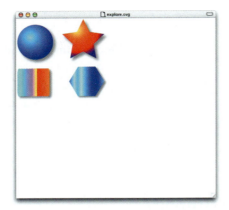

FIGURE 6.7

5 **Press Command/Control and click the Zoom tool on the approximate center of the four objects.**

You see the area where you clicked in the center of the window with the image enlarged to 200%.

FIGURE 6.8

6 **Continue holding Command/Control and click again on the center of the image.**

The image enlarges to 400%.

FIGURE 6.9

<u>7</u> **Press Command/Control-Shift and click the cursor on the center of the page to reduce the size back to 200%. Press only the Option/Alt key and drag the image to the right so the star is partly off the page.**

The cursor becomes a Hand tool and drags the image around, and even off, the page.

FIGURE 6.10

<u>8</u> **Press Command/Control-Shift and click the center of the page.**

The image reduces and centers on the page where you clicked the cursor.

FIGURE 6.11

9 **Continue holding Command/Control-Shift and click again on the center of the page.**

The image becomes even smaller.

FIGURE 6.12

10 **Press only the Option/Alt key and drag the image to the page's bottom-left corner.**

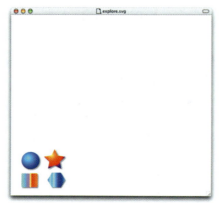

FIGURE 6.13

Chapter 6   SVG Graphics and Interactivity   **251**   **LEVEL 2**

11   **Refresh your browser window.**

The image reloads to its original position and size.

12   **Close the browser window.**

To Extend Your Knowledge . . .

BROWSERS AND SVG

Almost all browsers support "static" SVG images (ones that don't move or rely on JavaScript to perform assigned tasks). On the other hand, much of the appeal of SVG lies in its ability to incorporate JavaScript programs into vector illustrations, something that's becoming more frequently used by Webmasters.

LESSON 2 Adding Interactivity with JavaScript

SVG offers viewing and navigation options that aren't possible with raster image formats. SVG files become much more interesting when you add JavaScript. Thousands of Web developers and designers use the *JavaScript* scripting language to add interactivity to their pages.

When you combine SVG objects and JavaScript, you must change the Units & Display Performance preferences so objects are identified by their XML IDs. You do this in the following exercise. The XML code does not tolerate certain things like names beginning with numbers or spaces between words. The XML ID option automatically replaces spaces with an underscore symbol.

In order to create interactive SVG objects, you need to start with some JavaScript code, which you choose from the SVG Interactivity palette Options menu. The JavaScript files for the exercises in this chapter provide basic interactive functionality to the SVG format.

In the following exercise, you use SVG and JavaScript to add interactivity in the form of a color change. When you move your mouse over a tab, the tab changes color. When you move the mouse away from the tab, the tab reverts to its original color. This is known in Internet jargon as a "mouseover" or a "rollover."

Add Interactivity with JavaScript and Svg

1   **Open svg_tabs.ai from the WIP_06>SVG Interactivity folder. Open the Color, Layers, and SVG Interactivity palettes.**

This folder contains the files for this exercise.

2   **In the Preferences>Units & Display Performance dialog box, click the XML ID option and click OK to close the Preferences window.**

The names of layers, sublayers, and their objects must now adhere to the XML naming conventions. You cannot add spaces within names, nor can you duplicate names. When you show the Layers palette, Layer 1 will not take on the underscore in its name until you show its sublayers.

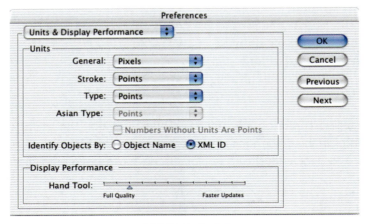

FIGURE 6.14

3 Select the rectangular path. In the Color palette, choose Web Safe RGB from the Options menu.

4 Set the Fill to R = 66, G = FF, B = FF. Set the Stroke to R = 00, G = 33, B = CC.

When listed as a hexadecimal color name, this fill color would be written as "#66FFFF". Note this name, as it will be used later in the exercise.

5 In the Layers palette, expand the sublayers so you can see the two objects listed.

The text block is named Home and the rectangle is named <Path>. Naming the sublayers that make up the drawing is a critical step in building interactive SVG documents.

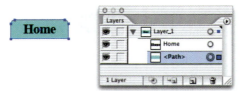

FIGURE 6.15

6 Double-click the <Path> sublayer and rename it "tab_01".

XML displays a warning message if there's a space between "tab" and "01". Remember to use an underscore to separate words, not a space.

FIGURE 6.16

Chapter 6   SVG Graphics and Interactivity   **253**   LEVEL 2

7   **Use the SVG Interactivity palette Options menu to choose the JavaScript Files option.**

When creating JavaScript interactivity with your SVG file, it is mandatory that an external JavaScript file be chosen to power the events you will set later.

8   **Click the Add button in the next dialog box that appears. In the Add JavaScript Files dialog box, click the Choose/Browse button.**

9   **Navigate to the WIP_06>SVG Interactivity folder. Choose events.js and click Open. In the Add JavaScript Files dialog box, click OK.**

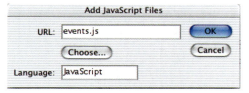

FIGURE 6.17

10   **In the JavaScript Files dialog box, click Done.**

The events.js file contains the JavaScript statements that allow this rollover effect to work. This file becomes associated with the SVG file you create later.

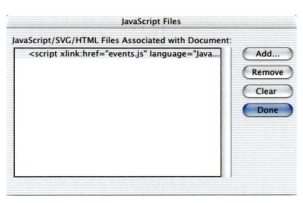

FIGURE 6.18

11   **Save your changes. Keep the document open for the next exercise.**

Add Events

1   **In the Layers palette, use the tab_01 Target button to select the sublayer's rectangular object.**

Objects must be selected when applying JavaScript events to them. If no objects are selected, the event defaults to the entire document. In this case, only certain events will work, such as "onload," which is executed when the HTML document loads in the browser.

2   **From the SVG Interactivity palette, choose onmouseout from the Event menu.**

This action sets an event to occur when a user moves the mouse off (out of the object region, thus the name "onmouseout") of the tab object.

FIGURE 6.19

3 **Type the following code (below) in the JavaScript field. Press Return/Enter after typing to apply the code.**

elemColor(evt, 'tab_01', '#66FFFF')

The "elemColor(evt" is the name of the event. The "tab_01" is the sublayer name, and its object, that the event is applied to. The "#66FFFF" is the hexadecimal code for the color given to the tab when the mouse moves away (out) from it.

Be sure to type the code exactly as shown here, including the letter case, such as the capital "C" in "Color." Use single quotes as specified. Illustrator automatically placed the double quotes you see in Figure 6.20.

FIGURE 6.20

4 **Return to the Event menu and choose onmouseover from the pop-up menu.**

This event applies its effects when the user moves the mouse over the object's region. This is where the "mouseover" term comes from.

Chapter 6 SVG Graphics and Interactivity   255   LEVEL 2

5 Type the following code in the JavaScript field. Press Return/Enter after typing to apply.

elemColor(evt, 'tab_01', '#0099CC')

The #0099CC is the hexadecimal code for the darker color the tab changes to when the mouse arrow touches it in the browser.

It is very important that you press Return/Enter after typing the code in order to apply it. You have now attributed two events to the object on the tab_01 sublayer.

FIGURE 6.21

6 From the File menu, choose Save As and choose SVG as the file format. Save the file as "svg_tabs.svg" to the WIP_06>SVG Interactivity folder.

7 In the SVG Options dialog box, click OK to accept the default settings.

8 From the desktop, open a new browser window. From the WIP_06>SVG Interactivity folder, drag svg_tabs.svg to the new browser window.

Always create a new browser window when you drag an SVG file to the browser. Depending on your browser, if a window already displays an SVG, it won't accept another SVG file you try dragging to it.

9 In the browser window, move your mouse over the tab and move it away.

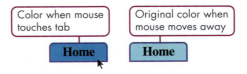

FIGURE 6.22

The tab turns a darker color when you pass the mouse pointer over it on the page. When you move the mouse pointer away from the tab, you trigger the onmouseout event, and the tab returns to its original color.

LEVEL 2 | **256** | Chapter 6 SVG Graphics and Interactivity

---

10 Return to the svg_tabs.svg document, which is now the current working document. Save your changes. Keep the document open for the next exercise.

To Extend Your Knowledge . . .

ACCURACY COUNTS

You must type JavaScript code with impeccable accuracy. If you enter one incorrect letter or quote, the entire event fails. If an event does not work, you must return to the code, ensure that you typed every item correctly and that you chose the correct JavaScript file. If any item in the production is out of place or typed incorrectly, the event will not operate as expected.

LESSON 3   JavaScript and XML Naming Conventions

Under normal circumstances, you can name any object by targeting it on the Layers palette and double-clicking the sublayer on which it resides. You can use spaces and ignore case (upper, lower, mixed) when you name a non-SVG object. You learned in Lesson 2 that these naming conventions don't work when you export the file as SVG or otherwise use the file in an XML workflow.

When you add JavaScript commands to a document, you run into problems if every object has the same name on the Layers palette, such as the default name of <Path>. JavaScript must be able to identify and single out objects according to their layer names.

In the previous exercise, you created a single navigation tab that changes color when the user touches it with the mouse pointer.

In this exercise, you complete the navigation object by duplicating the tab object and modifying the JavaScript associated with each of the clones. You also see how the proper use of naming conventions simplifies the development process.

Create Multiple Events in a Single File

1 Select both the Home text block and the rectangle button. Drag this to the right (holding the Shift key to constrain) so that the left side of the duplicate rectangle touches the right side of the original (see Figure 6.23).

2 When the dragged object is in position, press Option/Alt and release the mouse to duplicate. Hold down Command/Control and press the "D" key three times.

Three more duplicates appear to the right of the first duplicate.

Chapter 6 SVG Graphics and Interactivity **257** LEVEL 2

3 Use the Type tool to rename the duplicates on the Artboard: "Books", "Video", "Audio", and "Contact". Close the sublayers so they are not visible. Click Layer_1 to make it active.

FIGURE 6.23

4 At the bottom of the Layers palette, click the Create New Layer icon four times.

Four duplicate layers appear above Layer_1. The XML ID code renamed them with underscores replacing the spaces in the names: Layer_2, Layer_3, Layer_4, and Layer_5.

5 Rename Layer_1 to "Home", Layer_2 to "Books", Layer_3 to "Video", Layer_4 to "Audio", and Layer_5 to "Contact".

6 Select the Books rectangle path on the Artboard. Go to the layers palette and use the Selected Object icon to relocate it to the Books layer. Select the Books text block on the Artboard and relocate its sublayer to the Books layer.

FIGURE 6.24

7 Repeat step 6 to relocate the two Video sublayers (starting with the rectangle, then the text block) to the Video layer. Do the same to select and relocate the Audio and Contact objects.

Each named button should reside on its own layer.

FIGURE 6.25

8 Click the Sublayers icon of the Books layer to expand its sublayers.

Illustrator added "_2_" to the tab_01 name to identify the duplicate tab of the same name.

9 **Double-click the tab_01_2_ sublayer and rename it "tab_02".**

Pay close attention to letter case. If you accidentally replaced "tab" with "Tab", the JavaScript code looking for "tab" would fail. Remember, XML is case sensitive.

10 **Continue to show the other layers' sublayers and rename the tab_01 sublayers. Change the Video sublayer to "tab_03", the Audio sublayer to "tab_04", and the Contact sublayer to "tab_05".**

The sublayer for each tab on the Artboard is now named appropriately. All that remains is to customize the JavaScript code for each tab.

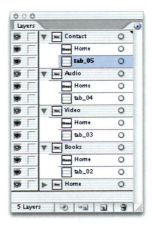

FIGURE 6.26

11 **Save your changes. Keep the document open for the next exercise.**

Customize the XML Code

1 **On the Artboard, click the rectangle of the Books object. Show the SVG Interactivity palette.**

You do not need to select the text block. The rectangle is the larger object and provides more area to trigger the mouseover.

2 **In the large lower section of the SVG Interactivity palette, the code of the two events appears in the event list. Click the top onmouseout option.**

When the onmouseout option is clicked, its code appears in the JavaScript field.

3 **In the JavaScript field, change tab_01 to "tab_02". Press Return/Enter to apply.**

4 **Click the onmouseover event in the event list. In the JavaScript field, change tab_01 to "tab_02". Press Return/Enter to apply.**

Chapter 6   SVG Graphics and Interactivity   **259**   LEVEL 2

The JavaScript for the second tab is now correctly applied to the tab_02 sublayer object. You must change the JavaScript associated with all the remaining tabs; right now, they still refer to the tab_01 object.

FIGURE 6.27

5 On the Artboard, select the rectangle of the Video object.

6 In the SVG Interactivity palette, change both of the tab_01 names to "tab_03", and apply the changes.

7 On the Artboard, select the rectangle of the Audio object.

8 In the SVG Interactivity palette, change both of the tab_01 names to "tab_04", and apply the changes.

9 Select the rectangle of the Contact object on the Artboard.

10 In the SVG Interactivity palette, change both of the tab_01 names to "tab_05", and apply the changes.

The naming and scripting are complete. The next step is to save the file and open it in a browser window.

FIGURE 6.28

11 Save your changes and close the document.

12 Return to the desktop. In your browser, create a new window. From the WIP_06>SVG Interactivity folder, drag the svg_tabs.svg file to the browser window.

13 Move the mouse over the various tabs in the browser window.

When the mouse touches the tab (*onmouseover*), the tab's color should become darker. When you move the mouse away (*onmouseout*), the tab should return to its original color.

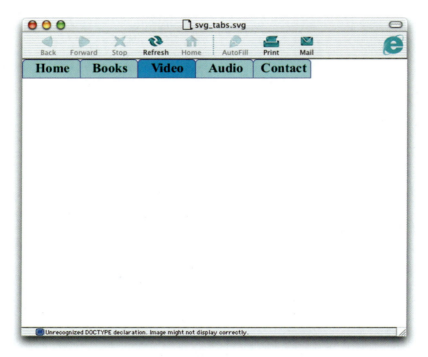

FIGURE 6.29

14 Close the browser window.

To Extend Your Knowledge . . .

ONMOUSEOVERS

Even though you may see this type of color-changing button on the Internet, it does not necessarily mean you are witnessing an SVG image enhanced with JavaScript and events. Various onmouseover methods are available in applets and other types of HTML coding. This SVG image, however, eliminates all HTML coding, other than embedding the SVG file. All of the onmouseover programming is contained within the SVG image, powered by the events.js file.

LESSON 4 JavaScript Events

JavaScript cannot affect an SVG file by itself. You must include an intermediary function relating the JavaScript code to the SVG file. This is known as an ***event***. Even though many events currently exist, Illustrator includes only the most commonly used mouse- and key-related events in its Event menu.

Events dictate which JavaScript operation takes place within the SVG image, which results in executing an action, such as onmouseover, onkeypress, or onmouseout. When the action takes place, we say the action was ***triggered***.

The events are named by the method that is used to trigger the JavaScript code associated with it. Events, such as "onmouseover," appropriately refer to the action that runs the script — in this case, when the browser mouse moves over the object. The onload event triggers when the HTML file loads in the browser.

FIGURE 6.30

Using JavaScript events in your SVG document must have all components in place:

- The objects receiving events must be named on their sublayers. This is necessary when the object is to be specified in the JavaScript code you type.

- An object must be selected before applying events to it from the SVG Interactivity palette. If the object is grouped with others, it is best to use the sublayer to target and isolate the single object.

- The external JavaScript file, such as events.js, must be attached to the SVG file (use the SVG Interactivity Options menu and select JavaScript Files).

- For best communication, the JavaScript file and the SVG document should be in the same folder. Otherwise, if files get moved around, the JavaScript file may not be accessible.

If you upload the SVG file to a folder on the Internet, be sure to include the JavaScript file as well. The SVG events will not work without this file being accessed. The most commonly used events on the Internet are the onmouseover and onmouseout, where the mouse pointer touches the image and causes an action to take place (onmouseover); the mouse moves away to return the object to its original state (onmouseout). Another name for the onmouseover technique is the ***rollover***.

In the previous exercise, you created objects that changed color when the mouse moved over their path regions. There are also rollovers that change the graphic image when a mouseover is triggered. In the following exercise, you create one of these rollovers.

Create an Image Rollover

1 **Create a new RGB document with the Artboard set for 640 × 480 in; set the units for pixels. Open the Layers and SVG Interactivity palettes.**

In a new document, the Artboard is centered on the screen. All placed objects default to the Artboard's center. This eliminates the need to align them with the Align palette. If you ever place images that do not align, use the Align palette to reposition them to one place.

2 **From the File menu, choose Place. Navigate to the WIP_06>SVG Interactivity folder and import jurassic_mall_2.jpg.**

The placed image is located in the middle of the Artboard.

3 **Choose File>Place again. Return to the same folder and place the jurassic_mall_1.jpg.**

Placing the object should position this image on top of the other in the Artboard. The two images are aligned correctly for the coming JavaScript events. When you create your own images for such a rollover, make certain that the two images are exactly the same size.

FIGURE 6.31

4 **In the Layers palette, expand the sublayers for Layer_1.**

5 **Double-click the top sublayer and rename it "image_1".**

Only sublayers need to be renamed for JavaScript. The layer possessing the sublayers does not need to be renamed.

6 **Double-click the bottom sublayer and rename it "image_2".**

Chapter 6 SVG Graphics and Interactivity   **263**   LEVEL 2

Naming sublayers is mandatory when working with JavaScript and events. When the code is written in the SVG Interactivity palette, it must know what object to apply its effects to.

FIGURE 6.32

7 Use the image_1 sublayer to target its object. In the SVG Interactivity palette, choose **onmouseover** from the Event menu.

8 In the JavaScript field, type the following text and press Return/Enter to apply:

elemHide(evt, 'image_1')

This event hides the top image (image_1) when the mouse moves over it in the browser window.

FIGURE 6.33

9 Press Command/Control-3 to hide the selected image.

10 Use the image_2 sublayer to target its object. In the SVG Interactivity palette, choose **onmouseout** from the Event menu.

11 In the JavaScript field, type the following text and press Return/Enter to apply:

elemShow(evt, 'image_1')

This event shows the top image_1 when the mouse moves off of image_2 in the browser window. Type this code correctly, as shown here. Yes, you are applying the code to the image_2 sublayer, but it refers to the showing of image_1.

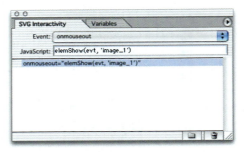

FIGURE 6.34

12. Use Show All in the Object menu to show the hidden image.

13. Name the document "jurassic_rollover.svg", and save it in SVG format to your WIP_06>SVG Interactivity folder. Keep the document open for the next exercise.

Apply a JavaScript File

1. In the open document, choose JavaScript Files from the SVG Interactivity palette Options menu.

2. In the JavaScript Files dialog box, click the Add button.

3. Click the Choose/Browse button in the Add JavaScript Files dialog box. Navigate to the WIP_06>SVG Interactivity folder and choose events.js. Click Open.

   The events.js file is not a single JavaScript event but contains several events that Adobe has collected in the file. As long as you correctly type the necessary code in the SVG Interactivity palette, these events should work.

4. Click OK in the Add JavaScript Files dialog box.

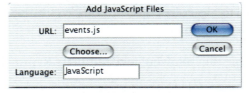

FIGURE 6.35

5. In the JavaScript Files dialog box, click Done.

   The events are now applied to the images, and the JavaScript file is attached to the document.

6. Save your changes and close the document.

Chapter 6 SVG Graphics and Interactivity **265** **LEVEL 2**

7 Go to your desktop and open a new browser window.

8 From the WIP_06>SVG Interactivity folder, drag the jurassic_rollover.svg file to the browser window.

9 In the window, move the mouse arrow over the Jurassic Mall image.

The image disappears because the onmouseover event tells the browser to hide it. The mouse is now hovering over the lower image in the SVG document.

10 Move the mouse off the remaining image.

The onmouseout event shows the original image (image_1) when the mouse leaves the image's region.

11 Move the mouse on and off the images.

12 After you experiment with the rollover, close the browser window.

To Extend Your Knowledge . . .

OTHER JAVASCRIPT EVENTS

After you study the Event menu and all its selections, you can use a bit of creative ingenuity to create some interesting effects for the objects that appear on your Web pages. The events.js JavaScript file includes several other events that we have not shown you:

To change the fill color of a path, type the following code in the event's JavaScript field:

elemColor(evt, 'object name', '#hexadecimal color')

To change the stroke weight, type the following JavaScript code, where the number represents the stroke thickness:

elemStroke(evt, 'object name', '1')

To change the color of the stroke, type:

elemStrokeColor(evt, 'object name, '#hexadecimal color')

? **If You Have Problems**

If you go through the process of applying events to objects and renaming the sublayers, and, after dragging the SVG file to a new browser window, find that the interactivity does not work, make sure you have attached the corresponding JavaScript file to the document. This oversight is the most common problem when an event does not work.

If you upload the SVG file to a folder on the Internet, be sure to include the JavaScript file as well. The SVG events will not work without this file being accessed.

| LEVEL 2 | **266** | Chapter 6   SVG Graphics and Interactivity |

LESSON 5   Embedding the SVG File

Sharing your SVG files with Web users is not as easy as creating them. On your own computer, you simply drag an SVG file to a browser window and then view the image. You cannot, however, supply all Web users with copies of the file to drag to their own browser windows. Instead, when users access your Web site, the HTML code is necessary to show the SVG image.

To present the SVG image properly, you must use the **<EMBED>** tag to *embed* the SVG file within the HTML file. The following code is an example of a typical **<EMBED>** tag:

> <EMBED SRC="filename.svg" TYPE="image/svg-xml" QUALITY=high
> BGCOLOR=#FFFFFF PLUGINSPAGE="http://www.adobe.com/svg/viewer/install/"
> WIDTH="400" HEIGHT="400">

For the browser to acknowledge the SVG file, you must identify the **SRC** and the **TYPE**. The **SRC** (source) names the SVG file you are using, and the **TYPE** tells the browser that this is an SVG or XML image. These two parts of the embedding tag are mandatory so the browser knows how to show the image.

The other components of the embedding code are optional. The **QUALITY** shows the image in low, medium, or high clarity. The **BGCOLOR** is the background color, which can be any hexadecimal color you prefer, but white (**#FFFFFF**) is most commonly used. The **PLUGINSPAGE** identifies the link to access or install any plug-ins that may be necessary for viewers to see the image.

You can use the **WIDTH** and **HEIGHT** attributes to make the image larger or smaller than the original object in the document. If you leave out the **WIDTH** and **HEIGHT** attributes, the SVG image in the browser window defaults to a very small size. It is necessary to find the image's exact width and height so the increments can be applied to the **WIDTH** and **HEIGHT** tags in the code.

In this exercise, you embed an SVG file into an HTML document.

Embed an SVG Image in HTML Code

1   Open embed_image.ai from the WIP_06>SVG Interactivity folder. Open the Info palette.

2   Press Command/Control-A to select all the objects on the page.

3   In the Info palette, note the W (width) and H (height) increments and write them down on a piece of paper.

4   Choose File>Save As to name the file "embed_image.svg" and to save it in SVG format to your WIP_06>SVG Interactivity folder. Close the file.

5 Go to your desktop. Use your word processor to open embed_image.html from the WIP_06>SVG Interactivity folder.

Be sure to open the file as "text only" or "plain text" and not RTF (Rich Text Format) or any other form. The Macintosh's SimpleText or TextEdit word processors are quite sufficient. TextEdit, however, must have its preferences set for Plain Text. Windows' Notepad word processor is strictly a "text only" program and is suggested.

? If You Have Problems

If you open any file with an ".html" extension in Microsoft Word, the program shows you a blank document. Do not be alarmed if this occurs. At the bottom of the View menu is a special option called "HTML Source." Choose this option to see the HTML code. The HTML Source option does not appear unless you open an HTML document.

---

6 Under the <body> tag, type the following:

<EMBED SRC="embed_image.svg" TYPE="image/svg-xml" QUALITY=high BGCOLOR=#FFFFFF PLUGINSPAGE="http://www.adobe.com/svg/viewer/install/" >

We purposely left out the **WIDTH** and **HEIGHT** attributes.

7 Save your changes and keep the HTML document open.

8 From your desktop, go to the WIP_06>SVG Interactivity folder. Open the embed_image.html in a browser window. Keep the browser window open.

Note the small size of the object, despite its larger size in the Illustrator document. We advise using Internet Explorer or Netscape. Not all browsers are compatible with SVG files. Also, you must have SVG Viewer installed on your computer.

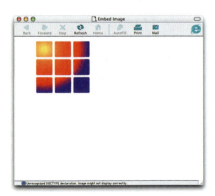

FIGURE 6.36

9 Return to the HTML file in your word processor. Add the Width and Height text to the code. Replace the "00" with the width and height increments you wrote down in Step 3.

Chapter 6   SVG Graphics and Interactivity

<EMBED SRC="embed_image.svg" TYPE="image/svg-xml" QUALITY=high
BGCOLOR=#FFFFFF PLUGINSPAGE="http://www.adobe.com/svg/viewer/install/"
WIDTH="00" HEIGHT="00" >

10 **Save your changes to the HTML file and close it.**

11 **Return to the browser window and refresh it.**

The image appears at the size you specified with the **WIDTH** and **HEIGHT** attributes. You can control how big the image appears in the browser by setting any width and height increments you wish.

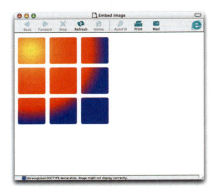

FIGURE 6.37

12 **Close the browser window.**

To Extend Your Knowledge . . .

JAVASCRIPT AND HTML

In any other case where you were using external JavaScript files referenced in an HTML document, you would have to include a tag in the HTML file that reads <script src="filename.js" language="JavaScript"></script> (the file name would be the actual name of the JavaScript file). The HTML file would then know to access this file for the events code. You do not have to do this in the HTML in which you embed an SVG file. As you have seen, you are already attaching a JavaScript file to the SVG document using the SVG Interactivity Options menu.

SVG FILES ON THE INTERNET

It is impressive to see your SVG files at work on your own computer's browser, but the ultimate test is to see them operate on a Web site. We show you how to do this in the final Challenge exercise, after you have created more SVG files from which to choose.

Chapter 6 SVG Graphics and Interactivity **269** LEVEL 2

LESSON 6 Using SVG Filters

Even though you can embed or link raster files in your SVG objects, this sometimes defeats the objective of keeping the file sizes small and keeping rasterization to a minimum. A good example of this is using filters. If you apply a regular filter to an SVG file, the image becomes rasterized when rendered in the browser window. Zooming in reveals the pixelization and produces a fuzzy, larger-than-necessary file.

To work around this problem, use the Effects>SVG Filters instead of regular raster filters. In the illustration in Figure 6.38, you see the SVG filters that ship with Illustrator.

FIGURE 6.38

In this exercise, you apply SVG filters to objects in an SVG file to create a Web button.

Apply SVG Filters

1 Create a new letter-size RGB document with units set for pixels.

2 In the Toolbox, click the Default Fill and Stroke box. Use the Ellipse tool to draw a 100-px circle in the top center of the page.

3 From the Effect>SVG Filters menu, choose Apply SVG Filter. Click the Preview button in the Apply SVG Filter dialog box.

Keep the dialog box located to the screen's right so it doesn't obscure the selected object. All the SVG filters are listed in the box. When you select an item in the list, you see the effect of the filter on the object on the page. This allows you to preview the effects of multiple SVG filters before you actually apply a filter to your image.

If You Have Problems

You can't preview two of these filter effects in the Illustrator document because they are animated effects: PixelPlay1 and PixelPlay2. To see how they work, load the svg_filters.html file into a browser window. You can find the file in the WIP_06>SVG Interactivity folder.

FIGURE 6.39

4 Select various filters in the Apply SVG Filter dialog box and observe how they affect the circle.

5 Keep the AI_Woodgrain filter selected, and click OK. Deselect the circle.

This particular filter eliminates the previous fill and stroke of the object.

FIGURE 6.40

6 Click the Default Fill and Stroke icon in the Toolbox. Use the Rectangle tool to draw a 150-px square. Position the square so it covers half of the circle.

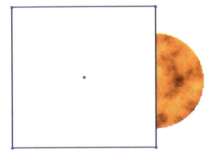

FIGURE 6.41

7 From the Effect>SVG Filters menu, choose AI_Alpha 1.

Chapter 6 SVG Graphics and Interactivity 271 LEVEL 2

This filter paints the square with a white fill and a black stroke. The white fill affects the Alpha 1 filter where the square object covers the circle.

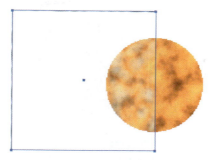

FIGURE 6.42

8 **Center the square on top of the circle.**

The circle's appearance changes slightly.

9 **Move the square down so its top almost touches the circle.**

The circle's appearance changes again.

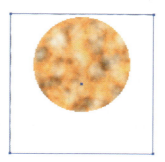

FIGURE 6.43

10 **In the Toolbox, click the Swap Fill and Stroke icon.**

Now you can see what happened: The white fill affected the square's filter. The Alpha 1 background is transparent, so laying the square on the circle distorted its appearance.

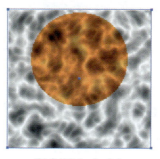

FIGURE 6.44

11 Click the Fill box in the Toolbox. In the Swatches palette, click the Aloha Blue swatch.

You can use the Fill box to paint the pixels in the Alpha 1 filter.

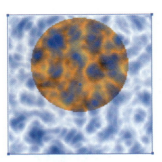

FIGURE 6.45

12 Save the document as "svg_filters_sample.svg" to your WIP_06>SVG Interactivity folder. In the SVG Options dialog box, click OK to accept the default settings. Keep the document open for the next exercise.

Add More SVG Filters

1 In the open document, the square should be selected. From the Select menu, choose Next Object Below. Copy the selected circle.

2 Select the square. Press Command/Control-F to paste the circle in front of the square. Keep the circle selected.

3 Open the Appearance palette and use the Options menu to choose Reduce to Basic Appearance. Copy the circle.

This option removes the applied SVG Filter from the pasted circle.

4 Select all the objects and press Command/Control-7 to mask them.

FIGURE 6.46

5 Press Command/Control-B to paste the copied circle behind the selected objects.

6 Change the Stroke to 8-pt Aloha Blue.

7 From the Effect menu, choose SVG Filters>AI_GaussianBlur_4.

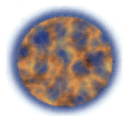

FIGURE 6.47

8 Press Command/Control-S to save your changes and close the document.

9 From the desktop, go to the WIP_06>SVG Interactivity folder.

10 Use your browser to create a new window. Drag the svg_filters_sample.svg file to the new window.

11 Press Option/Alt and drag the image to the window's center. Press Command/Control and zoom in several times.

Even though you scaled the image, the quality remains crisp and clear.

12 Close the browser window.

To Extend Your Knowledge . . .

SVG FILTERS AND TRANSPARENCY

Apply SVG filters to a few images and experiment with overlaying the images. Some of the filters are transparent and screen the objects underneath. You can use this method to create a variety of interesting effects impossible to produce with a single filter.

SUMMARY

In this chapter, you learned how to use SVG to create scalable graphics that you can use on a Web page. You discovered how the format supports zooming in the browser window. From there, you created interactive SVG files, which require JavaScript to invoke changes when specific events are triggered. You used onmouseover and onmouseout rollover effects to create interactive navigation elements, and you learned how to connect those elements to external URLs or HTML pages within the same site.

You also used JavaScript to trigger events that animate an SVG icon, and you discovered how to embed an SVG object within an HTML page. Lastly, you experimented with SVG filter effects, which allow you to apply raster-type effects while maintaining the integrity of your SVG objects.

LEVEL 2 **274** **Chapter 6 SVG Graphics and Interactivity**

KEY TERMS

embed	onload	Scalable Vector Graphics (SVG)
events	onmouseout	static
interactivity	onmouseover	SVG Viewer
JavaScript	pixelate	trigger
onclick	rollover	XML (eXtensible Markup Language)

CHECKING CONCEPTS AND TERMS

MULTIPLE CHOICE

Circle the letter that matches the correct answer for each of the following questions.

1. Which of the following describes the advantage of viewing an SVG graphic in a browser window?

   a. You can use a modifier key to zoom in and out of an SVG image.

   b. An SVG image remains crisp and clear, regardless of its viewing size.

   c. You can move an SVG image around in the browser window.

   d. All of the above.

2. To use an SVG image on a Web page, you must _____.

   a. use the <IMG SRC> tag in the HTML code

   b. embed the image with the <EMBED> tag

   c. write the image into a JavaScript file

   d. drag the image to a browser window

3. To make an object change color when the mouse pointer touches it requires _____.

   a. the objects to be painted with the alternating colors and placed on different layers

   b. a JavaScript file and the onmouseover event selected

   c. selecting only an event

   d. choosing only the JavaScript file

4. The width and height increments in an <EMBED> tag _____.

   a. control the browser window size

   b. are mandatory; you cannot see the image without them

   c. set the size of the image as it appears in the browser window

   d. must be set for one-half the actual size of the image

5. To name layers according to XML conventions, you must first select the XML ID option in the _____.

   a. Layers palette Options menu

   b. SVG Interactivity palette Options menu

   c. Units & Display Performance preferences dialog box

   d. JavaScript Files dialog box

6. In accordance with XML naming conventions, spaces in a name should be _____.

   a. a hyphen

   b. replaced with an underscore

   c. replaced with a hyphen

   d. None of the above.

7. Scaleable Vector Graphics are appropriately named because _____.

   a. as objects in the document, they have to be scaled to fit the design

   b. the graphics can be scaled but become pixelated

   c. the graphics can be scaled without becoming pixelated

   d. they can be scaled, but any raster images in the design become pixelated

Chapter 6   SVG Graphics and Interactivity   **275**   **LEVEL 2**

8. Which of the following is not an event from the SVG Interactivity palette Event menu?

   a. Onmouseover

   b. Onload

   c. Onkeypress

   d. Onimageclick

9. The Apply SVG Filters dialog box _____.

   a. is required if you want to apply an SVG filter to the selected object

   b. is an alternative method for applying SVG filters and shows a preview

   c. allows you to access other SVG filter libraries

   d. None of the above.

10. A unique characteristic of an SVG file is that it _____.

   a. must be embedded in an HTML file to function on the Web

   b. can contain JavaScript code and events

   c. cannot be placed in a publishing document, such as an EPS image

   d. All of the above.

DISCUSSION QUESTIONS

1. What are the advantages of SVG images over the standard raster images (GIF, JPEG, and PNG) on the Web?

2. How does including JavaScript in an SVG file affect the functionality of an image published on the Web?

3. Describe one example of using a static SVG image on the Internet.

SKILL DRILL

Skill Drills reinforce learned skills. Each skill that is reinforced is the same as, or nearly the same as, a skill we presented in the lessons. We provide detailed instructions in a step-by-step format. You should complete these exercises in order.

NOTE: To ensure that the following Skill Drill exercises work correctly, you should still have the Identify Objects By option set for XML ID in Preferences>Units & Display Performance. Change this setting before you perform any JavaScript interactivity and create the layer names. If you change the setting to XML ID after the fact, your layer and object names will not adhere to XML naming conventions, and the exercises will fail.

1. Create an SVG Document with Image Map

1. Open svg_link.ai from the WIP_06>SVG Interactivity folder. Show the Swatches and Align palettes.

2. Select the square on the Artboard and fill it with Mediterranean Blue. Set the stroke for None.

3. Draw a six-sided polygon within the boundaries of the square guide on the Artboard. Fill the polygon with Aloha Blue and Stroke it with 4-pt Yellow.

   Press Shift as you draw the polygon to constrain the object to 90 degrees. Go to Outline viewing mode to see the guide better if necessary.

4. With the polygon selected, go to the Effect>SVG Filters menu and choose the Apply SVG Filter option. Click the Preview button in the dialog box.

Move the dialog box to the right so you can see the effect on your selected object.

5. Experiment with various filters from the list, and choose the one you like best. Click OK to apply the filter.

6. Select the Type tool and click it on the Artboard, away from the painted objects. Set the Font to 10-pt Times or Times New Roman Bold. In the Paragraph palette, click the Align Center option.

7. In the text block, type the name of your favorite Web site.

    Type only the name of the Web site, not the entire URL.

8. Select all the objects and click the Horizontal Align Center and Vertical Align Center options in the Align palette.

9. With the Selection tool, select the text block, and fill the type with white. In the Attributes palette, assign a rectangular image map. Type in the URL of the Web site you named in Step 7 and press Return/Enter to apply this.

10. Save the file as "svg_link.svg" in SVG format to your WIP_06>SVG Interactivity folder. Close the document.

11. Go to the desktop and open a new browser window. Drag svg_link.svg to the window and click the text link in the image.

    The browser displays your favorite Web site. You can add image maps to SVG files and use them on the Internet.

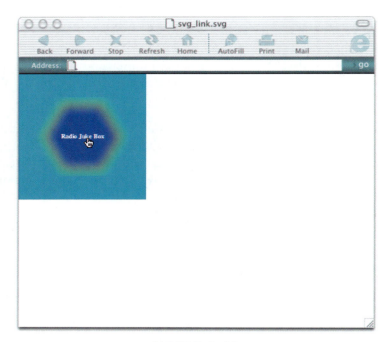

FIGURE 6.48

12. Close the browser window.

Chapter 6 SVG Graphics and Interactivity **277** LEVEL 2

2. Add Special Effects

You are a Webmaster and have converted your new client's logo into digital art to be used on their site, which you created. The client would like some added effects applied to the logo for when the user moves a mouse across it or clicks it. You know of some JavaScript events that can be added.

Note: Make certain that XML ID is selected in the Units & Display Performance preferences.

1. From your WIP_06>SVG Interactivity folder, open the dog_food.ai document. Show the SVG Interactivity and Layers palettes. Click the sublayers icon of Layer_1 to see the sublayers.

2. In the Layers palette, use the inner_circle sublayer to target its object.

   The small circle around the dog paw becomes selected.

3. In the SVG Interactivity palette, use the Events menu to select onmousedown. Type the following code into the JavaScript field and press Return/Enter to apply.

   elemColor(evt,'inner_circle','#FDC589')

   The onmousedown event does its work as the user presses the mouse and continues to hold it down on the object. In this case, the event changes the circle's fill color as long as the mouse is held down.

4. Return to the Events menu and select onmouseup. Type the following code into the JavaScript field and press Return/Enter to apply.

   elemColor(evt,'inner_circle','#FFFFFF')

   The onmouseup event changes to the color in the code when the mouse button is released. The color set here returns the object back to white.

5. In the Layers palette, use the outer_circle sublayer to target its object.

   The outer circle becomes selected.

6. In the SVG Activity palette, use the Events menu to select onmouseover. Type the following code into the JavaScript field and press Return/Enter to apply.

   elemStrokeColor(evt,'outer_circle','#0000CC')

   With this code, the onmouseover event changes the stroke color of the outer circle when the mouse touches its path.

7. Return to the Events menu and select onmouseout. Type the following code into the JavaScript field and press Return/Enter to apply.

   elemStrokeColor(evt,'outer_circle','#FF0000')

   With this code, the onmouseout event changes the stroke color back to its original red when the mouse moves away from the path.

8. From the SVG Activity palette Options menu, use JavaScript Files to go to the WIP_06>SVG Interactivity folder and attach the events.js file to the document.

9. Save the document as "dog_food.svg" in SVG format to the WIP_06>SVG Interactivity folder. Close the document.

10. Go to the desktop and create a new browser window. From the WIP_06>SVG Interactivity folder, drag the dog_food.svg file to the window.

11. Move the mouse arrow over the larger circle to see its stroke color change. Move the mouse away to see the original color return.

    You can make the image larger by pressing Command/Control and clicking the Zoom tool on the logo in the browser window.

12. Click-hold the mouse arrow on the white area of the logo's smaller circle to see its fill color change. Release the mouse to see it return to its white fill.

    Continue to click and hold the mouse briefly on the small circle, then release the mouse. Also, move the mouse over the larger circle border to see the color change.

FIGURE 6.49

13. Close the browser window.

3. Create Twinkling Stars with SVG Filters

1. Create a new letter-size RGB document with the orientation set for landscape and the units set for pixels. Show the page rulers. Open the Swatches palette.

2. Draw a 350 × 280 pixel rectangle on the Artboard's center. Fill the rectangle with Black and Stroke with None.

3. Copy the rectangle and press Command/Control-B to paste a copy in back. Press Command/Control-5 to convert the pasted object into a guide.

4. Select and hide the rectangle.

5. Click the Default Fill and Stroke icon in the Toolbox. Use the Star tool to draw eight stars of various sizes and angles.

6. Position the stars within the rectangular guide to create the impression of stars in the sky.

7. Select all the stars. From the Effect>SVG Filters menu, choose the AI_PixelPlay_2 filter.

8. Click OK in the warning dialog box that appears.

    The warning states that this particular filter cannot be viewed in the Illustrator document.

9. Show the hidden rectangle.

    Don't worry that the stars are barely visible against the black background. In the browser, the PixelPlay animation triggers in the browser and shows the stars.

10. Save the file as "starbursts.svg" in SVG format to your WIP_06>SVG Interactivity folder. Close the document.

11. Go to the desktop and open a new browser window. Drag starbursts.svg to the new window.

    The stars animate in a variety of appearances programmed into the filter.

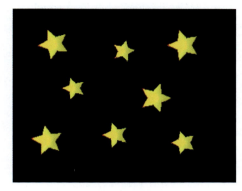

FIGURE 6.50

12. Close the browser window.

4. Use JavaScript to Change Stroke Width

1. Create a new RGB document with the Artboard set to 468 × 60 pixels and units set to pixels. Open the Swatches, Stroke, Layers, and SVG Interactivity palettes.

2. On the Artboard, use the Star tool to draw a star that is approximately 25 pixels in size. Press Shift while drawing to constrain the angle.

3. Fill the Star with Yellow and apply a Stroke of 1-pt Sunshine. In the Stroke palette, click the Round Join option.

4. In the Layers palette, expand the sublayers of Layer_1. Rename the <Path> sublayer to "star".

5. Keep the star selected. In the SVG Interactivity palette, use the Options menu to select JavaScript files.

6. Click Add. From the WIP_06>SVG Interactivity folder, choose events.js. Close the dialog boxes to return to the SVG Interactivity palette.

7. Choose onmouseover from the Events menu.

8. In the JavaScript field, type the following and press Return/Enter to apply.

    elemStrokeWidth(evt, 'star', '8')

   The "star" identifies the name of the object on the sublayer. The "8" indicates the weight of the stroke that appears when the mouse touches the object.

9. Choose onmouseout from the Events menu.

10. In the JavaScript field, type the following and press Return/Enter to apply.

    elemStrokeWidth(evt, 'star', '1')

   The stroke returns to its 1-pt weight when the mouse moves away from the star path in the browser.

11. Save the document as "star_stroke.svg" in SVG format to your WIP_06>SVG Interactivity folder. Close the document.

12. At the desktop, open a new browser window and drag star_stroke.svg to the new window. Move the mouse over the star to watch its stroke thicken when you touch it.

FIGURE 6.51

13. Close the browser window.

CHALLENGE

Challenge exercises expand on, or are somewhat related to, skills presented in the lessons. Each exercise provides a brief introduction, followed by numbered-step instructions that are not as detailed as those in the Skill Drill exercises. You should complete these exercises in order.

1. Create a Menu to Show/Hide with Onclick

You want to create a menu that does not take up too much space on a Web page but that extends to its full length when clicked. Your task is to create a pull-down menu using JavaScript and events.

1. Open the dropdown_menu.ai document from the WIP_06>SVG Interactivity folder. Open the Swatches and Layers palettes.

2. Use the Type tool to click a point text block above the rectangle.

3. Set the Font to 12-pt Times or Times New Roman and the paragraph alignment for Align Left.

4. Type the words "Click for Menu" in the text block. Position the block inside the rectangle, near the left side.

5. Select the text block, the rectangle, and the triangle.

6. In the Align palette, click the Vertical Align Center option. Deselect the objects.

7. In the Layers palette, double-click Layer_1 and rename it "menu_top".

8. Click the Create New Layer icon at the bottom of the Layers palette.

9. Rename the new layer "menu_bottom".

10. Select the menu_bottom layer and relocate it under the menu_top layer in the list.

FIGURE 6.52

11. Save the file as "dropdown_menu.svg" in SVG format to the WIP_06>SVG Interactivity folder. Keep the document open for the next exercise.

2. Create the Bottom Menu

Now that the top menu is in place, you need to create the bottom menu.

1. Click the bottom_menu layer to make it active.

2. Draw a 150 × 200 pixel rectangle and position it directly under the smaller rectangle. Keep the drawn rectangle selected.

   Make sure the top segment of the larger rectangle matches and aligns with the bottom segment of the smaller rectangle.

3. Use the Eyedropper tool to click the small rectangle to paint the selected large rectangle.

4. Select the text block and drag it to the top of the larger rectangle. Press Option/Alt to make a duplicate.

   Press Shift as you drag to constrain the move.

5. Use the Type tool to highlight the text of the duplicate text block and change the words to "Fave Site 1". Select the duplicate text block with the Selection tool.

6. In the Layers palette, drag the Selected Object square icon (small square on the far-right of the layer) from the menu_top layer to the menu_bottom layer.

   This relocates the duplicate text block to the menu_bottom layer.

7. Show the menu_bottom sublayers. Double-click the Fave Site 1 sublayer and rename it "fave_site_1".

   Illustrator does not automatically rename text layers with underscores in place of spaces. According to XML standards, lowercase letters are preferred but not required.

8. Use the Attributes palette to apply a rectangular image map to the text block. For the URL, type in one of your favorite Web sites, and press Return/Enter to apply.

9. With the text block still selected, go to the SVG Interactivity palette and choose onmouseover from the Events menu.

10. In the JavaScript field, type the following text and press Return/Enter to apply.

    elemColor(evt, 'fave_site_1', '#0000CC')

    When the mouse touches the text, the text turns blue in the browser window.

11. Return to the Events menu and choose onmouseout. In the JavaScript field, type the following text and press Return/Enter to apply.

    elemColor(evt, 'fave_site_1', '#000000')

    When the mouse moves away from the text, the text returns to its original black color.

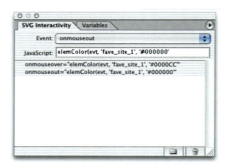

FIGURE 6.53

12. Save your changes. Keep the document open for the next exercise.

3. Organize the Layers Palette

The JavaScript has been applied to the objects. Next, the layers need to be named appropriately, and image maps need to be attached to the text blocks with URLs.

1. Select and drag the Fave Site 1 text block slightly underneath the original, pressing Option/Alt to duplicate.

    Press Shift as you drag to constrain the move.

2. Press Command/Control-D two times to make two more duplicate menu items.

3. Change the text of the three duplicate text blocks to "Fave Site 2", "Fave Site 3", and "Fave Site 4".

4. In the menu_bottom sublayers, rename the duplicate sublayers to the following: change fave_site_1_2_ to "fave_site_2"; change fave_site_1_3_ to "fave_site_3"; and change fave_site_1_4_ to "fave_site_4".

    When you duplicated the text blocks, the XML ID function added numbers to keep the names from conflicting.

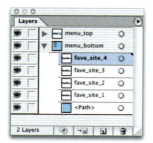

FIGURE 6.54

Chapter 6 SVG Graphics and Interactivity **283** LEVEL 2

5. One by one, select the Fave Site 2, Fave Site 3, and Fave Site 4 text blocks and change the assigned URL of each to another of your favorite Web sites, using the Attributes palette. Apply the change.

   Each text block should have a different URL address. Remember to press Return/Enter after changing each URL.

6. Select the Fave Site 2 text block on the Artboard. Go to the SVG Interactivity palette. Click the onmouseover event in the palette's event list section.

   Since this is a duplicate of Fave Site 1, the onmouseover and onmouseout events are already applied to it. You must change the numbers in the code names to accurately designate which object to affect.

7. In the JavaScript text field, change the 1 in the name to "2" to match its name in the Layers palette. Press Return/Enter to apply.

8. Click the onmouseout event in the palette's event list. In the JavaScript text field, change the 1 in the name to "2". Press Return/Enter to apply.

9. Select the Fave Site 3 text block on the Artboard. In the SVG Interactivity palette, change the 1 in the name to "3" in both the onmouseover and onmouseout events.

   Press Return/Enter to apply the changes.

10. Select the Fave Site 4 text block on the Artboard. In the SVG Interactivity palette, change the 1 to "4" in the two events appropriately.

    All four of the text blocks should have their own individual sublayer names and corresponding events that refer to those names.

11. Save your changes. Keep the document open for the next exercise.

4. Set the JavaScript and Events

The menu items have been named and organized. What remains is to set the JavaScript events and choose the external JavaScript file that will power them.

1. In the open document, select the larger rectangle and its four text blocks. Group the objects.

2. In the Layers palette, go to the bottom_menu layer to view its sublayers. Double-click its <group> sublayer and rename it "menu".

   With the objects grouped, you can apply one name to the entire group and assign an event to the group. The menu_bottom layer name does not work as an identifier. Only sublayers can receive events.

3. Select the top three objects: small rectangle, text block, and triangle. Group the objects and keep the group selected.

4. From the SVG Interactivity palette, choose onclick from the Events menu.

5. In the JavaScript field, type the following and press Return/Enter to apply.

   toggle(evt, 'menu')

   This event toggles the menu sublayer objects to show and hide them.

6. Deselect all objects. From the Events menu, choose onload.

With no objects selected, the event defaults to the entire document.

7. In the JavaScript field, type the following and press Return/Enter to apply.

    elemHide(evt, 'menu')

    This event hides the menu_bottom objects when the document loads into the browser window.

8. From the SVG Activity palette Options menu, use JavaScript Files to go to the WIP_06>SVG Interactivity folder and attach the menu.js file to the document.

    The menu.js JavaScript file is attached to the SVG document.

FIGURE 6.55

9. Save your changes and close the document.

5. See the Drop-down Menu in Action

The entire drop-down menu has been created and powered by JavaScript events and their corresponding JavaScript file. Now it is time to see all this work in action as you view the menu in a browser window.

1. On the desktop, create a new browser window.

2. Go to the WIP_06>SVG Interactivity folder. Drag dropdown_menu.svg to the new browser window.

    You see only the top portion of the menu. This is because you used the onload event to tell the JavaScript to hide the lower section when the file uploaded to the browser.

3. Click the menu to show the bottom menu selections.

FIGURE 6.56

Chapter 6   SVG Graphics and Interactivity   **285**

4. Move the mouse over the Fave Site links to see the change in color.

5. Click any of the Fave Site links to go to that site.

   Use Back in the browser to come back to the menu.

6. After you experiment with the menus, close the browser window.

6. Viewing SVG Files on the Internet

The SVG file and its HTML document it's embedded in, if used on a Web site, must be uploaded to the Internet. To do this, you must obtain storage space (free or paid) from a Web host, which requires just a quick account setup. You then use the host's file manager to upload the SVG, HTML, and JavaScript files to your new site. In your browser, you then type the URL address of your site and watch the SVG operate.

1. Choose any of your SVG files, such as one with a rollover or the menu in the previous exercise. Embed the file name into the index.html file supplied in the WIP_06>SVG Interactivity folder.

   Drag this HTML file to your browser to make sure it runs correctly. Remember, any referenced JavaScript files (such as events.js) must be in the folder with the SVG file it executes.

2. Use your browser to go to http:/www.741.com On their home page, click the Free Sign-Up link at the bottom of the left column, marked "FREE".

3. On the next page, in the Short Address box, type any short name you want for your site. Click the Continue Sign-Up button underneath this box.

   This will also be your User Name for when you log onto the site to upload files.

4. On the next page, fill out all the necessary personal information. At the bottom of the page, enter their Validation Code and click Create Your Account.

   The next page welcomes you as a new member and shows you the URL of your new site, which is http://yourname.741.com ("yourname" is the username you chose).

5. In the browser, press the Back button to return to the 741.com home page. Scroll down to 741 Client Login. Type "yourname.741.com" into the Username input field (the "yourname" should be the name you chose when creating the account). Type your password into the Password field and click Login.

6. On the next page, scroll down and click the HTML File Manager link (see Figure 6.57). In the upper right of the next page, under Upload Files from Your Computer, click Upload.

FIGURE 6.57

7. On the next page, click the top Browse button. Use the dialog box to navigate to the folder with the SVG and HTML files you wish to upload. Select the SVG file and click Open.

8. Back in the Upload Files page, click the second Browse button. Navigate to the same folder and select the index.html file. Click Open.

9. If you attached a JavaScript file (such as events.js or menu.js), click the third Browse button on the Upload Files page. Navigate to the same folder and select the appropriate file. Click Open.

   JavaScript files must accompany the SVG file wherever you use it. The SVG file internally references the external file and its information.

10. Back in the Upload Files page, scroll down and click Upload Files.

    The selected files will be uploaded to your new site.

11. The uploading is finished. You can close the 741.com browser page.

12. In your browser, type the URL address for your site http://yourname.741.com and press Return/Enter to execute this.

    Notice that "www" is not included in the address. Leave this out. What you have created is called a "subdomain," which resides on the main 741.com domain. When accessing subdomains on the Internet, you never use "www."

13. If your SVG file worked on your browser when you accessed it from your computer, the file should work on the Web site you created. Observe the operation of the SVG file and close the browser window.

PORTFOLIO BUILDER

Apply SVG Filters to Photos

You are a graphic designer who creates images for Webmasters. A client asked you to create a photo display where viewers can use zooming techniques to enlarge the photos for closer inspection, as well as move the images around on the Web page for better viewing.

1. Create a new RGB document with the Artboard set for 640 × 480 pixels.
2. Place several of your favorite photographs randomly around the Artboard page.
3. Select one of the photos and apply the SVG Filters>AI_Alpha_4 filter.

   Observe how the filter affects a raster object.

4. Return to the Effect menu and apply the AI_Shadow_2 filter to the same photo.

   Several filters may be applied to one object. Their order of application may be rearranged in the Appearance palette.

5. Apply other SVG filters to your other photos.
6. Save the document as "photo_filters.svg" in SVG format to your WIP_06>SVG Interactivity folder. Close the document.
7. Go to the desktop and drag the saved SVG file to a new browser window.
8. Use the zooming and image-moving capabilities to view the photos in the browser window.

LEVEL 2

C H A P T E R **7**

Working with Dynamic Graphics

O B J E C T I V E S

In this chapter, you learn how to:

- Connect Illustrator documents to external data

- Create and use variables

- Save data sets

- Modify XML files

- Build graphs

- Customize graphs

Why Would I Do This?

Imagine being able to develop a single ad and have a dozen variations automatically generated from data held in a spreadsheet or other data-management application. That's exactly what you can do when you include dynamic content in your workflow. **Dynamic content** includes layouts and designs created in Illustrator and populated by **variable** (changing) information. Using data from an external source to generate different versions and iterations of your artwork is a powerful and effective technique that saves considerable amounts of time, while ensuring that the text and pictures required for your layouts are accurate and error-free.

In this chapter, you work with XML (eXtensible Markup Language), a special type of markup language (similar to HTML code, complete with tags) that allows designers to use variable data in page layouts, drawings, and illustrations. After reading this chapter, you will have a solid understanding of how to apply XML as a competitive and time-saving tool.

VISUAL SUMMARY

In this chapter, you explore one of Illustrator's most exciting and flexible features — the ability to use variable data to automatically generate different versions of a design. Here you create graphs — powerful features that allow you to include data from external documents.

Using XML is outside a designer or an illustrator's normal requirements. To truly understand how to use variables and dynamic data, you need to learn how using external data speeds up production when designing with linked objects and text.

We show you how to connect an Illustrator document to external XML files and how the process updates any elements in the document assigned to variables. In an effort to streamline workflows, every graphic designer should investigate variables, especially if he or she produces multiple designs in the same format with only the objects changing on the page.

The variables in an Illustrator document must be organized and managed, tasks you perform in the **Variables palette**. You learn how to apply variables to objects and to keep track of them as you would layers. The Variables palette includes several components and icons that you can use to manage variables, shown in Figure 7.1.

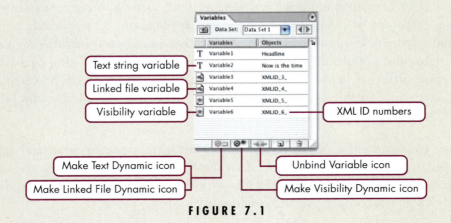

FIGURE 7.1

You also learn how to capture a data set and save it to an external XML file. **Data sets** are collections of variables for a specific design. When you import an XML file with a data set that replaces a data set of the same name (with same variables names) in the document, the bound variable objects and text take on the settings stored in the imported XML data set. One document can have several data sets and use the sets to show a variety of layouts that are saved to the sets. You discover the time-saving benefits of using variables and data sets to create multiple designs — all in the same layout but with changes in the objects that are included in the designs.

FIGURE 7.2

You look closely at XML text files and use the files to modify the variables in an Illustrator document. You discover that the XML tags, and the information you place within those tags, control the variables in your documents.

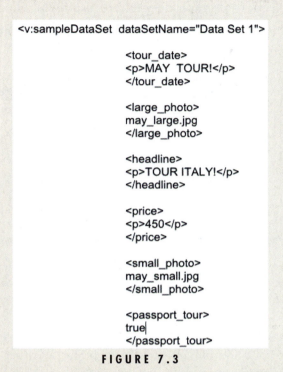

FIGURE 7.3

You work with the Graph tools to create several different graph types. You make column, bar, pie, and custom graphs. The Graph Type dialog box includes numerous settings for each graph type, allowing you to further control the graph's appearance and manage the values assigned to cells. You discover two ways to create a graph — using a dialog box for specific dimensions, or using the Graph tool to draw the graph manually.

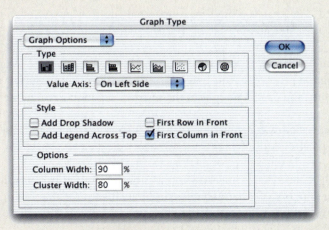

FIGURE 7.4

The lesson on customizing graphs shows you how to apply your own designs to the columns of the graph. You can convert any vector path object to a graph design and store it in the Illustrator document. Using the Graph Column dialog box, you can apply a design to the columns of existing graphs. You can keep a collection of graph designs and use them whenever necessary. The designs retain the colors and shapes of the original objects, which you can apply to the legends of the graphs.

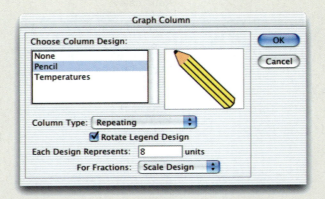

FIGURE 7.5

Exercise Setup:

Before you begin the exercises, go to your desktop and locate the Chapter_07 folder. Drag or copy the Watermelon Web Site, Tour Italy, Sports Banner, Italy Web Site, Weather Forecast, and Graphs folders to the WIP_07 folder. The documents and files must be together for the exercises to work.

LESSON 1 What Is Dynamic Data?

Dynamic data is formatted data that is stored in an external file that possesses the information necessary for your project. Mailing lists are a simple example of dynamic data.

When preparing a bulk-mail letter, the basic letter is written with a salutation of "Dear <name>" The <name> is a variable *tag*. Accompanying the printing of this letter is a separate file of thousands of real names linked to the letter. Each time the letter prints, the program replaces the <name> tag with a real name from the external list.

In this case, the <name> tag is a *variable*, meaning that the "name" is generic and can be replaced by information from an external file. The palette used for managing variables is called the Variables palette.

How can variables be used? What is their practical application when used in preparing designs in Illustrator? In the following exercise, you experience what variables do in an Illustrator document and can see their practical application when used with various projects that use the same layout but different objects.

Chapter 7   Working with Dynamic Graphics   293   LEVEL 2

Connect a Document to an External File

Preference Setup

Before starting the exercises, go to the Preferences>Units & Display Performance dialog box and make certain that the Identify Objects By option is set for **XML ID**. This ensures your variable names conform to XML naming conventions

1   Open watermelon_site.ai from the WIP_07>Watermelon Web Site folder. Open the Variables palette.

2   Study the page and note the characteristics of the page elements: the Watermelon Extravaganza logo, the two photos, the large text block, and the three watermelon link buttons at the bottom.

FIGURE 7.6

3   In the Variables palette, choose Load Variable Library from the Options menu.

A few variables are already in the palette. We assigned these variables to the objects on the Artboard. When you load the external XML file in the next step, new text will replace these variables.

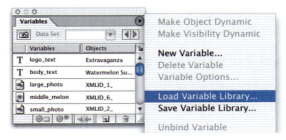

FIGURE 7.7

4   In the dialog box, navigate to the WIP_07>Watermelon Web Site folder and choose watermelons.xml. Click Open.

A warning dialog box appears, informing you that the document already contains variables and asks if you want to overwrite them.

5 **In the warning box that asks if you want to overwrite the current variables, click Yes.**

To get the current variables to change to the incoming data, they must be replaced. Even though you imported the XML file, it will not take effect in the document until you make the new data set active in the Variables palette.

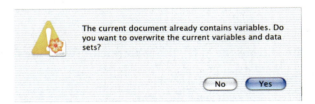

FIGURE 7.8

6 **In the top center of the Variables palette, to the right of the Data Set title, use the pop-up menu to choose Watermelons.**

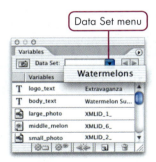

FIGURE 7.9

7 **Observe the changes that take place on the Artboard.**

The change happens very quickly. The XML information updates the page with new information, replacing some of the text and hiding the middle watermelon link.

8 **Press Command/Control-Z to undo the update.**

The Artboard returns to the original layout. The variable change happened so quickly, you need to undo and redo the action to see the difference.

9 **Press Shift-Command/Control-Z to redo the update.**

You can press the Undo and Redo keys to compare the layouts.

FIGURE 7.10

10 **Close the file without saving.**

To Extend Your Knowledge . . .

REPLACING OBJECTS

Even though you explore the details of replacing and hiding variable objects in the upcoming lessons, let's review the steps involved.

- Assign variables to the photos, text blocks, and other objects.
- Save the objects' variable information as a data set into an external XML file.
- Open the XML document (a text file) in a word processor.
- Edit the text file to include names of replacement photos, new text, and/or changes in visibility.
- Import the updated XML file back into the document to see the changes take effect on the objects bound to the variables.

LESSON 2 Assigning Variables

Once you comprehend the concept of variables and the XML markup language, it's not difficult to apply the technology. Using variables is a step-by-step process.

First, you create a design. You then select various types of objects and assign each to its own variable name in the Variables palette. Assigning an object to a variable is known as ***binding***. An object connected to a variable is "bound" to that variable.

Let's examine the Variable palette and its features that are used in defining variables:

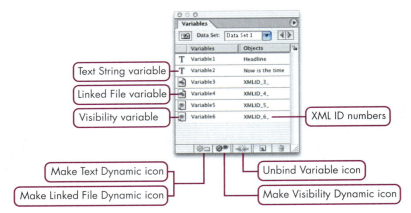

FIGURE 7.11

- ***Text String.*** Any text block that has not been converted to outlines can be assigned to a variable, which would be listed as a "Text String" category in the variable types. The text block can be either a point or area text block.

- ***Linked File.*** Only linked (not embedded) images can be defined as Linked File variables. A practical application of linked variables is using them in conjunction with Text String variables to generate 10 different ads with 10 different pictures.

- ***Visibility.*** The Visibility variable relates to objects in the document that are not (or cannot be) linked to outside sources. For example, if you drew a vector object in the document, this cannot be bound to a Linked File variable. Only the Visibility variable can work with it, which uses the visibility attribute of the layer it resides on to either show or hide the object.

- ***Make Text Dynamic/Make Linked File Dynamic.*** This icon has two names, depending on the object selected. If a text block is selected, it will be Make Text Dynamic. If a linked object is selected, it will be Make File Dynamic.

- ***Make Visibility Dynamic.*** This icon controls whether a selected object is shown or hidden in the document. This type of variable can be used on any object in the file, whether it has been created in the document (such as vector, raster, or text blocks) or is linked to an outside source.

- ***Unbind Variable.*** If you no longer desire an object to be bound to a variable, this icon disconnects the two.

- ***XML ID Numbers.*** Each object must have its own XML ID number, which Illustrator uses to organize its information in its data sets; Illustrator assigns this when the sets are administered.

Chapter 7   Working with Dynamic Graphics   297   LEVEL 2

Assign Variables

In this exercise, you assign variables to the ad's elements. Later, you modify the XML variables that are used later to change the ad.

1   **Open tour_italy.ai from the WIP_07>Tour Italy folder. Open the Variables and Layers palettes.**

You may not have these fonts on your computer. If you get a font warning, click "Continue". The type on the page will look slightly different, but this is just to show you how variables work.

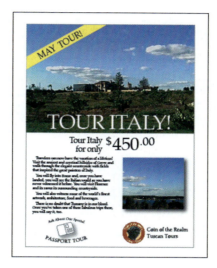

FIGURE 7.12

2   **Select the "MAY TOUR!" text block at the top of the page. In the Variables palette, click the Make Text Dynamic icon.**

The selected object becomes Variable 1 in the Variables column of the Variables palette. In the palette's Objects column, the first few words of the object's text are assigned as an identifier.

The "T" icon to the left of the Variable 1 name denotes text.

FIGURE 7.13

3   **Select the large photo at the ad's top.**

4   **In the Variables palette, click the same palette icon you clicked in Step 2, which is now the Make Linked File Dynamic icon.**

The icon's name changed because the photo is a linked file.

5 **In the Layers palette, expand Layer 1 so you can see its sublayers.**

The objects have different names, according to their file types. The text block variable name has a "T" icon next to it to show that it is text. The name of the text block includes the first few words of its text. The photo is an image assigned an XML_ID number for its name. The image has a graphic icon next to its name.

Do not rename the XML ID of any variable or sublayer. These names allow Illustrator to keep track of the objects and to update files correctly.

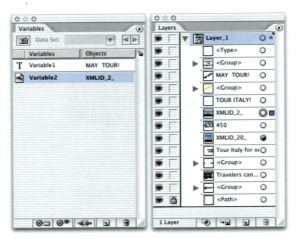

FIGURE 7.14

6 **Select the TOUR ITALY! text block. Click the Make Text Dynamic icon.**

This turns the text block into a variable.

7 **Select the 450 text block. Click the Make Text Dynamic icon.**

The price is now a variable, too.

8 **Select the smaller photograph in the ad's bottom right. Click the Make Linked File Dynamic icon.**

This allows you to replace the photograph with another image. Remember, to use placed images and variables, the images must be linked.

9 **Select the "Ask About Our Special Passport Tour!" object, which was created in the document and has no link. Click the Make Visibility Dynamic icon at the bottom of the Variables palette.**

An object created in an Illustrator document that has no link or connection with an external file cannot be updated as the Make Linked File Dynamic objects can. You can, however, assign a Visibility variable to the object, which allows you to control whether the object displays in the document.

FIGURE 7.15

10. **In the Variables palette, double-click Variable 1 and change it to "tour_date". Go on to change Variable 2 to "large_photo", Variable 3 to "headline", Variable 4 to "price", Variable 5 to "small_photo", and Variable 6 to "passport_tour".**

    These names allow you to quickly identify the variables. As you learned in Lesson 6 of Chapter 6, you should follow XML file-naming conventions when naming files: use lowercase letters and always use underscores to separate words (do not use spaces).

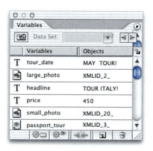

FIGURE 7.16

11. **Save your changes and close the document.**

Work with XML Data

1. **Open forecast.ai from the WIP_07>Weather Forecast folder. Open the Variables palette.**

    The artwork is a weather forecast panel with images denoting various types of weather.

    First, you must build the variables — a collection of data sets that allow you to enter forecasted weather conditions and temperatures for the next seven days; the artwork automatically generates a Web-ready seven-day forecast graphic.

2. **Select the weather graphic below the first SUN heading (Sunday). Make it a variable by clicking the Make Linked File Dynamic icon in the Variables palette.**

   Do not rename Variable 1 yet. You rename all the variables later.

3. **One at a time, select the 74, 57, and 35% text blocks in the Sun column. Make each a variable by clicking the Make Text Dynamic icon in the Variables palette.**

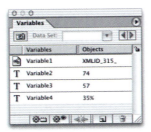

FIGURE 7.17

4. **Select the weather graphic below the MON heading (Monday). Make it a variable by clicking the Make Linked File Dynamic icon.**

5. **One at a time, select the 76, 59, and 30% text blocks in the MON column. Make each a variable by clicking the Make Text Dynamic icon.**

6. **Select the weather graphic below the TUE heading (Tuesday). Make it a variable by clicking the Make Linked File Dynamic icon.**

7. **One at a time, select the 75, 58, and 20% text blocks in the TUE column and make each a variable by clicking the Make Text Dynamic icon.**

   Let's stop with these three days of weather forecasts, rather than take the time to make variables for all seven days. This information allows you to see how a database of current weather conditions can change the variables in an Illustrator document.

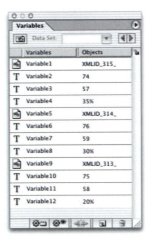

FIGURE 7.18

Chapter 7 Working with Dynamic Graphics | 301 | LEVEL 2

8 Double-click Variable 1 in the Variables palette and rename it "sunday_forecast".

9 Move down the Variables list in the Variables palette and change Variable 2 to "sunday_high", Variable 3 to "sunday_low", and Variable 4 to "sunday_rain".

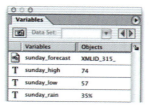

FIGURE 7.19

10 Change Variable 5 to "monday_forecast", Variable 6 to "monday _high", Variable 7 to "monday_low", and Variable 8 to "monday _rain".

11 Change Variable 9 to "tuesday_forecast", Variable 10 to "tuesday_high", Variable 11 to "tuesday_low", and Variable 12 to "tuesday_rain".

Each of the variables now has an appropriate name. The next step in the process is to save the variables into a data set, which is the focus of the next lesson.

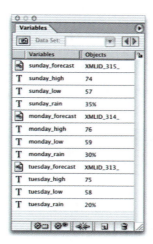

FIGURE 7.20

12 Save your changes and close the document.

To Extend Your Knowledge . . .

NON-SEQUENTIAL NAMES

The numbers Illustrator assigns to XML ID linked file names are not sequential. Do not be alarmed if these numbers are not in order and do not attempt to change them.

LESSON 3 Understanding Data Sets

The Variables palette provides the tools you need to connect design elements to external (or internal) data. In this palette, you can create any number of variables, but you cannot access the various layouts that include your variables until you save them as data sets.

You create a data set by *capturing* (combining them into a data set) the variables with the Capture Data Set icon of the Variables palette. Once captured, you assign a name to the data set, which stores the set information into the Illustrator document. You can access the set from the Data Set menu in the Variables palette. The data set provides several important functions.

Data sets contain all the pertinent information of only the objects bound to variables in the Variables palette, including the object's position on the page, its size, angle of transformation, color, and so on.

The Variables palette has the ability to name, retain, and load data sets, whether from inside the document (as you see in the next exercise) or from an external XML file. The data set changes all the bound objects in the document when selected. Using this function enables you to automatically generate multiple versions of any design or illustration. The practical application of this is to preserve, for instance, 10 designs in one Illustrator document, rather than having to save the designs in 10 different documents.

Create Data Sets

In this exercise, you assign variables to objects in various layouts and save them to data sets.

1   **Open sports_banner.ai from the WIP_07>Sports Banner folder. Open the Variables palette.**

This is a Web banner advertising mountain climbing in North Carolina.

FIGURE 7.21

2   **With the Selection tool, select the "climb" text block. Click the Make Text Dynamic icon in the Variables palette.**

A new variable named Variable 1 appears in the Variables palette. To the name's left is the "T" icon, indicating that it's a text variable.

3   **With the Selection tool, select the "NORTH CAROLINA" text block. Click the Make Text Dynamic icon.**

This is Variable 2.

4   **Select the mountains image at the banner's left end. Click the Make Linked File Dynamic icon.**

The selected image is now Variable 3.

5 **Change the Variable 1 name to "sport", Variable 2 to "state", and Variable 3 to "image".**

The variable names are not specific to the action, such as "climb." The various actions fit into the category "sport," which covers the other sports that we add next. Now that you have the three objects bound to variables, the next step is to store their information into a data set, better known as "capturing" the data set.

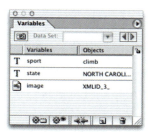

FIGURE 7.22

6 **In the Variables palette, click the Capture Data Set icon to the left of the Data Set name.**

The data set appears in the Data Set field and displays its default name, Data Set 1.

FIGURE 7.23

7 **Highlight Data Set 1 in the input box and name it "climb_nc".**

8 **Save your changes to the document. Keep the document open for the next exercise.**

Save Data Sets

1 **In the open file, select the mountains image on the banner's left side.**

2 **Choose File>Place and navigate to the WIP_07>Sports Banner folder. Click play.tif in the list of files. Select the Link and Replace options in the dialog box and click Place.**

3 **Use the Type tool to highlight the word "climb". Change it to "play".**

4 Highlight the word "NORTH CAROLINA" and change the text to "CALIFORNIA".

FIGURE 7.24

5 Click the Capture Data Set icon in the Variables palette. Change the data set's name to "play_ca".

6 Select the tennis image at the banner's end. Choose File>Place and navigate to the WIP_07>Sports Banner folder. Click ski.tif in the list of files. Select the Link and Replace options in the dialog box and click Place.

Make certain that the Link option is selected in the Place dialog box.

7 On the Artboard, change the word "play" to "ski", and change the word "CALIFORNIA" to "COLORADO".

FIGURE 7.25

8 Capture the data set and name it "ski_co".

9 Select the ski image at the banner's end and use File>Place to navigate to the WIP_07>Sports Banner folder. Select the fish.tif file in the files list. Select the Link and Replace options in the dialog box and click Place.

10 Use the Type tool to change the word "ski" to "fish", and change the word "COLORADO" to "FLORIDA".

FIGURE 7.26

11 Capture the data set and name it "fish_fl".

These four data sets are stored in the document; you do not need to export them to an external library.

12 In the Data Set menu of the Variables palette, choose one of the four data sets.

The banner changes according to the data set you choose.

13 One at a time, choose the other three data sets from the Data Set menu. To scroll through the sets, use the Previous Data Set and Next Data Set buttons to the right of the Data Set menu.

The advantage to variables and data sets is that you can store multiple ads, banners, or other designs within one document. Simply select a specific data set and it appears on your screen.

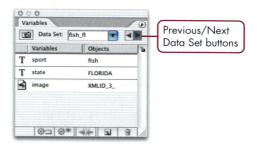

FIGURE 7.27

14 Save your changes and close the document.

Save Data Set for Weather Forecast

1 Open forecast.ai from the WIP_07>Weather Forecast folder.

2 In the Variables palette Options menu, click the Capture Data Set icon.

Choosing this option opens the New Data Set dialog box so you can name the data set. This is an alternate method of capturing a data set. By default, Illustrator saves the variables in a data set named Data Set 1 (or 2, depending if previous sets have been captured).

3 Change the Data Set 1 name to "forecast".

4 Choose Save Variable Library from the Variables palette Options menu.

5 Save the XML file as "forecast.xml" in the WIP_07>Weather Forecast folder.

This short exercise shows you how to save a data set to an external XML text file. We come back to this document in the next lesson.

6 Save your changes to the document. Close the document.

Save Data Set for Italian Ad

1 Open tour_italy.ai from the WIP_07>Tour Italy folder. Show the Variables palette.

Up to this point, the objects have been bound to variables and renamed in the Variables palette. The next step is to save the placement and names of the variables to a data set.

2 At the top left of the Variables palette, click the Capture Data Set icon.

The default name of the data set is Data Set 1.

FIGURE 7.28

3 In the Variables palette Options menu, choose Save Variable Library.

4 In the Save Variable Library dialog box, save the library file as "may_tour.xml" to the WIP_07>Tour Italy folder.

You modify this XML text file in the next lesson.

5 Save your changes to the document and close the file.

To Extend Your Knowledge . . .

ACCESSING DATA SETS

When you assign a name to a data set, it is automatically stored in the Illustrator document. If several data sets reside in a document, you can use the Data Set menu to choose the set you need. As long as the linked images are in the appropriate folder, you can use the sets wherever you use the document.

LESSON 4 Using the eXtensible Markup Language

In some ways, the eXtensible Markup Language (XML) is quite similar to HTML; in other ways, it's significantly different. If you use a word processor to look at an XML text file (in "text only" mode), you would see the tags that were created when the variable library was saved.

Apart from its own code and information, the XML file places the names of your variables within tags, such as `<variable 1>`, `<variable 2>`, or the name you assign to the variable. The information you place between the opening and closing variable tags tells Illustrator what image or text to show. For example:

<headline_1> <p> To sit in solemn silence, on a dull, dark dock. </p> </headline_1>

The variable name is in the tag `<headline_1>`. Text is the element to show, so a paragraph tag, `<p>`, precedes the text. A closing paragraph tag, `</p>`, follows the text, which is followed by the closing variable tag, `</headline_1>`. The forward slash denotes a tag's ending.

If the text between the paragraph tags was replaced in the XML text file and this file was loaded back into the Illustrator document with the same variable name "headline_1", all the text on the Artboard bound to the headline_1 variable would be replaced with the new text.

Chapter 7   Working with Dynamic Graphics   **307**   LEVEL 2

So far, you have created variables directly within Illustrator and have simply moved through the variables to see the different versions. In the following exercise, you edit an actual XML data file to make changes to the Illustrator document.

? Important Note:

There are many different word processors in the computer industry, but they all adhere to the most basic type of text format, which comes in various names: ASCII, text only, or plain text. Make sure that you open the XML files in your word processor with one of these various formats, or you will probably get an error messages stating that the file is not valid.

The SimpleText or TextEdit word processors of the Macintosh are quite sufficient. TextEdit, however, must have its preferences set for Plain Text.

The Notepad word processor in a Windows platform is strictly a "text only" program and is suggested. The Wordpad word processor also uses RTF and is not recommended.

In all of our editing exercises, make certain that you are opening and saving the XML files as one of the acceptable basic text formats.

Modify an XML File

In this exercise, you simulate how external information, such as from a database, can change the text and graphic elements in a dynamic Illustrator document.

1   **Go to the desktop and use your word-processing program to open forecast.xml from the WIP_07>Weather Forecast folder.**

Make sure the file's opening and saving format in your word processor is "text only" or "plain text." Any other formats, such as RTF, cause errors.

2   **Scroll down until you see the name of the first variable you created, `<sunday_forecast>`. The graphic bound to the variable is partly_cloudy.jpg. Change the name of this graphic to "rainy.jpg".**

A directory path precedes the image name in your computer. This path tells your computer the file's location. Change only the name in the path.

Note that the variable tag begins with <sunday_forecast> and ends with </sunday_forecast>. The slash denotes that this is the end of the variable tag. Any items inside these two tags belong to the variable.

```
<v:sampleDataSet  dataSetName="forecast">

         <sunday_forecast>
                  rainy.jpg
         </sunday_forecast>
```

FIGURE 7.29

3   **The next variable in the text should be sunday_high and its temperature 74. Change the temperature to "70".**

LEVEL 2   **308**   Chapter 7   Working with Dynamic Graphics

4 Continue moving down the list of variables in the XML file. Make the following changes that are listed in quotes:

sunday_low = "55"

sunday_rain = "50%"

monday_forecast = "sunny.jpg"

monday_high = "80"

monday_low = "63"

monday_rain = "25%"

tuesday_forecast = "partly_cloudy.jpg"

tuesday_high = "70"

tuesday_low = "60"

tuesday_rain = "10%"

```
<sunday_low>
        <p>55</p>
</sunday_low>

<sunday_rain>
        <p>50%</p>
</sunday_rain>

<monday_forecast>
        sunny.jpg
</monday_forecast>

<monday_high>
        <p>80</p>
</monday_high>

<monday_low>
        <p>63</p>
</monday_low>

<monday_rain>
        <p>25%</p>
</monday_rain>

<tuesday_forecast>
        partly_cloudy.jpg
</tuesday_forecast>

<tuesday_high>
        <p>70</p>
</tuesday_high>

<tuesday_low>
        <p>60</p>
</tuesday_low>

<tuesday_rain>
        <p>10%</p>
</tuesday_rain>
```

FIGURE 7.30

Chapter 7 Working with Dynamic Graphics 309 LEVEL 2

5 Save your changes to the word-processing document and close it.

6 Return to the Illustrator program and open forecast.ai from the WIP_07>Weather Forecast folder.

7 Choose Load Variable Library from the Variables palette Options menu.

8 Navigate to the WIP_07>Weather Forecast folder. Choose the forecast.xml variable library and click Open.

9 Click Yes when asked if you want to overwrite the existing variables.

Even though forecast.xml was accepted into the document, it has not yet been acknowledged as the active data set.

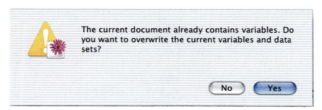

FIGURE 7.31

10 From the Data Set menu in the Variables palette, choose the "forecast" data set.

The document displays the text blocks and images that you changed in the XML file.

If this were a Web site connected to a database that could update the XML information, you would see how information can be updated.

FIGURE 7.32

11 Save your changes and close the file.

LEVEL 2 **310** Chapter 7 Working with Dynamic Graphics

Change the Italian Tour Ad

1 Go to your desktop and use your word-processing program to open may_tour.xml from the WIP_07>Tour Italy folder.

2 Scroll down to the `<dataSetName = "Data Set 1">` tag. Examine the names of the various elements underneath it.

The XML language is an extension of the HTML code and uses the same basic tags and techniques. Changing the information between tags changes how the objects appear in the Illustrator document.

Depending on your word-processing program, your text may not look lined up as we show here for better viewing. Also, the photo names show all the navigational directory paths on your computer that lead to the image. Do not ever delete these paths, because the Illustrator document will not know where to find them. We do not show our computer directory paths here; only the file name.

```
<v:sampleDataSet  dataSetName="Data Set 1">

    <tour_date>
    <p>MAY  TOUR!</p>
    </tour_date>

    <large_photo>
    may_large.jpg
    </large_photo>

    <headline>
    <p>TOUR ITALY!</p>
    </headline>

    <price>
    <p>450</p>
    </price>

    <small_photo>
    may_small.jpg
    </small_photo>

    <passport_tour>
    true|
    </passport_tour>
```

FIGURE 7.33

3 In the `<dataSetName>` tag, change Data Set 1 to "june_tour".

4 Change the `<large_photo>` photograph name from may_large.jpg to "june_large.jpg".

Your information will probably look different for linked objects, with your paths and folders showing appropriate information for your computer. Remember to change only the file name, and leave all the other information unchanged.

5 After the `<headline>` tag, change "TOUR ITALY!" to "TIME TRAVEL".

Chapter 7 Working with Dynamic Graphics **311** **LEVEL 2**

The text appears between two paragraph tags (`<p>` and `</p>`). This tells the Illustrator document that the variable is text.

6 After the `<price>` tag, change "450" to "395".

7 After the `<small_photo>` tag, change the photograph name from may_small.jpg to "june_small.jpg".

8 After the `<passport_tour>` tag, change the text from a true setting to "false".

This is the Visibility variable. A setting of "true" means the object is visible; a "false" setting hides the object.

```
<small_photo>
june_small.jpg
</small_photo>

<passport_tour>
false
</passport_tour>

</v:sampleDataSet>
```

FIGURE 7.34

9 Save the file as "june_tour.xml" to the WIP_07>Tour Italy folder. Close the word-processing document.

Load the XML File Into Illustrator

1 From Illustrator, open tour_italy.ai from the WIP_07>Tour Italy folder. Show the Variables palette.

You may not have these fonts on your computer. If you get a font warning, click "Continue". The type on the page will look slightly different, but this is just to show you how variables work.

2 From the palette Options menu, choose Load Variable Library.

3 Select june_tour.xml in the WIP_07>Tour Italy folder and click Open.

4 When asked if you want to overwrite the existing variables, click Yes.

Even though you have imported the XML, nothing happens on the Artboard. The new data set must be selected.

5 In the Variables palette Data Set menu, choose june_tour.

For the incoming variables to take effect, you must choose a data set. In a matter of seconds, the XML file changes the text, photographs, and graphics in the ad. The Passport Tour advertisement is hidden because it does not pertain to this ad.

FIGURE 7.35

6 Use the Undo and Redo options in the Edit menu to go back and forth between the two pages to see how cleanly Illustrator and the XML file executed the replacement.

7 Save your changes and close the file.

To Extend Your Knowledge . . .

CHANGING AREA TEXT BLOCKS

Using an XML file to change area text blocks in an Illustrator document is not a simple task. You are limited to only three paragraphs containing approximately 25–30 words each. If you continue to receive the "not a valid file" error, delete some words in your text block and try again. Keep in mind that some typographer's characters (such as quotes) do not translate well to a text-only file and may cause errors.

It is best to replace the text in individual paragraphs in the XML file, which are separated by the HTML <p> and </p> tags. Any changes you make to the words between these two tags will replace the corresponding text in the paragraphs in the Illustrator document.

Only the words change when you modify the text in indivdual paragraphs in the XML file. If the area text block in the Illustrator document has paragraph format settings, these settings will be retained.

Chapter 7 Working with Dynamic Graphics **313** LEVEL 2

LESSON 5 Using the Graph Tools

Much of the data we view is in the form of numbers. We've all become quite accustomed to seeing professionally made graphs that present financial figures, demographics, statistical data, and similar information in newspapers, on Web sites, in magazines, and on television. These facts and figures can be dry, sometimes boring, and possibly unintelligible when presented as straight text; but a well-designed graph can turn incomprehensible data into user-friendly information.

In Illustrator, the Graph tool's pop-out optional toolbar allows you to select the type of graph you want to create. Here's a short description of the graphs and their uses:

- Column and stacked column graphs show data changes over time or display comparisons between different items or categories. Categories display horizontally (usually across the bottom axis), and their values display vertically (usually on the graph's left side). Stacked columns show multiple values for each of the categories.

- Bar and stacked bar graphs are similar to column graphs, except their axes run the opposite way; the bars move from left to right horizontally, and the categories display on the left.

- Area and line graphs display volume or intensity over time (Area), or compare two or more data points as they change over time (Line).

- Scatter graphs are used primarily for statistical analysis to identify trends or clusters — visually highlighting groupings of similar values.

- Pie graphs rank alongside bar and column graphs as the most commonly seen graphs. If the total values add up to 100, the pie graph shows the relationship between each category.

- Radar graphs are statistical tools used to compare the aggregate values of two or more data ranges.

Create a Pie Graph

In this exercise, you create one of the more popular graphs and see how easy it is to apply and modify the information it contains.

1. Create a new letter-size CMYK document with orientation set for landscape and units set for inches.

2. Click-hold the mouse on the Graph tool in the Toolbox to show its optional tools. Select the Pie Graph Tool icon.

FIGURE 7.36

3 Hold Option/Alt and click the tool's cursor on the page's right side. In the Graph dialog box, set the Width and Height to 3 inches. Click OK. Move the data input box to the left to see the circular graph.

An unformatted pie graph appears as a black circle on the page, along with the data input box. In the Data Input dialog box, enter the increments you want reflected in the graph's slices. Type your numbers in the large input box in the upper-left corner. Select a cell in the dialog box to tell Illustrator where to place the numbers.

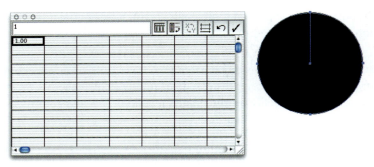

FIGURE 7.37

4 By default, the first cell is already selected. Type "125" and press the Tab key to move to the next cell to the right.

Pressing the Tab key is a fast way to advance from one cell to the next in the Data Input dialog box.

5 Type "200" in the cell and press Tab to move to the next cell.

6 Type "150" in the cell and press Tab. Type "175" in the cell.

7 Press Tab and type "225" in the cell. Click the Apply icon (see Figure 7.38) in the upper-right corner of the dialog box.

Starting at 12:00 on the pie graph, its slices reflect the increments you designated in the cells, starting from the first cell on the left of the Data Input dialog box. In this case, the graph pie slice to the right of 12:00 represents the 125 increment. Moving clock-wise, the next slice is 200, the next slice is 150, the next slice 175, and last slice 225.

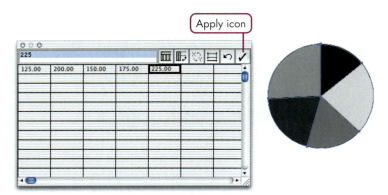

FIGURE 7.38

Chapter 7   Working with Dynamic Graphics   **315**   LEVEL 2

8 **Click the Close button in the Data Input dialog box.**

9 **Use the Direct Selection tool to select the different pie slices. Fill them with colors of your choice.**

Graphs are vector paths you can paint in various ways.

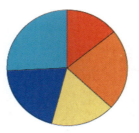

FIGURE 7.39

10 **Use the Selection tool to select the graph. From the Object>Graph menu, choose Data.**

The Data Input box appears again so you can modify the graph.

11 **By default, the first cell is selected. Type "100" and press Tab to go to the next cell. Type "145" and press Tab. Type "180" in the next cell.**

12 **Type "250" and "125" in the next two cells, respectively. Click the Apply icon.**

The graph reflects the modified settings. You can modify a graph at any time by changing colors or increments in the Data Input dialog box.

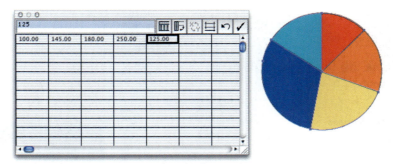

FIGURE 7.40

13 **Save the document as "pie_graph.ai" to your WIP_07>Graphs folder. Keep the document open for the next exercise.**

Experiment with Various Graph Types

1 Keep the pie graph selected on the Artboard. In the Toolbox, double-click the Graph Tool icon. In the Graph Type dialog box, click the Column graph icon. Click OK.

The pie graph on the Artboard transforms into a column graph, yet retains its painted colors.

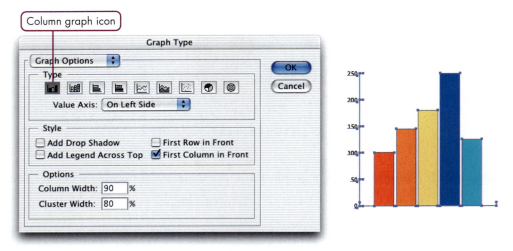

FIGURE 7.41

2 From the Object>Graph menu, choose Type. In the Graph Type dialog box, click the Bar icon (third from left). Click OK.

The bar graph turns the column graph sideways to show the increments along a horizontal axis.

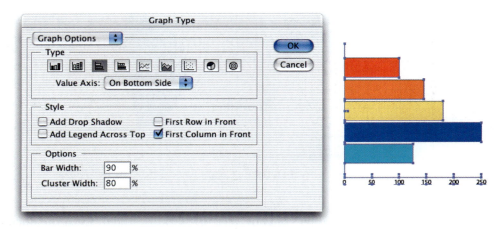

FIGURE 7.42

Not all graphs convert to other types very well. If you choose some of the other types, such as Line or Scatter, you won't see much — the data gets lost in the conversion.

3 **Select and delete the graph on the page.**

Chapter 7   Working with Dynamic Graphics   **317**   LEVEL 2

4 Click-hold the Graph tool in the Toolbox to choose the Column Graph tool from the pop-out toolbar.

5 On the page's right side, drag the cursor to draw a graph, approximately 3-inches square.

The Graph tool allows you to draw a graph according to your own size and shape specifications.

6 At the top of the Data Input dialog box, click the Import Data icon.

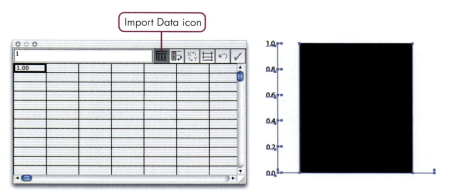

FIGURE 7.43

7 From the WIP_07>Graphs folder, choose the graph_import.txt file. Click Import/Open. Click the Apply icon in the Data Input dialog box.

The text file contains numbers separated by tabs in the document. You can insert your own graph data; use tabs to separate the numbers. Each tab-delimited figure fits within a cell across the top of the Data Input dialog box.

When you click Apply, the graph on the page immediately reflects the imported figures.

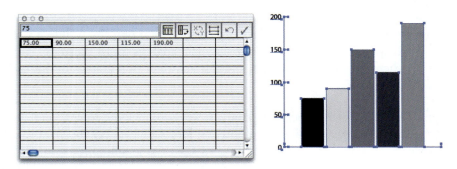

FIGURE 7.44

8 Close the Data Input dialog box. If asked if you want to save the data, click Yes. Keep the graph selected.

9 Double-click the Graph Tool icon in the Toolbox. Choose the Pie Graph option in the Graph Type dialog box. Click OK.

The column graph changes to a pie graph. Until they are expanded from the Object menu, graphs are dynamic and may have their graph type or data changed.

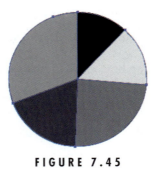

FIGURE 7.45

10 Save your changes and close the document.

To Extend Your Knowledge . . .

LEAVE GRAPHS UNGROUPED

Do not group the elements in a graph. If you do, the graph loses all its connections with the Data Input box, and you can no longer change to another graph type.

LESSON 6 Customizing Graphs

For a dedicated drawing program, Illustrator offers impressive graph options. While it's not as powerful as Microsoft Excel, which is specifically designed to provide data-analysis tools, Illustrator performs quite well. This is particularly true when you want to customize the appearance of your graphs. In this regard, no dedicated program comes close to Illustrator.

You can create graphs in several different ways. The simplest way is to pick the type of graph you want to create, and click the Graph tool on the page. Illustrator prompts you for a size. Let's say you want to create a simple pie graph, 100 pixels wide by 100 pixels high. Once you click OK, the graph appears on the Artboard. At this point, the Data Input dialog box contains no data, so nothing displays in the pie graph. Once you enter the data into the appropriate rows and columns and click Apply, the information appears in the graph. By default, all graph attributes are grayscale, but you can change a graph's attributes and create custom designs that you can apply with a few quick mouse clicks.

Chapter 7 Working with Dynamic Graphics **319** **LEVEL 2**

Customize Graphs

1 Open customize_graph.ai from the WIP_07>Graphs folder.

2 Use the Selection tool to select the thermometer above the Artboard. From the Object menu, choose Graph>Design.

For the following process to work, you must select the object before you choose the Graph>Design option.

FIGURE 7.46

3 In the Graph Design dialog box, click the New Design option. Click the Rename option and name the design "Temperatures". Click OK in both dialog boxes.

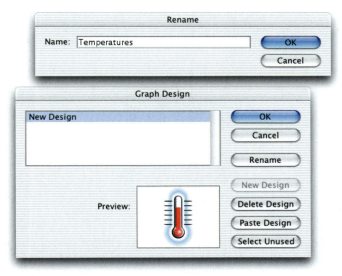

FIGURE 7.47

4 Use the Selection tool to select the graph at the Artboard's top.

5 From the Object menu, choose Graph>Column to access the Graph Column dialog box.

6 **Choose Temperatures from the Choose Column Design window, and choose Sliding from the Column Type pop-up menu. Click OK.**

The thermometer image replaces the column bars in the graph. The Sliding option lengthens (or shortens) parts of the design object to match the object in each column to its value.

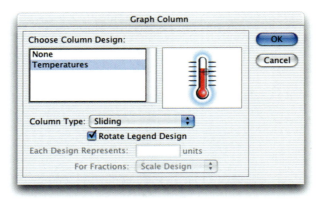

FIGURE 7.48

7 **Zoom in to the graph to see the columns better.**

All the columns in the selected graph receive the new design. As an alternative, you can use the Direct Selection tool to single out individual columns to receive the design.

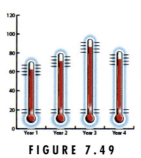

FIGURE 7.49

8 **Select the pencil object above the Artboard. From the Object menu, choose Graph>Design to create a new graph design. Rename the design "Pencil".**

9 **Select the bar graph in the middle of the Artboard. From the Object menu, choose Graph>Column.**

Chapter 7 Working with Dynamic Graphics   **321**   LEVEL 2

10 From the Graph Column dialog box, choose the Pencil design. Set the Column Type menu to Repeating. In the Each Design Represents field, type "12".

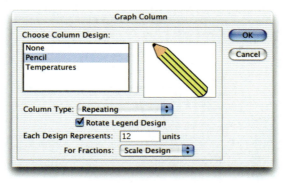

FIGURE 7.50

11 Click OK to apply this new column design.

The Pencil design fills the bars of the graph.

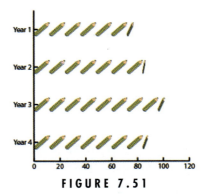

FIGURE 7.51

12 Save your changes to the document. Keep the document open for the next exercise.

Apply New Designs

1 To the right of the pencil object above the Artboard, select each painted rectangle and use the Object>Graph>Design dialog box to create three new designs named "Gold", "Ruby", and "Emerald".

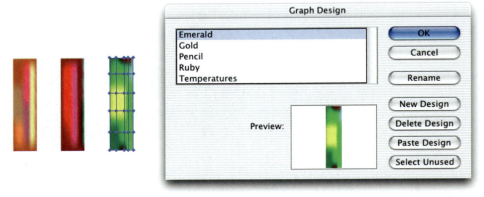

FIGURE 7.52

2 Zoom in to the stacked bar graph at the bottom of the Artboard and select it. From the Object>Graph menu, choose Data.

3 Click the Year 1 cell and rename it "Gold". Press Tab and rename the next cell "Ruby". Press Tab and rename the next cell "Emerald".

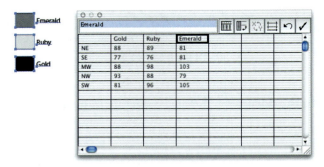

FIGURE 7.53

4 Click the Apply button to accept the changes. Close the Data Input dialog box. Deselect the graph.

Chapter 7   Working with Dynamic Graphics   **323**   LEVEL 2

5 **Press Option/Alt and use the Direct Selection tool to double-click the Emerald legend rectangle.**

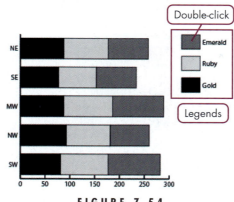

FIGURE 7.54

This automatically selects the corresponding column on the bar graph.

6 **With the Emerald graph column selected, use the Object>Graph>Column dialog box to apply the Emerald design.**

The shape of the legend rectangle changes to the Emerald design.

7 **Select the other two legend rectangles and apply the appropriate designs by name.**

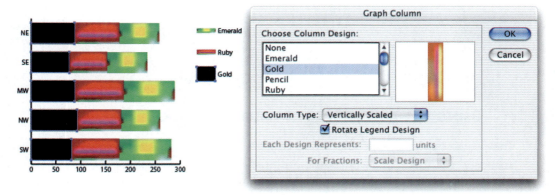

FIGURE 7.55

8 **When finished, the graph should resemble Figure 7.56.**

The graph is much more attractive in color than in grayscale.

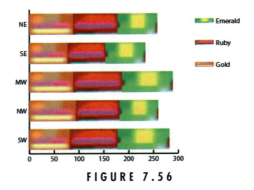

FIGURE 7.56

9 Save your changes and close the document.

To Extend Your Knowledge . . .

CHANGING GRAPH TYPES

New designs applied to the columns and bars of graphs are associated with their cells in the Data Input dialog box. If you change the graph type from column to bar, the new design remains intact. If you change a bar graph to a pie graph, however, the new design would not take effect.

CAREERS IN DESIGN

USING VARIABLE IMAGES IN YOUR PORTFOLIO

The use of dynamic, variable-based designs is cutting-edge technology, but you would be surprised by how many competent designers and illustrators don't use it in their workflow. Now that you've learned the basics of connecting your drawings to data coming from conventional sources (such as databases), you should consider creating a sample or two for your portfolio. Since you never know when a new opportunity for advancing your career might arise, being able to display your knowledge of connecting data to designs might prove invaluable.

You can find one idea for such a sample on your local news station—one you also used in this chapter. Creating a forecast graphic that shows long-range weather conditions is a perfect application of dynamic images. Set up a simple database that shows high and low temperatures, the days of the week, and file names that point to icons for clouds, rain, sun, snow, and fog. Construct a frame that automatically enters the correct values and imagery to generate a forecast graphic. Showing such an image to potential employers could result in a sunny professional outlook.

Chapter 7 Working with Dynamic Graphics **325** **LEVEL 2**

SUMMARY

In this chapter, you learned how to bind type and graphics to variables. You discovered that the Visibility variable can show or hide an object. You learned how to create and save data sets that retain variable settings. You saved and loaded variable libraries and made changes to an XML file that were automatically reflected in your drawings when you reloaded the file. You learned how to save a series of designs as variables and access those variables through their data sets.

You also created a variety of graph types. You used the Data Input dialog box to enter values, which were reflected in the graph. You also used the Data Input dialog box to modify values in a graph. You used the Graph>Design option to create designs you can administer to columns in a graph. Finally, you learned how to enhance a graph's appearance by applying painted designs to bars and columns.

KEY TERMS

area graph	dynamic content	variable
binding	Linked File	Variables palette
capture	tag	Visibility
data set	Text String	XML ID

CHECKING CONCEPTS AND TERMS

MULTIPLE CHOICE

Circle the letter that matches the correct answer for each of the following questions.

1. Which of the following can you use to create a variable?
   a. Text
   b. Image
   c. Visibility
   d. Graph data
   e. All of the above.

2. Which of the following is a false statement?
   a. Objects drawn in the document cannot be bound to variables.
   b. You can bind a linked image to a variable.
   c. You can bind a transformed object to a variable.
   d. You can bind a text block to a variable.

3. Which of the following can you save to a data set?
   a. Variables
   b. Paint attributes
   c. Images
   d. All of the above.

4. The document loading a variable library _____.
   a. must possess the same objects and variables
   b. allows the library to import and link the necessary objects
   c. must possess the same data set as the library
   d. must be the document that saved the variable library

5. When you save a data set to a variable library, the resulting file is _____.

   a. in Illustrator document format

   b. in HTML document format

   c. in XML document format

   d. in RTF document format

6. When you load a variable library into a document, _____.

   a. you must first delete the document variables of the same name

   b. Illustrator renames the incoming variables to avoid conflicting names

   c. you must allow the document variables of the same name to be replaced

   d. you must rename the variable names in the Variables palette

7. Once you create a graph in the document, _____.

   a. you cannot change it to another graph type

   b. you cannot modify its cell values

   c. you should ungroup it

   d. you can change the graph type and alter its cells

8. For a graphic object to become a graph design, you must _____.

   a. select the object and copy it to the clipboard

   b. select the object

   c. double-click the object with the Direct Selection tool

   d. None of the above.

9. What does the Graph Column dialog box do to the columns of a graph?

   a. Creates an extra column

   b. Applies designs created in the Graph Design dialog box

   c. Deletes a column

   d. Groups the columns

10. When importing data into a graph, you must separate the numbers in the text file with _____.

   a. the Tab key

   b. commas

   c. spaces

   d. hyphens

DISCUSSION QUESTIONS

1. Cite a situation where using variables to generate multiple versions of a design would save time and effort.

2. How would dynamic graphics benefit a designer preparing for a presentation to a new client?

3. How can importing text and switching graph types benefit an artist creating multiple charts?

SKILL DRILL

Skill Drills reinforce learned skills. Each skill that is reinforced is the same as, or nearly the same as, a skill we presented in the lessons. We provide detailed instructions in a step-by-step format. You should complete these exercises in order.

To ensure the following Skill Drill exercises work correctly, make certain that the Preferences>Units & Display Performance dialog box has its Identify Objects By option set to XML ID.

1. Create Variables for a Web Site

1. Open italy_web_site.ai from the WIP_07>Italy Web Site folder. Open the Variables palette. Show the page rulers.

   You may not have these fonts on your computer. If you get a font warning, click "Continue". The type on the page will look slightly different, but this is just to show you how variables work.

2. Drag a vertical guide to touch the left side of the "Take a Tour of Tuscany!" headline. Drag a horizontal guide to touch the top of the body text block on the page's right side.

3. Choose File>Place to go to the WIP_07>Italy Web Site folder and place tuscany_tour.jpg with the Link check box selected in the Place dialog box.

4. Scale the photo 50%. Rotate the photo 15 degrees.

5. From the Effect menu, apply the Stylize>Drop Shadow effect to the photo.

6. Position the photo so its top-left corner touches the vertical guide and its top-right corner touches the horizontal guide.

7. Select the headline text block and click the Make Text Dynamic icon in the Variables palette. Select the photo and click the Make Linked File Dynamic icon.

   If you try to make a photo dynamic, and the Make Linked File Dynamic icon will not activate, go to the Links palette and make certain that the photo is linked.

8. Select the body text block and make it dynamic.

9. Select the logo under the large text block and click the Make Visibility Dynamic icon.

10. Change Variable 1 to "headline", Variable 2 to "photo", Variable 3 to "body_text", and Variable 4 to "logo".

FIGURE 7.57

11. Save your changes to the document. Keep the document open for the next exercise.

2. Save a Data Set

1. In the open document, choose View>Guides>Clear Guides.
2. In the Variables palette Options menu, choose Capture Data Set.

   Using the Variables palette's Options menu to choose Capture Data Set shows a separate dialog box that allows you to enter a data set name of your choice.

3. In the New Data Set dialog box, enter "Home Page" and click OK.

   You created a data set that holds all the information about the elements on the page.

4. From the Variables palette Options menu, choose Save Variable Library.
5. Save the file with the name "home_page.xml" to the WIP_07>Italy Web Site folder.
6. Save your changes in the Illustrator document and close it.

3. Create a Text File for Importing Graph Data

1. From your desktop, use your word processor to create a new document.
2. Type the following words in the document, pressing the Tab key after each word. These words become the legend of graphs it is imported to.

   Watermelons   Squash   Tomatoes   Bananas   Green Peas

3. Press Return/Enter to create a new line. Type the following increments, pressing the Tab key after each number.

   100   174   200   135   90

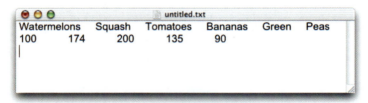

FIGURE 7.58

4. Name the file "pie_graph.txt" and save it in text-only or plain-text format to your WIP_07>Graphs folder.
5. Close the word-processing document.

4. Import Data to a Graph

1. In Illustrator, create a new letter-size CMYK document with the orientation set for landscape. Set the units for inches. Open the Swatches palette.
2. Double-click the Graph tool in the Toolbox.
3. From the Graph Type dialog box, choose the Pie type. Click the Add Drop Shadow option in the dialog box.

4. Set the Legend menu to Standard Legend. Set the Position to Stacked and the Sort menu to All. Click OK.

5. Drag the Graph tool cursor on the page, holding the Shift key to constrain the movement, and draw an approximate 4-inch square graph.

6. In the Data Input dialog box, click the Import Data icon. Go to the WIP_07>Graphs folder and import the pie_graph.txt file you created in the previous Skill Drill.

   The information appears in the Data Input dialog box with the legend names in the first row and the increments in the second.

7. Click the Apply icon at the top of the Data Input dialog box.

   The graph displays the values set in the imported file. The vegetable and fruit names become the legend, separate from the graph. The words are sorted alphabetically because you applied the Sort setting in the Data Input dialog box.

8. Activate the Direct Selection tool. Press Option/Alt and double-click the rectangle for the Green Peas legend. Fill the selected objects with the Mint Julep swatch from the Swatches palette.

9. Double-click each legend rectangle and paint the selected objects as follows: Bananas = Pure Yellow, Tomatoes = Red, Squash = Squash, Watermelon = Sunshine.

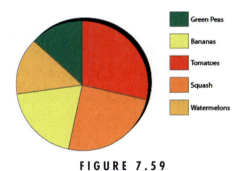

FIGURE 7.59

10. Save the document as "vegetable_chart.ai" to your WIP_07>Graphs folder. Close the document.

CHALLENGE

Challenge exercises expand on, or are somewhat related to, skills we presented in the lessons. Each exercise provides a brief introduction, followed by numbered-step instructions that are not as detailed as those in the Skill Drill exercises. You should complete these exercises in order.

To ensure the following Challenge exercises work correctly, open the Units & Display Performance Preferences dialog box and set the Identify Objects By option to XML ID. Change this setting before you perform any JavaScript interactivity and before you create any layers. If you change the setting to XML ID after the fact, your layer and object names will not adhere to XML naming conventions and the exercises will fail.

LEVEL 2 · **330** · Chapter 7 · Working with Dynamic Graphics

1. Modify Page 2 XML File

As the Webmaster creating a site for a travel agency, you applied variables to the content of a document. You saved the variables as a data set in an external XML file. In this exercise, you duplicate and modify the XML file to create two additional Web pages with identical layouts.

1. Go to your desktop and navigate to the WIP_07>Italy Web Site folder. Make two duplicates of the home_page.xml file.

    You should have the original file and two copies.

2. Rename the first duplicate as "page_2.xml", and rename the other duplicate as "page_3.xml".

3. Use your word processor to navigate to the WIP_07>Italy Web Site and open page_2.xml.

4. Scroll down to find the **dataSetName = "Home Page"** tag. Change the Home Page name to "Page 2".

    This changes the name of the data set.

5. In the **<headline>** variable tag, change "Take a Tuscany Tour" to "Go on a Photo Shoot".

6. In the **<photo>** variable tag, highlight tuscany_tour.jpg and change it to "photo_shoot.jpg".

    This changes the tuscany_tour.jpg image on the page to the photo_shoot.jpg image when this XML file is loaded back into the Illustrator document.

7. Next is the **<body_text>** variable tag. To change this variable, use your word processor to go to the WIP_07>Italy Web Site folder and open the photo_shoot.txt file.

8. Highlight the text in the document and copy it. Close the document without saving.

9. Back in the page_2.xml document, go to the **<body_text>** tag. Following it is the **<p>** tag, a body of text, and the **</p>** tag. Highlight all the text between the **<p>** and **</p>** tags and paste the copied text.

10. In the **<logo>** variable tag, change the true value to "false".

Chapter 7 Working with Dynamic Graphics **331** **LEVEL 2**

The "false" setting hides the logo on the page.

```
<v:sampleDataSet dataSetName="Page 2">

          <headline>
          <p>Go on a Photo Shoot</p>
          </headline>

          <photo>
          photo_shoot.jpg
          </photo>

          <body_text>
          <p> Now you can have the photo-shooting trip
of a lifetime! Visit the rustic hillsides of Tuscany and photograph their wealth of wonders.
Fly into Rome and, once you have landed, you will see Italian history unveiled as you
visit Florence and the surrounding countryside, home of the great masters. You will also
witness some of the world's finest artwork, architecture, food and beverages. The
splendor of Italy is unbelievable! </p>
          </body_text>

          <logo>
          false
          </logo>

     </v:sampleDataSet>
```

FIGURE 7.60

11. Save your changes and close the document.

2. Change Page 3 XML File

You modified the XML file for Page 2. Your next task is to alter the XML file for Page 3.

1. Go to your desktop and use your word processor to navigate to the WIP_07>Italy Web Site folder. Open page_3.xml.

2. Scroll down to find the **dataSetName="Home Page"** tag. Change "Home Page" to "Page 3".

    This changes the name of the data set.

3. In the **<headline>** variable tag, change "Take a Tuscany Tour" to "Visit the Italian Seaside".

4. In the **<photo>** variable tag, change the tuscany_tour.jpg name to "seaside.jpg".

5. Next is the **<body_text>** variable tag. To change this variable, use your word processor to go to the WIP_07>Italy Web Site folder and open seaside.txt.

6. Highlight the text in the document and copy it. Close the document without saving.

LEVEL 2 **332** Chapter 7 **Working with Dynamic Graphics**

7. Back in the page_3.xml document, highlight all the text between the two paragraph tags of the `<body_text>` tag and paste the copied text.

8. In the `<logo>` variable tag, change the true value to "false".

```
<v:sampleDataSet dataSetName="Page 3">

    <headline>
    <p>Visit the Italian Seaside</p>
    </headline>

    <photo>
    seaside.jpg
    </photo>

    <body_text>
    <p> Lovers of the sea can now have the
oceanic trip of a lifetime! Visit the seaside, harbors and beaches of Italy to see such
famous sights that line entire coastline of this famous peninsular known as Italy. You will
also witness some of the world's finest artwork, architecture, food and beverages. You
will see history unveiled as you visit Florence and the birthplace of the Renaissance.
There is no doubt that Tuscany is in our blood. </p>
    </body_text>

    <logo>
    false
    </logo>

</v:sampleDataSet>
```

FIGURE 7.61

9. Save your changes and close the word-processing document.

3. Update Page 2

Now that the Italy Web page XML files have been modified, you are ready to apply the changes to the Illustrator document.

1. In Illustrator, use File>Open to go to the WIP_07>Italy Web Site folder and open italy_web_site.ai.

   You may not have these fonts on your computer. If you get a font warning, click "Continue". The type on the page will look slightly different, but this is just to show you how variables work.

2. From the Variables palette Options menu, choose Load Variable Library.

3. Navigate to the WIP_07>Italy Web Site folder and open page_2.xml.

4. When asked if you want to overwrite the existing variables, click Yes.

5. In the Data Set menu in the Variables palette, choose the Page 2 set.

   The photo and text designated in the page_2.xml file replace those of the home page. The new photo automatically scales and rotates to fit the space on the page. Also, the drop shadow remains applied to the photo.

6. Choose Edit>Undo to return to the previous photo and text.

7. Choose Edit>Redo to go back to the Page 2 Web page.

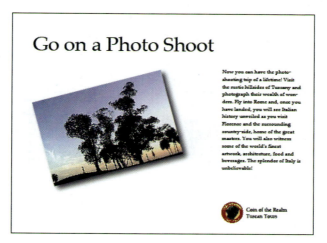

FIGURE 7.62

8. Keep the document open for the next exercise.

4. Apply Changes to Page 3

Page 2 is now complete, and you are ready to apply changes to Page 3 of the travel agency Web site.

1. In the open document, use the Variables palette Options menu to choose Load Variable Library.

2. Navigate to the WIP_07>Italy Web Site folder and open page_3.xml.

3. When asked if you want to overwrite the existing variables, click Yes.

4. From the Data Set menu in the Variables palette, choose the Page 3 set.

   The photo and text designated in the page_3.xml file replace those on the page.

5. Choose Edit>Undo to return to the Page 2 photo and text.

   Note the change of the photo and text in the text blocks.

6. Choose Edit>Redo to go back to the Page 3 Web page.

The XML file saved the time it would have taken to place the photo, type the text, and position the elements in their exact locations on the Artboard.

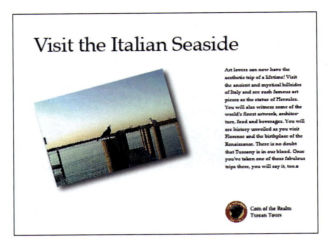

FIGURE 7.63

7. Save your changes and close the document.

PORTFOLIO BUILDER

Create a Visually Communicative Graph

You are a Webmaster and have taken on a new client who owns a car-racing team. He wants an artistic-looking graph to show the several years that his team has won races. Your task is to create such a graph and make it aesthetically pleasing.

1. Create a new letter-size CMYK document.
2. From the WIP_07>Graphs folder, place the checkered_flag.tif image without linking.
3. Select the Column Graph and drag its tool cursor to match the borders of the checkered flag photo.
4. In the Data Input dialog box, set the top cells with the six consecutive years the racing team has won: 1960, 1965, 1978, 1984, 1990, and 2003. Apply these figures and close the Data Input dialog box.
5. Select and ungroup the graph. With the Direct Selection tool, select the columns and compound them.

    Multiple objects must be compounded before being masked.

6. Select the columns and the photo. Press Command/Control-7 to mask them.

    The graph representing the years of victory is visually reinforced by the photograph of the checkered flag, which denotes the winning of a race.

7. Save the document as "checkered_flag.ai" to the WIP_07>Graphs folder. Close the document.

LEVEL 2

CHAPTER 8

Enhancing Your Workflow

OBJECTIVES

In this chapter, you learn how to:

- Create objects to use in Photoshop

- Add Photoshop effects to Illustrator objects

- Use the Actions palette

- Create and record actions

- Name objects and make menu selections for actions

- Combine Illustrator files

Why Would I Do This?

Illustrator is a powerful program, one that becomes increasingly useful as you add effective productivity techniques to your workflow. There are several ways to enhance the power of Illustrator. The first is to combine Illustrator with other programs, such as its image-editing counterpart, Adobe Photoshop. Applying Photoshop techniques to an Illustrator design can expedite the production process. Once you create an element in Illustrator, you can import the design into Photoshop, further enhance the piece, or use it as is.

A second workflow-accelerating feature is built-in *actions*, which are a series of processes that you record and then play back to automate repetitive and commonly used functions. Including actions in your day-to-day workflow saves considerable amounts of time — actions turn tedious tasks into single-click processes.

A third way to expand Illustrator's abilities is to use *Adobe Acrobat*, an application that allows you to manipulate and enhance *PDF (Portable Document Format)* documents. PDF is a method of delivering your digital content to anyone, anywhere, regardless of the platform on which the viewer works (Windows, Macintosh, UNIX, Linux). In addition to this improved distribution capability, PDF files preserve fonts and graphics with the same reliability as Adobe Illustrator. In this chapter, you learn to use both actions and PDFs to improve your productivity and to increase the chances that everyone in your audience can properly view your work.

VISUAL SUMMARY

This chapter explores the many ways to enhance and accelerate your workflow in producing designs that would otherwise require considerable time to create. As the old adage states, "Time is money," and anyone involved in the graphic arts industry will agree that high production rates coupled with short development cycles result in greater income — not to mention a long list of satisfied clients.

You explore Photoshop-related filters, palettes, and techniques in Illustrator. You also combine Illustrator features with Photoshop options to produce effects that neither program could create individually. Even though Photoshop and Illustrator are closely related in their abilities to create both vector and raster images, the two programs' methods and operations are dissimilar. You can use Photoshop to draw vectors to create clipping paths that mask objects, but Photoshop is not the correct choice for developing a solely vector design. You should use Illustrator to create vector objects, and then import the objects into a Photoshop document for further modification.

FIGURE 8.1

Illustrator borrowed the Transparency palette from Photoshop. This palette offers Photoshop-style options that allow you to achieve special effects never before possible in Illustrator, one of which is shown in Figure 8.2. These palette items use vector paths to alter the appearance of raster objects. After a little bit of practice with the Photoshop techniques, you will enjoy a considerable increase in your productivity.

FIGURE 8.2

If you complain about wasting valuable time creating a standard design or layout each time you begin a new project, then you will appreciate actions. From the *Actions palette*, you create, control, and use actions. You can record repetitive movements, menu selections, and drawing techniques into a single action. Once recorded, you play an action to automatically execute the movements, menu selections, and drawing techniques, one after another, as if you were performing the tasks manually. Using actions, you can draw designs, lay out pages, and rasterize objects — all from the convenience of the Actions palette.

FIGURE 8.3

The process of creating an action can be simple, but it can also prove frustrating. Drawing objects, painting and transforming objects, and recording movements and dialog box selections are the simple tasks involved in recording an action. Frustration enters the equation when you discover that you cannot record certain tasks, such as drawing with the Pen tool (you will find that some tools work and some tools don't). You may need to modify your drawing techniques when you use actions. Your drawing skills will probably increase sharply as you develop effective methods to achieve the final product.

FIGURE 8.4

As you continue your exploration of actions, you learn that you cannot select an object in an action unless it has an assigned name. You learn how to use the Note section of the Attributes palette to name the objects included in an action. You also discover that you cannot directly record many menu items into an action. To overcome this problem, you can use the Insert Menu Item option to successfully include a menu item in an action.

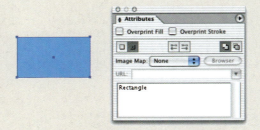

FIGURE 8.5

The final step in any workflow is showing your finished works to others — a critical step for graphic artists in search of a long list of clients. The best way to showcase your artwork to prospective clients is to combine your works into a PDF file. In this chapter, you learn how to use Adobe Acrobat to include multiple Illustrator documents into a single PDF, which you can open in Illustrator and modify as necessary. These files can be viewed by others possessing the program *Adobe* or *Acrobat Reader*, which is a read-only program, free from Adobe.com.

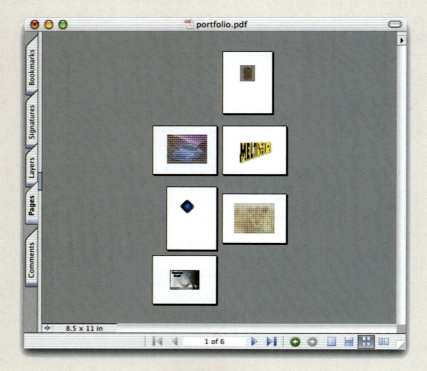

FIGURE 8.6

Chapter 8 **Enhancing Your Workflow** **341** **LEVEL 2**

NOTE: This chapter uses Adobe Photoshop and Adobe Acrobat. To use these particular lessons, you must own one or both programs to experience the additional design elements they add to Illustrator files. If you don't own these programs, go to http://www.adobe.com and download a free 30-day trial of Photoshop or Acrobat. You may also want to download a free copy of Adobe Reader (formerly Acrobat Reader).

LESSON 1 Modifying Objects for Use in Photoshop

Adobe Systems develops both Illustrator and Photoshop, whose features and functions are closely related. Illustrator includes Photoshop-type filters and offers the Photoshop Transparency palette and its options. Photoshop can draw vector paths, and then use the paths as masks or convert them to selections.

Illustrator performs some operations and techniques, such as text outline modifications and transformations, quite fluidly, while Photoshop cannot perform those operations or must use vastly different techniques to achieve the same effect. We suggest that you use Illustrator's more sophisticated drawing techniques to create the desired effect, and then open the document in Photoshop to apply the necessary final touch-ups.

Shear Perspective Type

1 **From the Chapter_08 folder, open the shear_perspective.ai document. Zoom out to 50% viewing.**

The shearing you do requires that you drag the Free Transform tool down quite a ways to fit the type. Zoom out to give yourself lots of room.

2 **Select the type outlines on the perspective grid. Press Command/Control-H to hide the edges.**

3 **Press the "E" key to activate the Free Transform tool.**

Make certain that the bounding box (from the View menu) is not showing. Its control handles can compete with those of the Free Transform tool.

4 **Click-hold the cursor on the tool's bottom-right corner handle.**

5 **Press Command/Control and drag the handle down (adding the Shift key to constrain the move) so the bottom of the letter "E" touches the bottom of the guide.**

Adding Command/Control shifts the tool into shearing mode. You shear the type outlines to fit the angular perspective created by the guides.

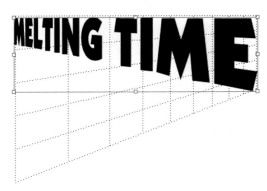

FIGURE 8.7

6 Release the mouse when you finish the shear.

7 Click-hold the Free Transform tool cursor on the bottom-left corner handle.

8 Press Command/Control and drag the handle down (adding the Shift key to constrain the move) so the bottom of the letter "M" touches the bottom of the perspective guide.

The text outlines should fit within the perspective guides, shrinking the text as it moves toward the vanishing point.

FIGURE 8.8

9 Deselect the text outlines. Use the Selection tool to select them again. Set the stroke to 1-pt Yellow. Hide the guides.

Chapter 8 Enhancing Your Workflow   **343**   LEVEL 2

10 From the Effect menu, choose Stylize>Drop Shadow. Make no changes in the dialog box and click OK.

FIGURE 8.9

11 Save the document with the same name to your WIP_08 folder. Close the document.

Modify with Photoshop

1 Go to the desktop and start Adobe Photoshop.

2 Use the File menu to go to the WIP_08 folder and open shear_perspective.ai.

3 The dialog box that appears lists the selected shear_perspective.ai file.

4 Depending on your version of Photoshop, apply the correct settings to open the Illustrator file as RGB color mode in 150 ppi resolution.

The Illustrator document is rasterized to Photoshop format.

5 Zoom out to see the image better.

6 From the Filter menu, choose Liquify. Use the cursor in this window to distort the type elements in the preview. When finished, click OK.

The Liquify filter is not available in Illustrator. To use the filter, you must place the Illustrator outlines into Photoshop and perform your modifications there.

FIGURE 8.10

7. **From the Layers palette Options menu, choose Flatten Image.**

   When you choose **Flatten Image**, all the layers in the Layers palette combine into one layer. This allows the file to be saved as TIFF format.

FIGURE 8.11

8. **Save the document in TIFF format as "shear_perspective.tif" to your WIP_08 folder. Close the Photoshop document and program.**

Chapter 8   Enhancing Your Workflow   **345**   **LEVEL 2**

To Extend Your Knowledge . . .

ILLUSTRATOR AND PHOTOSHOP

If you use both Illustrator and Photoshop, make mental notes about how each program performs certain operations. Photoshop is a raster program — designed and engineered to provide tools for working on bitmap (photographic) images — even though it offers certain vector functionalities, such as the Pen tool. By the same token, Illustrator is a drawing program, specifically designed to provide control over vector shapes and objects; but it also displays some degree of crossover, with functions such as rasterization and the ability to save images into bitmap formats. If you use both, make sure you consider which one is better suited as the primary application for a specific project.

LESSON 2   Using Photoshop Techniques in Illustrator

Until recently, Illustrator did not include the ***Transparency palette***. Illustrator "borrowed" the palette from Photoshop, and you can use it to perform the same types of operations as you can in Photoshop. This palette offers many options that allow you to apply a variety of effects to selected objects.

One of the Transparency palette's options is the ***Opacity slider***, which you move to adjust the opacity of an object, making it appear more or less transparent. The palette is commonly used to create masks that are transparent, rather than solid (opaque). Remember, a mask is a shape or object used to protect certain portions of an image while you modify other parts.

Illustrator offers an easy technique for masking called ***Make Clipping Mask***. This is found in the Layers palette Options menu. You can use clipping masks to mask one object at a time, or you can include several objects in one mask. Multiple objects must be compounded before they will all mask.

Another aspect of the clipping mask is apparent when you want the masking objects to retain some opacity but be transparent enough for the masked objects to show through. To attain this appearance, you need to create an ***opacity mask***. You can successfully accomplish a transparent opacity mask operation using the Transparency palette and its Opacity slider. The transparent objects are then combined with masked objects to create a unique appearance.

Opacity Masking

In this exercise, you create objects that become transparent, which you then combine with masked objects.

| 1 | From the Chapter_08 folder, open the opacity_truck.ai document. Open the Swatches, Layers, Info, and Transparency palettes. |

| 2 | Use the File>Place option to return to the Chapter_08 folder. |

| 3 | Place (without linking) the truck.tif image. |

The photo is positioned in the Artboard's center.

FIGURE 8.12

4 Select the photo and lock it. Change to Outline viewing mode.

5 Select the Ellipse tool and drag it, starting from the photo's upper-left corner, to draw an approximate 25-pixel circle.

Watch the Info palette as you draw the circle. You probably won't achieve an exact 25-pixel circle, but make the increments as close as possible.

Actions have their own quirks that you have to work with. Had you clicked the cursor on the photo corner and used the dialog box to draw the circle with exact increments, the circle would not have appeared in the same place during the action. To get an object to appear in the action in the exact place you drew it, you must draw it by hand. This applies to rectangles, squares, circles, and other objects drawn with the Geometric tools.

6 Fill the circle with the Vega Blue radial gradient from the Swatches palette. Set the Stroke for None.

7 From the Object>Transform menu, choose Move. In the Move dialog box set the Horizontal field to 25 px. Set the Vertical field to 0. Click Copy.

8 Hold down Command/Control and press the "D" key 18 times to create 18 more duplicates that extend to the photo's edge.

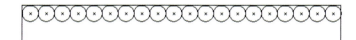

FIGURE 8.13

9 Select all the circles and return to the Move dialog box. Set the Horizontal field to 0 and set the Vertical field to −25. Click Copy.

Chapter 8   Enhancing Your Workflow   **347**   LEVEL 2

10 Hold down Command/Control and press the "D" key 13 times to create 13 more duplicates that extend to the photo's bottom.

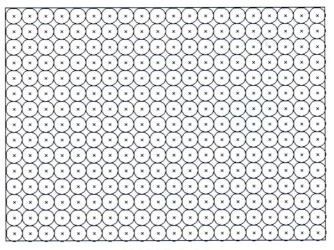

FIGURE 8.14

11 Save the document with the same name to your WIP_08 folder. Keep the document open for the next exercise.

Add Effects to the Opacity Mask

1 In the open document, return to Preview mode. Select all the circles on the photo.

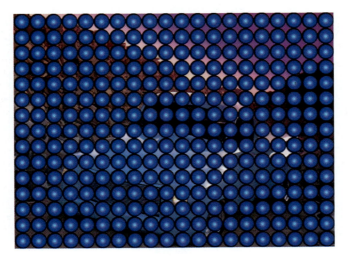

FIGURE 8.15

2 In the Transparency palette, set the Opacity slider to 40%. Copy the circles to the clipboard.

The selected circles become slightly transparent so you can see the photo through them.

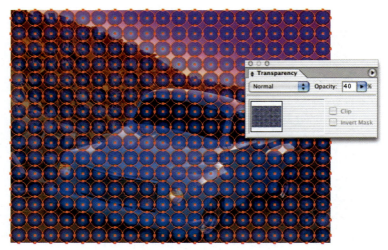

FIGURE 8.16

3 **From the Object menu, choose Compound Paths>Make.**

You must compound multiple objects before you can use them as masks. The keyboard shortcut for compounding is Command/Control-8.

4 **From the Layers palette Options menu, choose Make Clipping Mask.**

The compounded circles mask the photo. The circles lose their gradient-filled paint attributes.

5 **Press Command/Control-F to paste the copied transparent circles in front of the masked objects.**

The masked objects let the truck photo show through the transparent gradient-filled circles on top, creating an attractive hazy effect.

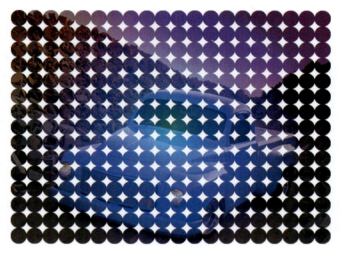

FIGURE 8.17

6 Save your changes and close the document.

Use a Transparency Screen

Sometimes you may want to fade a photograph from light to dark, creating an area on the picture where you can place type over the image without obscuring the type or cutting off parts of the photo. In the Transparency palette is a menu labeled "Normal". This menu has others options that allow you to apply fades and other effects to images.

1 From the Chapter_08 folder, open the vacation_now.ai document. Open the Swatches, Stroke, and Transparency palettes.

2 Use the View menu to zoom out to see the Artboard more clearly.

3. From the File menu, choose the Place option to go to the Chapter_08 folder and place (without linking) the hammock_sunset.tif image.

FIGURE 8.18

4. Change to Outline viewing mode.

5. Use the Rectangle tool to draw a rectangle the same size as the photo.

6. Fill the rectangle with the White, Black linear gradient from the Swatches palette. Set the Stroke to 1-pt Black.

7. Return to Preview mode. Keep the rectangle selected.

FIGURE 8.19

8. From the Transparency palette, open the Normal menu and choose Screen from its options.

Chapter 8 Enhancing Your Workflow 351 LEVEL 2

The gradient becomes a transparent screen that allows the photo to show through its lighter areas but become more opaque as the gradient turns black.

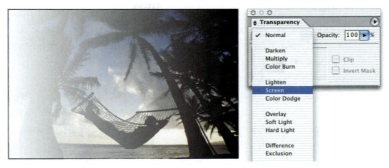

FIGURE 8.20

9. From above the Artboard, select the "Vacation Now!" text outlines. Bring the outlines to the front.

10. Position the outlines in the ad's upper-left corner (see Figure 8.21).

11. From above the Artboard, select the "*Hammock optional" text outlines. Bring the outlines to the front.

12. Position the outlines in the ad's bottom-left corner.

FIGURE 8.21

13. Save the document with the same name to your WIP_08 folder and close the document.

To Extend Your Knowledge

USING TRANSPARENCY OPTIONS

The Normal menu in the Transparency palette contains several image-altering options, including the Screen option. These menu options can change an image's color, lightness, and darkness, and perhaps create precisely the effect you need. Select a vector path or raster image and experiment with these options to see how they work.

LESSON 3 Using the Actions Palette

Adding actions to your workflow allows you to reduce the number of clicks and mouse moves you make and responding to dialog boxes when creating objects. These dialog boxes could include saving a file for the Web, rasterizing a series of images, or converting the color mode of multiple documents from RGB to CMYK. Almost any Illustrator function can be automated to a certain degree.

Fundamentally, actions are recordings of tasks you performed while using Illustrator. The Actions palette records actions in sequence and stores each action under a specific name. You can store related actions in sets that resemble folders when viewed in the Actions palette. You can edit actions, duplicate them, and automate them to run in a ***batch*** (several actions organized into a single group).

The Actions palette, shown in the following illustration, is the central location for everything action-related. To activate the Actions palette, choose Window>Actions; from here, you can run an action. However, when you assign a keyboard shortcut to an action, you simply press the appropriate key combination and the action runs automatically.

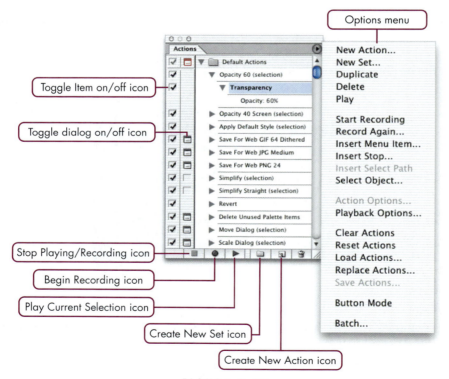

FIGURE 8.22

Notice the two columns on the palette's left side. The first one, displaying checkmarks in Figure 8.22, toggles individual actions on or off. If you want only a portion of an action to execute, turn off the steps you want to leave out of the action.

The next column indicates whether or not you can change values in a dialog box. If this icon is visible (as shown in Figure 8.22), any action that might require your input pauses so you can change values in that specific step's dialog box; if the icon is not visible, the action simply runs, using whatever values were entered when you initially recorded the steps.

Moving to the right, at the palette's bottom are three buttons that resemble those found on a video deck or tape player. The first button stops the recording process; the second button begins recording your action (until you stop recording); and the third button plays any action you selected in the palette.

Lastly, you can create a new set (the Folder icon), create a new action (the blank page icon), or delete selected sets, actions, or steps from the Actions palette.

Explore the Actions Palette

1. From the Chapter_08 folder, open the actions_palette.ai document. Show the Actions palette on the screen.

2. Enlarge the Actions palette downward so you can see all the actions in its list.

3. Click the Default Fill and Stroke icon in the Toolbox. Use the Ellipse tool to manually draw a 100-pt circle at the page's top.

4. Drag-duplicate the circle (hold down Shift to constrain the move) so the duplicate overlaps the original. Select the two objects.

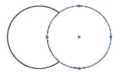

FIGURE 8.23

5. Choose the Unite (selection) action in the Actions palette. Click the triangle icon to the left of the Pathfinder name to see the details of the action.

You see Pathfinder and Unite. Unite is the name that used to be assigned to the Pathfinder paletter selection, which is now called Add to Shape Area. The action unites the selected paths into a single path. Clicking the small arrow icon to the left of an action expands the list so you can see each individual step.

FIGURE 8.24

6 **Click the Play Current Selection button at the bottom of the Actions palette.**

This button activates the action and applies all its elements to the selected object.

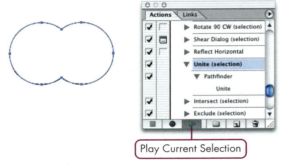

FIGURE 8.25

7 **Fill the new object with the Area Rug pattern from the Swatches palette.**

8 **Scroll down in the Actions palette and choose the Rasterize (selection) action. Click the triangle icon to show Rasterize, and then click the Rasterize triangle to see the details of the action.**

The color model listed in this action is RGB. This is a CMYK document, so you need to change the color model to CMYK. You do not, however, want to replace this RGB action, which you may need in the future.

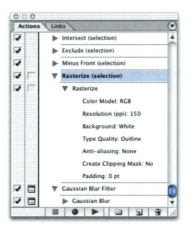

FIGURE 8.26

Chapter 8   Enhancing Your Workflow   **355**

9 **In the Action palette Options menu, choose Duplicate. Double-click the duplicate action and change its name to "Rasterize CMYK".**

You can duplicate and modify actions.

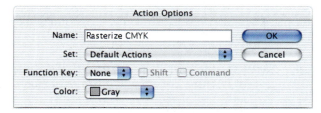

FIGURE 8.27

10 **Click the triangles of this new action to see the details. Double-click the Color Model RGB item in the new action's details.**

In most cases, double-clicking an item in an action opens the item's dialog box (assuming it has one), allowing you to customize the settings.

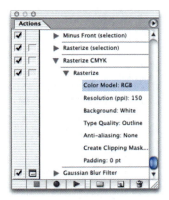

FIGURE 8.28

11 **In the Rasterize dialog box, set the Color Model to CMYK, and then click OK.**

12 **Save the document with the same name to your WIP_08 folder. Keep the document open for the next exercise.**

Use the Actions Palette

1   **Select the united object and choose the Rotate 90 CW (selection) action. Click the Play Current Selection button.**

There are two rotation actions. The Rotate Dialog (selection) shows a dialog box icon to the left of its name; when the action plays, a dialog appears so you can customize the settings. The Rotate 90 CW (selection) action offers no dialog box.

2   **Select the new Rasterize CMYK action and click the Play Current Selection button at the bottom of the palette.**

The object becomes rasterized with the CMYK color model.

3   **Scroll down to the bottom of the Actions palette and select the Gaussian Blur Filter action.**

4   **Click the checkmark to the left of its name.**

The checkmark icon toggles the action on and off. The icon does not hide anything; when toggled on, the action is functional; when toggled off, the action is nonfunctional.

FIGURE 8.29

5   **Click the Play Current Selection button.**

The action does not work because you turned it off. If shortcut keys were applied to particular actions, turning off an action eliminates the possibility of accidentally pressing the shortcut keys and inadvertently applying an action.

6   **Return to the Gaussian Blur Filter action and click the same checkmark area.**

This toggles the action on.

7   **Click the Play Current Selection button.**

Chapter 8 Enhancing Your Workflow **357**

The filter is not directly applied to the object. Instead, its dialog box appears. It can become quite a nuisance to continually stop and click the OK button in dialog boxes. You can click the dialog-box-shaped icon to the right of the checkmark to disable the dialog boxes.

FIGURE 8.30

8 In the Gaussian Blur dialog box, click Cancel.

9 In the Actions palette, click the dialog box icon to the checkmark's right.

The dialog box associated with the Gaussian Blur does not appear when the action runs.

10 Click the Play Current Selection button at the palette's bottom.

The object receives the Gaussian Blur raster filter effects.

11 Save your changes and keep the document open for the next exercise.

Create Shortcut Keys to Play Actions

1 In the open document, use the Rectangle tool to draw a 175 × 200 pt rectangle to the left of the rasterized object.

2 Select the Apply Default Style (selection) action and click the Play Current Selection button.

Default Style appears in the Graphic Styles palette and is based on the Default Fill and Stroke icon in the Toolbox. The Apply Default Style action applies the default fill and stroke to the rectangle.

3 Fill the rectangle with the Chinese Tiles pattern from the Swatches palette. Leave the Stroke set to Black.

4 Double-click the Opacity 60 (selection) action in the palette. Set the Function Key menu to any of the available F-keys. Click the Shift option and then click OK.

You can only use the function keys (F-keys) as the keyboard shortcuts for actions. You can also add modifier keys to the function key. If computer shortcuts have been applied to an F-key you prefer, add the Shift key to trigger the action.

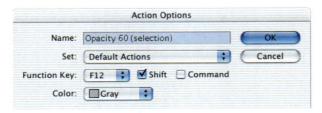

FIGURE 8.31

5. **With the rectangle selected, hold Shift and press your assigned F-key.**

   If your F-key does not work, click the Play Current Selection button to run the action.

6. **Move the rectangle over the united object.**

   The action uses the Transparency palette to set the Opacity to 60%, which explains the action's name.

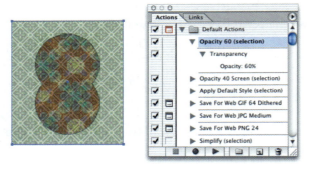

FIGURE 8.32

7. **Keep the rectangle selected.**

Chapter 8   Enhancing Your Workflow   **359**   LEVEL 2

8   Select the Save For Web GIF 64 Dithered action. Click its triangle icon to see the Save For Web element. Click the triangle icon to see its details.

FIGURE 8.33

9   Keep the dialog box icon next to the Save For Web GIF 64 Dithered action name. Click the **Play Current Selection** button.

The Save For Web feature requires you to type in a name for the saved file, so you need the dialog box in this case.

10   In the Save For Web dialog box, click Cancel.

You do not need to save the file. This exercise simply shows you how to (if necessary) make use of dialog boxes within an action.

11   Close the document without saving.

To Extend Your Knowledge . . .

VIEWING MODES

The Actions palette has two viewing modes. The **Normal mode** (the default) is how you see the palette when it first appears, with the action names listed in the palette in single file. To run one of the actions, you must select it and click the Play Current Selection button at the bottom of the palette.

In **Button mode**, which you choose from the palette's Options menu, a button is assigned to each action; you simply click a button, and an action executes.

LESSON 4 Creating Your Own Actions

Illustrator ships with a collection of predefined actions you see when you activate the Actions palette. If you can accomplish a task simply by clicking a button, there's not much advantage in creating a custom action for that job — one click is one click, whether you run an action or choose a button. There is also little value in creating an action for a task that you perform only once a year or for a job that requires so much creative attention that automation becomes impossible. On the other hand, tasks that require multiple mouse clicks to open standard menus, choose items in dialog boxes, and select palette commands are perfect candidates for actions.

Before you record a custom action, we recommend that you review all the actions already available to you. Once you determine that you need to create a new action, you can use the following exercise as a guide.

Create Your Own Action

1. From the Chapter_08 folder, open the rotate_square.ai document. Open the Swatches and Actions palettes.

2. Click the Create New Set button at the bottom of the Actions palette, and name the new set "my_actions". Click OK.

FIGURE 8.34

3. In the Actions palette, make sure the details of the Default Actions set are hidden. If they are visible, click the triangle icon to hide the details.

   The new my_actions set appears in the Actions palette (see Figure 8.35).

FIGURE 8.35

4. Click the Default Fill and Stroke icon in the Toolbox to begin with a white fill and black stroke.

Chapter 8   Enhancing Your Workflow   **361**   LEVEL 2

5   Select the my_actions set. Click the Create New Action button at the bottom of the palette.

6   Name the new action "Rotate Square", and then click Record.

From this point forward, any objects you draw with dialog boxes, and any palette options you click will record as part of this new action. If you make a mistake, you must click the Stop Recording button at the bottom of the palette and start over. The Edit>Undo option will not stop the recording or undo the action.

7   Select the Rectangle tool, hold Option/Alt, and click the cursor in the Artboard's top center area. Set the Width and Height for 100 points, and then click OK.

These steps will be a part of the Rectangle Tool heading that appears in the Actions palette.

FIGURE 8.36

8   In the Swatches palette, click the Show Gradient Swatches icon.

9   Fill the square with the Vega Blue gradient.

This becomes the next action in the action list. When the action plays, you must set the Swatches palette to the swatch section referenced in the action; otherwise, you receive an error message. For example, if the action calls for a gradient, and the Swatches palette is set to Show Color Swatches when the action plays, an error message displays.

FIGURE 8.37

10   Drag the Gradient tool on the square to change the gradient's angle.

Nothing appears in the Actions palette. The action is meant to record menu selections and specific values entered into the fields within dialog boxes.

11   Click the Stroke box in the Toolbox. Set the Stroke to None.

Clicking the Stroke box is the first Set color action; changing the stroke to None is the second Set color action.

FIGURE 8.38

12 You are still in the process of recording. Keep the square selected and continue to the next exercise.

Add to Your Action

1 With the square selected in the open document, double-click the Rotate tool in the Toolbox. Set the Angle to 45 and click OK.

The rotation becomes the next step in the action list.

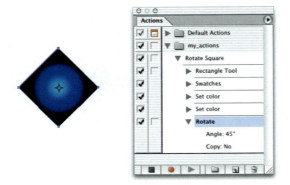

FIGURE 8.39

Chapter 8 Enhancing Your Workflow **363** LEVEL 2

2 **From the Filter menu, choose Stylize>Round Corners. Make no changes in the dialog box and click OK.**

All the options from the Filter menu record in an action.

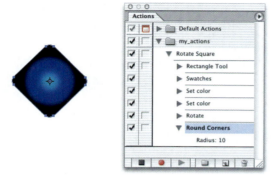

FIGURE 8.40

3 **From the Object menu, choose Path>Offset Path. Make no changes in the dialog box and click OK.**

There is no obvious change in the objects. The offset path received the Vega Blue gradient and blends with the original object.

4 **Click the Default Fill and Stroke icon in the Toolbox.**

The offset path takes on the default fill and stroke. This appears as a Set color item in the actions list.

FIGURE 8.41

5 **In the Stroke palette, change the Stroke Weight of the selected object to 3 pt.**

Note the addition of the Set Stroke action item and its details.

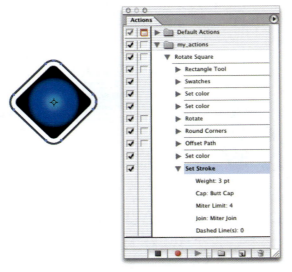

FIGURE 8.42

6. **From the Effect menu, choose Stylize>Drop Shadow. Make no changes in the dialog box and click OK.**

    The effect does not appear in the Actions palette—actions do not record effects. If you want a drop shadow, you must choose the option from the Filter menu.

7. **From the Filter menu, choose Stylize>Drop Shadow. Make no changes in the dialog box and click OK.**

    The drop shadow appears on the object, and the Drop Shadow item appears in the Actions palette.

FIGURE 8.43

8. **Click the Stop Playing/Recording button at the bottom of the Actions palette.**

Chapter 8   Enhancing Your Workflow   **365**   LEVEL **2**

Your action is complete and recorded. The next step is to replay the action.

9 **Select the object on the Artboard and delete it.**

10 **Select the Rotate Square action in the Actions palette. Click the Play Current Selection button.**

The action plays all the steps you recorded. Illustrator draws the square and applies all the attributes and transformations to the objects.

11 **In the Actions palette, choose the my_actions folder. In the palette Options menu, choose Save Actions.**

Save new action folders externally so you can access them from other Illustrator documents.

12 **Save the action set as "my_actions.aia" to the Illustrator CS2>Presets>Actions folder.**

The ".aia" extension is the standard extension for Illustrator's action sets. Make sure you always use it when saving actions for use in other documents.

13 **Save the document as "rotate_square.ai" to your WIP_08 folder. Close the document.**

To Extend Your Knowledge . . .

SAVE FOLDERS TO EXTERNAL FILES

Saving new action folders is a wise decision. New action folders appear in the Actions palette even if you quit the program and relaunch it. There is a chance, however, that the Illustrator Preferences file may become corrupt. If that happens, you must delete the Preferences file, which also deletes the new actions folder. If you save the actions folder to an external file, however, you can reload the folder at any time.

LESSON 5   Naming Objects and Menu Selections

Actions do not record every movement and menu selection you make during a recording. For instance, the Actions palette does not record the clicks you make with the Pen tool as you draw a free-form, multisided object; however, the Actions palette does record the objects you create with dialog boxes because they offer specific increments that successfully translate to actions.

Whenever you create an object that will be selected again in the action, it must be given a name in order for it to be valid within an action. In the Show Note section of the Attributes dialog box, you can name the object whatever you wish. The name should follow standard XML naming conventions: use all lowercase letters and don't use spaces or special characters. If you must separate words, use an underscore.

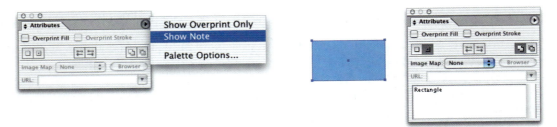

FIGURE 8.44

Once you name an object, Illustrator can select the object within an action. To name an object, choose the Set Selection option in the Actions palette Options menu and type in the name of the object you want Illustrator to select. When the action plays, Illustrator selects the specified object.

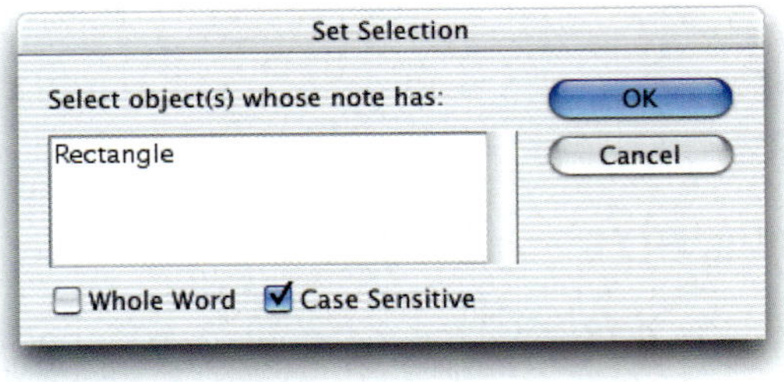

FIGURE 8.45

In the same vein, Illustrator cannot record most menu selections, but a few menu selections, including View>Guides>Make Guide, successfully record in an action. If a menu selection does not appear in an action, you can use the Insert Menu Item option to add the item to your action. The Insert Menu Item option is in the Actions palette Options menu.

Once the Insert Menu Item dialog box appears, you would choose a menu selection and click OK. The menu choice would then be added to the recording.

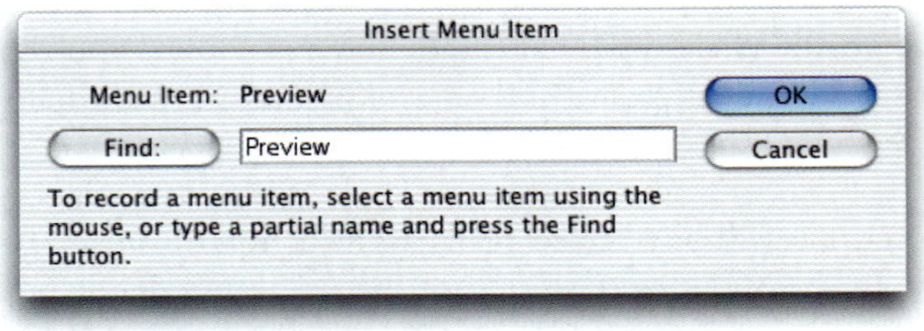

FIGURE 8.46

Chapter 8 Enhancing Your Workflow   367   LEVEL 2

Create an Action with Named Objects

1 Create a new letter-size RGB document with Units set to Pixels. Open the Swatches, Actions, Transform, Transparency, and Attributes palettes. Show the page rulers.

2 Choose View>Fit in Window, and then choose View>Zoom Out.

These commands center the Artboard and reduce the view.

3 From the Chapter_08 folder, place (without linking) the lion.tif image in the document and lock it.

The image centers on the Artboard.

FIGURE 8.47

4 Change to Outline view. Drag the ruler's Zero Point to the photo's top-left corner. In the upper-left grid of the Transform palette, click the top-left reference point.

In Steps 1–4, you completed the necessary setup to create tile objects that will rest on the photo. It was necessary to place the photo and set the Zero Point and reference point so the action could administer the X, Y attributes. You are now ready to begin recording.

5 In the Actions palette, choose the my_actions folder. Click the Create New Action button.

6 Name the new action "Tile Photo" and click Record.

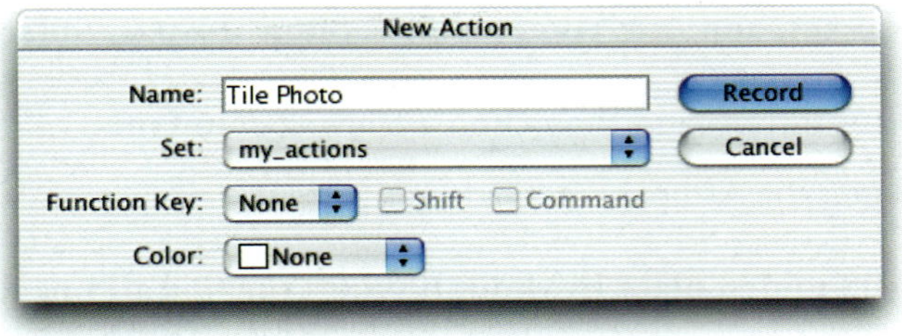

FIGURE 8.48

7 Click the Rectangle tool cursor anywhere in the photo's top-left corner.

This is another method of creating and positioning objects for actions. If you prefer to use dialog boxes to draw objects and place them in specific positions, you should draw the object and use the Transform palette to position it.

8 In the dialog box, set the Width and Height to 25 px. Click OK. Keep the drawn square selected.

9 In the Transform palette, set the X and Y fields to 0 (zero) px and press Return/Enter to apply.

The square relocates to fit the photo's top-left corner. The action can successfully record this tangible setting.

FIGURE 8.49

10 You are still in the process of recording. Keep the square selected and continue to the next exercise.

Chapter 8 Enhancing Your Workflow   **369**   LEVEL 2

Apply Tiles to a Photo

1   Fill the square with Sunshine and stroke it with 1-pt White.

2   In the Transparency palette, set the Opacity to 40%. Close the Transparency palette.

FIGURE 8.50

3   From the Attributes palette Options menu, choose Show Note. In the note section, type "Square". Close the Attributes palette.

FIGURE 8.51

4   From the Object>Transform menu, choose Move. In the Move dialog box set the Horizontal field to 25 px and the Vertical field to 0 px. Press the Tab key to apply. Click Copy.

5   Hold down Command/Control while you press the "D" key 18 times to create 18 more duplicates across the top of the photo.

FIGURE 8.52

6   From the Actions palette Options menu, choose Select Object. Type "Square" in the dialog box.

All the squares are selected because they are all named Square, being duplicates of the original Square object.

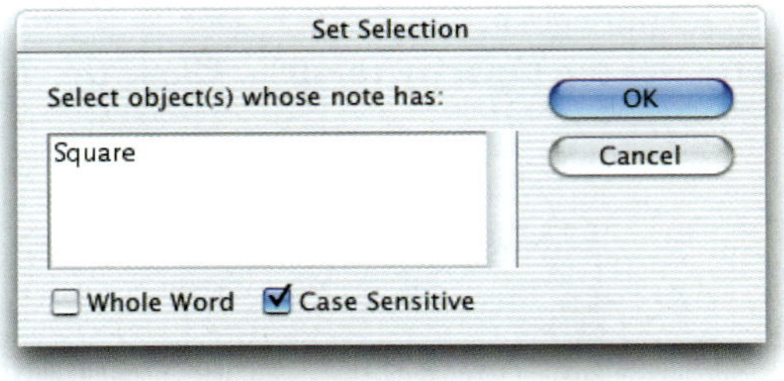

FIGURE 8.53

7 Return to the Move dialog box and set the Horizontal field to 0 px. Set the Vertical field to −25 px. Press the Tab key and click Copy.

8 Hold down Command/Control while you press the "D" key 13 times to create 13 more duplicates that extend to the bottom of the photo.

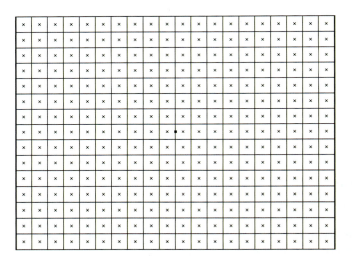

FIGURE 8.54

9 From the Actions palette Options menu, choose Insert Menu Item. With the dialog box showing, choose View>Fit in Window. Click OK.

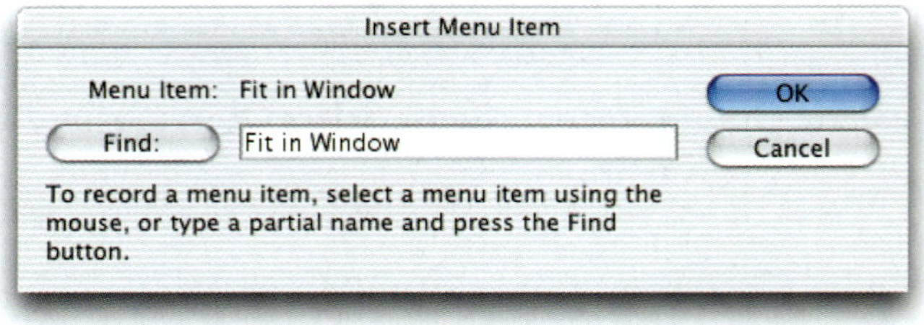

FIGURE 8.55

Chapter 8   Enhancing Your Workflow   **371**   LEVEL 2

10   Choose the Insert Menu Item again. With the dialog box showing, choose View>Zoom Out. Click OK.

11   Choose the Insert Menu Item again and choose View>Zoom Out. Click OK.

The Fit in Window menu item scales the document so you can see the entire image; zooming out twice allows you to see the finished product more clearly.

12   Click the Stop Playing/Recording button in the Actions palette.

13   Save the document as "tile_photo.ai" to your WIP_08 folder. Keep the document open for the next exercise.

Play the Recorded Action

1   In the open document, select all the squares on the Artboard and delete them.

2   Return the document to Preview mode.

3   Click the triangle to the left of the new Tile Photo action to remove all the action steps from view.

4   Use the view percentage menu in the screen's bottom left to set the page view to 50%.

5   In the Actions palette Options menu, choose Button Mode.

The palette's appearance changes to this alternative view. In Button mode, each button represents an action. When needed, you would click a button to play an action.

FIGURE 8.56

6 **Click the Tile Photo action button.**

The action runs through its recorded steps and places the transparent squares on top of the photo.

FIGURE 8.57

7 **Save your changes and close the document.**

To Extend Your Knowledge . . .

EXACT PLACEMENT

When you draw objects in specific locations on the Artboard, the action may record the location inaccurately. When you play back the steps you recorded while drawing an object with a dialog box, the object often appears in a different location. When you use the Transform palette, however, you provide exact X, Y increments, so the action knows precisely where to place the object.

TOGGLE-TYPE MENU ITEMS

When using the Insert Menu Item dialog box, the appropriate name of the menu selection may not appear. For example, to change the document view to Outline mode, you would use the Insert Menu Item dialog box to choose this option from the View menu. Once you choose View>Outline, you might be surprised to find the word "Preview" in the dialog box text field. Do not retype "Outline" in the field; this would result in an error. Instead, choose the Preview name. Since this is a menu toggle item, it switches the view from Preview to Outline. Remember this when you choose any toggle-type menu item.

Chapter 8   Enhancing Your Workflow   **373**   **LEVEL 2**

LESSON 6   Using Acrobat to Combine Illustrator Files

Even though Illustrator can create multiple pages in a single document, it is primarily a digital drawing program unsuitable for the intricacies of page manipulation. For those situations where you need to combine multiple Illustrator documents into a single file — such as when you want to show a portfolio of your work to potential employers — you can create a series of PDF files in Illustrator and use Adobe Acrobat to chain them together into a single viewing file.

You can use Illustrator to open any page in the Acrobat PDF document, modify the content, and then resave in the PDF format. Acrobat PDF is one of the three primary file formats that Illustrator supports, other than its native format (.ai) and Encapsulated PostScript (.eps).

This technique provides an excellent way to distribute your documents while ensuring they look exactly the way they did when you created them. Recipients see the same fonts (they are embedded in the PDF file), and all the graphics remain crisp and beautiful.

Combine Illustrator Documents in Acrobat

In this exercise, you combine six Illustrator documents into one PDF file created by Adobe Acrobat. You also modify an Illustrator document and update the PDF file.

1 **Go to your desktop and navigate to the WIP_08 folder. Inside this folder, create a new folder named "PDF Files".**

2 **Return to Illustrator. Choose File>Open to go to the WIP_08 folder.**

You should have six documents in this folder from Lessons 1–5.

3 **Open the six Illustrator documents and use Save As to save them each in PDF format. Be sure to add the ".pdf" extension to the name. Save these documents to the PDF Files folder you created in Step 1.**

In the Adobe PDF Options window, click OK/Save PDF. The default settings are correct.

4 **Go to the desktop and launch the Acrobat program (not Adobe or Acrobat Reader).**

5 **Choose File>Open and navigate to the PDF Files folder and open actions_palette.pdf.**

The objects you created in the Illustrator document appear in the Acrobat file as Page 1.

6 **From the Document menu, choose either Insert Pages or Pages>Insert (depending on your version of Acrobat).**

7 **In the WIP_08>PDF Files folder, choose opacity_truck.pdf.**

This should be the next PDF file in the list of names.

8 **In the next dialog box, make no changes and click OK.**

The dialog box asks if you want to insert the file after the first placed image.

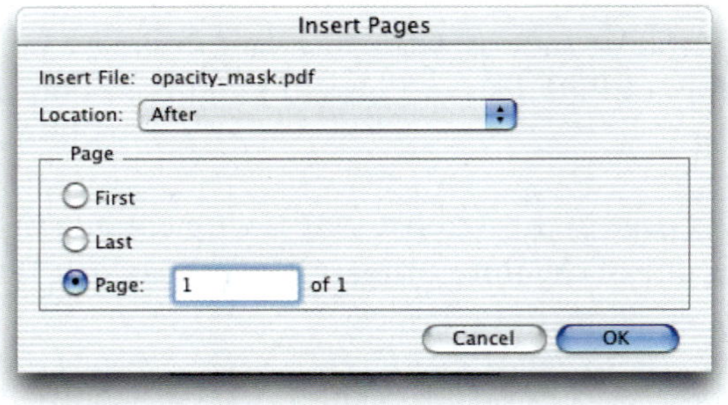

FIGURE 8.58

9 **Click the Next Page button at the bottom of the document window.**

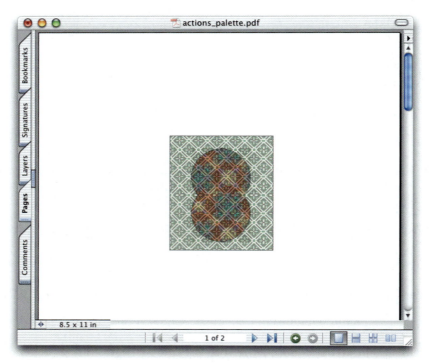

FIGURE 8.59

10 **Return to the Document menu and choose either Insert Pages or Pages>Insert. Insert shear_perspective.pdf. Make no changes in the Insert Pages dialog box and click OK.**

Since you are on Page 2, this inserts the new image after the current page.

Chapter 8 Enhancing Your Workflow **375** LEVEL 2

11 Click the Next Page button to go to Page 3.

12 Use the same Document menu method to insert all the remaining PDF documents into the Acrobat file.

Be certain to click the Next Page button before you insert each image.

13 Choose File>Save As to save the Acrobat document as "portfolio.pdf" to the WIP_08>PDF Files folder. Keep the Acrobat document open for the next exercise.

Modify the Acrobat File

1 In Acrobat, go to the View menu and choose either Continuous-Facing or Page Layout>Continuous Facing (depending on your version of Acrobat). Set the view percentage at the top of the screen to 12.5%.

All the pages appear in one window.

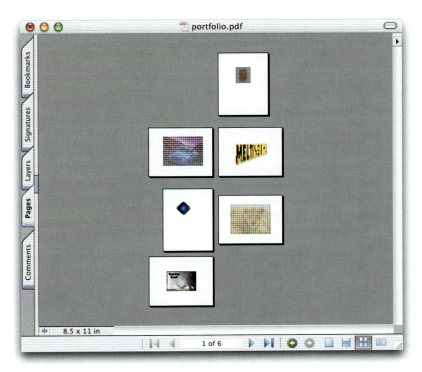

FIGURE 8.60

2 From the View menu, choose either Page Layout>Single or Single Page. Set the view percentage to 50%.

3 Use the page selector at the document's bottom to go to Page 3.

This image does not look quite right. In the Illustrator document, the type was only sheared. It was in the Photoshop file that the Liquify filter was applied to the image. This needs to be updated in the PDF file.

FIGURE 8.61

4   **Save your changes. Close the Acrobat document.**

5   **In Illustrator, choose File>Open to navigate to the WIP_08>PDF Files folder. Open portfolio.pdf.**

6   **In the dialog box, use the right arrow page selector to choose Page 3.**

Only Page 3 opens in the document. Even though this file resides in portfolio.pdf, the file opens as an Illustrator document with all the document features available.

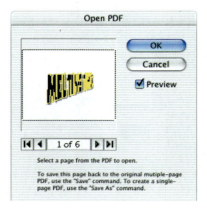

FIGURE 8.62

7   **Use File>Place to go to the WIP_08 folder and place (without linking) the shear_perspective.tif image.**

8   **Position the placed image over the paths on the Artboard. Hide the placed TIFF image.**

The placement on the paths does not have to be exact.

9   **Select the paths on the Artboard and delete them. Show the hidden image.**

Chapter 8 Enhancing Your Workflow   377   LEVEL 2

10 Save your changes and close the PDF document.

11 Return to Acrobat and open portfolio.pdf. Use the page selector to go to Page 3 and set the view percentage to 50%.

The modifications made in Illustrator were saved to the PDF file. Once you insert Illustrator documents into an Acrobat PDF, you can modify the Acrobat documents as necessary by opening the PDF document in Illustrator.

FIGURE 8.63

11 Close the file without saving.

To Extend Your Knowledge . . .

ADVANTAGES OF PDFS

When you load a multipage PDF document into Illustrator, you can only modify one page at a time. When you save the document, the modified page returns to its original position within the PDF file.

You can combine PDF pages of differing sizes and orientations into one Acrobat document. For example, you can include a tabloid-size map in an 8.5 × 11 inch document or mix landscape and portrait orientations.

LEVEL 2　**378**　　Chapter 8　Enhancing Your Workflow

SUMMARY

In this final chapter of the book, you learned how to improve workflow and simplify the creation of special effects by using Photoshop filters and the Transparency palette in an Illustrator document. You also learned how to create objects with effects in the Illustrator document and then transfer them over to Photoshop for further enhancement.

You learned about actions and how they record the creation of elements, dialog box selections, and menu commands. Once recorded, actions can be replayed with a single click of the mouse — dramatically improving efficiency by reducing the time it takes to perform routine and redundant tasks. You learned how to use the Actions palette and how to create, edit, and replay several different actions. You learned that some objects must be created manually and then named for later selection and attributes. You learned that most menu items in the Menu Bar cannot be recorded into an action and that you must use the Insert Menu Item option to record the menu selection.

You learned about Adobe Acrobat and Portable Document Format (PDF). You saw how Illustrator can be used to generate PDF files and how Acrobat can be used to produce multipage files that remain compatible with Illustrator and that can be opened and edited using Illustrator's drawing tools. You now understand that PDF files can be distributed to anyone having Adobe or Acrobat Reader installed on their system and that the graphic integrity — including all of your fonts and graphics — is protected by the file format.

KEY TERMS

action	Button mode	Opacity slider
Actions palette	Create Clipping Mask	PDF (Portable Document Format)
Adobe Acrobat	flatten image	Transparency palette
Adobe or Acrobat Reader	Normal mode	
batch	opacity mask	

CHECKING CONCEPTS AND TERMS

MULTIPLE CHOICE

Circle the letter that matches the correct answer for each of the following questions.

1. You can use Illustrator to create certain objects that _____.

a. Photoshop cannot produce

b. require further enhancements in Photoshop

c. use raster filters that Photoshop possesses but Illustrator does not

d. All of the above.

2. The Transparency palette was originally created in the _____ program.

a. PageMaker

b. Photoshop

c. Go Live

d. None of the above.

Chapter 8 Enhancing Your Workflow **379** **LEVEL 2**

3. The Opacity slider in the Transparency palette _____.
   a. makes the selected object darker
   b. makes the selected object lighter
   c. adjusts the object to make it appear more or less opaque
   d. does not work on raster objects

4. The _____ color model is the best choice when working with raster filters in Illustrator.
   a. CMYK
   b. RGB
   c. grayscale
   d. bitmap

5. The Actions palette is used for _____.
   a. recording actions
   b. playing actions
   c. modifying actions
   d. All of the above.

6. The Actions palette viewing modes are _____.
   a. List and Thumbnail
   b. Normal and Button
   c. By Name and By Subject
   d. Small Thumbnail and Large Thumbnail

7. When you must use a drawn object in an action, the object must first be _____.
   a. hidden
   b. put on its own layer
   c. named
   d. locked

8. To choose an option from a menu when recording an action, _____.
   a. you must use the Insert Menu Item option
   b. you must choose the menu item prior to recording the action
   c. you must choose the Select Object option
   d. You cannot choose options from a menu in an action

9. If an Acrobat PDF file contains Illustrator documents, and you need to modify one of the documents, you _____.
   a. must modify the document in Photoshop
   b. can modify the document in Illustrator
   c. must modify the document in Acrobat
   d. None of the above.

10. The Acrobat view that shows all the pages in one window is _____.
    a. Page Layout>Single
    b. Page Layout>Facing
    c. Page Layout>Continuous Facing
    d. Page Layout>Continuous

DISCUSSION QUESTIONS

1. What are some Illustrator elements that may be further enhanced in Photoshop?

2. The Transparency palette works on both vector paths and raster objects. What types of illustrations can you create with the features and functions of the Transparency palette?

3. List at least three illustrated projects that would lend themselves to actions.

4. What is a practical use of combining Illustrator documents into a PDF file?

LEVEL 2   **380**   Chapter 8   **Enhancing Your Workflow**

SKILL DRILL

Skill Drills reinforce learned skills. Each skill that is reinforced is the same as, or nearly the same as, a skill we presented in the lessons. We provide detailed instructions in a step-by-step format. You should complete these exercises in order.

1. Paint a Bitmap Image

Pizza Time pizza parlor asked you to produce a poster for them. They want the letters in their company name to resemble the texture of pizza dough. Your task is to produce this poster and the special effect.

1. From the Chapter_08 folder, open the pizza_time.ai document. Open the Color and Actions palettes. From the Actions palette Options menu, set the Actions palette to Button Mode.

2. From the Chapter_08 folder, place the pizza_time.tif image (without linking) and position it on the Artboard. Lock the photo.

3. From above the Artboard, select the "Pizza Time" text outlines and bring them to the front.

4. Select the Eyedropper tool and click it on the document's white background.

   This is a shortcut for painting the text white.

5. Position the white letters at the top of the pizza photo.

6. With the Rectangle tool, draw a rectangle that encloses the words. Fill the rectangle with White and set the Stroke to None.

7. Make certain that the Actions palette is set to Button Mode and click the Rasterize (selection) button in the Actions palette.

   This action rasterizes the white rectangle with the RGB color model.

8. Choose Filter>Pixelate>Mezzotint. In the dialog box, choose the Coarse Dots item. Click OK.

9. From the Objects menu, choose Rasterize, set the Color Model to Bitmap, and set the Background to Transparent. Click OK.

10. Click the Fill box in the Toolbox. Select the Eyedropper tool, press the Shift key, and click a light color in the pizza photo.

    Only the bitmap raster format allows you to paint the black parts of an image, which you must set as the Fill attribute.

11. Copy the bitmap image and press Command/Control-B to paste a duplicate behind it. Press the Left Arrow key and Down Arrow key 15 times each.

    This offsets the duplicate and adds extra bitmap pieces.

12. Select the Eyedropper tool, press the Shift key, and click a slightly darker color in the pizza photo.

FIGURE 8.64

13. Save the document with the same name to your WIP_08 folder. Keep the document open for the next exercise.

2. Finalize the Pizza Time Poster

1. In the open document, switch to Outline viewing mode.

2. Select the type outlines and bring them to the front. Press Command/Control-8 to compound the outlines.

   When you use multiple objects in a mask, you must first compound the items.

3. Press the Shift key and select the two bitmap images to add them to the selection. Press Command/Control-7 to mask the objects. Deselect the objects.

4. Select the Direct Selection tool, press Option/Alt, and click the "P" outline three times to select all the letter outlines.

5. Copy the outlines to the clipboard.

6. Return to Preview mode.

7. Press Command/Control-F to paste the copied letters in front of the selected outlines.

8. Fill the pasted letters with None and apply a Stroke of 3-pt White.

You filled the letters with a filtered raster object that resembles the pebbled texture of a pizza crust.

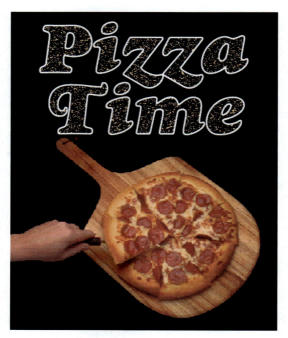

FIGURE 8.65

9. Save your changes and close the document.

3. Create a Screening Action

1. Create a new letter-size RGB document with units set to pixels. Show the page rulers.
2. Use File>Place to go to the Chapter_08 folder and place (without linking) the barn.tif image.
3. Position the photo so its upper-left corner matches the Artboard's upper-left corner.

    The dimensions of this sample image are 500 × 375 pixels. When you apply actions to your own photos, you will need to adjust the actions to match the dimensions of each image.

4. Change to Outline view.

    You can clearly see the borders of the image in Outline view.

5. In the Actions palette, use the Options menu to uncheck Button Mode (if checked) to return to Normal Mode. Choose the my_actions folder in the Actions palette.
6. Click the Create New Action button at the bottom of the palette. Name the action "Screen Photo" and click Record.
7. Click the default Fill and Stroke box in the Toolbox.

    Use the Rectangle tool to draw a rectangle that matches the borders of the photo. Start the rectangle in the upper-left corner.

Chapter 8   Enhancing Your Workflow   **383**   LEVEL 2

8. Fill the rectangle with the White, Black linear gradient from the Swatches palette. Leave the Stroke set to 1-pt Black.

9. In the Transparency palette, choose the Screen option from the Normal menu.

10. Click the Stop Playing/Recording button in the Actions palette.

11. Return to Preview mode.

FIGURE 8.66

12. Save the document as "screen_photo_action.ai" in your WIP_08 folder. Keep the document open for the next exercise.

4. Complete the Screening Action

1. Select the gradient path and delete it.

2. Select the photo and choose File>Place. Go to the Chapter_08 folder and select the parrot.tif photo. Make sure Replace is checked in the Place dialog box. Place the parrot photo to replace the barn photo.

3. In the Actions palette, choose Button Mode from the Options menu.

4. Click the Screen Photo action button.

    The action draws a rectangle, paints it with the gradient, and applies the Screen effect. If you have a photo of a different size, create a new action using that photo as the sample. Remember to place your own photo in the Artboard's upper-left corner so the action draws the rectangle in the correct place.

FIGURE 8.67

5. Choose the my_actions folder in the Actions palette. Select Save Actions from the Options menu.

   Only the folders and their actions, not the individual actions themselves, can be saved to an external file.

6. Save the file as "my_actions.aia" to the Illustrator CS2>Presets>Actions folder and replace the existing file of the same name.

7. Save your changes to the screen_photo_actions.ai document and close it.

CHALLENGE

Challenge exercises expand on, or are somewhat related to, skills we presented in the lessons. Each exercise provides a brief introduction, followed by numbered-step instructions that are not as detailed as those in the Skill Drill exercises. You should complete these exercises in order.

1. Create a Poster

You are a commercial artist who uses letter-size pages to produce magazine ads. In every project, you must apply 1/2-inch margins around the page and drag guides to mark the Artboard's center. In this exercise, your task is to create an action that applies the page margins and draws the guides.

1. Create a new letter-size CMYK document with portrait orientation and the units set to inches. Open the Actions and Transform palettes. Make certain that the center reference point is clicked in the Transform palette.

2. In the Actions palette select the my_actions folder. Click the Create New Action button. Name the new action "Margins" and click Record.

3. Select the Line Segment tool and click its cursor anywhere on the page. Set the Length to 13 inches and the Angle to 90. Click OK.

   The Line Segment tool name appears in the Actions palette.

4. In the Transform palette, set the X field to 4.25 and the Y field to 5.5. Press Return/Enter to apply. Press Command/Control-5 to convert the line to a guide.

   The vertical line centers on the page and becomes a guide. The Move item appears in the Actions palette.

5. Click the Line Segment tool cursor anywhere on the page. Set the Length to 11 inches and the Angle to 360. Click OK.

6. In the Transform palette, set the X field to 4.25 and the Y field to 5.5. Press Return/Enter to apply. Press Command/Control-5 to convert the line to a guide.

   The horizontal line centers on the page and becomes a guide.

7. Select the Rectangle tool, press Option/Alt, and click the cursor in the page's center, where the two guides intersect.

8. Set the Width to 7.5 inches and the Height to 10 inches. Click OK. Press Command/Control-5 to convert the rectangle to a guide.

9. Click the Stop Playing/Recording button in the Actions palette.

10. Use the View menu to clear the guides.

11. Select the Margins action and click the Play Current Selection button in the Actions palette.

    The action draws the objects, centers them, and converts them to guides. Whenever you need this layout, you can simply play the action and Illustrator does the work for you.

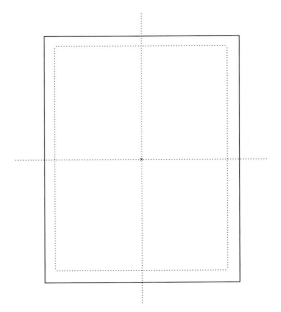

FIGURE 8.68

LEVEL 2 | **386** | Chapter 8 Enhancing Your Workflow

12. Close the document without saving.

Regardless of not saving the document, the new action remains in the Actions palette for future use.

2. Use the Transparency Palette

A company that produces children's apparel asked you to design a poster for a new ad campaign. The only creative suggestion was "the wilder, the better!" You have artistic freedom to create an interesting, eye-catching poster. In this exercise, your task is to use the Transparency palette to quickly alter the colors in the poster.

1. From the Chapter_08 folder, open the hightech_apparel.ai document. Open the Swatches, Actions, Align, and Transparency palettes.

2. In the Actions palette, show the actions in the my_actions folder.

3. Select the Margins action you created in the previous exercise.

4. Click the Play Current Selection icon at the bottom of the palette.

Margins appear and guides mark the page's center.

5. Select the Rectangle tool, press Option/Alt, and click the cursor on the marked center of the page.

6. Set the Width to 7.5 in and the Height to 10 in. Click OK.

7. Fill the rectangle with the Sensual Red gradient from the Swatches palette. Stroke the rectangle with 1-pt Black.

8. From the Chapter_08 folder, place (without linking) the kids.tif image.

9. Center the photo in the rectangle's lower area.

This leaves plenty of space above the image for a large-type headline.

10. Select the two objects and click the Horizontal Align Center option in the Align palette.

Chapter 8   Enhancing Your Workflow   **387**   LEVEL 2

If necessary, reposition the objects so the larger rectangle fits within the page margins.

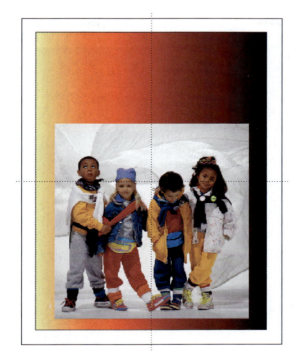

FIGURE 8.69

11. Save the document with the same name to your WIP_08 folder. Keep the document open for the next exercise.

3. Add to the Poster

The poster layout has been created. It is now necessary to add the text, convert it to outlines, apply a gradient, and give the text outlines a drop shadow.

1. In the open document, zoom out to see above the Artboard.
2. From above the Artboard, select the High Tech Apparel text outlines and bring them to the front.
3. Position the outlines in the rectangle's upper-left area. Keep the outlines selected.
4. Press Command/Control-Shift-B to show the bounding box.
5. Drag the middle-right handle of the bounding box to the right so the text outline fills the space above the photo.
6. Fill the outlines with the Blended Rainbow gradient from the Swatches palette.
7. Copy the outlines and paste them in back of the selected outlines. Fill the pasted copy with White.
8. Press the Right Arrow key and Down Arrow key three times to offset the white shadow.

9. Select the rainbow-filled text outlines. Drag the Gradient tool cursor from the upper-left to the bottom-right area of the outlines. Hide the guides.

FIGURE 8.70

10. Save your changes and keep the document open for the next exercise.

4. Complete the Poster

The poster elements are in place, so what now remains is applying Photoshop techniques to the gradient-filled elements.

1. In the open document, select the type outlines and send them to the back behind the rectangle.
2. Select the rectangle. Choose Color Dodge from the Normal menu in the Transparency palette.

   The type becomes visible because of the effect you applied to the rectangle.

3. Switch to Outline viewing mode.
4. Use the Rectangle tool to draw a rectangle that matches the photo's border.
5. Fill the rectangle with the Desert Horizon gradient from the Swatches palette. Set the Stroke to None.
6. Return to Preview mode.
7. With the rectangle on the photo selected, choose Color Burn from the Normal menu in the Transparency palette.

   The gradient's colors and the white area in the photo coalesce to create an interesting effect.

8. In the Swatches palette, click the various gradients to see how they affect the Difference transparency option.

9. Select the larger rectangle and click the various gradients to see how they affect the Exclusion transparency option.

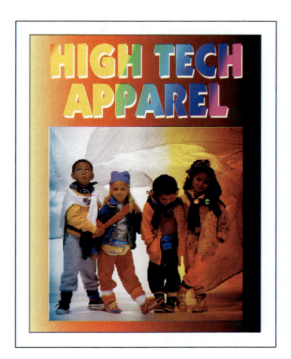

FIGURE 8.71

10. Save your changes and close the document.

PORTFOLIO BUILDER

Save PDF Files

As a freelance graphic designer, you are always searching for new clients. You have an impressive collection of art pieces you created in Illustrator, but you currently have no means of showing your work to prospective clients — short of gathering them around your computer. A better solution is to provide potential clients with files they can review in their own offices, at their leisure. You decide to save your work into a PDF file that viewers can scroll through, one image at a time.

1. In Illustrator, open hightech_apparel.ai and pizza_time.ai.
2. Save each file in PDF format to the WIP_08>PDF Files folder.
3. Launch Adobe Acrobat.
4. Use File>Open to go to the WIP_08>PDF Files folder and open the portfolio.pdf file.
5. From the View menu, choose Page Layout>Single, and then choose Go To>Last Page.
6. Insert hightech_apparel.pdf and pizza_time.pdf.
7. Go to the View menu and choose either Continuous-Facing or Page Layout>Continuous Facing (depending on your version of Acrobat). Also, set the viewing percentage to 12.5%.
8. Scroll down the list of images to see your work.

As long as prospective clients have Adobe or Acrobat Reader (which is free at www.adobe.com) installed on their systems, they can open and view the images in portfolio.pdf.

LEVEL 2

INTEGRATING PROJECT

Integrating Projects are, by their nature, challenging for us to develop and for you to complete. To incorporate a broad range of skills into a single cohesive learning tool, it's necessary to include several discrete components. Dividing the project into multiple sections allows us to cover more of the material presented in this Level 2 book, and create a Web site project that accurately mirrors a real-world assignment.

Tampa Bay Fitness Web Site

In this project, you apply the skills you learned in this book as you create a complete Web site. You use the Grid tools, apply effects from the Effect menu, create an onmouseover object, apply JavaScript, create SVG files, save new symbols, apply image maps, embed images, create a two-frame animation, and much more.

Exercise Setup:

Before starting this project, go to the Preferences>Units & Display Performance dialog box and make certain that the Identify Objects By option is set for XML ID.

The files you need to complete this project are located in the RF_Illustrator_L2>IP folder. Go to the desktop and drag all of the files from the RF_Illustrator_L2>IP folder to the WIP_IP folder. All the working files should now be in the WIP_IP folder.

Set Up the Web Site

1. From the WIP_IP folder, open the home_page.ai document.

   You may not have these fonts on your computer. If you get a font warning, click "Continue". The type on the page will look slightly different, but this is just to show you how variables work.

2. Open the Swatches and Layers palettes. Show the page rulers.

3. Drag the ruler's Zero Point to the Artboard's upper-left corner.

4. Select the Rectangular Grid tool and click its cursor on the Artboard's upper-left corner.

5. In the Rectangular Grid dialog box, set the Width to 640 pt and Height to 480 pt. Set the Horizontal and Vertical Dividers to 5. Click OK.

The grid appears on the Artboard.

6 Press Command/Control-5 to convert the grid to guides.

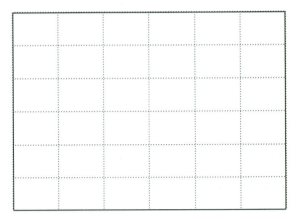

7 Save your changes to the document and keep it open. You come back to it after you create an image rollover in another file.

Create Image Rollover

1 From the WIP_IP folder, open fitness_logo.ai. Open the Align and Info palettes.

2 Select the logo and choose Stylize>Outer Glow from the Effect menu.

3 In the Outer Glow dialog box, set the Mode to Normal and click the color swatch to the right of the Mode menu. In the Color Picker, set the RGB sliders to R = 255, G = 255, B = 0, and then click OK.

The RGB settings create a yellow color that will be applied to the Outer Glow.

4 You are back in the Outer Glow dialog box. Set the Blur to 10 pt and the Opacity to 100%. Click OK. Keep the logo selected.

The logo takes on a glowing effect that extends outside the letter's bounding box.

5 In the Preferences>General dialog box, choose Use Preview Bounds and click OK. Press Command/Control-Shift-B to show the bounding box. Open the Info palette.

Note the distance between the bounding box and the objects. The extended space around the objects is created by the Outer Glow effect. Without the effect, the bounding box would be only around the paths. When two objects alternate in an animation or JavaScript event, both objects must possess the same dimensions to allow for true registration (alignment).

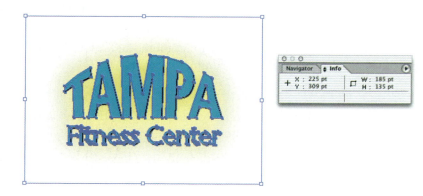

6 Write down the Width and Height increments in the Info palette. Deselect the logo object.

In our sample, the width was 185 points and the height was 135 points. The dimensions may be slightly different for your object.

7 Click the Default Fill and Stroke icon in the Toolbox. Change the Fill to None.

8 Press Option/Alt while you click the Rectangle tool on the logo. Set the Width and Height in the dialog box to the increments you wrote in Step 6. Click OK.

9 Select the rectangle and the logo. In the Align palette, click the Horizontal Align Center and Vertical Align Center options to center the two objects.

10 Select only the rectangle and change its stroke to None. Deselect the rectangle.

11 From the File menu, choose Export. Choose the JPEG format. Save the file as "logo_2.jpg" to your WIP_IP folder. Click Export.

12 In the JPEG Options dialog box, set the Quality to Medium, the Color Model to RGB, the Format Method to Baseline, and the Resolution to Medium. Click OK.

The logo and the unpainted rectangle are now exported as a JPEG image.

13 In the Preferences>General dialog box, deselect the Use Preview Bounds option. Keep the document open for the next exercise.

Remove the Effects

1. Select only the logo object. Open the Appearance and Layers palette.

2. In the Appearance palette, drag the Outer Glow item to the Trash icon.

   This removes the effect from the logo and ensures that an identical bounding box surrounds each of the objects in the rollover effect.

3. From the File menu, choose Export. Choose the JPEG format. Save the file as "logo_1.jpg" to your WIP_IP folder. Click Export.

4. In the JPEG Options dialog box, set the Quality to Medium, the Color Model to RGB, the Format Method to Baseline, and the Resolution to Medium. Click OK.

5. Select the logo and rectangle objects on the Artboard and delete them.

6. From the File menu, use the Place option to navigate to the WIP_IP folder and import logo_2.jpg. Position the image in the middle of the Artboard.

7. Choose File>Place to go back to the WIP_IP folder and place logo_1.jpg. Position the image over the other image on the Artboard.

8. Select the two images. In the Align palette, click the Horizontal Align Center and Vertical Align Center options.

   The two images become centered, one directly on top of the other.

9. Save your changes and keep the document open for the next exercise.

Add the Javascript Events

1. In the Layers palette, expand the sublayers for Layer_1.

2. Double-click the top sublayer and rename it "logo_1". Double-click the bottom sublayer and rename it "logo_2".

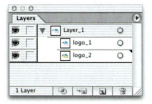

3. Select the top image on the Artboard. In the SVG Interactivity palette, choose onmouseover from the Events menu.

Integrating Project **395** **LEVEL 2**

4 In the JavaScript field, type the following text and press Return/Enter to apply.

elemHide(evt, 'logo_1')

This event hides the top image when the mouse moves over it in the browser window.

5 Hide the selected image. Select the glowing image that remains.

6 From the SVG Interactivity palette, choose onmouseout from the Events menu.

7 In the JavaScript field, type the following text and press Return/Enter to apply.

elemShow(evt, 'logo_1')

This event shows the top image when the mouse moves off the glowing image in the browser window.

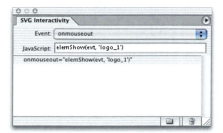

8 From the SVG Interactivity palette Options menu, choose JavaScript Files. Click Add in this dialog box.

9 Click the Choose/Browse button in the next dialog box, go to the WIP_IP folder, and choose events.js. Click Open/OK.

10 Close the Add JavaScript Files dialog box. In the JavaScript Files dialog box, click Done.

The events are now applied to the selected images, and the JavaScript file that powers the events is attached to the document.

Integrating Project

11 Show the hidden image.

12 Save the document as "fitness_logo.svg" in SVG format to your WIP_IP folder. Close the document.

Position the Logo Placeholder

1 Return to the home_page.ai document. Make certain the bounding box is active in the View menu.

2 Choose File>Place to navigate to the WIP_IP folder.

3 Place the logo_1.jpg image without linking.

4 Move the logo to the Artboard's upper-left corner.

5 Position the image so the middle handles of the bounding box touch the first vertical guide on the Artboard.

6 The left and right middle handles should touch the first horizontal guide.

The placement holder is in position. In the final Web site, you replace this image with the SVG file that uses the onmouseover event.

7 Press Command/Control-Shift-B to toggle the bounding box off.

8 Save your changes. Keep the document open for the next exercise.

Modify Symbols for Link Buttons

1 Select the Rounded Rectangle tool, press Option/Alt, and click the tool's cursor where the first vertical divider intersects the third horizontal divider.

With the addition of the Option/Alt key, the rectangle is drawn with its center originating from where the cursor was clicked.

Integrating Project **397** **LEVEL 2**

2 In the Rounded Rectangle dialog box, set the Width to 125 pt and the Height to 25 pt. Click OK.

3 Select the Eyedropper tool. Press the Shift key and click the tool on any of the TAMPA blue letters above the rectangle.

4 From the Window menu, select Symbol Libraries and choose Web Icons from the pop-out menu. Click the Home and Time symbols so they appear in the Symbols palette.

5 Return to the Window>Symbol Libraries option and choose Logo Elements from its pop-out menu. Click the Children and Runner symbols. Close the imported symbols palettes.

Drag the Home symbol from the Symbols palette to the rectangle's left side.

6 Activate the Bounding Box from the View menu and resize the Home instance to better fit in the rectangle. Keep the instance selected.

7 In the Symbols palette, click the Break Link to Symbol. Select the Eyedropper tool and click it on the Artboard's white background. Press Command/Control-8 to compound the object.

With compounding, the windows of the house become transparent so the rectangle's color shows through.

8. Drag the white house object to the Symbols palette. Rename the symbol "House".

9. Repeat the Steps 6, 7, and 8 so that from the Symbols palette you drag the Time, Children, and Runner symbols to the Artboard.

   One by one, they will be unlinked, resized, painted, and dragged back to the Symbols palette to create new symbols.

   The Time instance has only strokes to paint white. The Runner and Children instances require white fills.

10. Rename the new time symbol as "Hours", the children symbol as "Staff", and the runner symbol as "Activities".

    You have new symbols created that will fit the rectangle.

11. Save your changes and keep the document open for the next exercise.

Replace Symbols

1. Drag the House symbol to match the house on the rectangle and hide it. Select the white house object and delete it. Show the House symbol.

2. Select the Type tool and click its cursor on the Artboard to the rectangle's right. Set the font to 10-pt Verdana Bold (or an equivalent font). Set the alignment to Align Left.

3. Type the word "Home". Select the text block and position it so the "H" touches the vertical guide. Fill the text with White.

4. Select the rectangle, the Home instance, and the text block. In the Align palette, click the Vertical Align Center option. Group the objects.

5. Drag the selected group up (pressing the Shift key to constrain) so the rectangle's bottom segment touches the third horizontal guide. When in position, release the mouse. Click the group to select again.

6. Press Option/Alt and drag (pressing Shift to constrain) the group down to create a duplicate under the original.

Integrating Project **399** LEVEL 2

7 Hold Command/Control and press the "D" key two times.

This creates two additional copies.

8 Drag the bottom copy down so its bottom segment rests on the fifth horizontal guide.

9 Select the four rectangular buttons. In the Align palette, click the Vertical Distribute Center option.

The four objects distribute evenly between the top and bottom buttons.

10 Save your changes and keep the document open for the next exercise.

Customize the Buttons

1 Use the Direct Selection tool to select the Home instance in the second button. Select the Staff symbol in the Symbols palette and click the Replace Symbol icon.

The new symbol replaces the Home symbol on the rectangle.

2 Replace the text on this button with the word "Staff".

3 With the Direct Selection tool, select the instance in the third button and replace it with the Hours symbol. Replace the text on this button with "Hours".

4 With the Direct Selection tool, select the instance in the fourth button and replace it with the Activities symbol. Replace the text on this button with "Activities".

The buttons are in place with the correct symbols and text.

5 Use the Direct Selection tool to select (pressing the Shift key) the four rectangles.

Make sure you select all four rectangles.

6 From the Effect menu, choose Stylize>Drop Shadow. Make no changes in the dialog box and click OK. Deselect the rectangles.

A drop shadow appears on each rectangle.

7 Open the Attributes palette. Use the Direct Selection tool to select the top rectangle and apply a rectangle image map. Set the URL for "home_page.html". Press Return/Enter to apply.

Remember to press Return/Enter to apply URLs.

8 Apply image maps to the remaining rectangles. Set the Staff URL to "staff.html", the Hours URL to "hours.html", and the Activities URL to "activities.html". With each URL, press Return/Enter to apply.

Though you set the URL to the Hours button, to save time we are not going to make an Hours page in this project.

Integrating Project **401** LEVEL 2

9 Close the Attributes palette.

10 Save your changes. Keep the document open for the next exercise.

Import Text and Images

1 Select the text block to the Artboard's left and position it so its top-left corner matches the intersection where the second vertical guide and second horizontal guide meet.

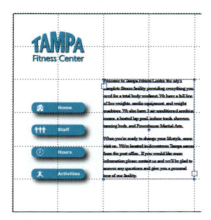

2 To the right of the Artboard, select the grouped photos and position them in the empty space to the right of the text block.

3 With the photo group selected, go to the Effect menu and choose Stylize>Drop Shadow.

4 Make no changes in the dialog box and click OK.

5 Save your changes. Keep the document open; you come back to it after you make an animation in another file.

Create an Animation

1 From the WIP_IP folder, open the weightlifter.ai document.

2 Zoom in to the weightlifter artwork.

3 In the Layers palette, drag Layer_1 to the Create New Layer icon. Rename the new layer "frame_2".

4 Double-click Layer_1 and rename it "frame_1".

5 Click the Visibility icon of frame_1. Select the frame_2 layer to make it active.

6 Use the Selection tool to click the barbells object, which is grouped with the two hands. Press the Up Arrow key five times.

The barbells are grouped with the hands, so they all move upward when you press the Up Arrow key. This provides a gap between the hands and the arms so you may make further alterations.

7 Use the Direct Selection tool to extend the paths of the arms downward to fill in the space between the arms and the hands on the barbells.

8 Click the Visibility icon of the frame_1 layer.

Integrating Project   **403**   LEVEL 2

You can see both objects. The difference between the frames and the objects is readily apparent.

9 Save your changes and keep the document open for the next exercise.

The animation frames are complete. The next step is to export a file for placement on the Artboard and in the SWF animation.

Export Animation Files

1 Choose File>Export and choose the JPEG format. Save the file as "weightlifter.jpg" to your WIP_IP folder.

2 In the JPEG Options dialog box, set the Quality to Medium, the Color Model to RGB, the Format Method to Baseline, and the Resolution to Medium. Click OK.

You insert this file on the home page as a placeholder for the actual animation. You cannot put an SWF file directly on the Artboard; you must embed the animation in the HTML file after you save the file for the Web, which you do later.

3 From the File menu, choose Export. In the dialog box that appears, set the format for Macromedia Flash (swf).

4 Save the file as "weightlifter.swf" to your WIP_IP folder.

5 In the Options dialog box, set the Export As menu to AI Layers to SWF Frames. Set the Frame Rate for 2 fps.

6 Click the Looping and Generate HTML check boxes. Animate Blends should not be selected.

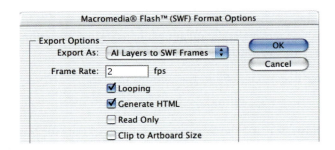

7 Leave all the other settings at their defaults. Click OK.

This saves both the weightlifter.swf animation and the weightlifter.html files.

8 Save the changes in weightlifter.ai and close the document.

9 Return to the home_page.ai document.

10 Use File>Place to go to the WIP_IP folder and place weightlifter.jpg without linking the file.

11 Position the image in the empty area directly above the body text block. Center the head where the two guides intersect.

This image appears in the HTML file, which you export later. You later replace this image with the real animation in the `<embed>` tag that contains the SWF animation.

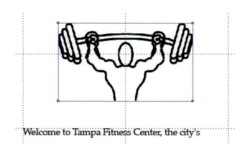

12 Save your changes and keep the document open for the next exercise.

Slice the Home Page

1 Show the Actions palette.

2 In the Actions palette, select the my_actions folder and click the Create New Action icon. Name the new action "Draw Rectangle" and click Record.

3 Use the Rectangle tool to manually draw a rectangle to match the Artboard. Keep the rectangle selected.

4 In the Toolbox, set the Fill and Stroke boxes to None.

When you manually draw rectangles or squares while recording an action, the object appears in the exact position on the Artboard when the action plays.

5 Click the Stop Playing/Recording icon in the Actions palette.

6 Keep the rectangle selected. Choose Object>Slice>Make.

This rectangle tells Illustrator that the Web page is 640 × 480 pts (or pixels) in size, which is the standard size of most 14-inch monitors. The information displays above the fold of the Web page. Without the rectangle, the sliced images would extend only as far as the bounding box of the objects on the Artboard.

Integrating Project   **405**   **LEVEL 2**

7 Select the Tampa Fitness Center logo and choose Object>Slice>Create from Selection.

8 Keep the document open for the next exercise.

Slice Other Home Page Objects

1 Select the four rectangular link buttons below the logo.

2 In the Object>Slice menu, choose Create from Selection.

This command combines all the buttons into one slice.

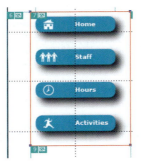

3 Select the weightlifter placeholder image and choose Object>Slice>Create from Selection.

4 Select the area text block and choose Object>Slice>Create from Selection.

5 Select the single group of photos to the right of the text block. Choose Object>Slice>Create from Selection.

6 The slices on the home page are finished. Hide the guides.

The two most important slices are those for the Tampa Fitness Center logo and the weightlifter animation. You use these image slices and their numbers again later.

Integrating Project 407 LEVEL 2

7 Return the guides to view. Save your changes and close the document.

The home page is finished. Next, you create the remainder of the Web pages.

Set Up a New Web Page

1 From the WIP_IP folder, open the staff.ai document. Show the rulers and drag the Zero Point to the Artboard's top-left corner.

You may not have these fonts on your computer. If you get a font warning, click "Continue". The type on the page will look slightly different, but this is just to show you how variables work.

2 Select the Rectangular Grid tool and click its cursor on the Artboard's upper-left corner.

3 In the Rectangular Grid dialog box, set the Width to 640 pt and the Height to 480 pt. Set the Horizontal Dividers to 11 and the Vertical Dividers to 1. Click OK.

The single vertical divider marks the vertical center of the Artboard.

4 Press Command/Control-5 to convert the grid to guides.

5 Drag vertical guides to the 348-pt and 603-pt ruler marks.

The first guide marks the left margin for the text blocks. The second guide marks a 36-pt margin along the page's right side.

6 Save your changes and keep the document open for the next exercise.

Add Page Elements

1 Select File>Place and go to the WIP_IP folder and place the staff.tif image. Make certain the Link option is selected in the Place dialog box. You apply a variable to the image later.

TIFF images are not acceptable file formats on the Internet; Illustrator saves all images in its Save for Web feature as GIF, JPG, or PNG files to ensure Web-compatibility.

2 Change to Outline view. Position the photo's upper-left corner to match the Artboard's upper-left corner.

The photo is in position on the Web page.

3 Select the Rectangle tool and draw a rectangle that matches the photo outline. Keep the rectangle selected through the following steps.

4 Fill the rectangle with the White, Black linear gradient from the Swatches palette. Set the Stroke for None.

5 Return to Preview mode. In the Gradient palette, change the Angle to 90. Press Return/Enter to apply.

6 From the Transparency palette, choose the Screen option from the Normal menu. Deselect the rectangle.

The photo becomes screened by the gradient's tones.

7 Select the Staff text block and position it so its left side touches the 348-pt vertical guide and rests on the second horizontal guide.

8 Select the area text block and position it so its top-left corner touches where the 348-pt guide intersects the third horizontal guide.

9 Select the remaining group of text blocks and position it so the "H" of "Home" touches the 348-pt guide and the block rests on the last horizontal guide.

10 Hide the guides to see the image more clearly.

11 Save your changes. Keep the document open for the next exercise.

Integrating Project 409 LEVEL 2

Set the Image Maps

1. Return the guides to view. Show the Attributes palette.
2. Click the Default Fill and Stroke box in the Toolbox. Change the Fill box to None.
3. Select the Rectangle tool and draw a rectangle around the Home, Staff and Activities text blocks at the bottom of the page.
4. Select the Home rectangle and use the Attributes palette to assign a rectangular image map.
5. Set the URL for the image map to "home_page.html". Press Return/Enter to apply this.
6. Change the rectangle's stroke to None.
7. Select the Staff rectangle and assign an image map with a URL of "staff.html". Apply this. Change the rectangle's stroke to None.
8. Select the Activities rectangle and assign an image map with a URL of "activities.html". Apply this. Change the rectangle's stroke to None.

   We are not going to create all the Web pages. We use only the Home and Activities pages for the project. The image maps aren't accessible until you apply the Save for Web command to generate HTML files, which is done later.

9. Save your changes to the document and keep it open for the next exercise.

Assign Variables

1. Open the Variables palette.
2. Select the Staff headline text block at the top of the Artboard. In the Variables palette, click the Make Text Dynamic icon.
3. Under the Staff text block, select the body copy's area text block. Click the Make Text Dynamic icon.
4. Select and hide the gradient rectangle. Select the photo and click the Make Linked File Dynamic. Return the gradient rectangle back to view.

   The icon changes its name because the photo you are clicking is a linked image.

5 Double-click Variable1 and rename it "headline". Rename Variable2 to "body_text" and Variable3 to "photo".

6 Click the Capture Data Set button in the Variables palette. Rename Data Set 1 to "Staff".

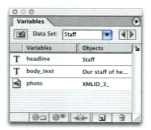

7 From the Variables palette Options menu, choose Save Variable Library. Save the file as staff.xml to your WIP_IP folder.

8 Press Command/Control-S to save your changes to the staff.ai document.

9 Use File>Save As to save the document as "activities.ai" to your WIP_IP folder. Close the activities.ai document.

Modify the Staff XML File

1 Go to the desktop and use your word processor to open the staff.xml file from the WIP_IP folder.

2 Scroll down to the `<dataSetName>` tag. Change the name from "Staff" to "Activities".

```
<v:sampleDataSets xmlns="&ns_custom;" xmlns:v="&ns_vars;">
    <v:sampleDataSet dataSetName="Activities">
```

3 Change the text in the `<headline>` variable tag from "Staff" to "Activities".

```
<v:sampleDataSet dataSetName="Activities">
    <headline>
        <p>Activities</p>
    </headline>
```

Integrating Project   **411**   LEVEL 2

4 Use your word processor to open activities.txt from the WIP_IP folder. Select the text in the document and copy it. Close the document.

5 Back in the staff.xml document, highlight all text between the **<body_text>** variable tags and paste the copied text to replace it.

The XML language is similar to HTML; both require paragraph tags at the beginning and end of paragraphs. We added these tags for you.

```
                        <body_text>
        <p>Tampa Fitness Center is not restricted to our Tampa, Florida headquarters.
        We have fitness centers in the other cities below.</p>

        <p>In each city our name is the same. As a Tampa Fitness Center member you
        may work out at any of our spas in the cities listed below.</p>

        <p>We would like to hear from you concerning our facilities or Web site. You
        may contact us at: Information@tampafitnesscenter.com</p>
                        </body_text>
```

6 In the **<photo>** variable tag, change the staff.tif name to "activities.tif".

```
                        </body_text>

                        <photo>
                                activities.tif
                        </photo>

                        </v:sampleDataSet>
```

7 Save the file to your WIP_IP folder as "activities.xml".

8 Close the activities.xml word-processing document.

Load the XML Variables

1 Return to the Illustrator program and open the activities.ai document from the WIP_IP folder.

You may not have these fonts on your computer. If you get a font warning, click "Continue". The type on the page will look slightly different, but this is just to show you how variables work.

2 From the Variables palette Options menu, choose Load Variable Library.

3 Navigate to the WIP_IP folder and open activities.xml.

4 When the warning dialog box asks if you want to overwrite existing variables, click Yes.

5 From the Data Set menu of the Variables palette, choose the Activities option.

The variables update and change the objects on the Artboard.

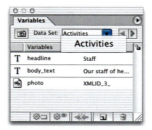

6 Save your changes and keep the document open for the next exercise.

Create a Graph for the Activities Page

1 In the Toolbox, double-click the Graph tool.

2 In the Graph Type dialog box, select the Column Graph tool. Under Style, click the Add Legend Across Top option. Click OK.

3 Click the tool cursor where the 348-pt vertical guide intersects the seventh horizontal guide.

4 In the Graph dialog box, set the Width for 200 pt and the Height for 100 pt. Click OK.

5 In the Data Input dialog box, click the Import Data icon at the top. Use the dialog box to go to the WIP_IP folder and choose graph.txt. Click Open.

6 In the Data Input dialog box, click the Apply icon in the top-right corner.

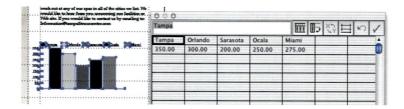

7 Close the Data Input dialog box. Move the graph to the right so the left sides of the numbers touch the 348-pt guide. Deselect the graph.

Integrating Project   413   **LEVEL 2**

The graph appears with its legend above the graph.

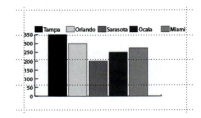

8 Select the Direct Selection tool, press Option/Alt, and double-click the rectangle of the Tampa legend.

9 Fill the selected rectangles with the color of your choice from the Swatches palette.

10 Use the same method to select the other legend rectangles and fill them with the colors of your choice.

11 Hide the guides to see the finished page.

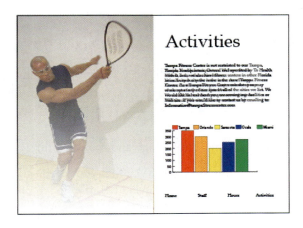

12 Save your changes to the document and close it.

Save the Home Page as HTML

1 From the WIP_IP folder, open the home_page.ai document. From the File menu, choose Save for Web.

You may not have these fonts on your computer. If you get a font warning, click "Continue". The type on the page will look slightly different, but this is just to show you how variables work.

There are no available settings on the right side of the Save for Web dialog box because you have not yet selected a slice.

2 Press Command/Control-A to select all the slices in the preview window. Click the Optimized tab above the preview window and make certain the Settings on the right are set for GIF format.

When objects are sliced, you must select one or more of the slices in the Save for Web preview window to see the available settings.

Each slice displays with its individual number. If you cannot see the slices and numbers, click the Toggle Slices Visibility button in the Save for Web dialog box's upper left, below the tools.

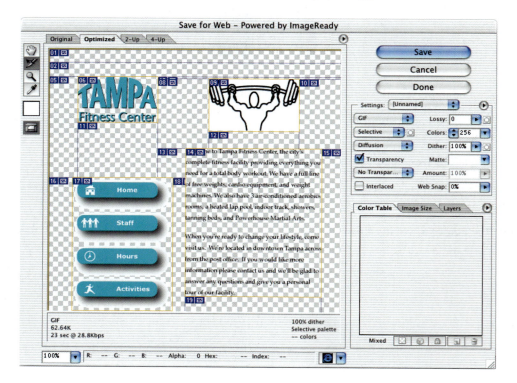

3 Write down the slice numbers for the Tampa logo and the weightlifter image.

These slices are placeholders for the SVG and SWF files you saved earlier. The number of the slice allows you to know what image to replace in the HTML file.

The numbers shown here may not match your slice numbers. Use your numbers, not ours.

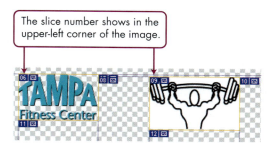

4 Click the Save button in the Save for Web dialog box.

5 In the next Save Optimized As dialog box, set the Format menu to HTML and Images. Save the file as "home_page.html" to your WIP_IP folder.

Integrating Project **415** **LEVEL 2**

6 At the bottom of the Save Optimized As dialog box, set the Settings menu to Default Settings and the Slices menu to All Slices.

7 Click the Save button in this dialog box.

The home_page.html file saves to the target folder. Along with this file, Illustrator creates an "images" folder and saves all the slices (in this case as GIF images) here.

8 Go to the desktop and open the WIP_IP>images folder. Observe its contents.

In the GIF images, the home_page name precedes the ".gif" extension. This naming structure avoids conflict when you save the other Web pages. As long as you save the HTML files to the WIP_IP folder, all slice images will be saved to the images folder.

9 Return to the Illustrator document. Close the home_page.ai document without saving.

Save Other Web Pages as HTML

1 From the WIP_IP folder, open the staff.ai document. Show the Actions palette.

You may not have these fonts on your computer. If you get a font warning, click "Continue". The type on the page will look slightly different, but this is just to show you how variables work.

2 Show the actions of the my_actions set.

3 Select the Draw Rectangle action and click the Play Current Selection icon in the Actions palette.

A 640 $\times$ 480 pt unpainted rectangle appears around the Artboard's border.

4 From the File menu, choose Save for Web. Click the Optimized tab above the preview window. Click the Save button in the dialog box.

In the Save Optimized As dialog box, the Format menu should still be set to HTML and Images. If not, select this.

5 Save the file as "staff.html" to your WIP_IP folder. Close the staff.ai document without saving.

6 From the WIP_IP folder, open the activities.ai document.

7 Play the Draw Rectangle action to create the unpainted rectangle.

8 From the File menu, choose Save for Web.

The Optimized tab should still be selected in the dialog box.

9 Click the Save button in the Save for Web dialog box.

In the Save Optimized As dialog box, the Format menu should still set to HTML and Images.

10 Save the file as "activities.html" to your WIP_IP folder.

11 Close the document without saving.

Earlier in this project, you created two special files: the fitness_logo.svg file with the onmouseover JavaScript event and the weightlifter animation saved as a Macromedia SWF file. These two file types cannot operate on their own; they must be embedded in the HTML file. In the final exercises, you embed the files so the HTML correctly displays them in a browser.

LEVEL 2 | **416** | Integrating Project

Embed the Javascript SVG Event

In this exercise, you embed the onmouseover event applied to the Tampa Fitness Center logo.

1 Go to the desktop and use your word processor to open embed.txt from the WIP_IP folder.

On the Macintosh, the Simple Text and TextEdit (OS X) word processors work well. On the Macintosh under OS X, you must change the TextEdit preferences from Rich Text to Plain Text. In the Windows platform, the Notepad text editor is preferred.

2 Highlight all of the text and copy it. Close the document without saving.

All the text copied is the <EMBED> tag that must appear in the HTML file so the JavaScript rollover event will function in a browser.

3 Use your word processor to open the home_page.html file from the WIP_IP folder.

Open HTML files in your word processors as text only (or plain text) so you can see the tags.

If you open an HTML file in MS Word, you see either a blank screen or the components formatted as they would appear in a browser. To see the code correctly, you must go to the View menu and choose HTML Source.

4 Scroll down in the HTML code until you find the GIF image whose name contains the slice number (of the Tampa Fitness logo) you wrote down earlier.

In our example, the slice is numbered 06, but yours may be different.

5 When you find the tag that contains the correct slice number, write down the width and height increments that appear in the tag.

In our example, the width is 186 and the height is 136, but yours may be different. Also, your slice number may be different from the one we show.

```
<TD COLSPAN=3 ROWSPAN=4 ALIGN=left VALIGN=top>

<IMG SRC="images/home_page_03.gif" WIDTH=186 HEIGHT=136 ALT="">

</TD>
```

6 Highlight the entire **<IMG SRC>** tag that holds the GIF image name. Paste the copied text to replace this tag.

The tag to replace begins with **<IMG SRC =** and ends with **ALT = "">** (see the figure above under step 5).

7 In the pasted text, change the generic.svg file name to "fitness_logo.svg". Change the width and height to the increments you wrote down in Step 5.

```
<TD COLSPAN=3 ROWSPAN=4 ALIGN=left VALIGN=top>

<EMBED SRC="fitness_logo.svg" TYPE="image/svg-xml"
PLUGINSPAGE="http://www.adobe.com/svg/viewer/install/"
WIDTH="186" HEIGHT="136"> </EMBED>

</TD>
```

The SVG file is embedded in the HTML file.

8 Save your changes and keep home_page.html open in the word processor.

Embed the SWF Animation

In this exercise, you embed the weightlifter.swf animation of the figure lifting barbells.

1 In your word-processing program, go to the WIP_IP folder and open weightlifter.html.

2 Highlight the text that starts with `<OBJECT>` and ends with `</OBJECT>`. Copy this text and close the document.

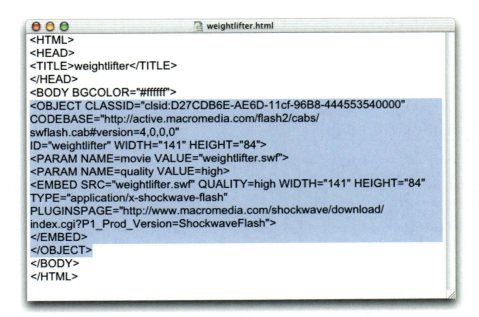

3 In the home_page.html document, scroll down to find the GIF image that contains the second slice number (of the weightlifter) you wrote down earlier.

LEVEL 2 **418** Integrating Project

Your slice number may be different from the one we show here.

```
<TD ALIGN=left VALIGN=top>

<IMG SRC="images/home_page_08.gif" WIDTH=140 HEIGHT=90 ALT="">

</TD>
```

4 Highlight the entire <IMG SRC . . . ALT=""> tag holding the GIF image.

5 Paste the copied text to replace the tag.

```
<TD ALIGN=left VALIGN=top>

<OBJECT CLASSID="clsid:D27CDB6E-AE6D-11cf-96B8-444553540000"
CODEBASE="http://active.macromedia.com/flash2/cabs/
swflash.cab#version=4,0,0,0"
ID="weightlifter" WIDTH="141" HEIGHT="84">
<PARAM NAME=movie VALUE="weightlifter.swf">
<PARAM NAME=quality VALUE=high>
<EMBED SRC="weightlifter.swf" QUALITY=high WIDTH="141" HEIGHT="84"
TYPE="application/x-shockwave-flash"
PLUGINSPAGE="http://www.macromedia.com/shockwave/download/
index.cgi?P1_Prod_Version=ShockwaveFlash">
</EMBED>
</OBJECT>

</TD>
```

The file is properly embedded in the HTML file.

6 Save your changes and close home_page.html.

Explore the Entire Web Site

1 Go to the desktop and use your browser to navigate to the WIP_IP folder. Open home_page.html.

2 Move your mouse over the Tampa Fitness Center logo to see it light up. Move the mouse away from the logo to see it return to normal.

3 Observe the weightlifter figure and note how the animation loops, with the barbells continually moving up and down.

4 Click either the Staff or Activities link buttons on the page's left side to see the other Web pages you created.

5 Click the other links you created and review the rest of the Web pages.

6 After you admire your work, close the browser window.

419 | **LEVEL 2**

TASK GUIDE

Task	Macintosh	Windows

Managing the Workspace

Invoke Help	F1	F1
Toggle between Standard screen, Full screen, and Full screen with menu bar	F	F
Fit imageable area in window	Double-click Hand tool	Double-click Hand tool
Magnify 100%	Double-click Zoom tool	Double-click Zoom tool
Move marquee while dragging with Zoom tool	Spacebar	Spacebar
Hide unselected artwork	Command-Option-Shift-3	Control-Alt-Shift-3

ACCESSING PALETTES

Show/Hide Brushes palette	F5	F5
Show/Hide Color palette	F6	F6
Show/Hide Layers palette	F7	F7
Show/Hide Info palette	F8	F8
Show/Hide Gradient palette	F9	F9
Show/Hide Stroke palette	F10	F10
Show/Hide Attributes palette	F11	F11
Show/Hide Styles palette	Shift-F5	Shift-F5
Show/Hide Appearance palette	Shift-F6	Shift-F6
Show/Hide Align palette	Shift-F7	Shift-F7
Show/Hide Transform palette	Shift-F8	Shift-F8
Show/Hide Pathfinder palette	Shift-F9	Shift-F9
Show/Hide Transparency palette	Shift-F10	Shift-F10
Show/Hide Symbols palette	Shift-F11	Shift-F11
Show/Hide all palettes	Tab	Tab
Show/Hide all palettes except the Toolbox	Shift-Tab	Shift-Tab

EDITING FILES

Cut	F2	F2
Copy	F3	F3
Paste	F4	F4
Revert to Saved	F12	F12

Task Guide

Task	Macintosh	Windows

Accessing Tools

Task	Macintosh	Windows
Selection tool	V	V
Direct Selection tool	A	A
Magic Wand tool	Y	Y
Lasso tool	Q	Q
Pen tool	P	P
Add Anchor Point tool	+ (plus)	+ (plus)
Delete Anchor Point tool	- (minus)	- (minus)
Convert Anchor Point tool	Shift-C	Shift-C
Type tool	T	T
Line Segment tool	\ (backslash)	\ (backslash)
Rectangle tool	M	M
Ellipse tool	L	L
Paintbrush tool	B	B
Pencil tool	N	N
Rotate tool	R	R
Reflect tool	O	O
Scale tool	S	S
Warp tool	Shift-R	Shift-R
Free Transform tool	E	E
Symbol Sprayer tool	Shift-S	Shift-S
Column Graph tool	J	J
Mesh tool	U	U
Gradient tool	G	G
Eyedropper tool	I	I
Paint Bucket tool	K	K
Blend tool	W	W
Slice tool	Shift-K	Shift-K
Scissors tool	C	C
Hand tool	H	H
Zoom tool	Z	Z
Switch to Hand tool (when not in text-edit mode)	Spacebar	Spacebar
Switch to Zoom tool (magnify)	Command-Spacebar	Control-Spacebar
Switch to Zoom tool (reduce)	Command-Option-Spacebar	Control-Alt-Spacebar

Task Guide   **421**   **LEVEL 2**

Task	Macintosh	Windows

Selecting and Moving Objects

Task	Macintosh	Windows
Switch from Direct Selection to Group Selection tool	Option	Alt
Add to a selection	Shift-click	Shift-click
Subtract from a selection	Shift-click	Shift-click
Add to selection (Lasso tool)	Shift-drag	Shift-drag
Subtract from a selection (Lasso tool)	Option-drag	Alt-drag
Move selection in user-defined increments*	Arrow keys	Arrow keys
Move selection 10x user-defined increments*	Shift-Arrow keys	Shift-Arrow keys
Lock all deselected artwork	Command-Option-Shift-2	Control-Alt-Shift-2
Constrain movement to 45° angle	Hold down Shift	Hold down Shift
Change pointer to crosshair for selected tool	Caps Lock	Caps Lock

* Set keyboard increments in General Preferences

Editing Paths

Task	Macintosh	Windows
Switch Pen to Convert Anchor Point tool	Option	Alt
Switch Scissors to Add Anchor Point tool	Option	Alt
Switch between Add Anchor Point and Delete Anchor Point tools	Option	Alt
Switch Pencil to Smooth tool	Option	Alt
Move current anchor point while drawing (Pen tool)	Spacebar-drag	Spacebar-drag
Cut a straight line (Knife tool)	Option-drag	Alt-drag
Cut at 45° or 90° (Knife tool)	Shift-Option-drag	Shift-Alt-drag

Transforming Objects

Task	Macintosh	Windows
Set origin point and open dialog box*	Option-click	Alt-click
Duplicate and transform selection*	Option-drag	Alt-drag
Transform pattern independent of object*	Tilde (~)-drag	Tilde (~)-drag

*Using the Rotate, Scale, Reflect, or Shear tool

Painting Objects

Task	Macintosh	Windows
Toggle between fill and stroke	X	X
Set fill and stroke to default	D	D
Swap fill and stroke	Shift-X	Shift-X
Select gradient fill mode	>	>

Task	Macintosh	Windows

Painting Objects (Cont'd)

Task	Macintosh	Windows
Select color fill mode	<	<
Select no stroke mode	/ (forward slash)	/ (forward slash)
Switch between Paint Bucket and Eyedropper tool	Option	Alt
Sample color from an image or intermediate color from gradient	Shift-Eyedropper tool	Shift-Eyedropper tool
Add new fill	Command-/ (forward slash)	Control-/ (forward slash)
Add new stroke	Command-Option-/ (forward slash)	Control-Alt-/ (forward slash)
Reset gradient to black and white	Command-click gradient button in Toolbox	Control-click gradient button in Toolbox

Using Palettes

Task	Macintosh	Windows
Apply value and keep field active	Shift-Return	Shift-Enter
Select range of items	Shift-click	Shift-click
Select noncontiguous items	Command-click	Control-click

ACTIONS PALETTE

Task	Macintosh	Windows
Expand/Collapse entire hierarchy for action set	Option-click expansion triangle	Alt-click expansion triangle
Set options for action set	Double-click folder icon	Double-click folder icon
Play a single command	Option-click Play button	Alt-click Play button
Play the current action	Command-double-click Play button	Control-double-click Play button
Begin recording actions without confirmation	Option-click New Action button	Alt-click New Action button

BRUSHES PALETTE

Task	Macintosh	Windows
Open Brush Options dialog box	Double-click brush	Double-click brush
Duplicate brush	Drag brush to New Brush icon	Drag brush to New Brush icon

CHARACTER PALETTE

Task	Macintosh	Windows
Highlight the font name field	Command-Option-Shift-F	Control-Alt-Shift-F

COLOR PALETTE

Task	Macintosh	Windows
Select the complement for the current color fill/stroke	Command-click color bar	Control-click color bar
Change the nonactive fill/stroke	Option-click color bar	Alt-click color bar
Select the complement for the nonactive fill/stroke	Command-Option-click color bar	Control-Alt-click color bar
Select the inverse for the current fill/stroke	Command-Shift-click color bar	Control-Shift-click color bar
Select the inverse for the nonactive fill/stroke	Command-Shift-Option-click color bar	Control-Shift-Alt-click color bar
Change color mode	Shift-click color bar	Shift-click color bar
Move color sliders in tandem	Shift-drag color slider	Shift-drag color slider

Task Guide **423** LEVEL 2

Task	Macintosh	Windows

Using Palettes (Cont'd)

GRADIENT PALETTE

Duplicate color stops	Option-drag	Alt-drag
Swap color stops	Option-drag stop onto another stop	Alt-drag stop onto another stop
Apply swatch color to active/selected color stop	Option-click swatch (Swatches palette)	Alt-click swatch (Swatches palette)

LAYERS PALETTE

Select all objects on layer	Option-click layer name	Alt-click layer name
Show/Hide all layers but the selected one	Option-click eye icon	Alt-click eye icon
Select Outline/Preview view for selected layer	Command-click eye icon	Control-click eye icon
Select Outline/Preview view for all other layers	Command-Option-click eye icon	Control-Alt-click eye icon
Lock/Unlock all other layers	Option-click lock icon	Alt-click lock icon
Expand all sublayers to display entire hierarchy	Option-click expansion triangle	Alt-click expansion triangle
Place new sublayer at bottom of layer list	Command-Option-click New Sublayer icon	Control-Alt-click New Sublayer icon
Place layer at top of layer list	Command-click New Layer icon	Control-click New Layer icon
Place layer below selected layer	Command-Option-click New Layer icon	Control-Alt-click New Layer icon
Copy selection to a new layer, sublayer, or group	Option-drag selection	Alt-drag selection

SWATCHES PALETTE

Create new spot color	Command-click New Swatch icon	Control-click New Swatch icon
Create new global process color	Command-Shift-click New Swatch icon	Control-Shift-click New Swatch icon
Replace swatch with another	Option-drag a swatch over another	Alt-drag a swatch over another
Select swatch by name (using keyboard)	Command-Option-click in swatch color list	Control-Alt-click in swatch color list

TRANSFORM PALETTE

Apply a value and keep focus in edit field	Shift-Return	Shift-Enter
Apply a value and copy object	Option-Return	Alt-Enter
Apply a value and scale option proportionately for width or height	Command-Return	Control-Enter

TRANSPARENCY PALETTE

Change mask to grayscale image for editing	Option-click mask thumbnail	Alt-click mask thumbnail
Disable opacity mask	Shift-click mask thumbnail	Shift-click mask thumbnail
Reenable opacity mask	Shift-click disabled mask thumbnail	Shift-click disabled mask thumbnail
Increase opacity in 1% increments	Click opacity field-Up Arrow	Click opacity field-Up Arrow
Decrease opacity in 1% increments	Click opacity field-Down Arrow	Click opacity field-Down Arrow
Increase opacity in 10% increments	Shift-click opacity field-Up Arrow	Shift-click opacity field-Up Arrow
Decrease opacity in 10% increments	Shift-click opacity field-Down Arrow	Shift-click opacity field-Down Arrow

Working with Text

NAVIGATING AND SELECTING TEXT

Move one character right or left*	Right Arrow or Left Arrow	Right Arrow or Left Arrow
Move up or down one line*	Up Arrow or Down Arrow	Up Arrow or Down Arrow
Move one word right or left*	Command-Right Arrow or Left Arrow	Control-Right Arrow or Left Arrow
Move up or down one paragraph*	Command-Up Arrow or Down Arrow	Control-Up Arrow or Down Arrow

Add the Shift key to select text

FORMATTING TEXT

Align paragraph left	Command-Shift-L	Control-Shift-L
Align paragraph right	Command-Shift-R	Control-Shift-R
Align paragraph center	Command-Shift-C	Control-Shift-C
Justify paragraph	Command-Shift-J	Control-Shift-J
Insert soft return	Shift-Return	Shift-Enter
Highlight kerning	Command-Option-K	Control-Alt-K
Reset horizontal scale to 100%	Command-Shift-X	Control-Shift-X
Increase point size*	Command-Shift->	Control-Shift->
Decrease point size*	Command-Shift-<	Control-Shift-<
Increase leading*	Option-Up Arrow	Alt-Up Arrow
Decrease leading*	Option-Down Arrow	Alt-Down Arrow
Set leading to font size	Double-click leading icon (Character palette)	Double-click leading icon (Character palette)
Reset tracking/kerning to 0	Command-Option-Q	Control-Alt-Q
Increase kerning (between two characters)*	Option-Right Arrow	Alt-Right Arrow
Decrease kerning (between two characters)*	Option-Left Arrow	Alt-Left Arrow
Increase kerning — 5X increment value*	Command-Option-Right Arrow	Control-Alt-Right Arrow
Decrease kerning — 5X increment value*	Command-Option-Left Arrow	Control-Alt-Left Arrow
Increase tracking (selected text)*	Option-Right Arrow	Alt-Right Arrow
Decrease tracking (selected text)*	Option-Left Arrow	Alt-Left Arrow
Increase tracking (selected text) — 5X increment value*	Command-Option-Right Arrow	Control-Alt-Right Arrow
Decrease tracking (selected text) — 5X increment value*	Command-Option-Left Arrow	Control-Alt-Left Arrow
Increase baseline shift*	Option-Shift-Up Arrow	Alt-Shift-Up Arrow
Decrease baseline shift*	Option-Shift-Down Arrow	Alt-Shift-Down Arrow

Set increment value in Type & Auto Tracing Preferences

425 LEVEL 2

GLOSSARY

above the fold 1. The top half of a newspaper, visible when the paper is folded. 2. The area of a Web page that a user can view without scrolling either vertically or horizontally.

actions Recorded sequence of clickings, attributes, and menu or palette selections that performs the selected sequence when Play Current Selection is clicked in the Actions palette.

additive color The process of mixing red, green, and blue light to achieve a wide range of colors, as on a color television screen.

alignment Positioning content to the left, right, center, top, or bottom.

animated graphics Images of any type that move.

animation The technique of simulating movement by creating slight changes to an object or objects over time.

appearance In Illustrator, the manner in which an object appears to be modified based on the settings you apply.

area graph A graph used to display volume or intensity over a period of time.

attribute Information included in the start tag of an element.

background A static object or color that lies behind all other objects.

banding 1. A visible stair-stepping of shades in a gradient. 2. Visible lines or stripes that often appear in artwork that is incorrectly formatted for use on the Web.

banner Common form of Web advertisement. Most banner ads are animated GIFs.

bar graph Similar to column graphs, except their axes run the opposite way; values move horizontally from left to right, and categories display on the left.

binding Assigning a selected object to a variable in the Variables palette by clicking the appropriate icon (i.e. Make Text Block Dynamic) at the bottom of the palette.

bitmapped Forming an image with a grid of pixels whose curved edges have discrete steps because of the approximation of the curve due to a finite number pixels.

bleed size An element of page geometry; the trim size plus the bleed allowance.

blend An Illustrator feature that performs a metamorphosis on two selected objects, creating additional objects of similar attributes between the two.

body copy The text portion of the copy on a page, as distinguished from headlines.

bounding box An area that defines the outer border of an object.

browser Software program that allows you to surf the Web. The most popular browsers are Netscape Navigator and Microsoft Internet Explorer. The very first browsers, such as Lynx, only allowed users to see text. Also called "Web browser."

build animation A type of animation in which the first object appears, and then the second, third, and so on, until all the objects in the animation are visible on your screen. Also called "cumulative animation."

capture To combine all the variables in the Variables palette into a "data set," which can be save and exported as an XML document for future use to modify the variables.

cell A unit of information within a table.

clipboard The portion of computer memory that holds data that has been cut or copied. The next item cut or copied replaces the data already in the clipboard.

clipping path A path that determines which parts of an image show on the page. Anything inside the path shows and prints; anything outside the path won't. The clipping path essentially knocks out the unwanted part of the image.

CMYK Cyan, Magenta, Yellow, Black. The subtractive primaries, or process colors, used in four-color printing.

color mode A system for describing color, such as RGB, HLS, CIELAB, or CMYK.

color picker A function within a graphics application that assists in selecting or setting a color.

color separation The process of transforming color artwork into components corresponding to the colors of ink being used, whether process or spot, or a combination of the two.

color shift The result of compressing out-of-gamut colors into colors that can be reproduced with a given model. Color shift can drastically change the appearance of the final output.

column 1. A vertical area for type, used to constrain line length to enhance design and readability. 2. A series of cells arranged vertically.

column graph A graph used to show how data changes over time, or display comparisons between different items or categories. Categories display horizontally (usually across the bottom axis) and values display vertically (usually on the left side of the graph).

control handle Nonprinting lines that define the shape or segments that connect two anchor points.

crop area The area that isolates a specific object (or objects) from the other objects in the document.

crop marks See *trim marks*.

cropping The elimination of parts of a photograph or other original that are not required to be printed.

cumulative animation See *build animation*.

cursor A small symbol that can be moved around a screen. Used to indicate the position where data will be entered or an action taken.

data sets Collections of variables for a specific design.

desktop 1. The area on a monitor on which the icons appear before an application is launched. 2. A reference to the size of computer equipment (system unit, monitor, printer) that can fit on a normal desk, thus, desktop publishing.

diameter The size of the tool cursor.

dimensionality Adding the traditional methods of perspective drawing to create the appearance of depth in a two-dimensional drawing.

dithering A technique in which a color is simulated by displaying or printing dots of two different colors very close together. Often used to compress digital images or to compress colors into the Web-safe palette.

document The general term for a computer file containing text and/or graphics.

drag To position the pointer on an object, press and hold the mouse button, move the mouse, and release the button.

drop shadow A duplicate of a graphic element or type placed behind and slightly offset, giving the effect of a shadow.

drop-down menu A selection list.

dynamic content Placeholder content that is populated by variable (changing) information.

effects list In Illustrator, a list of the effects that are applied to an object.

embedding Including a complete copy of a text file or image within a document, with or without a link. See *linking*.

event A JavaScript-related procedure that performs programmed actions on the elements residing in an SVG file.

facing pages A type of layout in which the pages of a design appear opposite each other, as in the pages of a book. See *nonfacing pages*.

field The section of a database record that holds one specific piece of information, such as a person's name, date of birth, or mailing address.

fill 1. Color that is applied to the background of a box or shape. 2. To add a color to the area inside a closed object in a graphic illustration program.

Flash Player Animation player from Macromedia.

fold The location at the bottom of a viewer's monitor, below which the user cannot see additional content without scrolling.

font The complete collection of all the characters (numbers, uppercase and lowercase letters, and in some cases, small caps and symbols) of a given typeface in a specific style; for example, Helvetica Bold.

four-color process See *process colors*.

FPS Frames per second. The number of frames in an animation or movie that play per second.

frame 1. The physical characteristics of a box edge. 2. An individual scene in a movie or animation.

global preferences Preference settings that affect all newly created files within an application.

gradient A gradual transition from one color to another. The shape of the gradient and the proportion of the two colors can be varied. Also known as blends, gradations, graduated fills, and vignettes.

gradient mesh A tool used to create realistic blends that follow the contours of a specific shape.

graph data The information that is used to make up a graph.

guide layer A special layer that is not output as part of the final file.

gutter Extra space between pages in a layout. Sometimes used interchangeably with "alley" to describe the space between columns on a page. Gutters can appear either between the top and bottom of two adjacent pages or between two sides of adjacent pages.

gutter width The amount of space between columns on a layout page.

hex values Numbers specified in the hexadecimal system, commonly used for specifying colors on Web pages.

home page Main page of a Web site. A Web site containing only one page is also called a home page.

horizon In perspective drawings, the imaginary line that marks the horizontal vanishing point.

hotspot A "live" area directly connected to an external or internal URL.

HTML Hypertext Mark-Up Language. A tagging language that allows content to be delivered over the World Wide Web and viewed by a browser.

icon A small graphic symbol used on the screen to indicate files, folders, or applications, activated by clicking with the mouse or pointing device.

image map A graphic containing hot areas, or areas of an image that are defined as links. When a viewer clicks the part of the image that is a hot area, they are actually clicking on a link.

import To bring a file generated in one application into another application.

indent The distance text is moved from the edge of a box or column.

instance In Illustrator, a copy of a symbol that has been placed in the document.

intensity An option that determines how heavily a tool affects an instance or symbol set.

JavaScript A scripting language, designed by Netscape, which can be embedded into HTML documents.

JPEG A compression algorithm that reduces the file size of bitmapped images, named for the Joint Photographic Experts Group, which created the standard. JPEG is "lossy" compression; image quality is reduced in direct proportion to the amount of compression.

landscape Printing from the left to right across the wider side of the page.

layers A function with which elements may be isolated from each other, so a group of elements can be hidden from view, reordered, or otherwise manipulated as a unit, without affecting other elements in the composition.

layout The arrangement of text and graphics on a page, usually produced in the preliminary design stage.

leading Space added between lines of type. Named after the strips of lead that used to be inserted between lines of metal type. In specifying type, lines of 12-pt type separated by a 14-pt space is abbreviated "12/14", or "twelve over fourteen."

left alignment Text having a straight left edge and a ragged (uneven) right edge.

line graph A graph used to display a change in data over time.

linking The act of placing a reference to one file (sound, graphic, or video) into another file. When the referenced file is modified, the placed reference is automatically (or manually, depending on the application) updated.

live area One of the elements of page geometry; the area of a page that can be safely printed without the possibility of being lost in the binding or cut off when the job is trimmed.

looping A technique used to play an animation or movie from start to finish, then start again at the beginning so the animation or movie plays continuously.

lossless compression A data compression method that does not throw away data at the highest (maximum) quality settings.

lossy compression A data compression method characterized by the loss of some data.

Macromedia Flash A program used for creating vector-based animations.

margin guides Guides that denote the live area of a layout page.

margins The nonprinting areas of a page, or the line at which text starts or stops.

marquee The blinking lines indicating the area selected with the selection tools. Also called "marching ants."

masking A technique used to display certain areas of an image or design; the shape and size of the top-most object or layer defines what is visible on lower layers.

matte color The intermediary color that bridges the range between the white pixels used by anti-alias (which cause artifacts) and the outer color that touches the background of the browser background.

matting   A technique used to minimize the artifacts that may appear on the edges of anti-aliased graphics.

mesh line   The connecting segment between mesh points.

mesh patch   The inner space of the mesh cells that displays the gradient's colors.

mesh points   Simliar to anchor points, but are actually smooth points that allow for adjustments.

morphing   Using a computer to animate the gradual transformation of one object into another.

mouseover   The event triggered when the user rolls the mouse cursor over an area or item on a Web page. Typically used to tell the browser to do something, such as execute a rollover script.

noncumulative animation   See *sequence animation*.

nonfacing pages   A type of layout in which the pages of a design do not appear opposite each other. See *facing pages*.

onmouseout   A JavaScript event that changes an object's appearance when the mouse cursor is moved away from it in a browser window.

onmouseover   A JavaScript event that changes an object's appearance when the mouse cursor touches it in a browser window.

opacity   1. The degree to which paper will show print through it. 2. The degree to which images or text below one object, whose opacity has been adjusted, are able to show through.

optimize   The technique of altering the file format, color palette, and uploading time for an image that will be used on the Internet.

page geometry   1. The division of a page into shapes and areas that hold the content you want to deliver. 2. The physical attributes of a layout page. See *trim size*, *live area*, *bleed size*.

palette   1. As derived from the term in the traditional art world, a collection of selectable colors. 2. Another name for a dialog box or menu of choices.

parallel view   See *single-point perspective*.

PDF   Portable Document Format. Developed by Adobe Systems, Inc. (read by Acrobat Reader), this format has become a de facto standard for document transfer across platforms.

perspective   The effect of distance in an image, achieved by aligning the edges of elements with imaginary lines directed toward one to three "vanishing points" on the horizon.

pie graph   A graph used to show the relationship between different categories. Each category is displayed as a percentage of a circle, which represents 100%.

pixel   Picture Element. One of the tiny rectangular areas or dots generated by a computer or output device to constitute images. A greater number of pixels per inch results in higher resolution on screen or in print.

pixelate   The ragged, bitmapped appearance of a raster image when it is either too low in resolution or has too few colors in its palette. The ragged edge is often referred to as "jaggies" because of the jagged appearance.

plug-in   Small piece of software, usually from a third-party developer, that adds new features to another (larger) software application.

PNG   Portable Network Graphics. A relatively new graphics format, similar to GIF. It is not yet widely supported by most browsers.

polygon   A geometric figure, consisting of three or more straight lines enclosing an area. The triangle, square, rectangle, and star are all polygons.

pop-up menu   A Web-page form element, with which users can choose one item from a specific set of options.

portrait   Printing from left to right across the narrow side of the page. Portrait orientation on a letter-size page uses a standard 8.5-inch width and 11-inch length.

PostScript   A page-description language, developed by Adobe Systems, Inc., that describes type and/or images and their positional relationships on the page.

preferences   A set of modifiable defaults for an application.

process colors   The four inks (cyan, magenta, yellow, and black) used in four-color process printing. A printing method in which a full range of colors is reproduced by combining four semi-transparent inks. See *color separation*, *CMYK*.

radar graph   A statistical tool used to compare the aggregate values of two or more data ranges.

record   An entry in a database, which contains all the fields and thus all of the data pertaining to a single item.

refresh   To reload.

registration marks   Printer's marks (often crossed lines and a circle) placed outside the trim edge on all color separations to provide a common element for proper alignment.

reload   To re-retrieve and redisplay a Web page in the browser.

RGB   1. The colors of projected light from a computer monitor that, when combined, simulate a subset of the visual spectrum. 2. The color mode of most digital artwork. See *CMYK*, *additive color*.

rollover   A Web-page element that changes appearance based on the position of the user's mouse cursor.

RTF   Rich Text Format. A text format that retains formatting information lost in pure ASCII text.

ruler guides   Horizontal and vertical guides that can be placed anywhere on the page by dragging from the rulers at the edge of the document window.

safe area   The area of the screen where content displays unobstructed.

sample   A method of selecting color; clicking the Eyedropper tool on any color in a vector or raster image applies the clicked color in either the Fill box (Illustrator) or the Foreground Color (Photoshop) in the Toolbox.

scatter graph   A graph used primarily for statistical analysis to identify trends or clusters, visually highlighting groupings of similar values.

select   To make an object active.

selection   The currently active object/s in a window. Often made by clicking with the mouse or by dragging a marquee around the desired object/s.

sequence animation   A type of animation in which one frame disappears as the next frame appears on the screen. Also called "noncumulative animation."

shortcut   1. A quick method for accessing a menu item or command, usually through a series of keystrokes. 2. The icon that can be created in Windows to open an application without having to penetrate layers of various folders.

single-point perspective   The simplest form of perspective, using a single vanishing point; the viewer directly faces the object as it recedes into the distance. Also called "parallel view."

slice   A specialized type of Web object that allows larger images to download faster.

stacked bar graph   A bar graph that shows multiple values for each category.

stacked column graph   A column graph that shows multiple values for each category.

stacking order 1. The order of elements on a PostScript page, where the topmost item can obscure underlying items. 2. The order in which elements are placed on a page; the first is at the bottom and the last is at the top. 3. The order of layers, from top to bottom.

startup disk The disk from which the computer is set to start.

storyboard A rough draft that describes what each frame of a movie or animation will show.

stroke The width and color attributes of a line.

SVG Scalable Vector Graphics. A form of XML (eXtensible Markup Language) that allows you to use JavaScript to add interactivity to your graphics.

SVG viewer A plug-in that enables the user to view SVG files in a browser.

symbol libraries Stored collections of symbols.

symbol set Defined groups of symbols.

symbols Virtual copies of existing elements, which can be used repeatedly without adding to the complexity or size of a drawing.

tags The various formats in a style sheet that indicate paragraph settings, margins and columns, page layouts, hyphenation and justification, widow and orphan control, and other parameters. An indication of the start and end of an element.

template A document file containing layout, styles, and repeating elements (such as logos) by which a series of documents can maintain the same look and feel. A model publication you can use as the basis for creating a new publication.

text The characters and words that form the main body of a publication.

text box A box into which users can type.

three-point perspective A perspective drawing technique in which the viewer sees the object from an angle, seeing its sides and top or bottom.

thumbnails 1. The preliminary sketches of a design. 2. Small images used to indicate the content of a computer file.

TIFF Tagged Image File Format. A common format used for scanned or computer-generated bitmapped images.

tool tip Small text explaining the item to which the mouse is pointing.

transparency 1. A full-color photographically-produced image on transparent film. 2. The quality of an image element that allows background elements to partially or entirely show through.

triggered action A JavaScript operation that is executed within an SVG image as the result of a specific action, such as onmouseover, onkeypress, or onmouseout.

trim marks Printer's marks that denote the edge of the page before it is cut from the press sheet to final size. Also called "crop marks."

trim size Area of the finished page after the job is printed, folded, bound, and cut.

tweening A process by which the in-between frames of an animation are automatically generated by the developing application.

tweens The in-between objects in an animation.

two-point perspective A perspective drawing technique that positions the viewer away from and to the side of an object, creating two vanishing points. Also called "angular perspective."

URL Uniform Resource Locator. Address of any resource on the Web.

vanishing point The exact location in a scene where objects disappear into the distance.

variable A unit of information that can be referred to by name.

vector graphics Graphics defined using coordinate points and mathematically drawn lines and curves, which may be freely scaled and rotated without image degradation in the final output.

visibility A variable that uses the visibility attribute of the layer on which an object resides to determine whether an object appears in a specific version of the design.

Web designer An individual who is the aesthetic and navigational architect of a Web site, determining how the site looks, how it is designed, and what components it contains.

Web page A single file or Web address containing HTML or XHTML information. Web pages typically include text and images, but may include links to other pages and other media.

Web-safe color A color palette used for images displayed on the Internet. The Web-safe color palette is a specific set that can be displayed by most computer-operating systems and monitors.

Web site A collection of HTML files and other content that visitors can access by means of a URL and view with a Web browser.

weight 1. The thickness of the strokes of a typeface. The weight of a typeface is usually denoted in the name of the font; for example, light, book, or ultra (thin, medium, and thick strokes, respectively). 2. The thickness of a line or rule.

XML eXtensible Markup Language. A special type of markup language that allows designers to use variable data in page layouts, drawings, and illustrations.

zero point The mathematical origin of the coordinates of the two-dimensional page. The zero point may be moved to any location on the page, and the ruler dimensions change accordingly.

zooming The process of electronically enlarging or reducing an image on a monitor to facilitate detailed design or editing and navigation.

INDEX

A

accuracy in typing   256
Acrobat   373, 375-377
Actions palette   338-339, 352-361, 364-365, 367-371, 404, 415
Add Anchor Point   88, 170
Add Legend Across Top   412
Align palette   26, 110-111, 151, 163, 392-394, 398-399
Anchor Point tools   88
animating blends   164-169
animation files   403-404
animations   147-149
    build (cumulative)   155-158
    creating   150-155, 402-403
    cumulative   148, 174-175
    raster   162-164
    sequence (noncumulative)   158-161
    SWF: embedding   417-418
anti-aliasing   209, 214
Appearance palette   40, 59-63, 70-71, 272, 394
appearances   47, 64
Apply Default Style (selection) action   357
Apply SVG Filter dialog box   269-270
area text blocks   312
Area Type Options   5-8
Arrows palette   121
artifacts   204, 209
    anti-alias, resolving   210-212
    eliminating by matting   212-214
Attributes dialog box   365
Attributes palette   214-216, 223, 369, 409

B

banding   191, 204-208
banners
    animated   155-158, 161, 165-169
    with raster effects   54-58
bar graphs   313, 316
batches   352
binding   295
Blend option   149
blends, animating   164-169
Books button   257
bounding box   109, 115-116, 119, 166, 394, 396-397
Break Link to Graphic Style   65
Break Link to Symbol   105-106, 110, 115, 117, 397
Bring to Front   171
broken links   108

C

browsers   251
build (cumulative) animation   148, 155-158, 174-175
Button mode   359, 371
Button 1 Mouse Down   117
buttons for links   396-401

Capture Data Set   303-305, 410
capturing   302
centering images   248-250
Choose Column Design   320
Clipping Mask   113
CMYK colors   19, 77, 79, 82-84, 86, 152, 354-355
CMYK documents   59, 105, 121-124, 133, 313
Color Model RGB   355, 393-394
Color palette   19, 69, 77, 79, 81-86, 130, 211, 252
Color picker   52, 55, 58, 152, 213, 392
Color Table   200, 206
column graphs   313, 316-317
combining documents   373-375
compounding   348
control handles   73, 86
Convert Anchor Point tool   170
Create from Selection   405-406
Create Gradient Mesh   78, 86
Create New Action   361, 367, 404
Create New Layer   5, 12, 151, 156, 159, 163, 167, 257
Create New Set   360
Crop Area   3, 13-17
Crop Artwork To menu   15
crop marks   14
cumulative animation   148, 155-158, 174-175
customizing
    buttons for links   399-401
    graphs   318-324
    objects on layers   168-169
    XML code   258-260

D

Data Input dialog box   314-315, 317, 412
Data Set menu   294, 304, 309, 311, 412
data sets   290, 299
    accessing   306
    creating   302-303
    saving   303-306

Default Fill and Stroke icon   11, 14, 16, 28-29, 54, 66, 113, 269, 353, 360, 363, 393, 409
Delete Anchor Point   88
Diameter setting   132
digital slide show with comments   163-164
dimensionality   2
directory paths   307, 310
Direct Selection tool   74-77, 80, 82, 88, 105, 110, 117-118, 159, 315, 320, 399-400, 402, 413
dithering   193, 199
dividers   22-23, 391, 407
dividing Web page components   12-13
documents
    connecting to external file   293-295
    Illustrator: combining   373-377
    saving as Web page   218-220
    startup   18-21
Draw Rectangle action   415
Drop Shadow   52, 56, 61-62, 67, 343, 364, 400-401
duplicating
    actions   355
    graphic styles   68-69
    objects   256, 346-347
    rectangles   11
    symbol instances   106
dynamic data   292-295

E

Effect menu   49-52, 56-60, 67, 273, 364
Ellipse tool   24-25, 66, 70, 110, 151, 216, 269, 346, 353
embedding
    JavaScript SVG event   416-417
    SVG file   266-268
Essentials palette   116
events
    adding   253-256
    JavaScript   261-265, 394-396, 416-417
    multiple   256-258
Expand Appearance   58
exporting
    animation files   403-404
    animations   151-154
    banners   157-158
    blends, into animation   169
    build animation   174-175
    objects, for the Web   15-17
Eyedropper tool   81, 83, 85, 397

430 Index

F

file formats
saving   201-203
setting   199-201
Fill box   19, 70, 76, 211, 272
Fill item   61-63, 70
Fill of None   113, 117, 393, 404, 409
Filter menu   343, 363-364
filters
vs. effects   53
SVG   269-273
Fit in Window   367, 370-371
Flatten Image   344
folders, action   365
fold of Web page   10
frame rate   153, 164, 169
frames   150-153, 173-174
frames per second (fps)   153
Free Transform tool   341-342
function keys   357-358

G

Gaussian Blur   57
Gaussian Blur Filter action   356-357
Generate HTML   174
GIF (Graphic Interchange Format)   193, 195-196, 202, 205, 210, 415
gradient meshes
creating   73-76
painting   76-78
using in design work   78-88
Gradient palette   69, 408
gradients   191, 350-351
Gradient Shadow style   67-71
Gradient tool   66, 71, 361
Graph Column dialog box   319-321, 323
Graph Design dialog box   319, 322
graphic styles
creating and applying   65-68
duplicating   68-69
modifying   69-71
tips on   72
Graphic Styles palette   48, 64-70, 109, 112, 116-117, 131
graphs. *See also* specific graph types
changing types of   324
creating   412-413
customizing   318-324
experimenting with   316-318
Graph tools   291, 313-318, 412
grids   21-27, 392, 407
guides   5-9, 23-26, 28-29, 166, 341-342, 392, 399, 406-407
gutters   6-9

H

Hand tool   198-199
Hide Slices   222
highlights   85-87
home page
saving as HTML   413-415
slicing   404-407
horizon line   27
Horizontal Align Center   151, 163, 169, 393-394
Horizontal Distribute Center   111
horizontal dividers   22, 391, 407
horizontal guides   28-29, 166, 408
hotspots   192, 214, 216-217, 223
HTML   155, 174-175, 202, 217-220, 245, 266-268, 403-404, 413-418
HTML Only   218

I

Illustrator documents   373-377
Illustrator Effects   49-50
Illustrator Symbol Libraries   120
Image Format   154
image maps   214-217, 409
image rollovers   262-264, 392-393
images
events applied to   395
importing   401
raster   113-114, 164
refining for the Web   209-214
SVG, embedding in HTML code   266-268
Image Size   201
Images Only   202-203, 208, 218
Import Data icon   317, 412
importing
symbol libraries   124
text and images   401
Info palette   266, 346, 392-393
Insert Menu Item   366, 370-371
Insert Pages   374
instances   102, 104-108, 110-113, 125-131
Intensity control   132-133
interactivity   251-256

J

JavaScript   244-245, 268
adding interactivity with   251-256
events   261-265, 394-396
SVG event: embedding   416-417
and XML naming conventions   256-260
JavaScript Files dialog box   264, 395
JPEG (jpg; Joint Photographic Experts Group)   16-17, 193, 200-201, 207-208, 393-394, 403

L

layer list   151, 163
layers
creating layouts on   5-7
customizing objects on   168-169
page elements retained on   9
Layers palette   5-7, 12-13, 149, 151, 155-156, 159, 162-164, 167, 171-172, 252-253, 257, 262, 298, 344, 394
layouts
adding to   7-9
creating on layers   5-7
perspective   27-31
Linked File   296
links
broken   108
buttons for   396-401
editing   115-119
hotspot   192
Liquify filter   343-344, 376
Load Variable Library   293, 309, 311, 411
Logo Elements palette   121-122, 397
logos   9, 392-396
Looping option   153, 158, 161, 163-164, 169
lossless compression   209
lossy compression   209

M

Macromedia Flash Export Options dialog box   158, 161, 163-164, 174
Macromedia Flash (SWF) file   150, 153-154, 169, 417-418
Make Clipping Mask   345, 348
Make Linked File Dynamic   296-298, 300, 302, 409
Make Text Dynamic   296-298, 300, 302, 409
Make Visibility Dynamic   296, 298
masking
objects   113-114
opacity   345-349
matte color   212
Matte menu   213, 225
matting   212-214
menu items, toggle-type   372
mesh line   73, 75-76, 79-87
mesh patch   73-74
mesh points   73-87
Mesh tool   76-77, 79, 83-84
Mode menu   152
modifying
Acrobat file   375-377
graphic styles   68-71
grids   27
objects   160-161, 341-344

startup document   18-19
symbols   116-118, 396-398
Web page   11-12
XML file   307-309, 410-411
Move dialog box   346, 369-370

N

naming objects   365-372
Nature palette   125-126, 133
New Graphic Style   65
New Symbol   105
New Window   78
Next Page button   374-375
noncumulative animation   148
Normal mode   359

O

objects. *See also* Web objects
compound multiple   348
customizing on layers   168-169
duplicating   256
exporting for the Web   15-17
extracting from blend   167
home page   405-407
in-between   149, 164-165, 170
isolating for printing   14-15
masking   113-114
modifying   160-161, 341-344
naming   365-372
nearing vanishing point   31
placing on sticker   25-26
replacing   295
Offset Path   363
onmouseout event   244, 253-255, 258, 263, 395
onmouseover event   244, 254, 258, 260, 394
opacity masking   345-349
Opacity 60 (selection) action   357
Opacity slider   345, 347
Open Symbol Library   121-124, 133
Optimized   195-196, 210, 212, 218, 413, 415
orientation   124, 313
Original   194-196, 207-208
Other Library   115-116, 120, 123, 127
Outer Glow dialog box   392
Outline view   51, 105-106, 346, 350, 408

P

page elements   407-408
page geometry   2
paragraph tags   411
parallel view   27
path, directory   307, 310
Path item   59, 61-63

PDF (Portable Document Format)   337, 340, 373, 376-377
pencil object   320-322
Pen tool   28, 30, 339
Percent   201-202
perspective
creating   28-31
shear   341-344
photo animations   162-163
Photoshop
modifying objects for use in   341-344
techniques: using in Illustrator   345-351
Photoshop Effects   53-58
pie graphs   313-315, 317-318
pixelate   246
placeholders   396, 414
Place Symbol Instance   105, 107, 111
Play Current Selection   354, 356-357, 359, 365, 415
PNG (Portable Network Graphic)   193, 203
Polar Grid tool   4, 23-25
Polygon tool   66
Preference setup   293-295
Preset menu   199-203, 205, 207
Preview mode   165, 347, 350, 371, 408
printing isolated objects   14-15
Pucker & Bloat effect   60-63

R

radar graphs   313
raster animations   162-164
raster effects   54-58, 62
raster formats   18
raster images   113-114, 164
Rasterize effect   48, 62-63
Rasterize option   48, 57
Rasterize (selection) action   354-356
Record   361-362, 368, 404
rectangles   11, 12, 55, 166, 211, 222, 256, 358, 399-400, 404, 408-409
Rectangle tool   11, 14, 29, 73, 110, 155, 173, 215, 223, 270, 350, 357, 361, 368, 393, 404, 408-409
Rectangular Grid tool   4, 22-23, 391, 407
Redefine Graphic Style "Gradient Shadow" option   70-71
Redo option   295, 312
Reduce to Basic Appearance   60, 272
Release to Layers   149
Release to Layers (Build)   158, 170-174
Release to Layers (Sequence)   170
Replace Symbol   105, 107, 109, 111-112, 117-119
replacing objects   295

replacing symbols   398-399
RGB color mode   165, 211, 343
RGB documents   262, 269, 367
rollovers   262-264, 392-393
Rotate   111, 362
Rotate 90 CW (selection) action   356
Rotate Square action   365
Round Cornered Rectangle tool   55
Rounded Rectangle tool   396-397
rulers   391

S

safe area   10
Save Actions   365
Save for Web   193-203, 205, 210-212, 218, 225, 413-415
Save for Web GIF 64 Dithered action   359
Save Optimized As   414-415
Save Symbol Library   123
Save Variable Library   306, 410
saving
action folders   365
data sets   303-306
document as Web page   218-220
document settings   21
file formats   201-203
home page as HTML   413-415
symbol libraries   122-124
scale settings   119
Scale tool   30, 166
scatter graphs   313
Scribble effect   51-52
Select All Instances   108-109
Select All Non-Web Safe Colors   206
Select All Unused   107, 123
Selected Object icon   257
Selection tool   5, 7, 126, 159, 222-223, 302, 315, 319, 342, 402
Select Object   369
Select Slice tool   225
sequence (noncumulative) animation   148, 158-161
Set color action item   363
Set Selection option   366
Set Stroke action item   364
shear perspective type   341-344
Shifts/Unshifts Selected Colors to Web Palette button   206
shortcut keys to play actions   357-359
Show Bounding Box   109
Show Gradient Swatches   19-20, 361
Show Note   365, 369
Show Pattern Swatches   19-20
single-point perspective   27
slices   192, 220-227, 404-407, 417-418
Slice tool   221-222
slide shows   163-164

LEVEL 2 · **432** · Index

Sliding option 320
Specified Steps option 167
stacked bar graphs 313
stacked column graphs 313
stacking order 175
startup documents
  modifying 18-19
  new 20-21
static images 246, 251
stickers 25-26
Stop Playing/Recording 364,
  371, 404
storyboard 162
Stroke of None 24-25, 29-30, 118,
  151, 346, 361-362, 404, 408-409
Stroke Weight 363
stroke width 279-280
sublayers 172-173, 252-253,
  257-258, 262-264, 394
SVG Interactivity palette 251-253,
  258-259, 261-264, 394-395
SVG (Scalable Vector Graphics)
  243-244
  event embedding 416-417
  exploring 246-251
  file embedding 266-268
  filters 269-273
SVG Viewer 243, 247
Swap Fill and Stroke icon 271
Swatches palette 19-20, 62, 66, 74,
  76, 77-78, 272, 345-346, 349-350,
  354, 408
symbolism tools 103-104,
  124-131
Symbolism Tools Options dialog
  box 132-134
symbol libraries 103, 115-116,
  120-124
symbols 101-102, 104
  adding 110-112
  creating 105-110, 112-113
  editing 115-119
  for link buttons 396-401
  modifying 116-118
  raster images and 113-114
  and Release to Layers (Build)
    171-174
Symbol Screener tool 131
Symbol Scruncher tool 128
symbol set 124, 135
Symbol Set Density 132-134
Symbol Shifter tool 128
Symbol Sizer tool 129
Symbols palette 102, 104-124,
  397-399
Symbol Spinner tool 129

Symbol Sprayer tool 103, 124-127,
  129-130, 133-134
Symbol Stainer tool 130-131
Symbol Styler tool 131

T

tags 292, 312, 410-411, 416, 418
Tearoff menu 124-125, 128-129,
  131-133
text editors 416
Text String 296
three-point perspective 32
Tile Photo action 372
tiles 369-371
Toggle Slices Visibility icon
  225, 414
toggle-type menu items 372
Transform palette 368
transparency 210-211, 214, 273
Transparency palette 338, 345, 347,
  349-351, 408
transparency screen 349-351
Trash icon 61-63, 394
trim marks 13
tweens 149, 164-165, 167, 170
Twist effect 50-51, 60-61
two-point perspective 32
type
  adding to sticker 25-26
  shear perspective 341-344
Type tool 5, 257, 303, 398

U

Unbind Variable 296
Undo option 295, 312
Ungroup 167
Units & Display Performance dialog
  box 251
Units & Display Preferences 14
2-Up 196
4-Up 196, 202-203, 205
upload times 209
URL (Universal Resource Locator)
  214-217, 409
Use Preview Bounds option 393

V

vanishing point 27-32
Variables palette 289-290, 292-306,
  409-412
vector effects 49-53
Vertical Align Center 151, 169,
  393-394, 398
Vertical Align Top 111, 163

Vertical Distribute Center 399
vertical dividers 22, 391, 407
vertical guides 28-29, 166, 407
viewing modes 359
View Percentage menu 198, 200,
  207, 212, 218, 371
Visibility 296, 298, 311
Visibility icon 7-9, 12, 152-153,
  156-157, 159-161, 168-169, 402

W

Weather palette 127, 129
Web Buttons and Bars
  palette 123
Web Icons palette 123
Web objects
  banding and color modification
    204-208
  creating image maps 214-217
  refining images for the Web
    209-214
  Saving for the Web—HTML
    217-220
  slicing images 220-227
  using Save for Web 193-203
Web pages
  home page 404-407, 413-415
  laying out 10-13
  setting up 407
  viewing 226-227
Web-safe colors 204, 207
Web Safe RGB 211
Web site creation 391-418
Window menu 78-79
word processors 307

X

XML code
  customizing 258-260
  loading variables 411-412
XML data 299-301
XML (eXtensible Markup
  Language) 243, 244, 289
XML file
  loading into Illustrator 311-312
  modifying 307-309, 410-411
XML ID numbers 296, 298
XML ID option 251, 293
XML naming conventions 256-260,
  299, 366

Z

Zero Point 367, 391, 407
Zoom tool 197, 199-200, 248